modern blackness

A book in the series

LATIN AMERICA OTHERWISE:

LANGUAGES, EMPIRES, NATIONS

Series editors:

Walter D. Mignolo, Duke University

Irene Silverblatt, Duke University

Sonia Saldívar-Hull, University of

California at Los Angeles

Deborah A. Thomas

MODERN BLACKNESS

Nationalism, Globalization, and

the Politics of Culture

in Jamaica

Duke University Press   Durham & London   2004

Library of Congress Cataloging-in-Publication Data

Thomas, Deborah A., 1966–

Modern blackness : nationalism, globalization and the politics of
culture in Jamaica / Deborah A. Thomas.

p. cm. — (Latin America otherwise)

Includes bibliographical references and index.

ISBN 0-8223-3408-9 (cloth : alk. paper)

ISBN 0-8223-3419-4 (pbk. : alk. paper)

1. Jamaica—Cultural policy. 2. Ethnicity—Jamaica. 3. Identity
(Psychology)—Jamaica. 4. Nationalism—Jamaica. 5. Politics and
culture—Jamaica—History. 6. Social classes—Jamaica. 7. Popular
culture—Jamaica. 8. Globalization—Social aspects—Jamaica.

I. Title. II. Series.

F1874.T46 2004

972.92—dc22   2004012453

Latin America Otherwise: Languages, Empires, Nations is a critical series. It aims to explore the emergence and consequences of concepts used to define "Latin America" while at the same time exploring the broad interplay of political, economic, and cultural practices that have shaped Latin American worlds. Latin America, at the crossroads of competing imperial designs and local responses, has been construed as a geocultural and geopolitical entity since the nineteenth century. This series provides a starting point to redefine Latin America as a configuration of political, linguistic, cultural, and economic intersections that demands a continuous reappraisal of the role of the Americas in history, and of the ongoing process of globalization and the relocation of people and cultures that have characterized Latin America's experience. *Latin America Otherwise: Languages, Empires, Nations* is a forum that confronts established geocultural constructions, that rethinks area studies and disciplinary boundaries, that assesses convictions of the academy and of public policy, and that, correspondingly, demands that the practices through which we produce knowledge and understanding about and from Latin America be subject to rigorous and critical scrutiny.

Modern Blackness is a history and ethnography of the cultural politics of nationalism in Jamaica. Starting with the years after independence, Thomas presents the changing valence of nationalist ideologies—from the awakenings of "the people" as a creole nation to today's nation, rooted in an ethos of urban "blackness." Thomas places nationalism in several contexts: from the history of Jamaica in a changing world, to the history of Mango Mount in a changing Jamaica. With great analytical sophistication, Thomas gives, then, a three-dimensional view of the dynamics linking global forces, the Jamaican nation, and local possibilities: and all this with attention to political, economic, and cultural factors.

Modern Blackness is an ambitious book that manages to tell a big story of national and global transformations without sacrificing what matters—the day-to-day lives of "ordinary" Jamaicans. Thomas's generous vision, then, is a lesson in how to see otherwise: to appreciate the simultaneous workings of global, national, and local forces, without forgetting the human beings that constitute them; to understand that "culture" (like dance) is part of this dynamic; and to remember that the Caribbean, including the English-speaking Caribbean, and "Latin" America are part of each others' being in the history of the modern/colonial world.

for my family and my posse

contents

acknowledgments

Because this exploration into the politics of culture in postcolonial Jamaica has spanned ten years and several sites, I have racked up innumerable debts. First, I am deeply indebted to Rex Nettleford, Artistic Director of the National Dance Theatre Company of Jamaica; L'Antoinette Stines, Artistic Director of L'ACADCO; and all the performers in these companies for allowing me to participate in Company classes and rehearsals, sitting through countless interviews and engaging me in innumerable discussions, and giving me special access to performances. Several individuals based at other national institutions were also central to the conceptual and practical implementation of this project. At the Jamaica Cultural Development Commission, Maria Smith (then Director of Performing Arts) and Joyce Campbell (Consultant for Traditional Folk Forms) provided me with access to the Commission's materials, included me (as an arts practitioner) in several teacher training workshops throughout Jamaica, and invited me to participate (as an adjudicator) in the dance competitions of the 1997 National Festival of the Arts. Barbara Requa (Dean of the Performing Arts) and Alaine Grant (Director of the School of Dance) at the Edna Manley College of the Visual and Performing Arts offered their time, institutional records, and ideas with patience, candor, and a sense of humor.

Michael Cooke at the Institute of Jamaica, Bernard Jankee at the African-Caribbean Institute of Jamaica, and Alwin Bully at UNESCO were amenable sounding boards early on in my research; Sidney Bartley invited me to the Consultations on Cultural Policy in December 1996; and the Honorable Burchell Whiteman (Minister of Education, Youth and Culture) provided me with the report of the proceedings. Additionally, Mrs. Joan Young-Davis, who in 1997 was based at the Emancipation Secretariat, and the library staffs at the National Library, the archives in Spanish Town, the West Indies Collection at the University of the West Indies, and the Statistical Institute of Jamaica also offered much-needed assistance. Finally, Barry Chevannes at the Faculty of Social Sciences and Neville Duncan at the Institute for Social and Economic Research provided me with institutional affiliation at the University of the West Indies. For the generosity and graciousness with which these individuals opened their doors, hearts, and minds, I am grateful.

I have also incurred debts I will never be able to repay in the community of Mango Mount (a pseudonym). I thank the Executive Committee of the Mango Mount Community Council for providing me with unlimited access to their archives, involving me in their meetings, and inviting me to participate in programming at the Community Center. My deepest respect goes to the community members who permitted me to enter their lives. This book cannot possibly reflect the immeasurable gratitude I feel for the ways they opened their homes and hearts (and often their kitchens) to me. Nor could it ever indicate the numerous and profound ways they have influenced my life. For teaching me, laughing with me, arguing with me, and most of all, for including me, I am deeply thankful.

At New York University, I could not have asked for a more helpful and interested dissertation committee. The intellectual engagement and professional support of Constance Sutton, Fred Myers, Lila Abu-Lughod, Claudio Lomnitz, and Don Robotham have been unwavering. Connie especially has provided guidance, inspiration, and personal support over the years in incalculable ways, and I am thankful for her example. At the Center for the Americas at Wesleyan University, Ann Wightman, Patricia Hill, Claire Potter, Kehaulani Kauanui, María Elena García, and Joanne Palmer were supportive—and more importantly, fun—colleagues. And my current colleagues at Duke University have been generous intellectual interlocutors. I'm particularly thankful to Ann Wightman and Anne Allison for critically engaging earlier versions of this book. My students at New York University, Wesleyan, and Duke deserve special mention as well for helping me to think through the themes raised in the book, and for contributing comparisons based on their own experiences. The three Wesleyan students who were brave enough to travel with me to Jamaica for six weeks during the summer of 2001 in order to conduct research projects of their own design—Zuleka Henderson, Tamisha Navarro, and Tiesha Sargeant—also helped me to see old issues through fresh eyes and taught me countless lessons about mentoring.

Financially speaking, the Center for Latin American and Caribbean Studies at New York University provided me with the opportunity to conduct summer research in Jamaica in 1993 and funded me to present my first academic paper at the March 1996 Conference on Caribbean Culture in Kingston, Jamaica. My research in Jamaica from October 1996 to December 1997 was supported by a predoctoral grant from the Wenner-Gren Foundation for Anthropological Research (no. 6063), and a Dissertation Fellowship from the Ford Foundation Doctoral Fellowship Program for Minorities in 1998 sustained me during my last year of graduate school.

Outside the university, I also have many people to thank. Jawole Zollar, Laurie Uprichard, Rhoda Cerretelli, and the rest of the Urban Bush Women—past and present—continued to find ways for me to be involved with the Company (both as a performer and administrator) despite my "graduation" from full-time performance. And Linda Basch, Liz Horton, and the rest of the staff and network of the National Council for Research on Women were incredibly flexible about my working hours while I was finishing my doctorate, read drafts of chapters, and inspired my current research into globalization and female labor migration from Jamaica to the United States. Because Linda Basch is also an anthropologist and a former student of Professor Sutton, she provided a comparative perspective and a sense of intellectual generational continuity.

Many, many other people have also read various incarnations of sections (or all) of what follows and have been gracious enough to serve as intellectual sparring partners. For the generosity with which they have offered their time and insights, I would like to especially thank Gage Averill, Lee Baker, Tina Campt, Ginetta Candelario, Barry Chevannes, Kamari Clarke, Carolyn Cooper, Crystal Feimster, Faye Harrison, Cheryl Hicks, Antonio Lauria, Maureen Mahon, Sue Makiesky-Barrow, Liza McAlister, Brian Meeks, Pat Mohammed, Harvey Neptune, David Scott, Anu Sharma, Irene Silverblatt, and Kevin Yelvington. Various additional individuals provided encouragement and comments in both formal and informal settings, including Eudine Barriteau, A. Lynn Bolles, Kamala Kempadoo, Rhoda Reddock, Karla Slocum, Faith Smith, and students and faculty members within the Department of Cultural Anthropology at Duke University, the Department of Anthropology and the Program in African-American Studies at Wesleyan University, and the Center for African-American Studies at the University of California, Los Angeles. I am grateful as well for the support of Ken Wissoker, my editor at Duke Press, as well as the insights of the various anonymous readers of this manuscript. Finally, I want to thank Mahmood Mamdani, who was present at a small seminar in 1999 at Columbia University when I was presenting my work and who asked me a question that I couldn't answer about the transformative potential of the politics of contemporary lower-class Jamaican popular cultural production. His question has gnawed at me ever since that time, and I hope this current iteration of my ideas offers a more explicit rendering of the complex political ideologies and processes that are prevalent. In spite of the considerable wisdom offered by all these interlocutors, I have not always heeded their advice. The responsibility for errors in analysis and judgment, and for leaving out far more than I explain in these pages, is therefore exclusively mine.

Lastly, I want to thank my family and friends. My parents, Doris and Delroy Thomas, have sustained me (emotionally and financially) when I needed it most and provided a place for me to crash when I was overwhelmed. I hope what they both read here will convince them that going back to Jamaica for my research was, indeed, worth it. In Jamaica, Roy and Kamala Dickson graciously took me into their home and included me in their family. Patient and loving friends—both nearby and far away—always provided much needed relief from the alienation and isolation often engendered by the academic enterprise. Thanks are particularly due to Yoko Akagi, Catherine Barnett, Ann and John Buttrick, Noah and Mariana Byrd, Charles Campbell, Tina Campt, Sharon Craddock, Dawn Crossland, Thulani Davis, Kwesi and Martha Dickson, Sita Dickson and Tim Littlewood, Mark Winston Griffith, Andrew Janiak, Judy Markes, Francine McKenzie, Angela Mitchell, Negar Mottahedeh, Toshi Reagon, Queenie Robinson, Lotti Silber, Vanessa Spence, and Rebecca Stein. To those of you who have had to share a roof with me at various points during the process of researching and writing this book go both my apologies and undying gratitude. Last, I want to thank Junior "Gabu" Wedderburn for inspiring this project through his music, laughter, and spirit, and Diana E. Wells for her unwavering friendship over the years as well as her acute editorial eye for theoretical nuance. And my abiding appreciation and everlasting love are due to John L. Jackson Jr., who consistently teaches me about the arts of profound support, engaged listening, and caring collaboration.

introduction

"OUT OF MANY, ONE (BLACK) PEOPLE"

During a rehearsal for a dance performance in Kingston, Jamaica, I was stretching and talking with members of one of the country's premiere concert dance companies. I noticed a fair-skinned woman with long, dark, slightly wavy hair who was warming up with some of the other dancers in the opposite corner of the studio. She looked familiar to me, so I asked the artistic director whether she was the British woman who had performed with the Company some years before. "Who? She?!" the director responded. "No, she is very, very Jamaican!" When I asked what it meant to be "very, very Jamaican," the director replied, "You know, very, very Jamaican. You eat plenty ackee and saltfish. You love reggae music. You talk patois." I probed further, asking whether one had to do those things all the time to be "very, very Jamaican." "Jamaica very broad you know," she answered. "Very cosmopolitan. Plenty Jamaicans even eat lasagna, but them don't love it more than them ackee and saltfish. And there are plenty Jamaicans in America who are more Jamaican than Jamaicans here. Some high class Jamaicans don't act very, very Jamaican at all."

By this time, another dancer had joined the conversation. "Let me tell you," she offered, "I am so into my culture, the least thing will bring tears to my eyes":

> Going to a craft fair, seeing the women selling dukoonoo and wearing them traditional headwrap. Going to a dance, jooksing in a corner, reasoning with a Rastaman while him smoke him herb, watching the dancehall girls skinning out on the floor. We are very brash, brash and colorful. It's the way the dancehall girls dress, the way them leave them belly out, the way them walk, the way them wear them big earrings, the way them color their hair. It's a true and natural expression of how we are deep inside.

A third dancer ultimately had the last word. "In Jamaica," she said, "we are a culture of tricksters, we are a culture of loud mouth people, we are a culture of expressive people. If I had to use words to describe Jamaican culture, I would say it's big. We do everything in a very big, loud, attention-getting way. We are clever people, you know. Very clever. You can't keep Jamaicans out of anything."

This conversation took place near the beginning of my longest period of fieldwork in Kingston during the late 1990s. I didn't know it at the time, but it would become iconic, occurring over and over in various permutations, in various venues, and with various people. Because they evoke several popular constructions of Jamaicanness, these dancers' reflections introduce the themes I consider salient to an exploration of cultural identity in late-twentieth- and early-twenty-first-century Jamaica. In some contexts, they define Jamaican identity through the local production and consumption of the foods (ackee and saltfish), music (reggae and dancehall), and language (patois) associated with black lower-class Jamaicans. The emotional resonance of nationality was sometimes inspired by performances of the cultural practices developed by Jamaicans during slavery and in the postemancipation period (cooking dukoonoo, a cornmeal pone wrapped in a banana leaf, and wearing headwraps). More often, however, popular expressions—dancehall style, loudmouth bigness, cunning cleverness—were the more common and immediate indicators of being Jamaican, especially among a younger generation.

Additionally, although the default referents of nationhood were here associated with black lower-class cultural practices, Jamaicanness was portrayed as something that could be chosen. That is, one would not necessarily be any less Jamaican because one had access to other (foreign) foods and music or fluency in Standard English. As a result, being "very, very Jamaican" wasn't inherently rooted in one's color or class or even in having been born on the island. Indeed, the fact that Jamaican migrants in the United States could be perceived as more "authentically" Jamaican than Jamaicans "on the rock" destabilizes the oft-presumed link between culture and territory. It also, in conjunction with the references to Jamaica's cosmopolitanism ("broadness") and the fact that "you can't keep Jamaicans out of anything," evokes how central migration has been, not only with respect to Jamaica's economic development but also in terms of Jamaicans' sense of themselves and their place in the world. If one's Jamaicanness were embedded in, and assessed through, ongoing negotiations of color, class, gender, generation, and cultural practice in local venues, it was also always constituted and evaluated in relation to a transnational community.

The various versions of cultural identity evoked by the dancers also circulate broadly within diverse sectors of the Jamaican public sphere and so raise several questions that have become increasingly significant to scholars, policy makers, and activists in recent years. For example, what is the role of the state in shaping, institutionalizing, and socializing cultural identities that reflect nationalist concerns? What kinds of alternative nationalist identities circulate alongside these institutionalized ideals? Who do these appeal to and what kinds of histories ground them? What are the relationships among global political and economic processes, cultural production, and subject formation? How are individuals, families, and communities negotiating changing geopolitical and economic terrain and conceptualizing cultural belonging in the contemporary period?

This book explores these questions by analyzing the changing relationships among nationalism, popular culture, and the political economy of development in postcolonial Jamaica. It is an attempt to ethnographically ground the ongoing tensions between Blackness, Africanness, and Jamaicanness—competing identities that have been used to mobilize Jamaicans locally and to represent Jamaicans internationally—within the contexts of postcolonial nation building and current neoliberal capitalist globalization. It demonstrates how the institutionalization of aspects of these identities by a nationalist state structures the ways that belonging (to a community, to a nation, to a culture) and ownership (of resources, of a cultural heritage, of property) have been conceptualized and experienced over time at both national and local levels. At the same time, it charts the ways individuals not explicitly connected to various nationalist projects represented themselves as well as how they assessed the efforts of creole nationalist cultural mobilizers.

These emphases reflect my own curiosity about nationalism's effects. In other words, I was interested in how people who were diversely located within Jamaica's social system viewed their actions and practices not only with respect to local state and civic initiatives, but also in relation to the transnational circuits in which they were personally embedded as well as to those pan-Africanist and migratory routes that provided meaningful referents for their own experiences. Moreover, I was concerned with finding a way to understand popular visions of national belonging as more than simply alternative, reactive, subversive, or resistant to a hegemonic norm. As a result, I embarked upon a research odyssey designed to clarify the various contexts in which, processes by which, and purposes for which Jamaican men and women produced culture.

Forging Cultural Futures

British imperialism was not merely a system of economic exploitation and political domination but also one of cultural control that attempted to socialize colonial populations into accepting the moral and cultural superiority of Englishness. The British colonial state throughout the West Indies and elsewhere legitimated its rule by transforming space and linking hierarchies of education and status to color, class, culture, and gender.[1] As a result, the decolonization process involved not only an agitation for political and, to some extent, economic self-determination, but also a cultural reevaluation. In fact, as many scholars have pointed out, some of the most difficult battles within anticolonial struggles have been fought within the domain of culture, for it is through cultural politics that "relations of power are asserted, accepted, contested, or subverted by means of ideas, values, symbols, and daily practices" (Glick Schiller 1997a:2).[2]

When the most populous Anglophone Caribbean territories gained independence in the 1960s,[3] the leaders of these new nations pursued political and economic modernization through parliamentary democracy and state-sponsored capitalist development. At the same time, nationalist intellectuals and artists—many of whom had been educated in Great Britain—were concerned to build or maintain a national cultural identity that would meet two objectives: (1) assert a distinctive way of life at a time when cultural influences from the United States were becoming increasingly pervasive; and (2) recuperate and revitalize those practices that were either actively prohibited or quietly discouraged throughout colonial rule. As in many post–World War II new nations, then, artistic representations of nationhood became critical arenas in which anticolonial struggles were waged.

In Jamaica, the creole multiracial nationalist project that was consolidated between the 1940s and the 1960s is reflected through the country's national motto, "Out of Many, One People." This project encompassed efforts to legitimize selected elements of previously disparaged Afro-Jamaican cultural practices in order to foster a sense of national belonging among Jamaica's (majority black) population.[4] Jamaica's independence from Britain in 1962 was marked, therefore, with the establishment of a cultural policy that sought to promote a new idea of cultural citizenship by bestowing a new public prominence upon aspects of Jamaica's "folk" culture, now understood as part of the country's "African heritage."[5] In this way, selected Afro-Jamaican practices—those religious and secular rituals, speech patterns, foods, musical forms, and dances associated with the rural peasantry—came to enjoy some measure of legitimacy by the state. This was significant, in part, because at the time, members of the striving middle classes and ruling political and economic elites—as well as sectors of the respectable poor—considered "Africa" a symbolic representation for much of what was viewed negatively in society.

While the government's legitimation of aspects of Jamaica's African cultural heritage broadened the public space in which notions of national identity could be debated, the actual process of privileging particular elements of Jamaica's African cultural heritage also marginalized alternative visions. The attempt to consolidate a nationalist state, to inculcate soon-to-be-ex-subjects with a sense of national belonging and loyalty that would naturalize new relations of authority,[6] validated a particular kind of citizen and a specific vision of cultural "progress" and "development." Intense debates regarding who and what should represent the nation have therefore been ongoing and have been shaped by changing internal and international political economies. Ultimately, these debates have also been about the extent to which national representations have reproduced colonial racial, ethnic, class, cultural, and gendered hierarchies of power throughout the postindependence period, both institutionally and interpersonally, a reproduction that Brackette Williams has called "ghost hegemony" (B. Williams 1991; see also B. Williams 1993, 1996b; Munasinghe 2001).[7] They have also called into question the legitimacy of nationalist leadership, typically "men of moderation and modernity" (F. Cooper 1996:260) who would advocate on behalf of their populations while remaining invested in colonial hierarchies of education and status. In other words, though race became a "cornerstone of national identity" (Safa 1987:119) throughout the Anglophone Caribbean during the nationalist period,[8] revalorizing rural Afro-Jamaican cultural practices neither tended to appreciably alter the structural position of rural Afro-Jamaicans, nor to significantly reinvent the ideological systems through which modern "progress" had been measured and "development" evaluated.

By selecting certain cultural practices (those of the postemancipation rural peasantry) and excluding others (those of the rapidly growing urban unemployed), the cultural policy adopted at Jamaica's independence reflected a vision of cultural "progress" and "development" that prioritized "respectability." Respectability, here, is a value complex emphasizing the cultivation of education, thrift, industry, self-sufficiency via land ownership, moderate Christian living, community uplift, the constitution of family through legal marriage and related gendered expectations, and leadership by the educated middle classes. This vision of progress has its roots in the postemancipation establishment of "free villages," Baptist church communities that were established to provide former slaves with the opportunity to purchase land, reconstitute families, and educate their children. It was also this vision that was ultimately institutionalized through the initiation of social welfare work and democratic political nationalism in the late 1930s, providing the parameters to distinguish citizens-in-the-making from other individuals, seen as atavistic, uncritical, and unready for independence (see Bogues 2002).

Of course, this was not the only vision of progress available to Jamaicans at the time of independence. As Jamaican political scientist Brian Meeks has pointed out, "it has been the constant feature of social movements in Jamaica in the last hundred years, that while the leaders may define the movement in terms of national, class, or social goals, the people have invariably redefined it in terms of race" (2000:169). In other words, the vision of progress nationalist cultural mobilizers associated with the rural peasantry was in constant tension with other, more explicitly racialized visions and values. These visions and values have typically been framed transnationally and, as a result, have challenged the legitimacy of territorially bounded governmental bodies. Moreover, some of these visions, though not all, have been ideologically linked to a mythical or actual Africa. The conflict over the meanings of Africa and its place in Jamaica's past and present, therefore, has been linked to ongoing tensions between race and nation as markers of citizenship and (trans)national belonging as well as to ideas about governance and development.

If many twentieth century political and cultural nationalist elites have tended to reproduce colonial hierarchies of power, even as they agitated against colonial rule, then perhaps the most productive way to conceptualize postcolonial nationalisms is as dialectical contests between the hegemonic project of nationalist modernity and popular challenges to that project at various levels (Joseph and Nugent 1994). In other words, despite the uneven power relations that contextualize the terrain of this struggle, processes of state formation and popular cultural production are mutually constitutive. Among nonelite sectors of the population, particular forms of popular practice—and most obviously, popular music—have provided windows through which to parse what Gilroy has termed "a distinctive counterculture of modernity" (Gilroy 1993:36)—alternative, and potentially counterhegemonic, visions of both the past and the future.[9] However, because these countercultures are forged not outside of, but through engagement with, Western modernity (Gilroy 1993; Gupta 1995; Ong and Nonini 1997; Piot 1999), popular cultural production is multifaceted and multivalent.

Indeed, creolized and other innovative cultural structures have raised questions about "authenticity," the political implications of cultural improvisation, and the ethnic, racial, gendered, and class "ownership" of particular forms. Assertions of ownership, in turn, have had various and changing implications for making cultural and political claims about "belonging" to both national and transnational communities. In Jamaica, while the countercultural space of the dancehall, for example, opens the possibility of black solidarity, it is also the location where "social divisions of race, class, gender, sexuality, religion, and political affiliation are made, reinforced, and undone" (Stolzoff 2000:6). The contemporary popular music scene also both transcends and, in a way, redraws the territorial boundaries dividing Jamaicans in Jamaica from those in the diaspora, as well as those between Jamaicans in different locations within diaspora— New York, Miami, Toronto, London, etc. Popular cultural production is therefore flexible, reflecting the changing relationships among nationalism, historical consciousness, the political economy of development, and the politics of culture.

Popular cultural practices, however, do more than merely reflect the hidden histories and alternative visions of Caribbean (and other) subalterns. They are also integral nodes through which people experience and mediate their relationships to global processes, thereby producing nationalist modernities for themselves (Comaroff and Comaroff 1993, 1997; Donham 1999; Ferguson 1999; Ong 1999; Piot 1999; Rofel 1999). The Caribbean, as a region, has always been modern, insofar as the agroindustrial plantation system inaugurated a new phase of capitalist development and a learned openness to cultural variety and creolization. Moreover, the innovation of mass production for export and the exploitation of labor did not preclude the generation of specialized labor roles through which workers developed modern forms of subjectivity, even during the period of slavery (Mintz 1996, 1998; Trouillot 2002). Yet, though black bodies were central to the generation of Western modernity during the initial period of imperial conquest, slavery, and racial domination, the promises of modernization were not held out in any substantial way until after World War II, when development dreams positioned Africa, Latin America, and the Caribbean as "backward" but ultimately recuperable. Nevertheless, despite apparent formal political and economic marginalization, as Paul Gilroy and others have argued, modernities have been coproduced through ongoing encounters that occur within fields characterized by inequality. By engaging, appropriating, and resignifying dominant Euro-American cultural—and to a degree political and economic—practices, poor and working-class Jamaicans have aspired to a modernity of their own making within the context of their own history. Rather than seeing this engagement as false consciousness, assimilation, or acquiescence to the hegemony of neoliberal capitalist globalization, then, we must see it as laying claim to an as yet unfulfilled promise. This is especially so in the contemporary period when, as James Ferguson has demonstrated so eloquently, processes of globalization have created "new, up-to-date ways not only of connecting places but of bypassing and ignoring them" (1999:243).

Like many scholars interested in these issues, I have found it helpful to focus on cultural production in socially differentiated local, national, and transnational spaces.[10] Looking at the ways power is expressed through the idiom of culture at various institutional levels shows us where the reproduction of hegemonic ideologies is at its most tenuous, and therefore where the ability of these ideologies to constitute particular subjectivities is most fragile. It also allows us to more clearly identify the spaces that have facilitated (counter)cultural production among different sectors of the population. Hegemony, in this view, does not imply a shared ideology, but is instead the process of negotiating "a common material and meaningful framework for living through, talking about, and acting upon social orders characterized by domination" (Roseberry 1994:361). From this perspective, change, incompleteness, and complexity emerge as foundational theoretical and analytical principles. My attempt to understand the relationships between creole multiracial nationalism and popular cultural practices in Jamaica, therefore, is situated in relation to a historical political economy of race and nation that is contextualized by changing transnational circuits of ideas, opportunities, and constraints.

Globalization and Transnational Blackness

While the first postindependence government privileged aspects of Jamaica's African cultural heritage through its cultural policy, it also continued to pursue development strategies initiated in the 1950s that were geared toward modernizing Jamaica's economy through foreign invest-ment and industrial development. The land shortage that began in Jamaica during the mid-nineteenth century continued throughout the twentieth, and the rural lifestyles that generated and nurtured the majority of the newly celebrated "folk" practices were increasingly destabilized. Despite the fact that these practices had begun to "die out," creole nationalist cultural mobilizers continued to assert their relevance and encourage their perpetuation even at the turn of the twenty-first century, not only because they served as proof of a dynamic and creative history, but also because they might provide a base from which to cope with the rapid changes facing Jamaicans after independence and into the contemporary period.

By now it has become commonplace to speak of processes of globaliza-tion and the ways in which they are continually restructuring our lives. The massive decentralization of capital accumulation worldwide over the past two decades has resulted in the growth of new centers of economic expan-sion, while older centers have declined. Simultaneously, rapid advances in information and transportation technology have changed the ways in which space and place are both conceptualized and experienced. While massive movements of people, and with them their ideas and customs, have been documented throughout the historical record, recent global reconfigurations mark an intensification of both the speed and character of these processes.[11]

Scholars and activists alike have critically reflected upon the impact of privatization policies, and neoliberal capitalist globalization more gen-erally, both within and between nations. They have demonstrated how worldwide deindustrialization and the concomitant rise of the service and informal economic sectors, the phenomenal proliferation of information technologies, and (throughout the Third World) the implementation of structural adjustment policies have widened the gaps between rich and poor, developed and underdeveloped, north and south, resulting in what Michel Rolph Trouillot has called a "fragmented globality" (2001:129).[12] Indeed, throughout the Caribbean, current processes of neoliberal capital-ist globalization have engendered crises within many states, especially as they attempt to manage the various "adjustments" mandated by interna-tional lending agencies.

Within the Anglophone Caribbean, the past two decades of economic crisis have eroded many of the previous gains in health and nutrition, literacy and education, employment and social services, gender empowerment, and political stability (Barrow 1998b; Dupuy 2001). Structural adjustment programs have mandated repeated currency devaluations, which, alongside privatization drives, have resulted in an escalated cost of living and an increase in poverty. Unemployment has escalated, especially among women and youth, and crime rates have skyrocketed, especially those related to drug trafficking and domestic violence. Caribbean nations, though rich in natural resources, are increasingly competing with each other in addition to competing as a region with other regions. The key economic sectors—agriculture, mineral extraction, offshore assembly production, and tourism—are dominated by foreign firms and are dependent on external demand or foreign consumers for their services. As a result, the region is increasingly reliant upon exporting more of its workforce to the United States, and at the same time it is becoming a magnet for illegal drug trafficking and money laundering (Dupuy 2001:524–26, 529). In Jamaica, as elsewhere, these processes have had particular gendered and generational effects. While we know that women have suffered disproportionately from the repatriation of social services to the household, it is also the case that undereducated and unskilled young men have become increasingly marginalized from any promise of "development." This is, in part, because the shift to service- and information-based industries worldwide has increasingly encouraged female-generated labor migration at the same time that local opportunities for both men and women have contracted.

Since capital has become increasingly flexible and labor markets have become increasingly differentiated (within and across national borders), it has become more difficult for states throughout the Global South to provide for and socialize their citizens. As a result, many state functions have been redirected to new sites (Sassen 2000; Trouillot 2001). It has also become progressively more of a challenge for states to legislate the "cultural content" of the nation (Trouillot 2001). This does not mean, however, that globalization has heralded some postnationalist order, or a complete transcendence of the nation-state,[13] because the nation-state "continues to define, discipline, control, and regulate all kinds of populations, whether in movement or in residence" (Ong 1999:15). Instead, states themselves, as well as the relationships between states and citizenries, have changed. Paying attention to the specifics of these changes, and to their effects, helps us to arrive at more sophisticated understandings of the relationships between contemporary political and economic processes and cultural production.[14]

In the Caribbean and elsewhere, shifts in the balance of power between state administrations and transnational capital over the past two decades have closed many of the traditional means by which citizenries have met their needs. However, new avenues of survival and expression have also emerged. That is, while current privatization drives and structural adjustment programs have had hugely deleterious effects on local communities—and especially on women's lives—recent reconfigurations of capitalism have also allowed some individuals to enter global markets in new, and sometimes lucrative, ways. In turn, they have developed new forms of subjectivity.

These are the processes that concern me because they provide the parameters that shape peoples' claims to being "very, very Jamaican." I will develop several overlapping arguments in these pages. First, there is a struggle for public representational power in Jamaica between what I am calling the "respectable state" and popular culture that has been ongoing and that has been discursively framed through references to "values." Values, in turn, have been linked to class-coded cultural forms and practices. The parameters of this struggle for power were defined during the colonial period and then reproduced—at least in part—by advocates of creole multiracial nationalism. In order to understand how these hierarchies of value are both reproduced and potentially transformed, we must look closely at the ways individuals and groups enter into (and define) relationships with each other, with local institutional structures at the community level, and with the transnational circuits that encompass their familial, educational, occupational, and political lives. Because local structures articulate with those at the national level, they tend to reproduce national hierarchies of value and parameters for progress and development. However, because national hierarchies of value and structures of opportunity are also integrated within, and conditioned by, a changing global political economy, there has always been an element of instability to this reproduction. Yet, when the hegemony of the respectable state has been threatened, what often emerges is a discourse that foregrounds a sense of crisis rather than one that acknowledges or celebrates a particular kind of liberation.

The second argument I will develop is that by the late 1990s, a significant shift had occurred within Jamaica's public sphere whereby the creole vision of Jamaicanness, consolidated by political and intellectual elites at the time of independence, became publicly superseded by a racialized vision of citizenship that I am calling "modern blackness." By this, I mean that urban popular expressions of blackness that had been marginalized within the cultural policy designed at independence have, despite intense debates concerning their appropriateness as national representations, become paramount within contemporary understandings of Jamaican particularity. This shift has not been due to any one specific social movement or even to the work of several different movements. It is, instead, the result of a confluence of factors that have had a variety of (sometimes unexpected) effects.

First, since the 1960s there has been a significant decline in the influence of that sector of the professional middle classes who gained state power at independence as cultural and political brokers in the lives of poorer Jamaicans. This decline has bolstered the autonomy of working-class and poor Jamaicans, giving them relatively greater ability to eschew conventional middle-class modes of respectability. Second, the current prime minister, P. J. Patterson—the first prime minister elected by popular vote who is regarded as black by Jamaicans—has himself changed the racial landscape of Jamaica's public sphere. His public projection of a more explicitly racialized concept of citizenship and leadership has opened a space for other expressions of blackness to become "louder." Third, the intensification of transnational migration and the proliferation of media technologies have facilitated the amplification of a diasporic consciousness. Here, I mean to suggest that while certain aspects of "folk" culture are codified by states, others are not and remain in the changing folk public sphere. As a result, the new technologies and institutions that have evolved are spaces where old ideas (about blackness, about gender, about nationhood) continue to be debated, though now more instantaneously across space and time. And finally, the increased political, economic, and social influence of the United States has opened avenues for many black Jamaicans to evade the colonial constructions of the relationships between color, class, gender, culture, and progress that were institutionalized by the British. I do not mean to argue that new, potentially more deleterious constructions have not emerged with the intensification of neoliberal capitalist expansion. However, the decline in the specific hegemony of British colonial class and color hierarchies is, in itself, critical.

"Modern blackness," then, is a term I'm using to provide a rejoinder to the creole nationalist slogan—"Out of Many, One People"—an aspirational slogan that nevertheless reproduces colonial social hierarchies by parenthesizing blackness, thus pushing out the possibility of a hegemonic blackness within the public sphere. Yet, modern blackness is not a new nationalism. This is an important point, because elements of modern blackness recall ideologies and aesthetics that have been associated with earlier generations of working-class black Jamaicans, while other elements could only have been generated within the contemporary political and economic context. More accurately, therefore, modern blackness is a subaltern aesthetic and politics from which to make claims upon the earlier forms of nationalism that gained state power in Jamaica. Indeed, what I am calling modern blackness and creole multiracialism are always side by side, jockeying for position. This is what I have tried to reflect in the title of this introduction, a bracketed blackness that continually deconstructs the creole nationalist motto by calling attention to the relations of power that are often erased within the creole formulation.

Because the ascendance of modern blackness within the public sphere coincides with a period of intensified economic contraction and political and drug-related violence in Jamaica, its challenge to the dominance of creole multiracial nationalism has also generated a resurgence of crisis-oriented discourse. However, modern blackness itself constitutes a crisis only for the maintenance of a particular color, class, gender, and culture nexus that reproduces colonial relations of power and hierarchies of value.

There are spatial and temporal dimensions to the shift I'm examining here. "Folk" blackness, or the emphasis on Jamaica's African heritage, has a territorially grounded past-tenseness about it. In attempting to define what was distinctive about Jamaican culture, creole multiracial nationalism posited blackness not just in the past, but also in the future. This was a utopianist vision of what blackness could do, could be, if it were to get with the creole program, a vision of a "tamed" blackness that mirrored the values that have come to be associated with the creole professional middle classes. It was also a blackness that was locally rooted. Within this conceptualization, blackness was used as dominant raw material in the assertion of "authentic" national culture, but rejected as a tool for political mobilization. Modern blackness, however, doesn't need the past to ground it and doesn't posit an utopianist or revolutionary future. Instead, it is unapologetically presentist and decidedly mobile. It challenges the past-tenseness of "folk" blackness and African heritage as well as the notion of an evolving future based on creole nationalists' modernist visions. It is a notion of blackness in the here and now that accepts and validates the immediacy of contemporary popular cultural practices, such as dancehall, and reflects the transnational experiences of the majority of the population.

Finally, modern blackness is not the harbinger of some revolutionary transformative social order. In fact, aspects of modern blackness appear to reproduce some of the discourses regarding consumerism and individualism that are associated with neoliberal capitalism. Yet, as contemporary public invocations of blackness and black progress in Jamaica become increasingly unmoored from notions of communal morality expressed by earlier black nationalists, the individualism they advance is strategic and contextually specific. Here, the discourse of individualism is infused with a notion of racial progress designed to challenge stereotypical assumptions about racial possibilities. This challenge is also reflected through patterns of consumption, as elements of American cultural products are incorporated into Jamaican stylistic and ideological repertoires.

It is this process that has generated the most intense concern among sectors of both popular and academic communities, in part because it is seen to indicate the death of collectively mobilized, transformative political action. It is true that while consumption has emerged, as the Comaroffs have noted, as a "privileged site for the fabrication of self and society, of culture and identity" (2001:9), and as the culture of neoliberalism "re-visions persons not as producers from a particular community, but as consumers in a planetary marketplace" (2001:13), the extent to which different consumers have been able to access or influence this market remains clearly uneven. Moreover, this is a marketplace that privileges First World (and especially United States) markets, styles, and tastes, which then encompass those of the Global South in a more totalizing manner than previously. At the same time, if we reorient our vision of politics in a way that decenters totalizing revolutionary narratives and pays special attention to very locally grounded negotiations, incorporations, and rejections, we are able to more clearly conceptualize the ways people confront and revise both structural and ideological systems of power and domination. From this perspective, black Jamaicans use "America" to simultaneously critique, selectively appropriate, and creatively redefine those aspects of the dominant capitalist ethos that they believe benefit themselves and their communities, both materially and psychologically.

When I invoke the term modern blackness, then, I mean to evoke both a sense of historical consciousness and a sense of promise. I use this term rather than, for example, "postmodern blackness" in order to signal that modern blackness in Jamaica is not predicated upon a fundamental break with the past. Invocations of Africa and of African-Jamaican historical struggles still resonate powerfully for many black Jamaicans and provide a symbolic basis for pride at specific junctures. However, everyday experiences of blackness within local and global racial hierarchies emerge as most salient in people's material and emotional lives currently. This is because current processes of globalization have reinscribed racial and cultural hierarchies within and between nations, communities, and regions in ways that recall the centrality of racial categorization and racism to processes of modernization, nationalism, and state formation (Friedman 1994; S. Hall 1997). In Jamaica, as a result, the "postmodern" condition does not present itself as the harbinger of unlimited opportunities, possibilities, and hybridities. I also use the formulation modern blackness rather than Afro-Modernity (Hanchard 2001) to direct attention to everyday life in contrast to the self-conscious development of social, cultural, and political movements and identities at various levels. If we understand modernity as, to borrow Donald Donham's definition, "the discursive space in which an *argument* takes place, one in which certain positions continually get constructed and reconstructed" (2002:245), then we are better positioned to parse the relationships between changing political economies and cultural production over time. Analyzing the ways respectable citizenship and transnational blackness have been reconfigured and mobilized at particular historical junctures also forces us to look at global processes from the ground up. This, in turn, allows us to make better connections between analyses of systems (of international financial institutions, multilateral organizations, governments) and strategies (of individuals, families, communities). This is the point of departure from which I believe we might most fruitfully approach the dialectic between creole multiracial nationalism and modern blackness.

Taking modern blackness seriously, therefore, requires that we abandon the binaries of hegemony and resistance, global and local, and instead try to understand the range of contemporary cultural formations among black Jamaicans—indeed, among African-descended people throughout the diaspora—vis-à-vis an ongoing negotiation of dynamic systems of power and domination at historically specific junctures.[15] This requires a head-on confrontation with both sides of the Janus-faces of nationalism, modernity, and what John and Jean Comaroff (2001) have called "millennial capitalism" in order to critically and respectfully engage the complicated maneuvers people perform in order to advance their interests as individuals, families, and communities.

Genealogies and Sites

I began this introduction with dancers' ideas about Jamaican culture not only to introduce the broad themes of the book but also to honor the origins of this project. I became interested in the issues I address here while I was dancing professionally in New York City. The company with which I was performing—the Urban Bush Women—had begun to supplement its touring schedule with local development initiatives we called Community Engagement Projects. These were six- to twelve-week residencies during which we would work, at a community's invitation, in conjunction with various grassroots organizations toward catalyzing the kinds of changes they wanted to see within their own neighborhoods. For example, one group of company members would use music and movement counting drills to help a boys' basketball team improve their math scores; another group would develop movement games and writing exercises that would assist clients at a welfare rights organization to negotiate their options; while still another would meet with a group of young women to discuss their concerns regarding physical, mental, and spiritual health. The small individual and collective breakthroughs engendered by this working process—among both community and company members— inspired my already at times overzealous commitment to viewing the performing arts as a means to create a consciousness of social, political, and economic inequalities that would lead people to mobilize around efforts to challenge and redefine their circumstances. As a result, when I entered graduate school in 1992, I was interested in gaining a deeper understanding of the issues surrounding these kinds of processes within the context of postcolonial nationalism. Toward this end, between 1993 and 2003, I conducted a total of two years of ethnographic research in Jamaica, using dance as a point of entry.[16]

I trace this genealogy in order to point out that these are processes in which I have also had a personal and professional stake as a half-Jamaican, half-German-American, *browning/red girl/light-skinned*, dreadlocked, middle-class artist and intellectual. Therefore, I make no pretense to some abstracted sense of objectivity in this discussion about cultural politics, popular culture, and nationalism. I am quite certain that both my persona and my prior involvement in cultural development projects have shaped my data-gathering and analytic processes in a variety of ways. At the same time,

I trust that the deep historical and political-economic contextualization provided here, as well as the leveling effects of collaborative checks and balances offered by colleagues and community members both in the United States and Jamaica, have mitigated some of the more personal biases and concerns that might have found their way into these pages.

Because the issues I address have simultaneously local, national, and global implications, the research for this project was multisited (Marcus 1995; Roseberry 1994). I investigated the political economy surrounding the evolution and implementation of Jamaica's cultural policy from independence to the late 1990s as well as the initiatives and events promoted by the institutions that were established to develop and represent Jamaican culture and history to the population. I worked extensively with members of the artistic community—performers, teachers, administrators, and policy makers. I participated in classes; observed rehearsals and performances; and conducted interviews regarding their participation in the arts, their understanding of the mission statements of the various organizations with which they worked, their assessment of the impact of expressive cultural action in helping to define a national cultural identity, and their views with respect to the ways in which Jamaica has changed since independence. Additionally, I served as an adjudicator for the parish and national finals of the National Festival of the Arts organized by the Jamaica Cultural Development Commission and attended a conference in December 1996 that was held to revise Jamaica's national cultural policy. Finally, I followed the debates and activities surrounding a committee that was also established in 1996 to reevaluate the country's national symbols and observances.

In order to comprehend the significance of these various activities geared toward defining and redefining Jamaican cultural identity to those not directly involved in their conceptualization and implementation, I also conducted research in a rural hillside community just outside Kingston that I call Mango Mount.[17] In Mango Mount, the relatively rich lived side by side with the relatively poor, an unusual situation in and around Kingston where middle- and upper-class Jamaicans tend to live in segregated residential enclaves. Mango Mount maintains a distinct community identity because unlike other rural villages in the foothills of the Blue Mountains, the roads to the village lead nowhere but there. In other words, one does not drive through Mango Mount on the way to somewhere else, yet the community is only a ten-minute taxi or minivan ride to one of the main transportation squares in greater Kingston. In 1997, villagers estimated that the entire community was home to some 2,500 people. According to 1991 census figures, the area in which my fieldwork was concentrated— one of the two enumeration (voter's registration) districts comprising the village—had a population of 1,343 (Statistical Institute of Jamaica 1991:xi).

In the community, my research was focused on what nationalism meant at the grassroots level. I paid particular attention to the ways local institutions (such as the churches, political party groups, and the neighborhood's Community Council) structured class and status distinctions between people in the village based on their varying degrees of control over economic and social resources. I also performed extensive thematic and genealogical interviews regarding individuals' perceptions of Jamaican history and its effects on the present; attitudes toward national symbols and observances; ideas about the meaning of "culture" and its relationship to race, class, gender, nation building, and migration; awareness of the various projects of national cultural institutions; reflections about Jamaica's changing political culture; and understandings of the place of their community in relation to other communities, the nation, the Jamaican diaspora, and the world.[18] Additionally, through oral histories, I gleaned different perspectives on the "origin" and growth of the community and its various institutions, such as the Anglican and Seventh-Day Adventist Churches and the All Age School.[19]

I also conducted considerable archival and participant-observation research with the Community Council, the local organization for social, cultural, and economic development that was established in October 1978 as a result of the then democratic socialist government's emphasis on self-reliance, local mobilization, and community-based problem solving. During the early 1980s, it was identified as one of the most effective community councils in Jamaica, having built a community center and encouraged recreational activities, obtained public transportation for the district, opened a small health clinic, and supported a revolving loan fund. In the years just prior to my arrival, the community center had been closed. However, it was reopened during the period of my fieldwork. This provided me with the opportunity to involve myself more fully in some of the Council's initiatives. I made myself available to participate in whatever ways community leaders saw fit and ended up teaching a dance/theatre class to some of the younger children who frequented the center. As will become clear in chapter 5, I was also integrally involved in the organization of the community's first commemoration of Emancipation Day.

This kind of direct involvement in events related to my research concerns renders particularly explicit the fact that the presence of ethnographers affects community life and, therefore, ultimately our own analyses of local processes. That this involvement does not stop when one "leaves the field" was made clear to me upon one of my return visits during the summer of 2000. I had brought a copy of my dissertation to circulate within the community, and the United States Peace Corps volunteer who was working with the Community Council asked to read the sections that explicitly addressed life in Mango Mount. By the summer of 2001 when I returned again with three students from Wesleyan University, the volunteer was writing her final report to both the Council and the Peace Corps. In it, she cited sections of what appears here as chapter 3 in order to substantiate her own observations regarding the level of community participation in the Council's various programs. Her report circulated, in turn, to other community members who had not yet read the results of my many intrusive questions, and I was subsequently asked to provide a summary report of my own. It is my hope that this kind of dialogue will continue and that members of both the artistic and village communities will not find their words or actions severely misrepresented in these pages.

Structure of the Book

Multisited research requires multileveled analysis, and so this book is divided into three sections: the global-national, the national-local, and the local-global. I have borrowed this tripartite structure from Michel Rolph Trouillot's ethnography of peasants in Dominica (1988) in order to clarify the links between global processes, nationalist visions, and local practices.[20] My own use of the tripartite structure here is meant to underscore that each of these levels articulates with the others and that these articulations change over time. The first section, then, emphasizes the ways the global contexts of imperialism and modernization have shaped anticolonial and postcolonial nationalist efforts to define both cultural distinctiveness and political and economic progress. The second section is primarily concerned with how these definitions at the national level have been reproduced at the village level through a variety of institutional structures. Finally, the third section outlines various alternative (and in some cases oppositional) definitions of progress, development, and community belonging current among individuals within Mango Mount and demonstrates how their mobilization of these alternative definitions links them more directly to global political economies of labor and cultural production.

Within all three sections there is a sense of struggle. In other words, these are not one-way processes but are dialectical levels of experience that require an analytic frame positioning them as simultaneous, dynamic, and ongoing. I use dual pairings, therefore, to draw attention to how the global constitutes the national, which constitutes the local, which reconstitutes both the national and the global, not in some hydraulic and linear way, but through myriad dialogic interactions of which I have tried to capture a few in the chapters that follow. This means that the distinctions between the global-national, the national-local, and the local-global are not always so clear-cut at the level of experience. Nor is it the case that the "content" of one or another section can only fruitfully be addressed within those particular parameters. Nevertheless, the pairings I have chosen do suggest a particular temporality. By this, I mean that the analytic focus shifts—both in space and in time—from the ways the nation-state has responded to global directives throughout the early postcolonial period to the ways individuals—and the networks they mobilize—shape global trends. In this way, the structure of the book mirrors the movement of the argument. That is, it chronicles the shift from the post–World War II struggle to establish a definition of nationalist progress and development within the parameters of respectable citizenship embodied through the figure of the rural Afro-Jamaican peasant to the popular contemporary constructions of racialized belonging that are rooted in—but also transcend—the boundaries of the Jamaican state.

The two chapters in part I introduce late-nineteenth- and mid-twentieth-century nationalists, scholars, and cultural activists; their visions of progress and development; and their efforts to formulate, disseminate, and institutionalize a cultural policy and other mandates regarding Jamaican cultural production. It traces the consolidation of a creole political and sociocultural hegemony. Chapter I explores the relationship between emergent identities rooted in blackness and Jamaicanness—race and nation—and how these mobilizing identities have been influenced by perceptions of Africa, by a history of consistent and extensive migration, and by the emphasis on the part of middle-class mobilizers upon cultural modernization and progress rooted in the "respectable" values of the sectarian churches. Here, I discuss how the various ideological developments toward the end of the nineteenth century placed early black nationalists in the precarious position of proving, to local and international publics, both their equality (to "civilized" whites) and their difference (from the "backward" masses). By proving their progress, early black nationalists and later creole nationalists were able to demand equality, first as human beings and later as citizens. At the same time, by actively containing the development of other mobilizing ideologies along class or racial lines and by placing emphasis upon the transformation of black lower-class Jamaicans' social, political, and cultural practices, they also reproduced aspects of the colonial nexus of color, class, gender, and culture—a nexus that was coded through a concern with "values." By independence in 1962, then, race became sublimated into the universalizing ideology of the modern creole nation, despite the persistence of alternative nationalist ideologies among other sectors of the population.

Chapter 2 investigates the evolution of cultural development initiatives during the period of Crown Colony rule (1865–1944) and the ways these became institutionalized at independence through the development of a cultural policy reflecting the creole ideology. I trace alterations to this policy throughout the postindependence period by foregrounding the tensions between creole multiracial nationalism and various more explicitly racialized understandings of belonging that emerged at different points in time. By analyzing these tensions within the context of a changing local and global political economy, I show how the state has responded to popular challenges to its hegemony at various moments. Throughout this discussion, I examine questions regarding the definition of culture, its purported relationships with values, and the links posited between culture and development at the national level.

Part 2 takes us to the community level in order to explore the ways both nationalist policies and popular ideologies regarding progress and development have been evaluated, interpreted, reproduced, and/or transformed locally. Here, I ground the sphere of ideological production in everyday practice. Throughout part 2, I highlight the ways people negotiate a range of ideologies and experiences to construct their own sense of belonging, both to the community and to the nation. In chapter 3, belonging is defined in relation to villagers' differing levels of control over social, economic, and political resources. By paying attention to the ways community members evaluate these differences, I chart the processes by which national hierarchies of value are mapped onto individuals and groups at the local level. This chapter also begins to trace the ways these hierarchies of value are reproduced through community members' interactions with local institutions and are transformed as a result of generational mobility among poorer community members. Chapter 4 turns to address the implications of local class divisions and status distinctions for community members' expectations regarding leadership as well as their diverse definitions of "development." It investigates some of the contexts in which status distinctions among poorer community members are overridden and the extent to which this is related to an apprehension of their common designation as black people within a national hierarchy of races.

In chapter 5, I examine how the structural and ideological differences among community members influence their various assessments of state-driven initiatives geared toward encouraging pride in Jamaica's history and African cultural heritage. I analyze local responses to one of the more recent attempts to foster the values of unity, collective work, and national pride—the government's 1997 reinstatement of Emancipation Day as a public holiday. Here, I counterpose villagers' ambivalences regarding "Africanness" to their concerns about "blackness" to explain why poorer Mango Mount community members—whose lives were increasingly urban and transnational—did not conceptualize their problems in terms of "culture." Because they did not perceive their inability to "move forward in life" as related to a negative evaluation of Jamaica's African cultural heritage, they could appreciate the symbolism associated with state-sponsored cultural development initiatives, but did not see them as providing a basis for their own progress and development.

Part 3 explores the actual strategies poorer community members did pursue to "move forward in life" as well as the ways these strategies were represented within their own cultural production. It defines these strategies and representations as embodiments of a "modern blackness" and repositions the transformations I have been noting all along as aspects of a single shift from creole multiracialism to modern blackness. I explore modern blackness at two levels. While chapter 6 examines lower-class Jamaicans' visions of progress, modernity, and (hoped for) mobility, chapter 7 highlights popular representations of these visions. Both chapters attempt to show that community members, and Jamaicans more generally, are intensely aware of their own relationships to a changing global political economy and that this awareness influences their evaluations of their political options, their economic opportunities, their social potential, their cultural choices, and their sense of both social and physical place—locally, nationally, regionally, and globally.

In chapter 6, I demonstrate that by the late 1990s, poorer families in the community more easily bypassed local middle-class leadership to achieve their goals than previously, and I argue that their strategies in doing so have been supported by recent processes of globalization. Following Lisa Rofel (1999), I highlight the importance of generation, both as an analytic category and as a critical factor in the formation of sociopolitical cohorts. My ulterior motive here is to demonstrate that analytically speaking, people's political and economic ambitions on one hand and their sociocultural beliefs and practices on the other cannot be reduced to a simple one-to-one relationship and that the contemporary context brings this into greater relief. Chapter 7 returns to a discussion of representation in order to concretize my definition of modern blackness as urban, migratory, based in youth-oriented popular culture and influenced by African American popular style, individualist, "radically consumerist," and "ghetto feminist." I use the issues raised through a local theatrical production to speak in more general theoretical terms about how individuals at the local level negotiated the publicly powerful ideologies associated with modern blackness and related them to their own lives and experiences. I also position modern blackness in terms of its relationship to earlier black nationalisms, views of America and Americanization, cultural imperialism and appropriation, consumerism and individualism in Jamaican society, and the cultivation of respectability as a mechanism for policing social difference. In doing so, I suggest where we might position modern blackness in relation to a continuum of lower-class political visions and action within Jamaica. I end the book with a conclusion that considers some of the implications of these changes for both nationalist institutions and alternative ideological and practical expressions of belonging, and an epilogue that notes some of the changes that have occurred since the bulk of the research for the book was conducted.

An Important Terminological Note

Throughout this book, I identify individuals' racial and class designations with terms used by Mango Mount community members. When I use the term "middle class," I am referring to that segment of the national middle class that predominates within the civil service and professions: lawyers, doctors, journalists, intellectuals, and artists. "Middle class," here, connotes the acquisition of at least a secondary, but often also a tertiary, education. It also connotes "brownness," an intermediary color and class construction that is linked historically with the population of free people of color that emerged during the slavery period. In the community ethnography, most (but not all) of those variously referred to as "the middle class," "the more fortunate," the "rich people," and the "upper sets" fall into the range of color categories usually referred to as "brown." This is because the village lacks the substantial black middle- (and upper-) class population that exists at the national level. "Brown" is as much a way of life as it is a phenotype, however, as it also signifies respectability or at least aspirations toward respectability. This is the segment of the national middle class most often associated with the creole multiracial nationalist project and with the values and visions of progress I define in part 1 of the book. As a result, "middle class" additionally implies a generational frame of reference. My usage of the term "middle class," then, does not refer to the newer (post-1970s) managerial middle class nor does it signify those involved in the trade or industrial professions. These distinctions will be parsed in the chapters that follow.

In the village, the group of tradespeople, farmers, itinerant laborers, and unemployed men and women, who are overwhelmingly phenotypically black, will be alternatively called "the poorer set," "the poorer class of people," "the local people," and "Mango Mount people." This is the segment of the national population usually coded as "working class" or "lower class." Very occasionally, I use the term "Afro-Jamaicans," but this is generally a capitulation to dominant trends of racial and cultural identification in the United States. "Afro-Jamaican" or "African-Jamaican" are not widely circulated designations in Jamaica, and with one exception, they were never used by Mango Mount community members.

I have usually identified those speaking by their age, class position, and gender, but sometimes have not. In these cases, it is often clear which sector of the Mango Mount community the speaker belongs to by their language, but it should be noted that many in the "poorer class of people" also spoke a variant of Jamaican English that more fully approximated that of the "upper sets." These tended to be older villagers and, often, women, a fact that underscores some of my broader arguments regarding gender and generation throughout the book, particularly in chapter 7. Therefore, it should not be assumed that because a quotation is not presented in patois, the speaker was middle class. Additionally, with the exception of a few "slang" words that wouldn't necessarily be recognizable to a non-Jamaican audience, I have not translated people's statements from Jamaican English or patois to Standard American English. While the general meaning of the remarks will always be evident in context, this is a deliberate attempt on my part to force the reader to personally experience, albeit in a very minor way, one of the dimensions through which modern blackness has constituted a degree of cultural and political autonomy for lower-class black Jamaicans. It is also a small, yet important, reminder that despite the often deep level of intimacy generated by anthropological methods, there are always limits to understanding.

It is my hope that this book will not only offer something of value to Caribbeanists, and to people specifically interested in Jamaica, but also to those concerned with the notion of diaspora more broadly. Many of the issues I discuss in these pages will not be unrecognizable to scholars who have researched the experiences of people of African descent in other locations. For example, the crisis-oriented discourse that surrounds popular cultural production and the conceptualizations of respectable citizenship will sound familiar to African Americanists who have worked on these themes. Familiar, yet not identical. But this is not only because their specific iterations in Jamaica have been shaped by a different, though related, historical political economic context. It is also because our different scholarly preoccupations and political projects—in short, our different vernaculars—sometimes render translation difficult. This is an important point because it touches on a larger issue shaping attention to black communities worldwide: the tendency to privilege similarity, or unity, among African diasporic populations rather than difference, disunity, and asymmetry. This is an issue that has garnered more attention recently as anthropologists, literary critics, and historians have attempted to explore implications of the observation that "diaspora may very well constitute an identity of passions; but these passions, and the means of pursuing them, may not be identical within particular communities" (Brown 1998:298; see also Carr 2002; Campt 2003; Edwards 2003).

If our starting point in diasporic discussions always assumes similarity and unity, we cannot help but privilege particular narratives, assessing other narratives primarily in relation to the extent to which they accede to or diverge from that which seems normative. Often, this leads us to pay less attention not only to those aspects of particular diasporic formations that might not be readily translatable, but also to the broader contexts and relations of power within which diasporic cultural and political formulations are created and re-created *in relation to one another* over time. My intention in what follows is to clarify some of these contexts, some of these changes, some of these power dynamics, and some of these instances of lateral borrowing, anticipating that this will help to provide a foundation from which to more profoundly engage popular cultural production and modern blackness in Jamaica—its relationships to anticolonial nationalism; its visions of modernity; its processes of racial, gender, and class formation; and its articulations (and disarticulations) with other blacknesses.

PART I

The Global-National

chapter 1

THE "PROBLEM" OF NATIONALISM

IN THE BRITISH WEST INDIES; OR,

"WHAT WE ARE AND WHAT

WE HOPE TO BE"

It has long been asserted that the growth of nationalist sentiment has been particularly weak in the British West Indies. In the prologue to her memoir *Drumblair: Memories of a Jamaican Childhood*, Rachel Manley recalls someone —maybe her grandfather Norman Manley, the "father" of the Jamaican nation—stating, " 'We lack that hammock of national belonging which cradles a people against historical falls' " (1996:3). The imagery used here suggests that what is fundamental to creating nations out of newly independent states is a seemingly autochthonous identity that would cushion, sustain, and nurture a citizenry whose primary historical and current reality hinges upon the various and varying dynamics of international capitalism. Significantly, the tone of the phrase, indeed of the whole book, is one of nostalgia—more specifically, a nostalgia generated by the assessment that the dreams of a particular generation were not only deferred, but also debunked, even derailed. It is a nostalgia borne of the nagging notion that the nationalist project in Jamaica, despite formal political independence, has failed, that the "hammock" has gaping holes.

The discussion that follows outlines the ideological and practical foundations of mid-twentieth-century creole nationalism in Jamaica, exploring the relationships between blackness (a racial identity) and Jamaicanness (a national identity), and between both of these concepts, class and gender. My purpose here is not merely to rehearse some of the more interesting historical developments in postemancipation Jamaica. Rather, it is to recast these developments in light of their relevance to the twentieth-century project of defining who and what should represent the national community.

Toward this end, what I assert is that the ideology of national belonging that became publicly hegemonic by Jamaica's independence in 1962—that of creole multiracial nationalism—had its roots in late-nineteenth-century perceptions of Africa, in the history of consistent and extensive migration, and in the emphasis on the part of (black *and* brown) middle-class mobilizers upon cultural modernization and progress rooted in the values promoted by the sectarian churches. As a result especially of the latter, the creole multiracial nationalist perspective ultimately emphasized self-help through moderate middle-class leadership and the transformation of (lower-class) people's cultural practices, without substantial reform of the larger political and economic context. This perspective, however, never existed in a vacuum. As a result, I juxtapose its development with the consistent challenges offered up by advocates of more explicitly racially based blueprints for independent development.[1] What is key here is that at the core of concerns regarding the relationship between Race and Nation is one of the most fundamental issues addressed by both scholars and activists throughout the twentieth century—the place of black people in the modern West.

Nation Building and Race Making: The "Failure" to Develop an "Authentic" Nationalism, or, "Fear of a Black Planet"

Between the late nineteenth century and the labor rebellions of the late 1930s, the predominant ideology that unified Jamaicans across race and class was that of pride in Empire (Bryan 1991). Though the strength of this ideology had begun to decline by the mid-twentieth century, at the moment of the formal transfer of sovereignty in 1962 there still appeared to be very little commitment to the idea of Jamaica as an autonomous political (and cultural) entity among either the mass of the population or the elites. This was a phenomenon noted by contemporary observers such as Katrin Norris, a radical English leftist who viewed Jamaican society as lacking faith in itself in light of its adherence to a colonial educational curriculum and the readiness of the population to migrate:

> On the eve of her constitutional independence, instead of being filled with real passion for its achievement, Jamaica is still colonial at heart, drawing her values from foreign sources; this is the greatest wrong colonialism has done her (Norris 1962:71).

Norris, like many others, argued that anticolonial nationalism in Jamaica was a weakly rooted ideology due to the lack of an "authentically" local worldview around which the entire population could be mobilized toward self-government.

Historians have explained this lack in several ways. Some have attributed purportedly weak nationalist sentiment to the prevalence of absenteeism among the planters during the period of slavery, a practice that they believe prevented the development of local colonial pride and nationalism (Burn 1937 [1970]; Curtin [1955]; Patterson 1967; Ragatz 1928). Others have argued that what protonationalist thought did develop among the urban Creole intelligentsia during slavery and after emancipation in 1838 was a sort of "colonial Whiggism" that maintained a pro-English bias and presumed that the old slave society would yield to a Victorian-like class society tempered by the civilizing influence of Christianity (G. Lewis 1968, 1983). Richard Hart, a Marxist historian and a founding member of the People's National Party, viewed the slave masses (rather than the Creole elites) as the Jamaican nation in embryo. Therefore, the factors he has emphasized as responsible for a slow development of nationalist agitation after emancipation were a pervasive loyalty to Great Britain among free blacks and people of color coupled with an imperial education policy that, in his view, successfully convinced the mass of the Jamaican population that they were racially inferior (1970). Still other historians have attributed the early dearth of nationalist sentiment to an aborted creolization process that resulted in the elaboration of a cultural dichotomy that was sustained not only by former planters but also by slaves, who failed to use their "folk" culture to develop group self-consciousness (Brathwaite 1971a).[2]

The general consensus among these scholars is that despite the fact that a type of group self-consciousness was manifest in Jamaica throughout the period of slavery (the first slave rebellion occurred in 1673, not twenty years after the British took Jamaica from Spain in 1655, and it is estimated that there was an average of one rebellion for every five years throughout the eighteenth century), and despite the fact that these rebellions were often undergirded by the creole religio-political worldviews slaves developed within Jamaica, after "full free" in 1838,[3] the momentum initiated by these revolts was not carried over into a nation-building project.

The development of nationalism became even more of a "problem" with the strengthening of British political, social, and cultural institutions after the establishment of Crown Colony rule in 1866. Prior to this point, Ja-

maica's white oligarchy had considerable autonomy from the metropolitan government in that they elected their own Legislative Assembly
locally in Jamaica and constituted a particularly powerful lobby in British
Parliament. The 1865 Morant Bay Rebellion led by Paul Bogle inspired a
change in these political relationships for the first time.

   Paul Bogle, a black Baptist preacher and literate landowner with voting
privileges, led a march of several hundred armed men and women to
Morant Bay, the capital city of the parish of St. Thomas, in order to articulate their grievances against a colonial government that had turned a blind
eye to their increasingly unbearable living conditions. This march—one of
several that Bogle led—protested then Governor Eyre's refusal to address
the supplications made on behalf of St. Thomas' black peasant population
by George William Gordon, a colored landowner who was a minister in
Bogle's church and who was elected to the local legislature.[4] It was designed to challenge the power of the white planter class and to catalyze a
more general rebellion throughout Jamaica. Bogle motivated his followers
with the rallying cry "Cleave to the Black!" (quoted in Post 1978:34), and
they quickly overwhelmed the small militia that met them, taking control
of Morant Bay. For the next few days, hundreds of additional followers
patrolled the St. Thomas countryside, killing two white planters and forc-
ing others to flee. Governor Eyre sent troops to regain control of the area.
His soldiers shot or hanged anyone they suspected of being one of the
rebels and burned down hundreds of houses. Paul Bogle was among those
hanged, and George William Gordon, tried in connection with the rebellion, was found guilty despite a lack of evidence against him and was
murdered. While Eyre's retaliations produced popular public outcry in
Britain, British elites and several intellectuals (including Thomas Carlyle,
Lord Tennyson, and Charles Dickens) rallied behind Eyre in one of the
foundational moments of modern British racism.[5]

   In the aftermath of the rebellion, planters voted to dissolve the local
Legislative Assembly and establish a system of direct nondemocratic rule
from the metropole through a governor and his representatives (Crown
Colony rule). This was significant because it demonstrated that planters'
fear of potential black retribution was stronger than their commitment to
local political participation. As Richard Hart has explained, "Those who
for two centuries had upheld the principle of political self-determination
readily jettisoned it when the disenfranchised masses appeared to threaten
their economic and social security" (1970:9). Since the Assembly had be-

come one channel through which nonelite Jamaicans were attempting to exert influence over the political and economic direction of the island, the acceptance of Crown Colony rule by the local oligarchy is perhaps not particularly surprising.

During the late nineteenth century, the colonial institutions that had been strengthened by Crown Colony government were significantly transformed with the trend toward secularization and the rapid expansion of empire, yet imperial racism was not attenuated. The "new imperialism"— justified through the pretense of philanthropy, now defined as the bestowal of civilization—emerged as part and parcel of Social Darwinist principles of progress.[6] Within this context, a new racism, now intellectually legitimized as science, was used to justify paternalistic class domination and white social authority and (tropical) people's cultural practices were placed on the agenda of change. Would-be nationalists, then, were placed in the awkward position of having to prove both their equality (to the civilized British) and their difference (from the uncivilized masses).[7] At the same time, they were required to destabilize aspects of Social Darwinism in order to generate support for their cause. That is, they had to demonstrate the debilitating effects of Jamaica's history of plantation slavery. As a result, early nationalists were led to emphasize reform rather than political and economic radicalism. This emphasis persisted despite the emergence of alternative nationalist ideologies and was ultimately consolidated within the creole multiracial nationalism that became hegemonic by the time of Jamaica's constitutional independence.

Early Black Nationalism: Jamaica's Jubilee

The 1888 publication of Jamaica's Jubilee; or, What We Are and What We Hope to Be was the first published work by black Jamaicans that codified a critique of racism.[8] The book was geared toward demonstrating to a British audience the progress of ex-slaves in Jamaica during the fifty years since emancipation and toward assuring them that blacks held no feelings of revenge (C. Wilson 1929). The five authors, all of whom had substantial connections to the nonconformist missionary churches,[9] attempted to convince their readership that fifty years of freedom and missionary effort had benefited the people of Jamaica who, with continued assistance, would progress even further:

We launch [this book] forth upon a considerable public, in the earnest hope that it will, in this Jubilee year of our country's Emancipation, awaken in the bosoms of our friends in Britain and Jamaica a still livelier interest in us, and evoke still more persistent and hopeful efforts on our behalf; while we trust that the wholesome advice, the faithful admonitions, and the encouraging facts contained in it, will produce their legitimate effect on ourselves, the struggling children of Afric in the West. (JJ 10)

The book is divided into five essays, each of which tackles an aspect of Jamaica's past, present, and future, illuminating the meanings of freedom and progress for the authors at the turn of the century.

In their attempt to refute the widespread belief that black Jamaicans were incapable of possessing "those mental and moral qualities so indispensably necessary to his rise in the scale of true civilisation" (JJ 12), the authors outlined several advances since emancipation. The increase in elementary schools after the abolition of slavery was cited as evidence of the ex-slaves' ability and desire to learn. The authors also placed great emphasis upon the increased number of mutual improvement societies, reading clubs, and Christian associations, the proliferation of musical and social gatherings during Christmastime, and the increase of legal marriage. In their estimation, these indicators of the former slaves' progress had been due to fifty years of "social liberty and equality, of religious privileges, of educational advantages, and of intercourse in various ways with civilized and Christian men" (JJ 75). The "Jubilee Five" also cautioned the readership against censuring Jamaicans for not having advanced further in the fifty years since emancipation, arguing that *"no other people could, under similar circumstances, have reached a greater height on the ladder of social advancement within the same period of time"* (JJ 83, italics in original):[10]

> That a nation is not born in a day is a truth that holds good here. Those who are expecting to find our people higher up the moral, social, and intellectual ladder, have certainly forgotten how many centuries it took other nations and peoples enjoying superior advantages to be what they are to-day: notably, the British nation, now the foremost, on the whole, in science, art, commerce, literature and religion. (JJ 16–17)

Notably, the authors attributed the postemancipation developments in Jamaican society to the nonconformist missionaries, whom they viewed as having instilled in the slaves a desire for freedom and progress during slavery and as having worked to counteract the effects of the slavery system that had continued after emancipation, including, as they saw it, laziness and apathy. The British colonial government, on the other hand, was indicted for having abandoned the ex-slaves after emancipation and for having failed to initiate any policy that would counter the destabilizing influences of slavery. The authors' view was that Britain left "Africa and her children" derailed on the path to civilization:

> Has [the Jamaican negro] been happily positioned since his introduction into this island? Have his advantages been of the best and most favorable kind? Has sufficient encouragement been held out to him? The only answer to these questions that can have any show of fairness and justice, must be in the *negative*. (JJ 13, italics in original)

The authors' acceptance of an evolutionary paradigm with respect to progress—or, in the terminology of the day, civilization—is clear, but here they used Social Darwinism to critique postemancipation British colonial policy by invoking history. Further, their assertion that despite their African ancestry, black Jamaicans' positions as British subjects gave them the right to claim both a history and "the interest, sympathy, and protection of those who were instrumental in effecting the expatriation of [their] ancestors" (JJ 12) indicated that they expected some degree of reparations based on their legal equality as British subjects.

The writers' vision for future progress can be divided into two categories, with the first addressing the need to strengthen Jamaica's infrastructure. In this respect, they called for more effective management of the colony, greater access to training in scientific agriculture, a greater reliance on locally grown goods rather than imports, and the construction of more and better parochial roads. The second category of the authors' vision for the future concerned the need to strengthen Jamaicans' values. Progress, as they saw it, rested on the pillars of industry (thoughtful and focused labor), economy (thrift and frugality), and godliness (Christian living). They located these values in the persona of the independent peasant, based on their view that working on the sugar estates exerted a demoralizing influence that ultimately would hinder the development of respectable practices and values. Respectability, here, was defined as owning a small plot of land in the mountains, being able to support a family through small-scale agricultural production, having a quiet disposition, and living simply. In their elaboration of these values, the authors consistently evoked the principle that individual effort was related to national development, arguing that the cultivation of respectability would give black Jamaicans entrance into "the brotherhood of nations" (JJ 48):

Our defamers shall be constrained to acknowledge us, as, with themselves, the common denizens of a common world, the children of a common Father, the subjects of a common king, the servants of a common Maker; possessing the same rights, entitled to the same privileges, claiming the same regard and affection, and having the same destiny. (JJ 21)

Finally, the authors made a plea for greater unity among Jamaicans. They argued that "internal jealousy" in the guise of racism and class prejudice "prevents steady advancement as a civilized people" (JJ 30), and that unless blacks in Jamaica united, the development of a national spirit would be inhibited. Here, it is notable that though their argument was general, they were also speaking on behalf of their race, as it were: "We form the bulk by far of Jamaica's people" and, therefore, "Jamaica is emphatically ours" (JJ 111). The potential for the articulation of such a vision of ownership had terrified both the local elite and colonial administrators since the establishment of Jamaica as a plantation colony. Its appearance here allows us, I believe, to position *Jamaica's Jubilee* as the first published espousal of black nationalism. The volume concludes on an optimistic note, proclaiming hope for Jamaica's future as a united and prosperous nation:

We seem born to live! Other savage nations have perished under oppression and vanished before the advance of civilization; but, in the most inhospitable climates of the globe, the children of Africa have lived and increased through centuries of different climates of the globe, and there treated as anything but men and women; and yet they have lived, and instead of being crushed beneath the tread of advancing civilization, they have joined the ranks of progress, and are to-day marching after the nations already in the van. . . . 'Ethiopia shall soon stretch forth her hands unto God.' (JJ 115, 128)

Rebutting Racism

There are several reasons that the publication of the *Jamaica's Jubilee* volume is so critical to an understanding of the development of nationalist thought in Jamaica throughout the twentieth century. The first is that despite the authors' reproduction of Social Darwinist premises regarding progress through imperial guidance, the book offers a counterpoint to the revival of the racist prejudices of the old planter histories, such as James

Anthony Froude's *The English in the West Indies*, published in the same year as *Jamaica's Jubilee* (1888). An English essayist and historian and Thomas Carlyle's biographer,[11] Froude railed against both imperial absenteeism and self-government for the Caribbean colonies, ultimately arguing for a change in British imperial policy for the West Indies toward the model of the British Raj in India. He viewed West Indian blacks as innately inferior —"of another stock" (1888:50)—and as incapable of ruling themselves, let alone whites. While Froude's work is generally seen as an aberration within the growing liberalism of the late nineteenth century, at the same time his association of imperialism with all that was new, modern, and civilized and his conviction that the emancipation of black West Indians began with their removal from Africa as slaves (1888:236) reflected the growing ideology within Britain that Britain had an imperial responsibility, defined as both *right* and *duty*, to lead "weak nations" toward true freedom (1888:207).

Froude's polemic did not go unanswered.[12] Nevertheless, even Froude's detractors tended to accept the conventional paternalistic view that emancipation was an act of English benevolence. This reveals the extent to which Social Darwinism, as an ideology of racial progress, pervaded the analyses of even the most progressive or purportedly sympathetic observers. Indeed, even the Jubilee authors, in their refutation of scientific racism, also framed their remarks within a vision of progress consistent with Social Darwinist ideas.[13] While this should underscore for us the difficulty of transcending context, it also points us toward consequences. By capitulating to the sectarian churches' view that the combination of religiously inspired behavioral and institutional change in conjunction with small (though significant) postemancipation reforms would lead to improved conditions for the mass of the population, the Jubilee writers relegated both systemic overhaul and explicitly racial mobilization to back burners. In this way, the vindicationist arguments put forth by the authors of *Jamaica's Jubilee* ultimately foreshadowed those formulated by mid-twentieth-century creole nationalist elites.

Privileging the Peasant

A second contribution of the *Jamaica's Jubilee* collection of essays to our understanding of twentieth-century creole nationalism in Jamaica is the authors' equation of progress in conditions of freedom with the development of an independent peasantry. Those improvements they delineated as necessary —more schools, more and better parochial roads, training in scientific agriculture, a stronger institutional infrastructure—were all pol-icy matters that would facilitate the growth of a peasantry, rather than an estate-based wage-laboring population. The authors' privileging of a "respectable" peasant lifestyle over that of the sugar plantation worker directly countered the intentions of both Jamaican planters and British policy makers at the moment of emancipation.

Historian Thomas Holt has argued that abolitionists and policy makers sought to solve the "problem of freedom" by transforming slaves into reliable wage laborers. This would be done by socializing former slaves to respond to the work incentives of free people and expanding their material aspirations (1992).[14] Many of the apprentices and former slaves, however, had other aspirations, aspirations that surprised missionaries and other observers from England and the United States who traveled throughout the West Indies to assess the results of the "great experiment" of eman-cipation.[15] For example, during their sojourn in Jamaica, James Thome and J. Horace Kimball documented several instances of apprentices work-ing on estates other than their own during their free time where wages were known to be higher, as well as refusing to work on the estates when they could make more money by selling the proceeds from their own provision grounds in the market. These trends led them to conclude that the former slaves' "notion of freedom was precisely the reverse of that which slaves are generally supposed to entertain; instead of associating it with a *release from labor*, they connected it with an *increase of labor*" (1838:404, italics in original). John Bigelow, a West Indian planter, understood these trends as examples of the ex-slaves playing their options off each other since it was well known that Jamaican wages were below subsistence level (1851 [1970]). Bigelow also associated the desire among ex-slaves to own land with their growing participation in the political process, countering the view more generally held by planters that Jamaican small freeholders were politically apathetic. Because postemancipation legislation deline-ated property and literacy qualifications for voting in order to keep the former slaves tied to the estates, land ownership not only represented an alternative to working full time on the plantations and an opportunity to bargain with planters over the conditions of their labor, but also their first chance to participate directly in the civic and political life of the colony as free subjects.[16]

Among the former slaves, then, land rights emerged as the central theme of both freedom and community. Within this context, the Baptist Church played a major role in postemancipation rural settlement by buying and subdividing properties in order to establish church communities called "free villages." While the missionary churches and schools provided the slaves with opportunities to establish new claims to status, to acquire new skills, and to question "why Christian values were not practiced in the society they knew" (Turner 1982:94), it is also evident that even the nonconformist churches encouraged the development of values that legitimated the system of domination, both during slavery and after emancipation. For example, as historical sociologist Nigel Bolland has pointed out, the Baptists' paternalism stressed white cultural superiority, fostered dependency, and promoted passivity rather than critical thinking (1992). As a result, during the 1830s and 1840s, Jamaicans aspiring to be Christian blacks faced a dilemma because those who supported their freedom from slavery were simultaneously engaged in a project to reconstruct their selves and their souls.

Moreover, as historian Catherine Hall has demonstrated, Baptist missionaries also mobilized new gender ideologies to support their view of restructured economic, political, and social life after emancipation. Hall argues that Baptists viewed slavery as having produced a situation by which male slaves, dependent upon their masters, were unable to become "real men." That is, they were unable to live up to the standards of middle-class Englishmen at the time—seen as "being married, being independent in 'pecuniary affairs,' working for wages, being a householder, paying for medical care and education, celebrating the voluntary principle which was at the heart of dissenting politics, [and] refusing state intervention in church, school and welfare" (1995:53). For the Baptists, emancipation marked the potential for the former slaves to become "white"—but not like the white men and women of plantation society. Rather, black men would become "responsible, independent, industrious, domesticated Christians" and black women, now focused on marriage and child rearing, would "no longer be sexually subjugated to their masters but properly dependent on their husbands" (1995:54). However, in order to facilitate this "whitening," Baptist missionaries embarked upon a campaign to eradicate the social and religious ideologies held by the population during slavery, ideologies understood to have been African in derivation.

This campaign, however, did not go unchallenged. Women, in particular, distressed the missionaries by continuing to work outside the home as well as by playing important roles in politics (Wilmot 1995). And various other religious sects and revivalist movements emerged throughout the postemancipation period, attracting large numbers of poorer Jamaicans in what Diane Austin-Broos has identified as an attempt to "supersede the persona of the Christian black" (1997:39). The Baptist missionaries' fatal flaw, then, was their refusal to recognize an existing black culture and their related inability to apprehend the fact that marriage failed to become popular, that the birth of children outside of wedlock remained the norm, and that women's labor and land tenure continued to be of utmost importance to the communities they were supposed to serve. Nevertheless, their rhetoric of an idealized respectability survived well beyond the mid-nineteenth century when the missionary communities began to decline.

In spite of the church's role in buttressing the colonial authority structure and in imposing new (though contested) ideologies with respect to social organization, it is clear that the Baptist communities represented an alternative to hegemonic economic and political relations; it has been estimated that by 1845, 19,000 ex-slaves had purchased land in these church villages (Besson 1992:191).[17] Several contemporary historians and anthropologists have celebrated this fact in their efforts to show that far from being passive recipients of a freedom benevolently bestowed by the British imperial government, the former slaves played an active role in defining emancipation for themselves and, therefore, in shaping the contours of postemancipation society more generally. Indeed, the former slaves' movement away from the estates represented not only a desire to avoid new forms of surveillance and coercion, but also the possibility of shaping new social relations unlike both those imposed during slavery and those envisioned by their former masters. Land ownership, kinship and community-based production, and the development of the institution of family land—land whose inheritance generally dates back to an original freeholder, which is subdivided equally among the offspring of each generation, and which is considered inalienable and therefore unsalable, either in parts or in totality (Carnegie 1987b; Besson 2002)—represented new forms of economic and political participation and provided the foundations for an alternative interpretation of freedom (Besson 1992; Bolland 1992).

By the mid-nineteenth century, funding for the Baptist free villages had begun to dry up, and Jamaica's small farmer class became increasingly dispersed due to the collapse of the sugar industry, the takeover of peasant banana production by the United Fruit Company, and the expansion of Crown Lands during the 1880s and 1890s. Because it had become progressively more difficult to buy land, the peasantry was also increasingly unable to avoid being exploited as proletariats.[18] This thwarted desire to own land would be among the principal factors leading to the Morant Bay Rebellion in 1865, the massive rural-to-urban and international labor migration during the 1880s and continuing throughout the early 1920s, and the labor rebellions of the late 1930s. As a result, by advocating reforms that would improve conditions for the peasantry, late-nineteenth-century intellectuals and nationalists like the authors of *Jamaica's Jubilee* continued to legitimize *both* the popular ideology that linked land rights to independence—culturally and socially, but also economically and politically—*and* the religious conviction that the figure of the independent peasant represented a more respectable type of human being. These ideologies have not waned. Land ownership and small-scale peasant production continued to signify a modicum of independence not only from the state but also from the more deleterious effects of increasing global capitalist integration throughout the second half of the twentieth century. On the issue of land reform in particular, then, the *Jubilee* five articulated an abiding concern with which twentieth-century nationalists would also have to continuously contend.

Subjects and Nationalists

Changes toward a more interventionist imperial policy by the late nineteenth century, despite the emergence of the free trade movement and laissez-faire opinion, reflected the growing conviction within Britain that the state should play a greater role in the lives of its citizens. By the time the five *Jamaica's Jubilee* authors penned their essays, then, the concept of empire as a mobilizing ideology designed to bridge racial and class-based divisions both in the colonies and in England was reaching its peak. This brings us to the third critical contribution of *Jamaica's Jubilee* to understanding the ideological and practical foundations of twentieth-century nationalism in Jamaica—the simultaneous proclamation of loyalty to Jamaica and to Great Britain within the context of an emergent diasporic sensibility.

The insistence that black people in Jamaica could claim a history based on their position as British subjects (JJ 12), the vision of Queen Victoria as the Great Ruler of the Universe and of emancipation as a great act of elevation (JJ 90), and the assertion that Britain—as "the most enlightened Christian nation on the face of the earth"—had a duty to assist the former slaves (JJ 14) all reflected the identification of the British Crown (with whom many former slaves associated the Baptists) with benevolent and fair rule. The British government was viewed as protecting the interests of the former slaves from both direct persecution by local whites as well as from the planters' intermittent dalliances with the idea of annexation to the United States (Bakan 1990; Bryan 1991; Hart 1970; Holt 1992; Robotham 1981). The former slaves' understanding of the relationship between the planters and the colonial government as antagonistic was long standing and would be long lasting.[19]

It is important to note, however, that the identification of the British Crown as protector among the former slaves and their descendants did not generally translate into loyalty to British imperialism or colonialism as an economic and political system, either on the part of the mass of the population or the emergent black intelligentsia.[20] That the Jamaica's Jubilee authors ultimately regarded Jamaica as a nation, albeit an embryonic one, is incontrovertible. It is also apparent that their simultaneous loyalty to Britain and to Jamaica coexisted with their recognition that the position of blacks in Jamaica was part of a worldwide conception of blacks, Africa, and African civilization as having "as yet achieved nothing" (JJ 111). Indeed, this belief would lead many contemporary educated blacks to proselytize for the Christian church in Africa in an attempt to prove that blacks were capable of civilization, and that Africa, though currently wild and backward, could rise to prominence again with the transference of Western civilization.[21] The Jamaica's Jubilee authors' identification with Africa, then, was with its potential future rather than its present. Of course, this is an attitude that would alter with the emergence of Garveyism, which, in its recognition of the significance of racism as a factor retarding black social, economic, and political progress, presented a more radical challenge to hegemonic ideas regarding progress consolidated around the tenets of Christianity. What emerges as most significant here, however, is that the authors' self-assessments as British, as Jamaican, and as "children of Africa" were not presented as either/or propositions. Rather, they were able to express intense loyalty to all three aspects of their identity.[22]

Here, it is critical to consider the role of Jamaicans' increased mobility during the second half of the nineteenth century, as well as technological developments and the growing economic penetration by the United States during this period. Following emancipation there was a rapid increase of communication within the island, complemented by extensive migration beyond Jamaica's shores. For the first time, an alternative to plantation wage labor or subsistence farming emerged. After 1880, Jamaican laborers traveled to Panama to participate in the initial attempt by a French company to construct the canal. This wave of migration peaked in 1883 with a total of 24,301 workers leaving the island (Eisner 1961:148). Between 1880 and 1889, there was also a net outflow of about 24,000 Jamaicans to Costa Rica to construct railroads (Eisner 1961:149). After 1900, there was another movement of Jamaicans to Panama for work on the Canal, this time under a U.S. company, and back to Costa Rica for work in the banana industry. Prior to 1911, Panama received 62 percent of all emigrants (about 43,000) and the United States received 16,000, but after this year, approximately 30,000 Jamaicans migrated to the United States (Roberts 1957:139,140). Finally, between 1912 and 1920, 75,000 Jamaicans traveled to Cuba for work on the sugar plantations after the World War I boom in production (E. Petras 1988:232), and after 1943, Jamaicans were increasingly recruited for agricultural labor in the United States on Farm Work schemes. While mobility had become a taken-for-granted feature of life among Jamaica's laboring population by the fourth quarter of the nineteenth century, it has only been since the beginning of the twentieth century that the United States has become migrants' primary destination.

With the development of the banana industry under the auspices of American multinationals in the late 1800s, the United States displaced Great Britain as the dominant trading partner, and Jamaica became increasingly dependent upon American imports. Until the closing of immigration channels as a result of the U.S. Immigration Act of 1924—the act that extended, for the first time, a national origins quota system for immigrants from the Americas, including the Caribbean—greater economic interaction with the United States also provided thousands of Jamaicans with opportunities to increase their wages through both formal and informal emigration channels. Though aware of the potential social tensions that might arise as Jamaicans confronted post-Reconstruction racial relations and ideologies in America, many, including the Jamaica's Jubilee authors, celebrated the economic implications of an American-centered future:

[Here we are] just a stone's throw from America—America, whose prophets proclaim her a giant in embryo, and, what Jamaica is especially glad of, a giant whose increasingly capacious stomach will always be huge enough to demand all that little Jamaica can produce. (JJ 104)

While extensive labor migration and increased U.S. capital penetration may have facilitated the development of new economic opportunities for lower-class Jamaicans, it also occasioned significant shifts within Jamaica's gendered division of labor. Prior to the 1880s, Jamaican women had worked mainly in agriculture, but the fragmentation of rural holdings during the last two decades of the nineteenth century led many to seek other avenues for work. Meanwhile, the growth of the banana industry catalyzed the growth of a middle class, which itself created a demand for new services, including domestic work. When domestic service work was at its peak in 1943, many rural women migrated to urban areas to seek jobs within this industry. As maids within middle-class households, these newly urban women were confronted with a considerably diminished autonomy and were also subjected more directly to class and racial discrimination. As Diane Austin-Broos (1997) has pointed out, therefore, the proliferation of domestic service—especially after the 1920s and 1930s when migrated men returned home and resumed their places within the agricultural labor force—marked one of the most dramatic restructurings of female labor in twentieth-century Jamaica, both in terms of occupation and with respect to the conditions under which women were laboring. This restructuring disadvantageously incorporated black lower-class women more squarely within the colonial color, class, gender, and culture nexus in terms that devalued their customary political, economic, and sociocultural practices.

While migrated men also "faced a heightened experience of subordination that collapsed the issues of race and class into a sense of heritable condition" (Austin-Broos 1997:25), the experience of migration and participating in a regional labor force also provided men with access to a wider range of ideas and experiences than those locally rooted in Jamaica. Here, I do not mean to suggest that a more global exchange of ideas *began* in the late nineteenth century, as instances of prior cross-territorial interactions between people of African descent are well documented. For example, black Baptists from the thirteen colonies were among the thousands of black loyalists and slaves who arrived in Jamaica toward the end of the

American Revolution (Pulis 1999), and Haitians were among those advocating for colored Jamaicans' political rights after emancipation (Heuman 1981). What was different about these interactions at the turn of the twentieth century was their scale. Changes in Jamaica's political economy during the late nineteenth century, therefore, also had implications for the ways working-class men and women conceptualized their own positions in relation to wider polities of state, region, and world.

What emerged was an increasingly diasporic consciousness and experience that provided the potential for an organized *political* movement from multiple loyalties and locations. Indeed, while the five authors of *Jamaica's Jubilee* put forth their arguments primarily in economic and socioreligious terms, other late-nineteenth-century black nationalists like Dr. Robert Love agitated for increased participation in electoral politics as well as the establishment of alternative opportunities for political organization and involvement for black Jamaicans.[23] Moreover, Panama, Costa Rica, and Cuba were fields that bred many new leaders within Jamaican popular movements such as Marcus Garvey, Alexander Bedward, and the three founders of the Rastafari movement (about all of whom, more below).[24] While Garvey, Bedward, and the Rastafari took somewhat different positions from the *Jamaica's Jubilee* authors, the debates in which these various nationalists were integral participants were some of the first regarding the relevance of race to political identity and participation, and to sociocultural and economic development.

For example, Marcus Garvey's establishment of the Universal Negro Improvement Association (UNIA) in Kingston (1914) and later in New York City (1917) marked an attempt to mobilize West Indians and African Americans toward a black nationalist and pan-African point of view that included among its tenets racial pride, self-help, and repatriation to the African continent.[25] After Garvey was deported from the United States in 1927, he returned to Jamaica to launch the People's Political Party and the Jamaica Workers' and Labourers' Association. Though he failed to win a seat in the Legislative Council in the 1930 elections, between 1927 and 1935 (the year he exiled himself to London), Garvey organized support for an electoral manifesto that embraced self-government, the protection of labor through minimum wage legislation and land reform, and the establishment of institutions of higher education and training. The UNIA laid the foundation in Jamaica and worldwide for self-respect and organized nationalism among both the working and middle classes. In Jamaica, this came at a time of significant alterations in the local class structure, since the early-twentieth-century movement toward industrial modernization that generated the growth of both a (black) proletariat and an increasingly vocal black and brown bourgeoisie coincided with the in-migration of South Asian agricultural laborers, and Chinese and Syrian traders (J. Carnegie 1973). In fact, Garvey's following among upper- and middle-class small businessmen was due, in part, to their efforts to protect and expand the stake of black and brown Jamaicans in the island's businesses in the face of increasing competition from Chinese and Syrian immigrants.[26]

Mussolini's October 1935 invasion of Ethiopia—the only African country to successfully resist European colonization—also heightened the impact of black nationalist ideologies among all except the upper and upper-middle classes. The influence of Ethiopianism upon the Jamaican masses had most likely taken hold long before Mussolini's military action, since the first black Baptist church (the Ethiopian Baptist Church established by George Liele) had been founded in Kingston in 1784. However, as Ken Post has argued, this second Italian invasion (the first was in 1895) brought middle-class Jamaicans to a new ideological interpretation of Jamaica's poverty that "stressed the wickedness and inevitable consequent decline of the white man" (Post 1978:205). The Ethiopian crisis, however, also split nationalist tendencies. Some Jamaicans, influenced by Garvey's prophecy that a black king would be crowned in Africa, as well as by their experiences with racism as migrants in the United States and Costa Rica, developed the religious/sociopolitical worldview of Rastafari. Others among the middle classes and small land holders withdrew from Ethiopianism due to its growing association with aspects of the Rastafarian anti-imperialist doctrine. This was a doctrine that singled out England (by which was also meant the United States) in particular, and the white race in general, as the main enemies of Africans (Chevannes 1976). These Jamaicans developed instead a nationalist sensibility that, though influenced by black nationalism, was framed in terms of Westminster constitutionalism.

That Ethiopianism would have such a decisive impact on emergent nationalisms also highlights the extent to which religious ideologies have been central vehicles for forging (and enacting) alternative visions of the present and the future, particularly after the early-nineteenth-century religious revival in Europe that swept through Jamaica by the mid-1860s. Several scholars have argued that protest in Jamaica has generally been undergirded by a religious philosophy of black deliverance geared toward exposing racial and economic inequality (Bakan 1990; Bogues 2003; Burton 1997; Chevannes 1998; C. Price 2003; Yelvington 1999). Abigail Bakan (1990) has traced the persistence of a racially radical variant of Christianity as the impetus for the Sam Sharpe Rebellion in 1831 that precipitated the end of slavery throughout the British West Indies,[27] the Morant Bay Rebellion in 1865, and the labor rebellions of 1938 that inaugurated the move toward self-government. A similar trajectory can be traced for Ethiopianism. However, this ideological framework, as Charles Price has explained, has tended to posit a more explicitly millenarian vision of black redemption and white malevolence since it "predicted the fall of slavery and the West, the rise of Africa in the future, the return of Blacks to their imagined glory in precolonial Africa, all under the direction of a coming Black Messiah and redeemer" (2003:36).

Alexander Bedward, for example, led a revival movement—the Native Baptist Free church—for the better part of thirty years in August Town, a neighborhood in greater Kingston near what is now the University of the West Indies. Bedward's sermons emphasized the colonial oppression of black Jamaicans, criticized the Anglican and other established churches, and positioned himself as the deliverer of the black race. Colonial officials viewed Bedward as a threat to the government and so arrested him on numerous occasions on the grounds of sedition, treason, and vagrancy and ultimately committed him to the lunatic asylum in 1921, where he died in 1930 (C. Price 2003). Bedward's following was comprised mainly of poor peasants and working-class people who were drawn to what Price calls a black "moral economy." That is, they were attracted to Bedward's vision of "the need for land and justice, the injustices associated with White rule, and the necessity of setting up social welfare schemes that addressed the needs of the aged, infants, sick, and illiterate" (2003:46). This is the sector of Jamaica's population that was least incorporated within the Anglican, Methodist, and other more established churches. Ethiopianist leaders, then, tended to explicitly identify with the bulk of Jamaica's poor, using ecstatic religious idioms to challenge the legitimacy of Jamaica's social and political arrangements.

While the *Jamaica's Jubilee* authors struggled for postemancipation economic and political development for the masses of Jamaicans, they nevertheless disassociated with these same masses both socially and culturally. This was, in part, a result of their own position within Jamaica's late-nineteenth-century black middle class, a relatively unstable grouping of teachers, religious ministers, small-scale farmers, artisans, and constables (Bryan 1991). As black intellectuals, the *Jubilee* writers insisted that they articulated important mass concerns on the basis of their shared blackness, but they distanced themselves from lower-class blacks and African-derived cultural expressions as a result of their own education and goals toward personal progress. The various ideological developments toward the end of the nineteenth century—the ascendance of Social Darwinism as a new justification for stratified race relations, the privileging of the formation of an independent peasantry, and the simultaneous assertion of allegiance to Great Britain and Jamaica within the context of an emerging diasporic consciousness—reinforced these class and cultural cleavages. Early Creole nationalists, therefore, were in the precarious position of proving, to local and international publics, both their equality and their difference.

This was a trend that would continue among some sections of the nationalist movement in which respectability and status were based on the achievement of a formal education and the adherence to an idealized Victorian middle-class gender and family ideology. Indeed, the dual pillars upon which mid-twentieth-century creole multiracial nationalism rested echoed late-nineteenth-century emphases upon the moral economy of the peasant.

Reforming the Polity I: Fixing the Family

By the 1930s, the already poor living conditions of the Jamaican lower classes had become exacerbated by the global economic depression. Intensified poverty and unemployment, a reduction in wages, the return of migrant workers from overseas, a frustration over the lack of substantial land reform, and increased workers' mobilization all led to the labor rebellions that erupted at the Frome sugar estate in April 1938. Fearing increasing instability in the region, the colonial government sent a delegation to probe the causes of discontent. The report of this West Indian Royal Commission (WIRC) initiated several important shifts in post–World War II colonial policy, shifts reflecting the growing influence in Britain of Keynesian economic policies that suggested, among other things, that societies could be morally reformed without altering their basic socioeconomic or political structures (Bakan 1990; Bryan 1990). In Jamaica, this represented a marked departure from the earlier laissez-faire attitude, and it inaugurated the move toward self-government.

Prior to the WIRC Report, the Colonial Development and Welfare Act earmarked a mere £1,000,000 per year for the entire colonial empire, arguing that the colonies should have only such services as they could afford from their own local revenue. That act, passed in 1929, further stipulated that these funds could only be applied toward profit-generating projects. That is, these monies were not to be spent on "social programs" like the expansion of the health care or education systems. After the labor rebellions, the new Colonial Development and Welfare Act of 1940 provided £5,000,000 yearly for general purposes and £500,000 for research within the West Indies alone.[28] The 1940 act, therefore, reoriented colonial development policy toward the implementation of social welfare policies—policies buttressed by academic research—that were geared toward bringing the West Indies in line with a "universal 'modern' practice" (R. T. Smith 1996:81).

An important aspect of this project had to do with a renewed emphasis upon the formation of "modern" conjugal families comprised of a male breadwinner and his dependent housewife. This unit was seen as central not only for social development but also as the motor of modern economic development because familial conditions were now viewed as affecting labor productivity, absenteeism, occupational aspirations, training and performance, attitudes toward saving, birth control, farm development, and programs of individual and community self-help (M. G. Smith 1966). The social ills of poverty and underdevelopment came to be blamed on the family, or seeming lack of it. Thus, the high rates of illegitimate births, the "loose" family organization, and the "careless" upbringing of children in the West Indies cited in the report of the WIRC became utmost concerns. Family formation, therefore, was to be a key component of postwar policy toward the West Indies (Reddock 1994; M. G. Smith 1966; R. T. Smith 1996).

This would pose special problems in the West Indies where, during the slavery period and throughout the nineteenth century, there existed neither substantial evidence of gender being used to prevent women from agricultural or other forms of work, nor a general acceptance of legal marriage as the fundamental basis of family formation or household composition among the mass of the population (Beckles 1989; Mathurin 1975; Senior 1991). Popular patterns of family formation persisted despite the growing association of sectarian Christianity and marriage with increased social status among the rural middle class by the end of the nineteenth century (Austin-Broos 1997). Nevertheless, programs were designed to address the WIRC's concerns, one of which was the infamous Mass Marriage Movement initiated in 1944 by Lady Huggins, the wife of the then governor of Jamaica. The failure of this movement (it petered out by 1955) was attributed to the erroneous assumption that marriage had the same meaning and value among different social strata. That it did not convinced researchers that there was a need for systematic sociological studies of patterns of family formation among black lower-class Jamaicans, among whom promiscuity, marital instability, "defective" paternity and child socialization, and high rates of illegitimacy were all thought to be connected. The idea was that sociological research would not only provide insight into these "problems," but also blueprints for policy-oriented solutions that would ultimately facilitate Jamaica's transition from British Crown Colony to internal self-rule.

The appointment of T. S. Simey as the first Social Welfare Adviser to the Comptroller for Development and Welfare in the West Indies, a post created by the 1940 Colonial Development and Welfare Act, reflected a move in this direction.[29] A sociologist by training, Simey adopted the Frazierian position that the social and economic conditions of slavery had precluded the development of stable nuclear families. He also identified the contemporary "disorganization" of West Indian family life as the cause of lower-class Jamaicans' continued marginalization as an economically and socially depressed group. His survey of social conditions in Jamaica set the pattern for future family studies by delineating types of mating practices and by arguing that there seemed to be a close correlation between color, occupation or economic level, and family type (1946).[30] This would lead to the formulation of a model of social stratification whereby differences in cultural practice were ranked hierarchically according to social positions and roles, though ultimately integrated through a common value system (Braithwaite 1953; R. T. Smith 1956, 1967).[31] While the theoretical positions advanced within these early studies have since been significantly modified,[32] their importance lies in the belief, current at the time, that the implementation of land settlement policies, as well as other public health, housing, and educational programs, was contingent upon the existence of a cohesive nuclear family unit.

Reforming the Polity II:
The Consolidation of Moderate Middle-Class Leadership

Simey's initial study was also significant because of his vision for the future. He imagined the West Indies as polities "ruled by an elite, a specifically West Indian elite to be sure, guided by cadres of social researchers

providing blueprints for middle class leaders" (R. T. Smith 1996:84). Despite the fact that all major shifts in colonial policy toward the West Indies
emerged as the result of struggles, protests, and violent uprisings led by
those who had been most marginalized, Simey insisted that "the future
lies with the middle classes" (1946:258), and that there existed "no possibility of founding a new culture on working-class society alone" (1946:
103). Therefore, for Simey, independent, democratic societies could only
emerge under "brown" middle-class leadership. However, the "brown"
middle classes, seen as having originated from the free colored offspring
of plantation owners and their slave concubines, have always occupied a
rather problematic structural position in relation to the majority of the
population. As the class born in Jamaica, they have been seen as the most
creole of Jamaicans (in the sense of being a "new" social group, the result
of the new socioeconomic conditions of plantation-based production)
and, like the Jamaica's Jubilee authors, as exhibiting the greatest loyalty both
to Jamaica and to Great Britain (Curtin [1955]; Campbell 1976; D. Hall
1972; Heuman 1981). At the same time and for the same reasons, they have
been viewed with suspicion due to the extent to which they have distanced
themselves—materially and socially—from the insecurities faced by the
majority of the population.[33] Nevertheless, beginning in the 1930s and
continuing throughout the 1940s and 1950s, the working-class influence
on local politics was taken over by the emerging middle-class strata who,
as lawyers, journalists, and civil servants, emphasized law, due process,
and established British institutions. They understood the 1938 rebellions
as workers' riots, but felt the working class needed middle-class leadership in order to articulate their problems in a clear voice to both colonial
representatives and to local capitalists.[34]

Creole Multiracialism Ascendant

Political scientist Selwyn Ryan has argued that nationalist feeling during
the postwar period was fueled by the experience of black middle-class
students and war veterans returning from England, the victory of the Labour party in Britain, and the struggles for independence in other areas of
the British Empire (1972). By this time, a substantial Jamaican community
had been established in the United States. In Harlem in 1936, the Jamaica
Progressive League (JPL) was established by Wilfred Domingo (who in

Jamaica had served alongside Garvey as an assistant secretary of the National Club), W. Adolphe Roberts, Rev. Ethelred Brown, Jaime O'Malley, and other Jamaican residents in New York City who had been active in immigrant associations such as the Jamaican Benevolent Association and the Jamaican-American Industrial League. In opposition to Garvey's racialist approach, the JPL's objective was to agitate for nationalist self-determination, and in 1937, Domingo and Roberts traveled to Jamaica in order to establish a local branch.[35] Also in 1937 Ken Hill, in conjunction with Noel Nethersole, established the National Reform Association (NRA), an organization with a broad nationalist objective, though one that was less radical than that of the Jamaica Progressive League. The NRA's positions were made public in the *Jamaica Standard* launched in February 1938. Both these organizations advocated for the development of a political party to give the new nationalism an organizational form.

Meanwhile, other kinds of middle-class social action had also developed during this period. In 1936, the Citizen's Associations that had been forming since the early 1930s to improve standards of living in Kingston were grouped into the Federation of Citizens' Associations. Numerous charitable and remedial organizations were also established, and there was an attempt to encourage and develop elements of the plastic arts, music, and folktales of the Jamaican peasantry in order to provide the foundation for an emerging Jamaican national culture. Most significant among these various efforts was Norman Manley's 1937 establishment of Jamaica Welfare, an organization that focused on land reform, the development of community-based small industries, and community uplift (Marier 1953). By 1943, Thomas Simey, impressed with the way Jamaica Welfare linked social and economic objectives as well as with its programs geared toward rural development and the organization of village improvement associations, proposed that funding be made available to the organization through the Colonial Development and Welfare Scheme.[36]

The ideology undergirding Jamaica Welfare's program of community work in rural areas held that the "responsibility for social betterment must be left with the people themselves, but they must nevertheless be given both the desire and the means of self improvement" (Marier 1953:27). Toward this end, staff members made efforts to develop local leadership and to dismantle the paternalist dependent-provider relationship that often obtained between the middle and lower classes, but in their statements of activities, they often remarked upon the difficulties they faced in doing so. Nevertheless, Jamaica Welfare was used as a model for social welfare development not only in additional British West Indian territories, but also in other areas of the empire.[37]

Prior to his establishment of Jamaica Welfare, Norman Manley had been asked to become president of the National Reform Association but had refused due to his belief that Jamaica's problems were economic and social but not political. After the labor rebellions in 1938, however, he was persuaded to launch the People's National Party (PNP) at the Ward Theatre on September 18, 1938. The PNP brought the unions into a politics of labor that ultimately embraced wider anticolonial aims.[38] This relationship articulated readily with the changes in colonial policy focused on preparing Jamaicans for self-government and independence. In the belief that "Jamaica has suffered too long because Jamaicans have been willing to sit down and wait for other people to do the work" (PNP 1939), the PNP launched an extensive educational program in order to develop a "new spirit of love of Jamaica" (PNP 1939) and to foster the political consciousness of the mass of Jamaican people. In order to promote this mass education, the PNP held open-air meetings in Kingston's business district, many in cooperation with the unions, and encouraged the formation of small study groups throughout the island, each of which was visited fortnightly by a party worker from Kingston until leadership could be provided locally. These groups were provided with pamphlets, published by the PNP, which were geared toward facilitating discussions regarding the difference between colonies and sovereign states, the rights and duties of citizens to an independent government, and the meaning of socialism (PNP 1941). The study groups were also designed to educate Jamaicans about the PNP's proposed programs,[39] programs that would ultimately require Jamaicans to reform their practices—economically, socially, and politically:

> People will have to learn that all men must have a chance to live well; they will have to cooperate instead of striving to do each other down; they will have to work harder and better, they will have to develop a strong sense of responsibility for the conditions of their own community so that all those who share the desire for progress will work to make progress real. (PNP 1940:4)

In seeking to find an answer to Jamaica's problems, Manley and others within the PNP focused on the development of a cooperatively organized independent peasantry in order to curtail the power of large-scale agriculture and to diminish the dependence of poor Jamaicans on wage labor. This focus was rooted in the party leaders' belief that independent peasants had achieved a "higher standard of civilisation and prosperity and outlook on life than the labourers" (Post 1978:370), a belief that should remind us of postemancipation missionary ideologies. However, this essentially populist position was largely untenable, as a complete disengagement of peasant production from that of the multinational and local capitalist class was impossible. It also proved unattractive to many poorer Jamaicans who were urban industrial workers rather than rural agriculturalists. These working-class Jamaicans were largely drawn to Alexander Bustamante's unions and bread and butter political platform. Bustamante originally stood against independence for Jamaica, arguing that self-government would equal "brown man rule," in this way evoking not only racial cleavages but also class-based antagonisms between the middle-class professionals in leadership positions within the nationalist movement and the Jamaican masses. Ironically, Bustamante was no less phenotypically "brown"—and indeed quite a bit fairer—than his cousin Norman Manley. What Bustamante's early anti-independence position suggests, therefore, is not an advocacy of black leadership but rather an indictment of what he saw as a needlessly paternalistic orientation among the PNP leadership toward personal and individual reform, and here I mean "reform" in the sense of transforming people's practices and consciousness through collective study and mobilization. Bustamante's 1943 split from the PNP and subsequent formation of the Jamaica Labour Party (JLP) set the stage for the factionalism that has plagued politics in Jamaica through to the present.[40]

While the creole nationalism that developed in Jamaica after the 1938 labor rebellions—and that was consolidated after the expulsion of the leftist wing from organized party politics in 1952—involved a revived appreciation of indigenous Caribbean culture, thereby calling into question the natural superiority of all ideas emerging from England, it also solidified Western political and economic structures administered by the local middle-class intelligentsia. Within the political and economic spheres, however, this nationalist leadership sought to enter the world of nations not singly and directly, but by the retention of special relationships— economically, through privileged trade arrangements, and politically, as members of the British Commonwealth of Nations. Here, the concept of self-determination got a new twist. While anticolonialist, it was not anti-imperialist since the PNP had begun encouraging direct investment of foreign capital by the mid-1950s.[41]

Moreover, the Jamaican nationalism of the PNP was not a black nationalism viewing all those of African descent as sharing the same destiny. In fact, anthropologist Don Robotham has argued that the retention of special political and economic relationships with Britain "could not but generate identities dominated by concepts of the inferiority of blackness and the superiority of all things white, especially British" (1998b:311). Instead, creole multiracial nationalism was a narrower assertion of a specifically Jamaican identity more closely resembling classical European nationalism. That is, it was founded on a concept of common history and culture rather than race and, as in Europe, obscured the conflation of class with race. Additionally, the nationalist political and intellectual elite's emphasis on the equality of all racial groups in the building of the new nation, while striving for universalism and inclusiveness, facilitated the continued hegemony of colonial values, thus legitimizing class domination whereby new ruling groups would function as guardians for the lower classes.

Conclusion: Consolidating a Respectable State

In spite of pervasive hopes that anticolonial nationalisms would catalyze more egalitarian social relations than those that obtained under imperial rule, newly independent states have often reproduced the exclusions of the colonial period because post–World War II anticolonial nationalist elites did not entirely eschew the precepts upon which European nationalisms were based. Because European nationalisms linked culture to power by establishing the dominant classes as the producers of superior standards of civilization, subordinated populations were required to manipulate the definition of culture and its relation to power—in other words, to reformulate understandings of who could possess culture—in order to reposition themselves within the state (B. Williams 1993). Anticolonial nationalists within the British Empire, faced with the challenge of consolidating their legitimacy as leaders to both their colonial custodians and their own populations, responded similarly. That is, in order to achieve their political objectives, Jamaican nationalists were compelled to distance themselves both from the "backwardness" of Africa and from the rural and urban proletariat whose practices—and values—were seen as a throwback to the slavery period and, therefore, as disruptive to a modern social order presided over by middle-class leaders.

Indeed, creole multiracial nationalists in Jamaica were the ideological heirs of the perspective on progress held by late-nineteenth-century black nationalists like the five authors of *Jamaica's Jubilee*. Again, this perspective privileged the postemancipation establishment of an independent peasantry that would embody the values of middle-class respectability: thrift, temperance, industry, and community spirit. While this vision of progress —socialized through the churches and missionary schools—imposed new ideologies regarding social and domestic organization, it also stood as a response to attempts by the local planter class to maintain the labor and social relations that had obtained during the slavery period. By the mid-twentieth century, the figure of the independent peasant had also come to represent a degree of relative autonomy within the context of increasing capitalist integration. From the abolition of slavery to independence, then, black and brown Jamaicans have defined freedom and progress through land ownership, education, and community self-help in their attempts to foster their own independence. Local nationalists, therefore, were able to manipulate the racist ideology of imperialism as a civilizing mission during the late nineteenth century to shame British imperial authorities into greater accountability toward their colonial subjects and in the mid-twentieth century to argue for self-government. By proving their progress, both early black nationalists and later creole nationalists were able to demand equality either as human beings within the "brotherhood of Christians" or as citizens within the "brotherhood of nations."

My use of the masculine relational term here is intentional, for as we have seen, the cultivation of nationalist respectability has been gendered. Indeed, the period from emancipation to independence in Jamaica has been characterized by a decline in lower-class black women's public social, economic, and political power. This is not to say that individual women were not prominent within various kinds of political movements throughout the twentieth century. Rather, I am suggesting that late-nineteenth-century transformations in the local political economy were structurally and ideologically disadvantageous to women of all classes in Jamaica. The emphasis placed upon privatizing women to the realm of the family and social reproduction has not only obscured our understandings of women's work, but has also tended to frame women's struggles within the rubric of welfare. In this way, women's roles were naturalized rather than opened up for debate and reconsideration within an explicitly political sphere, and paternalistic social relations that were rooted in late-nineteenth-century patriarchal hierarchies of class, color, and culture were solidified rather than transformed.

As Britain's empire was disintegrating, then, Jamaicans seeking self-government found themselves in the contradictory position of reproducing the colonial value system that had been strengthened during the period of Crown Colony rule in order to legitimize their leadership and provide for their population. The subtly racial blueprint for independent development within the work of the *Jamaica's Jubilee* authors was thereby dropped, and other forms of racially, class-, or gender-based affirmation and mobilization were marginalized within a public sphere dominated by the projection of a territorially based multiracial harmony. In order to vindicate their colony and legitimize themselves as the most natural and reasonable leaders of its population, creole multiracial nationalists fashioned a "hammock of national belonging" that knotted anticolonial mobilization to middle-class respectability and cultural creolization. During the period immediately surrounding independence in 1962, this hammock was tethered to the establishment of cultural institutions and the development of a cultural policy that would reflect and support the creole nation-building project.

chapter 2

POLITICAL ECONOMIES OF CULTURE

Black Jamaicans have always created and maintained their own forms of cultural expression. These forms have emerged from and been supported by the social, economic, and religious institutions developed from the period of slavery to the present and have also been shaped by interactions with those institutions imposed upon them. Some of these cultural forms —such as *jonkonnu* and various forms of worship—have been extensively documented by early planter historians and colonial officials or their wives.[1] Others became part of the written record with the emergence of folklore as a discipline and with historians' attempts to recover the social worlds of slaves.[2] There has also always existed in Jamaica an exposure to elite expressive cultural forms from abroad. For example, as early as the mid-1700s, theatrical companies from England and the North American colonies toured the island, and during the late 1800s and early 1900s, European opera companies often stopped in Jamaica on their way from Cuba to South America (R. Wright 1937; Baxter 1970). It was not until the establishment of Crown Colony rule in 1866, however, that institutions were established locally to cater to a growing middle-class audience within Jamaica. While these institutions tended to uphold an ideology of British cultural superiority, they nevertheless provided the structures within which elite and middle-class Jamaicans would reframe the parameters of "legitimate" culture by encouraging more conscious attention to the needs and experiences of the population. In doing so, they ultimately challenged the legitimacy of a colonial rule that had defined the culture of Jamaicans as inferior and, therefore, as an inadequate foundation for independent economic and political equality.

While the previous chapter outlined the ongoing tension between blackness and creole multiracialism in relation to the development of political nationalism from emancipation in 1838 to independence in 1962, this chapter foregrounds the ways this tension has informed cultural politics from the establishment of Crown Colony rule through the late twentieth century. Here, the emphasis is on the evolution of what I call "folk blackness"—the sense of Jamaicanness that became linked to the creole multi-racial nationalist project—and outlines the institutionalization of this sense through the formulation of a cultural policy and the establishment of various cultural institutions in newly independent Jamaica. While these processes have typically been viewed as emancipatory moments in the transition from colonial rule, it is also the case that the consolidation of a creole cultural hegemony has been contingent upon policing, and some-times violently suppressing, popular cultural expressions and practices.

At the same time, popular challenges to the hegemony of creole multi-racial nationalism and "folk blackness" have catalyzed changes in Ja-maica's cultural policy and institutions throughout the postindependence period. These challenges, rooted in more racialized visions of national and global belonging, have been both cultural and explicitly political, ranging from the spiritual politics of Rasta, the antiauthoritarianism of Rudie, and the in-your-face brazenness of dancehall, to the antistate hostility of vari-ous grassroots political uprisings, the refined race-conscious socialism of the Abeng and New World Groups, and the modified black nationalism of the 1990s People's National Party (PNP). Throughout this chapter, I define these various challenges, and explore the ways they have influenced Jamai-cans' understandings of how the concept of culture is linked to class, color, and gender.

I am particularly interested in tying the negotiations between creole multiracial nationalism and popular culture to the wider (national and global) political and economic contexts in which they are occurring in order to understand people's varying material experiences and their ideo-logical and expressive worldviews as relational, that is, as mutually con-stitutive. Furthermore, I connect the relative power of racial visions of citizenship to the changing power of the Jamaican state over time. That is, the fact that popular challenges to creole multiracial nationalism were more successful in the late 1990s than they had been previously is partially due to the ways processes of neoliberal capitalist globalization have eroded the power of states, particularly those states presiding over vulner-able economies. Of course, those elected to positions of state power have also changed, and this generational shift has influenced the publicly pro-jected image of Jamaican culture. Indeed, the question of leadership is critical throughout these discussions, not only in terms of who holds political power but also with respect to who commands the legitimacy to direct the processes of cultural progress and development. This is the arena in which we see perhaps most starkly the persistence of the colonial link between socioeconomic mobility and cultural transformation. The ongoing emphasis upon transforming the cultural practices of black lower-class Jamaicans stands as an attempt to contain the influence of popular challenges to creole multiracial nationalism, not only within lower-class communities but also upon the middle and upper classes— that is, to prevent particular sectors of lower-class Jamaicans from taking cultural leadership of the nation.

Consolidating "Creole" Culture

In 1879, thirteen years after the imposition of Crown Colony rule, the Institute of Jamaica was founded by then Governor Sir Anthony Musgrave, replacing the Royal Society of Arts that had been established in 1854.[3] The Institute was conceived as a central clearinghouse of sorts for the cultivation of the arts, sciences, and letters among the educated elite in Jamaica, and as such it had many functions. It administered the Cambridge examinations, organized the Jamaica Scholarship awards enabling students to study at British universities, promoted exhibitions and took the leading role in organizing the Jamaica International Exhibition in 1891, sponsored art classes, and stimulated the development of instrumental and vocal music by sponsoring the music exams of the Royal Academy of Music. In its early days, the Institute also served as information office, tourist board, and learned society.

Locally published newspapers and journals also served to consolidate a middle-class audience for West Indian artistic and literary production in Jamaica. After emancipation in 1838, more than thirty-six newspapers and literary journals began printing, many of which lasted only a year or two. By the 1920s, several journals reflected a growing cultural consciousness in Jamaica that was related, in part, to the success of several expatriate Jamaicans within artistic movements such as the Harlem Renaissance as well as to the heightened folkloric interest in rural Jamaicans' songs, dances, and stories.[4] The 1920s and 1930s were also the heyday of literary and debating societies, forums for intellectual and artistic expression among many of the young men who would later become active in the political nationalist movement through the People's National Party. During this period of growing political and cultural nationalist sentiment, several programming changes were introduced at the Institute of Jamaica. Among these was the extension of art classes to artisans, plumbers, sign painters, and many other aspiring artists who had never before come under the aegis of the Institute. These classes were directed by Edna Manley, the wife of Norman Manley and an acclaimed sculptor who would ultimately found the Jamaica School of Art in the early 1940s.

Many of the activities geared toward the development of a greater local cultural awareness were underwritten by the British Council, established in the late-1930s, which awarded scholarships in Jamaica for artistic study in Great Britain and encouraged the development of drama and music by funding the travel of performers from England to Jamaica. The 1940 passage of the Colonial Development and Welfare Act placed these kinds of activities more solidly within the purview of colonial tutelage. This meant that while the colonial government was now providing long-overdue financial and institutional support for local development initiatives, it was also more directly involved in shaping the form and content of these initiatives. As a result, individuals who advocated other assertions of "cultural consciousness" that were developing at the same time, assertions that did not conform to the colonial ethos of moderate multiracialism, did not receive support through these channels.

Marcus Garvey, for example, also envisioned the arts as an integral part of the assertion of black nationalism. Garvey believed that in order to subvert their oppression, black people needed to develop their own cultural norms and aesthetics for literature, music, dance, and visual art and that black artists had a duty to create works that were uplifting. By the time Garvey returned to Jamaica from the United States in 1927, he had also come to argue that the state should support local artistic activity. Part of his platform during his 1930 run for the Jamaican Legislative Council, therefore, was the establishment of a national performing arts center. Having lost the election, Garvey founded the Edelweiss Park Amusement Company in 1931, through which he showcased dramatic presentations, musical revues, vaudevilles, comedies, films, fairs, and elocution, singing, and dancing contests. Edelweiss Park also became the home base for a dance troupe called the Follies, a troupe that performed a varied repertoire of Broadway-inspired compositions as well as presentations of Jamaican folk music and dance (Hamilton 1994).

During the 1940s and 1950s, several additional organizations and events fostered the development of a local cultural aesthetic. The Little Theatre

Movement, founded in 1942 by Henry and Greta Fowler, began production of annual pantomime musicals based on West Indian themes using Jamaican language and inspired the establishment of the Jamaica Drama League in 1955, which organized an annual adult drama festival. The social welfare movement also helped to mobilize Jamaicans around the assertion of a local cultural identity by offering instruction in dance, music, and handiwork. At the end of training periods in the villages, Jamaica Welfare workers would organize local festivals that included performances of Jamaican folk songs and dance. This kind of work at the community level was legitimized through the Extra-Mural Department of the University College of the West Indies (established in 1948 as a branch of the University of London), which facilitated the development of locally rooted performing arts by means of lectures, seminars, and workshops; through summer school workshops in music, drama, dance, literature, and art; and by the publication of the journal *Caribbean Quarterly*.

During the 1950s, a greater regional cultural awareness was promoted, in part due to efforts to establish a political federation among British West Indian countries that were in various stages of self-government. The first Caribbean Festival of the Arts, for example, brought together dancers, singers, visual artists, and musicians from fourteen Caribbean territories to generate a heightened consciousness of the kinds of cultural production occurring throughout the Caribbean.[5] At the same time, a notably different cultural image was projected within Jamaica, both to the population and to visiting dignitaries. For example, the ascension of Queen Elizabeth to the throne in 1952 was recognized in Jamaica with a government- and military-financed celebration that included performances of Jamaican folk dance and music. Where previous civic celebrations had been characterized by military parades and patriotic anthems, this event showcased local expressive cultural forms as part of the acceptable material for display in an official occasion for the first time.

In December 1954, the Jamaican government announced its plans for a National Arts Festival, sponsored by the Ministry of Education and Social Welfare, as part of the Jamaica Tercentenary celebrations that would commemorate three hundred years of British colonial rule the following year. This was the first national attempt to showcase—and therefore also delimit—a Jamaican cultural heritage. The festival incorporated the secondary schools' drama festival, the speech festival for elementary and secondary schools, and an all-island music competition. Also planned were a one-act play competition; an art exhibition held at the Institute of Jamaica; a literary competition; a beauty competition entitled "Ten Types, One People"[6]; and recitals in folk, ballet, and modern creative dance. A National Planning Committee was established to develop syllabi, to supply judges for the competitions, and to provide lectures and workshops for teachers and other interested parties. Once written, syllabi for the festival were distributed indicating that festival entries should address West Indian themes or should "otherwise reflect contact with the West Indian environment" (Daily Gleaner 1955b). The festival climaxed in December with two events. Mr. W. Adolphe Roberts and Mrs. Elise Benjamin-Barsoe wrote a pageant that outlined "the salient points in the history of the people who make up the present population of the island" (Daily Gleaner 1955b), and Madame Soohih choreographed a ballet. The latter was publicized as the "first ballet on a Jamaican historical theme, written, choreographed and directed by a Jamaican, interpreted by thirty dancers and singers who are all Jamaican, and premiered in Kingston, the capital of Jamaica" (Daily Gleaner 1955c).

One newspaper account of Jamaica 300 reported that "all the cosmopolitanism which has gone to the building of this unique Jamaican society was there on parade," and that the festival "reflected a sense of present achievement and awareness that the sordidness of the past was being left behind." This same author concluded that the event should be an annual celebration of "the transition of a fully prepared people from the irresponsibility and humility of an infant to the responsibility and pride of an adult" (King 1955). The minister of education and social welfare viewed the Tercentenary Festival as a "spontaneous expression of national aspiration and achievement" (Lloyd 1955), and Sir Hugh Foot, the governor general at the time, saw Jamaica 300 as having positively influenced Jamaica's reputation internationally and strengthened Jamaica's integration internally:

> As we look back on all these events . . . we can ask ourselves: what is the outcome, what is the result, what is the benefit to the Island of all this? . . . First, the reputation of Jamaica, as it strides towards self-government, has been greatly enhanced throughout the Caribbean and far beyond. Secondly, national self-consciousness and self-respect have been immeasurably increased; increased by the evidence throughout the island of bubbling springs of new life and new hope and new enthusiasm. Thirdly, there has been the remarkable response and participation of

every parish in the celebrations with the result that the ties which bind the parishes together in a national unity have been permanently strengthened. (*Daily Gleaner* 1955a)

So much enthusiasm was generated by the Tercentenary Festival, in fact, that in 1959 then Chief Minister Norman Manley promised a yearly All-Island Arts Festival. Also during that year, an Arts Advisory Council to the government Ministry of Housing and Social Welfare was formed, and a total of £1,000 was administered as prize money for the performing and creative arts and later for commissioning murals by Jamaican artists in government buildings. With this support, Edward Seaga—then the Minister of Development and Welfare—began planning an arts festival in May 1961 for the following year's independence celebrations. Seaga, a white Jamaican of Lebanese descent who received his master's degree in social anthropology from Harvard University, appointed a committee to organize a series of celebrations in at least *one thousand* rural villages. These celebrations would include activities such as digging songs, quadrille dances, maroon dances, jonkonnu, kumina rituals, fisherman regattas, children's games, speech, drama, singing, and dance and would serve as preliminaries to the parish finals that would, in turn, determine the participants for the existing all-island festivals and exhibitions. The competition was to culminate in a national finale toward the end of the year. The Ministry of Housing and Social Welfare sponsored the development of a General Syllabus for the National Arts Festival,[7] which was then sent to island-wide agencies, schools, and cultural and social groups in order to "encourage the development of such folkloric and other artistic traditions as are vital to an authentic expression of the Jamaican genius" (Ministry of Housing and Social Welfare 1961).

These syllabi stipulated the appropriate materials and themes of festival entries in different arts categories. Within the literary competition, for example, writers were asked to consider the following topics: the West Indian novel; the development of West Indian poetry; some problems of the West Indian playwright; religious cultism as a solace for social frustrations; the national idea in West Indian literature, or H. G. de Lisser as a novelist. For the exhibition of art and craft work, entries were accepted in indigenous media such as jippi-joppa and other straws, sisal, gourd, calabash, loofah, and coconut shells. The music syllabus included categories for all ages, instruments, and musical forms including Jamaican folk songs and diggings songs; and the drama syllabus encouraged the writing and production of specifically West Indian plays. Finally, acceptable entries for the dance competition included square dancing, West Indian and English folk dances, and creative (modern) dance. Like the artistic flowering during the 1940s and the Tercentenary Festival, the National Arts Festival was to contribute to the development of a broader local cultural awareness and unity among Jamaicans throughout the island, "and to the generation of a regional pride as West Indians."

The Political Economy of "Policing" Culture

A Cultural Policy for Independent Jamaica

The efforts of the nationalist intelligentsia during these years prior to Jamaica's independence were geared toward elevating aspects of Jamaican "folk" culture to the realm of the "cultured" in order to prove to their colonial rulers that Jamaica too possessed a culture that was not only as legitimate as British culture, but also more relevant to the surroundings and experiences of the majority of the population. By showcasing this culture through national arts festivals, nationalist elites also demonstrated that Jamaicans' culture was something around which people all over the island could be mobilized toward a unified national spirit. In this way, they legitimized Jamaica as a country ready to take its place within an international community of nations. The people involved as leaders in this process—mostly "brown" and middle class—emphasized Jamaica's diversity as an assertion of their legitimate membership to the nation.

Their project was, therefore, primarily a creole one. Unlike Garvey or the Rastafarians, theirs was not a vision that explicitly connected Jamaica's "blackness" to a contemporary "Africanness," however conceived. Rather, they were focused on presenting, within "acceptable" theatrical fora, an "indigenous" cultural history, a "folk blackness" that was understood as constituting Jamaica's African heritage. As a result, the early movement to cultivate a local aesthetic and promote a new vision of cultural citizenship was double-edged. It remained wedded to British institutions and to the idea that these institutions would socialize the population into values that had, by then, been constructed as uniquely belonging to the middle classes—discipline, temperance, collective work, thrift, industry, Christian living, community uplift, and respect for the leadership of the educated middle classes. The idea, then, was to officially give symbolic primacy to historical events and cultural practices deemed relevant to the majority of the population, while at the same time focusing on social modernization defined through "middle-class values" as expressed through "respectable" family structure, community mobilization, and political participation in order to facilitate Jamaica's economic growth. The message advanced could be summarized as follows: look back, take pride, but move forward.

The success of the nationalist intelligentsia's efforts to socialize the idea that the arts had a special role to play in nation building can be measured, in part, by the fact that when Edward Seaga wrote his five-year development plan for independent Jamaica in 1963, it included a cultural policy whose agenda was to democratize participation in the plastic and performing arts. In an effort to increase access to participation in the arts among a wider cross section of the population and to broaden the cultural content upon which Jamaican cultural institutions would bestow legitimacy, Seaga's policy was designed to provide an institutional infrastructure for the preservation and presentation of the "folk" blackness that had come to represent Jamaica's African heritage. He sought to establish the following: (1) a national auditorium and various training institutes for music, dance, drama, and art in order to encourage fledgling arts organizations to merge into national performing companies; (2) a folk art center that would, through exchange programs with the training institutes, encourage "the growth of a national art" (1963:203); (3) an art development agency that would stimulate creative work in literature, music, and dance based on folk themes and presented in the folk idiom at the village level to encourage a sense of local pride; (4) intervillage arts competitions that would ultimately coalesce into the annual National Festival of the Arts, itself conceived "as an annual report to the Nation on all its phases of development" (1963:204)[8]; (5) a major entertainment center in each tourist area with Jamaican decor, featuring Jamaican food, and providing Jamaican entertainment; and (6) arts exchange programs with other countries, especially with African nations "which share a similar cultural background" (1963:204).

Here we are presented for the first time with a cultural policy in which the Jamaican state officially recognized and foregrounded the African aspects of Jamaica's cultural heritage. Seaga's insistence upon the development and dissemination of local forms of "high" culture rooted in an ongoing and state-sponsored interaction between middle-class and "folk" artists officially validated those activities in which many artists had been engaged prior to independence, for example, the founders of the National Dance Theatre Company of Jamaica (NDTC), Rex Nettleford and Eddy Thomas.[9] What was especially significant about Seaga's policy was that he extended the privilege accorded to the lifestyle and cultural practices of the rural peasantry to similar practices among the urban poor, having himself conducted ethnographic research upon the religious culture of those living in urban ghettos (and particularly Revivalism). However, the emphasis on a "folk" culture was not intended to support lower- and working-class black Jamaicans' efforts toward racial and economic justice and self-determination. Instead, it reflected an apprehension, on the part of the nationalist leadership, of the need to give more respect to "blackness" within a country stratified along lines of race and class at a point when the government was attempting to mobilize the population toward accepting a particular strategy of political and economic development.

During the 1950s, after the expulsion of the left wing from the People's National Party leadership, the government established the Jamaica Industrial Development Corporation (JIDC) in order to provide more employment opportunities for the rapidly increasing urban poor population through the development of a manufacturing sector. Jamaica's industrialization program was financed primarily by North American capital and was based on the use of cheap labor and imported raw materials and components.[10] Incentives such as income tax concessions and import duty relief were given to foreign investors in the hopes of realizing the levels of economic growth witnessed in Puerto Rico.[11] As the public and private sectors expanded rapidly, new jobs and occupations were created and many working- and middle-class Jamaicans enjoyed greater economic security in the early years. However, these new centers of Jamaica's wealth—manufacturing, bauxite mining, construction, and tourism—ultimately employed fewer Jamaicans than had estate-based agricultural production. In fact, the limited inroads into land reform after the 1930s were, to a large extent, reversed with the development of the bauxite and tourism industries, both of which alienated large acreages of land from the peasantry. For the first time, urban industrial service workers outnumbered agricultural workers among the working classes and black rural poverty became entrenched.

In the face of a rural economic depression and rapid population growth, many Jamaicans migrated to Kingston where urban unemployment and vagrancy increased exponentially. Many others, whose heightened aspirations for a better life were frustrated, joined the exodus to Britain that remained steady until the closing of immigration channels in 1962. Furthermore, while foreign capital financed and provided the technology for a tremendous diversification of the economy, the newly created sectors had no links among themselves and developed few links with agriculture (Beckford and Witter 1982). As a result, despite an average annual economic growth rate of 7 percent during the period between 1945 and 1971, income gaps widened (Robotham 1998a:312). It is estimated that between 1958 and 1968, the real income of 30 percent of the population was cut in half (Girvan et al. 1980:115).

At the same time, foreign capital investment reorganized the class structure locally (Stone 1991). The economic dominance of the rural-based planter class was dismantled by JIDC initiatives as the fortunes of an indigenous capitalist class rose. Economic power shifted to the urban-based entrepreneurs—Jewish, Lebanese, Chinese, and "brown" Jamaicans—whose capitalist expansion included the whites but eliminated their dominance. Concurrently, black Jamaicans used the expanded educational opportunities created by the new political leaders to enter the middle classes through white collar and professional employment in the public sector and in the independent professions. While middle- and upper-level positions in these industries remained reserved for members of ethnic minorities, black Jamaicans became the largest ethnic group within the middle classes.[12] This sector of black Jamaicans typically supported neither the Rastafarian movement nor other black nationalist ideologies, instead looking to the traditional political party structure for their own advancement (Stone 1991). These transformations in Jamaica's political economy—the growth in foreign investment, the newly consolidated hegemony of a capitalist class composed primarily of ethnic minorities, and the expansion of the black middle classes—potentially posed contradictory challenges to the cohesion of a creole multiracial nationalist politics. These were challenges that Seaga attempted to resolve, in part, within the realm of culture.

While Seaga's policy undoubtedly reveals a respect for the cultural practices of poor black Jamaicans, it also reflects the interests of the new ruling Jamaica Labour Party elite consolidated at the time of independence. This was a group that, like the post-1952 People's National Party, generally held the view that only industrial growth along Western lines could provide the basis for modernization and development in Jamaica. However, due to their own status as ethnic minorities, they also recognized that a mass base of support for the JLP would depend on the party's patronizing particular popular cultural forms, despite their view of the cultural practices of the rural poor as backwards and of the urban poor as threatening to their socioeconomic and political interests.[13] What was unique about Seaga's conviction was that he felt that by mobilizing the growing urban poor along cultural lines, it was possible (and essential) for the JLP to secure a mass base among the urban middle and working classes independently of the trade union movement.[14] This sector of the population was often unemployed, semiemployed, underemployed, or self-employed and therefore not amenable to unionization and organization. As a result, it tended to be ignored by both the left- and right-leaning middle classes, and was politically "homeless." Most among the urban poor retained very strong rural connections, however, having only recently migrated to the city. Furthermore, many of these newly urban Jamaicans also originated from the very group in the countryside that had supported the JLP's platform of conservative modernization. As such, they were a potential constituency for the ruling party at independence. By successfully mobilizing these individuals through the same religious practices into which he had conducted research, Seaga extended the JLP's base of support.[15]

Seaga's cultural policy, therefore, while officially validating Jamaica's African heritage, emphasized only selected elements of this heritage—those that privileged the lifestyle of the rural peasantry as well as those that could mobilize a particular stratum of the (recently) urban poor. It remained a creole project, providing a space for "blackness" while maintaining the "Out of Many, One People" ideology. In no way did Seaga's cultural policy support the kinds of black nationalism espoused during that period by Rastafarians or the Ethiopian World Federation, an international organization that was originally established in New York City by Ethiopian Emperor Haile Selassie in 1937 in order to generate support for Ethiopia's struggle against Mussolini among Africans throughout the Americas.[16] Nor was Seaga's policy intended to sustain alternative political visions such as the "Blackman's Party." This was Millard Johnson's attempt to contest the 1962 elections by reprising Garvey's People's Political Party (PPP). A founding member of the Marxist-oriented People's Freedom Movement and former president of the Afro-West Indian Society,

Johnson was a Garveyite but not a Rastafarian. Reflecting the aspirations of the black middle and entrepreneurial classes at the time of independence, the PPP advocated a reduction of foreign capital's dominance in the economy, assistance to small businesses, an end to racial discrimination in employment, and the strengthening of cultural ties with Africa (Gray 1991; R. Lewis 1994). Though ultimately annihilated in the elections, the PPP demonstrated, in its ability to attract thousands to its meetings, that "racial politics were strongly ingrained in the Jamaican people, and that . . . a mass following could quickly be assembled for a movement appealing specifically to black Jamaicans" (Lacey 1977:55).

By emphasizing preservation and presentation rather than racially based mobilization, Seaga's policy, on the other hand, deflected an active contemporary relationship to Africa and other areas in the diaspora where individuals were developing alternative cultural frames of reference from which to engage in "modern" development.[17] As such, it served to stabilize the established social and cultural order at a time when the ideologies and mobilizing strategies of other sectors of the population potentially threatened the integrity of both political parties' vision of multiracial development.

State-Suppressed Blackness: The 1960s

What the continued support for Rastafari, Ethiopianism, and alternative organizational forms of black nationalist political expression suggests is that at the time of independence, many poorer Jamaicans were hostile to the Jamaican state and its policies, viewing both Norman Manley and Alexander Bustamante as stooges of imperialism. As Jamaican political scientist Rupert Lewis has argued, the proliferation of Rastafarian sects throughout the 1950s "placed the racial question, the character of Jamaica's multiracialism, and the island's relationship with Africa on the national agenda" (R. Lewis 1994:12). Additionally, the Cuban Revolution, the various strains of the U.S. Black Power movement, and national liberation struggles in sub-Saharan Africa further inspired the development of both racial and socialist consciousness.

The 1960s, then, were a period of intense ideological and cultural upheaval during which cultural politics informed the class and color conflicts that challenged the newly independent Jamaican state. Several varieties of radicalism developed during this decade, and instances of grassroots action mobilized poor Jamaicans around racialized visions of community and solidarity (Gray 1991; Lacey 1977; Stone 1973). Of particular significance here is the 1960 Henry Rebellion, since it stood as an attempt just prior to independence to organize an armed rebellion against both the colonial and the impending nationalist Jamaican governments and security forces with the goal of establishing a black government in Jamaica, and, ultimately, of repatriation to Africa.[18] As with earlier instances of black resistance, migration and the mobilization of people of African descent throughout the diaspora, and particularly those in the United States, are central to the story of the rebellion.

Claudius Henry and his family migrated from Jamaica to the United States during World War II, where they stayed for thirteen years until 1957. After their return, Henry—by then a Rastafarian who came to be known as the "Repairer of the Breach"—began proselytizing among landless migrant workers in Kingston, recruiting them for his insurrection and repatriation movement. His political philosophy, as Anthony Bogues (2002) has argued, fit squarely within the trajectory of the black redemptive tradition discussed in the previous chapter. That is, Henry synthesized ideas about Ethiopianism, repatriation, and utopia with a critique of creole nationalism that was rooted in black internationalism. As a result, he and his organization were targeted as threats to the colonial state. In 1960, police raided Henry's headquarters and seized over five thousand detonators, several sticks of dynamite, ammunition cartridges, a shotgun, a revolver, and swords, clubs, batons, and a spear (Chevannes 1976). They also found a letter to Fidel Castro asking for advice and assistance, the text of which is reproduced in full below:

> We wish to draw your attention to the conditions which confronts (sic) us today as poor, underprivileged people which were brought here from Africa by the British slave traders over 400 years ago to serve as slaves. We now desire to return home in peace, to live under our own vine and fig tree, otherwise a government like yours that give justice to the poor. All our efforts to have a peaceful repatriation have proven a total failure. Hence we must fight a war for what is ours by right. Therefore, we want to assure you Sir, and your government that Jamaica and the rest of the British West Indies will be turned over to you and your Government, after this war which we are preparing to start for Africa's freedom is completed; and we her scattered children are restored. We are getting ready for Invasion on the Jamaican Government therefore we need your help

and personal advice. We have the necessary men for the job. Since you cannot know sir without our information, the Black people of Jamaica are with you and your Government one hundred percent and desire to see Jamaica gets into your hands before we leave for Africa. (cited in Chevannes 1976:277)

Henry and twelve of his followers were charged on four counts of intent and conspiracy to " 'subvert, overawe, and intimidate the Government of Jamaica' " (Chevannes 1976:277). After raiding Henry's headquarters, the police also searched his base in the Red Hills area outside of Kingston where his son Ronald and several African American recruits trained and stored ammunitions. During that operation a skirmish ensued and two British soldiers were killed. Ronald Henry and four others were subsequently found guilty not only of subversion but also of the murder of the British soldiers.

Coming on the eve of independence, the Henry Rebellion galvanized middle-class Jamaicans' fear of Rastafarians. Now Rastafarians were viewed not only as "uncivilized" or "unclean," but also as hostile to the state and its ideology of creole multiracial nationalism. This view was crystallized by the Coral Gardens disturbance in 1963, an event that—in conjunction with the Henry Rebellion—triggered massive repression of Rastafarians at the hands of the security forces throughout the 1960s and beyond.[19] On April 22, six Rastafarians attacked a Shell gas station in Coral Gardens, a community outside of Jamaica's "second city," Montego Bay. While the motives for the incident were unclear—some have opined that it signaled a Rasta uprising, others that it was the result of land scarcity in the rural areas[20]—the response was unequivocal. A party of police and civilians pursued the men. Ultimately, eight people were killed, and the three surviving Rastafarians were subsequently hanged.

Rastafari was not the only ideological framework through which the urban poor articulated their critiques of multiracial harmony during the 1960s. It was not the primary impetus, for example, behind the anti-Chinese disturbances during August and September 1965 that were sparked by a violent fight between a black Jamaican shop worker and the Chinese proprietors.[21] An additional phenomenon—that of the "rude boy," or Rudie, best personified through Jimmy Cliff's character in the movie The Harder They Come—combined racial protest with a class-antagonistic morality among militant poor black men. A sector of the urban unemployed population in the early 1960s that was growing alongside a burgeoning

Rastafarian movement, rude boys tended to be young, unskilled, and unorganized. They developed rituals and ideas associated with but distinct from those of Rastafarians, who, in constructing an alternative sociopolitical sensibility, strengthened their moral dominance among sections of the urban poor (Gray 1991). Attracted to Rastas' political dissidence and notions of black emancipation but turned off by their discipline, asceticism, and metaphysics, rudies drew haphazardly from Rasta ideology in order to celebrate and affirm the legitimacy of what sociologist Obika Gray has called "the moralities of ghetto culture"—political cynicism, aspirations for a better life, the celebration of instinctual needs, and in-group camaraderie, as well as the cultivation of a fearsome, violent personality (Gray 1991:75). As a result, their pride in blackness, their rejection of the status quo, and their claims for social justice competed with an antisocial temper that was also influenced by cowboy movies imported from the United States and shown almost exclusively in working class communities.[22]

Despite the popularity of these American Westerns and their filmic examples of heroic personae, the soundtrack for rudies' exploits was the developing local musical form of ska. In the decades immediately prior to World War II, a significant transition had occurred within the expressive cultural production of lower-class Jamaicans—urban commercial music began to supplant rural village-based mento bands (White 1984; Stolzoff 2000).[23] This transition was facilitated by the development of new communications technologies and the growing influence of the music industry in the United States. With the advent of the sound-system dance catering largely to lower-class Jamaicans, African American rhythm and blues enjoyed growing popularity after World War II. By the mid-1950s as rock and roll began to dominate the United States musical scene, access to rhythm and blues recordings declined, especially for the lower classes. To fill this demand, a local commercial music industry developed that initially produced and recorded Jamaican covers of popular rhythm and blues songs to play at sound-system dances. By the late 1950s as studios began pressing these "dub versions," the rhythm and blues sound was combined with local folk music to create the genre known as ska (Stolzoff 2000:57–59).

As ska became a driving force not only of black lower-class culture but also, increasingly, of national culture, it more openly challenged the dominant sociopolitical system and became progressively more militant throughout the 1960s. This alarmed many among the middle and upper classes, who viewed the rude boys' affirmation of ghetto culture and ideology in terms of a lack of breeding. Contemporary scholars, on the other hand, tended to celebrate those aspects of rude boy ideology that could not be incorporated within the dominant creole vision:

> In inventing what might be called a culture of resistance, the youths selected those aspects of the moral codes most cherished by the middle and upper classes and inverted them . . . This antagonistic morality, expressing a growing defiance and an erosion of deference, radiated throughout the lower ranks of the unemployed, marking them with a sensibility which called into question the adhesion of the urban poor to the official consensualist ideology. (Gray 1991:73)[24]

Both Rasta and Rudie emerged within poor urban communities and galvanized a denial of the notion of racial harmony as the norm in Jamaica, highlighting instead a conception of the country as a place where black people were oppressed. In doing so, both demonstrated the limited attraction of Jamaican nationalism among significant sectors of the population and encouraged, to different degrees, interest in a broader pan-African sensibility.

This reassertion of black nationalism presented a major political and ideological dilemma for the state, not least because the articulation of protest in explicitly racial terms began to block the traditional paternalistic alliance between middle- and lower-class Jamaicans. If on one hand, however, the articulation of black nationalism was seen as a national security concern and was suppressed as such throughout the 1960s, on the other, it was simply ignored. Seaga's cultural policy recognized neither Rasta nor Rudie, and instead focused on "folk blackness"—those aspects of Jamaica's African heritage that weren't seen to challenge the integrity of a creole multiracial nationalist state. Unlike those artists who continually borrowed from and reinvigorated "folk" or "traditional" sources as they created and produced new popular cultural forms, such as ska and later reggae, that spoke to people's contemporary realities (Bilby 1995), Seaga's vision of an Afro-Jamaican "folk" culture was one that relegated its relevance to heritage. Jamaica's first cultural policy, then, celebrated aspects of African ancestry but contained Afro-Jamaican efforts toward self-determination.[25]

The Challenge of the 1970s: Culture and Development

In 1971, political scientist and celebrated pollster Carl Stone conducted a survey designed to glean the extent of support for the new political structures and dominant ideologies of nationhood across class sectors. Stone

reported that the two polarized views of Jamaican nationalism—multiracialism, and a conception of citizenship based on racial community and
solidarity—correlated to class in ways we might expect, with the upper and
middle classes as well as the upwardly aspiring working classes supporting multiracialism and the lower classes rejecting it. However, his findings
also revealed the importance of employment as a variable shaping individuals' nationalist visions *across class*. That is, support of multiracialism declined with employment in *each* class stratum, with the chronically unemployed being the most hostile to the political parties, to the ideology of
multiracialism, and to whites and other ethnic minorities within Jamaica
(Stone 1991: 147, table 9.6). While some members of the Jamaican middle
classes viewed the return of racial sentiment within the public sphere of
politics and culture as atavistic, others were inspired by the proliferation of
Rasta and Rudie to value their own African past (Brodber 1987; Brodber
and Greene 1988; Chevannes 1976, 1998; Nettleford 1970). In other words,
it was not just the urban poor whose social and political consciousness
was galvanized by black nationalist ideologies. Together, Rasta and Rudie
were also the two principal cultural reference points for the generation of
middle-class radicals that became politicized during the 1960s (R. Lewis
1994).

For many among the professional middle classes, the attraction of racially based conceptions of citizenship lay in the central contradiction
confronting them after independence. They had acquired political power
and social mobility, but because they were excluded from any significant
control over economic resources in land and in the growing manufacturing and tourism industries, their wealth did not grow. This is because
though many white individuals and families (many of whom were involved
either directly or indirectly with the British colonial infrastructure) left the
country after independence, big corporate enterprises remained in the
hands of Jamaica's ethnic minorities who had consolidated themselves as
a local capitalist class. For those middle-class intellectuals who were connected to the Mona campus of the University of the West Indies, then, a
heightened politicization of racial identity was complemented by an espousal of a more left-leaning pan-Caribbean, anti-imperial vision which
was complementary to, but not necessarily identified with, pan-Africanism and other explicitly racial formulations.[26]

Ironically, one of the Jamaican government's attempts to curtail the
influence of these intellectuals committed to popular education—the ban-

ning of Walter Rodney, the Guyanese Marxist historian and activist, from reentering Jamaica after attending a conference abroad in 1968—instead served as a catalyst for increased cross-class mobilization. Though by profession an academic, Rodney's influence was felt far beyond the university campus. Because he believed in the revolutionary potential of the urban youth who had been radicalized by Rastafari, he had been deeply involved in helping to catalyze the development of political consciousness among the urban poor (R. Lewis 1994). His expulsion by the Jamaican government spoke to a fear on the part of the JLP that forging links between university intellectuals and grassroots leaders could result in radical political mobilization powerful enough to threaten the young state. Students and community leaders alike took to the streets to protest the government's action. As protests turned into riots, a number of North American properties—seen as symbolic of increased foreign penetration and intensified economic dislocation among poorer Jamaicans—were attacked, burned, and looted. Both the students and community groups involved in what became known as the "Rodney Riots" were met with violent reprisals by the police and the army, but the protest demonstrated the existence of significant and organized discontent beyond the control of the conventional political system (Lacey 1977).

In the wake of these riots, an alliance of intellectuals and grassroots leaders came together under the umbrella of the Abeng movement. Among other activities, this group published a weekly newsletter calling for the assumption of power by the black Jamaican masses and a cultural reconstruction of society in the image of blacks. In its heyday, The Abeng National Weekly enjoyed a reported circulation of fifteen to twenty thousand readers (Nettleford 1970:134). By this time, the New World Group—a group of radical social scientists—had also crystallized at the University of the West Indies. While the New World and Abeng groups tended to criticize both political parties, advocating more traditionally socialist solutions to Jamaica's development issues, their activism also restored the left-leaning foundations of the PNP (Robotham 1998a).

Indeed, by 1972 Michael Manley, Norman's son and the leader of the PNP between 1969 and 1991, managed to construct a broad alliance of nationalist and progressive elements within the local middle classes, workers, peasantry, and unemployed—especially youth and Rastafarians. The newly radicalized members of the middle classes attempted to develop, through the PNP, a strong state sector in order to circumscribe the power of the old elite and to consolidate the economic and political power of the new rising elite. Manley's government nationalized key sectors of Jamaica's economy and initiated several new social programs. The state also played an active role in repositioning Jamaica internationally and in redefining national identity internally. Membership in the Non-Aligned Movement diverted focus from the British Commonwealth by promoting a strong identification with Africa and the rest of the Third World.[27] In the atmosphere of increased international racial and feminist consciousness, Jamaicans were encouraged to organize for local development around identities that did not have local boundaries—as workers, as black people, as women.

One of Manley's first acts as prime minister was to organize the Exploratory Committee on Arts and Culture, the report of which was to form the basis of a new policy on cultural development (Nettleford 1978). This committee made several recommendations, the most notable of which was to place Jamaica's cultural policy within the context of human resource development. Here, cultural development became linked with social and economic development through educational policy, adult education, and youth community programs, as well as through direct assistance to national cultural bodies and groups. The changes in the cultural policy during the 1970s, therefore, reflected a more general attempt to position Jamaica's "blackness" and African heritage as bases for new kinds of mobilization. These types of institutional changes reflected an apprehension, on the part of Jamaica's leadership, of the need not only to elevate aspects of popular culture but also to link these cultural forms to more general development initiatives. The state no longer viewed Jamaica's African heritage merely in terms of preservation and presentation, but as having the potential to positively influence individual and national growth.

Still, this new focus was not explicitly a black nationalist one. Despite heightened racial consciousness, Jamaica's struggles during this period were framed within the language of class and class conflict, socialist formulations that were to absorb and eventually neutralize blackness into working-class comradeship. Nevertheless, by 1968 the emergent class consciousness among poorer Jamaicans converged with an increasing cultural assertiveness, and Rasta's emphasis on African roots, black redemption, and social awareness began to displace the rude boy variety of socioeconomic and political critique. The marriage of Rasta consciousness with reggae music affected the entire society, not least during the elections in 1972 and 1976 when the PNP successfully mobilized around these symbols of black lower-class experience (A. Waters 1985).

Ultimately, the 1970s challenge to some of the tenets of creole multiracial nationalism failed in part because, like the JLP before it, the government was unable to transform the economy. The local elite and many among Jamaica's middle classes were alarmed by the PNP's declaration of democratic socialism in 1976 and the subsequent escalation of violent crime. In the midst of serious personal economic decline, many of these families left the country during this period, taking their money with them. The Jamaican government's renewed ties with Cuba fueled the JLP's anticommunist campaign and worried the United States enough to launch a Central Intelligence Agency (CIA) campaign to destabilize the Manley administration (Bolles 1996a:29).[28] Both private sector organizations and sections of the religious establishment[29] defected from the PNP and began to respond to the JLP or at least to endorse anticommunism. The 1980 election campaign also sharpened the polarization of the media, the security forces, and civil servants. By the middle of its second term, the PNP had become unable to finance the employment or housing programs it initiated, had to cut spending on health and education, and finally in 1977 signed Jamaica's first agreement with the International Monetary Fund (IMF). Because the government of the 1970s could not realize the programs designed to improve the standard of living of the black population, their nationalist slogans rang hollow. The PNP lost political power and, with it, the ability to shape the country's cultural direction.

The 1980s: Marketing Jamaica

While large-scale emigration contributed to steady economic decline throughout the 1970s, it also created unanticipated and unexpected openings for some black Jamaicans to become socially and economically mobile. Widening employment opportunities in the private sector motivated many gifted, highly trained, and experienced black Jamaicans to abandon public sector careers in favor of more lucrative private sector employment, and blacks emerged to occupy 40 to 50 percent of top- and middle-level private sector technical and managerial jobs (Stone 1991:254). Despite consistent national economic decline, then, the 1970s witnessed some of the most far-reaching changes in Jamaica's ethnic economic division of labor. Increases in both import trading (higglering) and the illegal drug trade placed significant wealth in the hands of some lower-class black Jamaicans. Concurrently, many middle-class black Jamaicans became established within the corporate managerial elite. At the same time, black entrepreneurship got a foothold in part due to the PNP's nationalization of Barclay's bank, which as the National Commercial Bank became an aggressive lender to small- and medium-sized businesses. As a result of these changes, by the end of the 1970s ethnic minorities no longer dominated the ownership of medium-scale and smaller manufacturing and commercial enterprises.

With the 1980 election of the JLP under Edward Seaga, many of the gains of these black middle entrepreneurial classes were eroded. As prime minister, Seaga ended Manley's social programs, shifted Jamaica's economy from import substitution to free market capitalism, and cut diplomatic relations with Cuba. With the new pro-business political atmosphere, many among the ethnic minorities who had migrated returned, thereby both displacing black proprietors who had rented their properties and run their businesses and competing with newly established black businesses, many of which folded as a result.[30] Additionally, layoffs and employment cutbacks in the public sector weakened the position of middle-class black Jamaicans. Seaga's collaboration with Ronald Reagan on the Caribbean Basin Initiative realigned Jamaica's foreign relations with the United States and, through that country, toward the IMF and the World Bank. As a result, structural adjustment policies designed to make Jamaica hospitable to foreign investment subjected the population more directly to the whims of international capital, and severe anti-ganja campaigns reduced a significant source of capital accumulation. The increase in international aid also reduced the market share of commerce for higglers since the foreign exchange shortages that had facilitated the growth of the higgler trade throughout the 1970s were removed. Moreover, import deregulation policies placed local manufacturers and farmers in the position of having to compete with imported goods that were selling at lower prices. These policy shifts resulted not only in an escalation of poverty, social and political violence, and migration, but also in a reestablishment of the hegemony of whiteness and a "quiet ridiculing and denigration of blackness" (Robotham 1993:12). The message to the local population was that blackness, nonalignment, and democratic socialism had brought the country to ruin, and the JLP's economic policies helped to restore old class and color hierarchies.

As housing, public transportation, education, and health budgets were cut, and as teaching and nursing salaries were frozen or increased only nominally, the lower sections of the black middle classes experienced a downward mobility and a decline in the public services that had been available to them previously. These shifts undermined the conventional clientelistic relationships between the black middle and lower classes and the elite. Further, the sharp fall in real wages forced many poorer Jamaicans into the less secure service and informal sectors of the economy. Women, especially, were economically dislocated and close to 40 percent (as compared with 12 percent of the male labor force) turned to informal sector employment, mainly in domestic service and petty commerce. Because IMF-inspired structural adjustment programs redirect funds from the most costly elements of national expenditures (such as education, health care, social housing, and subsidized food and transportation) at precisely the time when demand for these services increases, poor Jamaicans' ability to acquire the basics of human subsistence and social welfare services was drastically reduced.

As has been extensively documented, poor and working-class women feel the impact of these policies most keenly because the rising cost of living imposes a disproportionate burden on those with primary responsibility for the well-being of households and the care and socialization of children, and because the coping strategies women employ for economic survival within this context tend to be less secure.[31] The irony of this is that during the 1980s, national development strategies targeted female labor on an unprecedented scale. Women ultimately displaced the traditional male working class as priority plans for economic development were based on the expansion of free trade zones, offshore data processing, and tourism (Ford-Smith 1997). Moreover, women came to represent the bulk of Jamaica's internationally mobile labor force. These simultaneous trends marked as significant a shift within Jamaica's gendered division of labor in the late twentieth century as did the transformations that occurred during the late nineteenth century.

During the 1980s, then, national cultural policy became a secondary governmental concern to international capitalist integration. At the same time, there was widespread debate regarding emergent popular cultural forms. Dancehall—the music and associated culture of a new generation of "sufferers" and rude boys—became increasingly popular in the mid-1980s and especially after the death of Bob Marley. Where previous reggae music had emphasized social critique and a belief in redemption, early dancehall music reflected a ghetto glorification of sex, guns, and the drug trade. This led many observers to refer to dancehall derisively as "slackness" music, vulgarly degrading to Jamaica's moral fiber. These assessments of dancehall spoke to an ongoing concern, a fear even, among the middle classes regarding the relative power of popular culture to shape both behavior and public perceptions of Jamaica and Jamaicans. The diatribe against dancehall, however, has not merely been moored in morality. Dancehall's distancing from the revolutionary politics of the 1970s and its reflection of the personal melodramas of making it in the marketplace have led some to characterize it as politically conservative. This critique is associated not only with the left-leaning Jamaican intelligentsia but also with sectors of poorer Jamaicans, including prominent Rastafarians. These critics have viewed dancehall as demeaning to black people, especially women, and therefore as serving the ruling elements in society. However, cultural critic Patricia Saunders reminds us that "the line separating these two forms of Jamaican music (conscious vibes and dancehall music) is not at all solid" (2003:96). Anti-Western and oftentimes sexist and homophobic sentiments are also common within conscious vibes music, though they receive considerably less scrutiny because they are "veiled in ethical, moral, and religious discourses" (2003:96).

While several organizations have taken a public stance against the explicit misogyny and homophobia that characterize some dancehall lyrics,[32] some scholars have viewed the cultural space of dancehall as facilitating a form of female liberation. Carolyn Cooper, a Jamaican literary critic, has argued that dancehall is a kind of "verbal marronage" (1989:12) through which singers critique the conservatism of Jamaican social relations. Similarly, ethnomusicologist Ken Bilby's view is that dancehall discourse simply rehearses ideologies espoused more generally within Jamaican society. Bilby also ties dancehall's language—both literally and figuratively—to a move toward increased local cultural autonomy among the black lower classes:

> The sexual "slackness" of many lyrics, overblown and sexist as it may have become, is nonetheless part of a tradition of sexual banter and double entendre in Jamaican popular music that goes back to mento and before. The violence of "gun lyrics" reveals the harsh reality of life in a desperately poor part of Kingston that continues to be ravaged by political warfare, drugs, and crime. And the strident vilification of homosex-

uality is rooted in local values that have been shaped by a fundamentalist reading of biblical scripture. As young, downtown deejays have reclaimed Jamaica's indigenous popular music from the pretensions of international marketers aiming to please cosmopolitan audiences, it has become harder for foreign consumers of that music to romanticize the experience from which it springs or to see it in an entirely "progressive" response to social injustice. (Bilby 1995:178)

What these kinds of assessments flag is the need to analyze dancehall within a historical framework that links popular cultural representations of gender and sexuality to the continuities and changes within more general societal norms, because in spite of its adversaries, dancehall has remained the most popular music in Jamaica.

The 1990s: "Black Man Time Now"

The intense privatization drive that began in the 1980s—one of the largest in the IMF-controlled Third World—continued throughout the 1990s, this time facilitated by a newly elected PNP government. One of the consequences of privatization has been an intensified division between those Jewish business families connected to the old sugar economy, newer brown businessmen who became affluent through the insurance and finance industries, and Lebanese clothing traders and tourism developers (Robotham 1998a; Douglass 1992). Tourism entrepreneurs, in particular, have reestablished the economic power of the old white and brown elites because they have been able to transition from agriculture and commerce to owning and managing hotels, travel agencies, tour companies, and related services. A rising brown and black propertied class has joined these elites, and, as a result, the economic and social gaps between the nascent black bourgeoisie, the black professional upper-middle class, and the black lower classes have widened (Robotham 2000). This intensified ethnic and class polarization, of course, is not unique to Jamaica, but has been shown to be one of the effects of globalization worldwide.

Migration patterns also shifted somewhat during the 1990s. While emigration from Jamaica had risen in the late 1980s, net migration actually decreased throughout the 1990s from a total of 17,000 migrants in 1990 (or 0.7 percent of a total population of approximately 2.37 million) to 13,000 in 2000 (0.5 percent of a total Jamaican population of approximately 2.57 million) (United Nations 2002:201). This decrease reflects the tightening of immigration policies in Canada, the United States, and the United Kingdom. The April 1997 implementation of the Illegal Immigration Reform and Immigrant Responsibility Act, for example, resulted in a dramatic rise in total deportations of Jamaicans from the United States. While 14,420 Jamaicans were returned to Jamaica in 1996, 125,840 Jamaicans were deported in 1997 (Criminal Justice Research Unit 2001:1). Despite a decrease in actual numbers, however, the amount of money sent back to Jamaica by migrants increased sixfold. Workers remittances increased from US$136 million in 1990 (or 3.2 percent of Jamaica's GDP) to US$789 million in 2000 (or 10.9 percent of Jamaica's GDP). This reflects an almost 600 percent per person increase from US$58 to US$306 (United Nations 2002:201). By the year 2001, remittances had reached 13.6 percent of the GDP at US$1,058,700, which represents almost US$400 per person in Jamaica (International Monetary Fund 2003). These numbers would rise considerably if remittances sent by extralegal migrants were also calculated. This is significant because while tourism is Jamaica's principle source of foreign exchange, a migrant labor force whose numbers have decreased in recent years is actually generating an increasing percentage of Jamaica's gross domestic product. This trend evokes some of the more general spatial transformations that have been associated with current processes of neoliberal capitalist globalization. It has also both reflected and inspired a shift in the political sphere vis-à-vis diaspora.

Since Michael Manley's retirement in 1991, the PNP has been led by Prime Minister P. J. Patterson. Patterson's governing cohort is not drawn from either the old or new elite in terms of wealth or social status. Rather, they are black professionals who have advanced mainly through education and not through business. They are a direct product of the expansion of public, especially university, education in the 1950s and 1960s that produced a professional upper-middle class of brown and black civil servants. This cohort of engineers, lawyers, accountants, and managers gained power and position rapidly with the expansion of the state sector during the 1970s, and despite a contracting economy, the PNP government won an unprecedented third term in the 1997 elections.

This is, in part, due to the party's advocacy of a sort of modified black nationalism. Since 1992, Prime Minister Patterson has issued subtle but significant public challenges to the ideology of creole multiracial nationalism. For example, when Patterson took on the leadership of the PNP in 1991, he framed his electoral victory as a triumph for "me and my kind."

He has invited various African heads of state to visit Jamaica for independence and other celebrations and has promoted a sense of pan-Africanism, urging African Americans to invest in Jamaica and encouraging Jamaicans abroad to fully participate in political and civic activities in their adopted countries in order to effect policy changes that would benefit Jamaica (*Daily Gleaner* 1997e, 1997f). The more general idea projected both popularly and by the government has been that "brown" people, whether in the private sector or in national politics, have failed the country and so must step down. The new government's thrust, therefore, reflected the triumph of the notion that Jamaica is a black country that should be led by black people. This is a notion that has been of critical importance in realigning cultural and political hierarchies of racial value in the contemporary period. It has had important implications for the ways black people are positioned in relation to political power, to an older local and expatriate economic elite that maintains control over Jamaica's significant national resources as well as both daily newspapers and to an educational system that continues to promote assumptions of creole superiority and black subordination, particularly in the history, social science, and literature curricula (Robotham 2000). In other words, the modified black nationalism advocated within institutional politics has opened the potential for other expressions of black nationalism to become ascendant within the public sphere.

At the same time, because purveyors of modified black nationalism were socialized within institutions established during the creole period, they have maintained aspects of the creole multiracial ideology, most notably those related to the values that had been delineated as progress oriented. As a result, they often arrive at a negative assessment of the kinds of values they see as emanating from more popular assertions of blackness, like dancehall. In fact, the extraordinary increase in drug- and politically related violent crimes in the late 1990s had Jamaicans of all socioeconomic levels decrying what they saw as a complete degeneration of culture and values throughout the society. As a result, recent efforts of the nationalist intelligentsia to shift the course of Jamaica's future have centered in part on attempts to (re-) socialize the population into a code of moral conduct rooted in an idealized peasant past.

"Accentuate the Positive, Eliminate the Negative": The 1996 Consultations on Cultural Policy

In December 1996, Prime Minister Patterson convened public consultations on Jamaica's cultural policy in order to reconsider the role of culture in national development, education, industry, and tourism. These consultations were the first since the late-1970s, and representatives from government ministries, educational and vocational training institutions, arts organizations, tourism interests, and industrial training and promotional organizations were invited to participate. Additional meetings addressing issues surrounding cultural development were also held in rural communities where individuals and groups—including churches, trade unions, educators, and youth groups—also became involved. These consultations were held to develop recommendations for the formulation of a new national cultural policy, one that echoed some of the concerns of the 1970s in the attempt to move away from the goal of preserving a "cultural patrimony" and toward that of repositioning culture "as a motivational and development tool to take Jamaicans into the 21st century" (Ministry of Education, Youth, and Culture 1997:1).[33]

This change in focus was accompanied by an attempt to promote adherence to a more holistic definition of culture. During his opening address in Kingston, Patterson defined culture as "the way of life of a people . . . those things we do and how we do them . . . [those] peculiar characteristics that make us different from other countries and societies." To the Minister of Education, Youth, and Culture this definition marked a shift from earlier policy elaborations he characterized as being mainly concerned with creative and artistic expressions. It also represented an alignment with the way development had been reconceptualized among multilateral agencies like UNESCO, but also the World Bank.[34] Nevertheless, despite exhortations that participants maintain a holistic and dynamic definition of culture as "what people do" in all spheres of life, two rather static visions of culture emerged as paramount: culture as possession and culture as either positive or negative, in other words, as articulated by UNESCO Representative Dr. Simon A. Clarke, Education Advisor for the Caribbean, culture as "either a help or a hindrance to overall development."

With respect to the former, consultation participants commented extensively on cultural "loss" and pled for a return to "values." The perceived decline in values was linked to what they saw as a decrease in the influence of local institutions—such as churches, schools, extended families, and communities—vis-à-vis the socialization of children. It was also attributed to the increasing encroachment of globalized (American) media as well as new telecommunications and computer technology. The dominant representation throughout the meetings was one of Jamaican culture "under siege" by "foreign cultural influences." As such, concerns regarding cultural "authenticity" persisted to the extent that Patterson proposed the establishment of "cultural conduits" to "filter" the information arriving from outside Jamaica. This way, he argued, foreign cultural influences would operate within the context of a strong Jamaican culture.

There was also significant discussion regarding the purportedly "positive" or "negative" aspects of culture. Here, participants focused on developing ways to encourage the "desirable" aspects of Jamaican (and "foreign") culture while discouraging those that were "undesirable." That this delineation of aspects of culture as positive or negative was related to practices usually associated with particular classes of people did not go unarticulated. Many spoke of the "two cultures in Jamaica" and of a "constant collision between the culture of those who rule and the culture of those who are ruled." Relatedly, several participants also acknowledged that some forms of cultural expression were perceived as more valued and respected by the "validating elite," those individuals who most often attend public consultations, while others were ignored because their practitioners were not invited. As one individual asked,

> Is there any representation from grassroots communities anywhere in this conference? Does anyone want to hear what the average Jamaican has to say about anything? It is always the same people who know each other at these kinds of meetings. The problem is not information filtering down, but coming back up so that people feel what they have to say is respected. If you are invisible, what you are doing is invisible.

Notwithstanding critiques like these, issues of race and class were never explicitly addressed. They were, however, evoked through a coded concern with values. That is, participants argued that as a multiethnic society, Jamaica should follow a cultural policy that highlights the "cultural positives" of each ethnic group in order to delimit a universal national system of morality.

The idea that culture could be lost or maintained, and the related idea that culture could be divided into aspects designated as either positive or negative, lead to a view that culture itself is both the problem to solve and the recipe to follow. This view presents various dilemmas for cultural mobilizers and has several consequences for the general population. For example, at the final meeting in Kingston, one representative from the Jamaica Cultural Development Commission (JCDC) noted that while the JCDC had been successful at maintaining the expressive aspects of various folk forms, she felt that the values embedded within these music and dance traditions had been left behind. Here, she was arguing that the effort to preserve the music and dance forms was not complemented by development policies that would have supported the lifestyles from which these forms emerged. An analysis of the entries in the dance competition of the JCDC-sponsored National Festival of the Arts, however, suggests that in many cases even the expressive aspects of "folk" cultural forms had been "left behind." The dance syllabus for the festival competition divided entries into the categories of ring games, Jamaican folk, other Caribbean folk, modern contemporary, jazz, dance drama, integrated song and dance, popular skit, and popular dance. Of the approximately 110 dances entered in the folk category during the 1997 festival parish finals, only 43 were renditions of Jamaican folk dances. The rest were calypso dances set to soca music culled, in the majority of cases, from the 1996 and 1997 carnivals in Trinidad. During the National Finals, this led the executive director of the JCDC to complain to the adjudicators. "We are losing our traditions," he remarked. "I don't know that this is the direction in which we want to be going as we move into the future."

A seemingly equally undesirable direction has to do with the proliferation of dancehall. During JCDC-sponsored teacher workshops prior to the actual competition, emphasis was placed on appropriate music and movement selections for the popular dance category based on the stated desire to maintain "moral standards." While their previous guidelines had approved any musical accompaniment that was played by the local radio stations, JCDC representatives now ask that teachers be more selective in their choices of music for the dances, especially for the younger children. They argued this because they felt that in recent years, "slackness" music had been getting more airplay. Several adjudicators also expressed the view that it was inappropriate to choreograph pieces using dancehall idioms in their "raw" form for young girls. They suggested instead that greater use be made of a wider range of dancehall movement vocabulary, and that some of the more sexually suggestive movements be "toned down."[35] At the St. James parish finals, which were held in a Methodist church hall, the children were cheering a particularly vibrant dancehall piece and the director of the performing arts for the JCDC stopped the dance to remind the children that they were in a church. She shouted, "You will not turn this place into a dancehall!" She later said that the JCDC highlights the dancehall form because it is part of a Jamaican movement vocabulary but that this doesn't mean that everything else that accompanies dancehall style must be brought into the competition.

This example illuminates two consequences of straying from a holistic concept of culture. First, the representative's initial remarks show how easily the view of culture as possession can slide into the equation of culture with heritage. As heritage implies "past," change implies loss.[36] It is true that economic and political modernization has, to a great extent, decimated the base from which rural "folk" culture emerged. Younger Jamaicans, therefore, no longer had the social frame of reference for the cultural practices many of the participants in the Consultations have struggled to preserve as central to Jamaica's identity. Second, changes in the global political economy as well as the exigencies imposed by international lending institutions have greatly reduced the power of individual states to socialize their citizens. The preoccupation with the "positive" aspects of Jamaica's cultural heritage, in this context, was related to these leaders' apprehension of a real loss of independence. Highlighting the cultural practices of the rural peasantry, then, was a means by which to remember and resocialize a sense of relative autonomy and, to some extent, unity. The urban-based youth culture associated with the strata of the population most (dis-) affected by these global trends, however, because it so forcefully reflected the increased polarizations in Jamaican society, was viewed as retrogressive and therefore "cultureless." The class implications here were clear—some people possessed "good" culture, and others did not. The conviction of many participants in the Consultations, however, was that the "problematic" culture of those in the latter category could be reformed and redirected through an engagement with a (creole multiracial and not a black nationalist) history and cultural heritage with which they should ostensibly identify and from which they should derive inspiration.

Toward this end, the most general recommendations emerging from the Kingston meetings addressed the training and sensitization of bureaucrats, teachers, and politicians regarding the importance of local artistic expression; an evaluation of the country's "moral codes" through a greater emphasis on Jamaican history in the schools; a more general overhaul of curricular content and pedagogical approaches; and a repositioning of culture as an industry.[37] In theory, emphasis in these areas would stimulate the development of self-esteem, which would result in greater national pride. This pride, in turn, would serve as the foundation for a more productive economy.

Conclusion: The Arts of Domination and Resistance

Virginia Dominguez has evocatively argued that the whole enterprise of postcolonial cultural policy development is not, as it has generally been perceived, an act of resistance. Rather, she has framed it as a continuation of a form of European ideological hegemony that positions "culture" as a sphere of life separate from other spheres such as political organization, economic production, and technological innovation (Dominguez 1992; cf. Marriott 1963). While this tendency was generally perceived by participants in the 1996 Consultations, it was also true that the policy makers, educators, and others involved were attempting, through the idiom of culture, to devise a strategy that would address their most serious concerns including poverty, crime, and un- and underemployment at the end of a year that saw the highest murder rate in Jamaica's history. Their efforts to do so also existed within the context of wider perceptions of Jamaica's development relative to other postcolonial states within an international hierarchy of nations. The difficulty of sustaining a holistic and dynamic concept of culture, then, is also a profound testament to the persistent ideological hegemony positioning the cultural practices of formerly colonized peoples as either irrelevant or inherently inferior, unproductive, retrogressive, and even dangerous.

This is an ideological position that nationalist elites have tended to reproduce because they have not been able to transform more general institutionalized inequalities within their societies. In attempting to secure the hegemony of the state and to manage the tension between creole multiracial nationalism and popular racialized conceptualizations of citizenship, therefore, nationalist elites have (sometimes unwittingly) upheld a bifurcated rather than holistic concept of culture. In this way, culturally coded binaries—positive:negative, progressive:retrogressive, middle class:lower class, creole:racial, elite:popular, culture:slackness, urban: rural—all of which revolve around the same axis, have been institutionalized through policy. As the Jamaican case makes clear, while nationalists have often responded to colonial cultural hegemony by turning the binary on its head, that is, encouraging a shift in valuation from elite to more popular cultural forms, they have not been able to remove the binary itself.

Throughout this chapter, we have seen that the creole multinationalist state has never enjoyed uncontested dominance. In fact, it could even be argued that the Jamaican state has not, throughout the postindependence period, been genuinely proactive with respect to cultural policy development. Rather, the various political leaderships have merely been in the position of responding and reacting to intellectuals, artists, and other popular forces and attempting to shape and/or contain them in ways that have suited their own objectives. If in the 1960s the Jamaican state actively suppressed racialized popular challenges to creole nationalism by unleashing its security forces, in the 1970s Manley's PNP recognized, negotiated, and at least symbolically appropriated those cultural and political ideologies emanating from black lower-class communities. In many ways, the JLP of the 1980s temporarily shelved official cultural development policy, though Seaga's links to the music industry ensured that he had a hand on the popular pulse of the nation. In the 1990s, despite a continuing concern with the morality and political viability of lower-class Jamaican cultural forms and practices, there was also somewhat of a public convergence of popular and state interests with respect to racial ideology, with blackness enjoying more explicit articulation with power after the accession of P. J. Patterson to prime minister. Here, I do not mean to imply that Patterson has unequivocally supported dancehall culture, nor that the majority of Jamaicans have supported his policies on the basis of a shared blackness. Rather, I am arguing that Patterson's somatic blackness and his articulations of modified black nationalism have resonated powerfully among black Jamaicans across class and gender lines.

These changes in the state's relationship to popular cultural practices and racialized ideologies of belonging have to do, in part, with transformations in the strength of the Jamaican state since the 1960s. These transformations have been, in large measure, the result of Jamaica's disadvantageous position vis-à-vis increased global economic integration. Because the process of this integration has been increasingly managed by transnational corporations and multilateral financial institutions, the state's capacity to formulate social policies that would meet the basic needs of Jamaicans has declined. One result of this decline has been that the legitimacy of the state's role in cultural leadership has been openly called into question, and it has been less able to contain popular cultural practices and ideologies. Despite this, or perhaps because of it, the creole multiracial nationalist emphasis on modernization and progress through moderate middle-class leadership has endured. That it has remained difficult for many Jamaicans to sustain the imagination of a community whose primary political, economic, and sociocultural institutions have been developed by black lower-class Jamaicans, despite their acknowledgment of (and pride in) an African heritage, speaks to the strength of racialized class antagonisms whose persistence is rooted in the ongoing experience of economic insecurity within national, regional and global contexts.

PART II

The National-Local

chapter 3

STRANGERS AND FRIENDS

Where part 1 provided a template for understanding the critical issues animating nationalist cultural politics in Jamaica since independence, this section directs attention to the community level in order to analyze the ways both nationalist policies and popular ideologies regarding progress and development have been interpreted, evaluated, reproduced, and/or transformed locally. Here, I ground the sphere of ideological production in everyday experience and practice in order to make visible how the persistent tension between globalizing and localizing forces shapes ideas about belonging, leadership, progress, and development. At the state level, these ideas have been framed in relation to a color, class, gender, and culture nexus that has been institutionalized both politically and culturally in ways that have typically excluded racially explicit mobilization. This section outlines how the ideologies that became hegemonic at the national level were reproduced at the community level. It also traces the ways community members' own experiences shaped alternative visions and begins to examine the parameters of these visions.

The three chapters in this section, then, are concerned especially with how people at the local level conceptualized color, class, gender, and cultural differences, how they related these differences to Jamaica's historical development, and how they positioned themselves vis-à-vis ethnic and gendered divisions of labor locally, nationally, and globally. Throughout, I place particular emphasis on local institutions, such as schools, churches, political party groups, and the Community Council. This is because these institutions structured the parameters of class and status in the village, and therefore also shaped community members' diverse ideological perspectives. They also provided the framework for how villagers were articulated within national institutions, and therefore also global hierarchies of race, culture, and power. To poorer community members, these hierarchies often seemed static. As a result, they portrayed the class differences and status distinctions among villagers as rigid and fixed, even though they often experienced them as individually flexible and situationally specific. At the same time, villagers were also able to challenge the agendas of these local institutions, either directly by working within them or indirectly by placing themselves outside of their purview.

Community members' ideas about belonging to the community, about the markers of class and status, about leadership, and about development (and especially cultural development) also reveal something about subject formation. That is, the ways community members engaged with local institutions had an impact on their senses of themselves as Africans, as Jamaicans, and as black people. The reverse is also true, of course. Villagers' various levels of commitment to these three aspects of their identities influenced how, and the extent to which, they engaged with community institutions. Paying close attention to these dynamics lends insight into the ways villagers both reproduced and challenged a nationalist ideology whose project it has been to socialize them into the vision of national unity and development that I have been calling creole multiracial nationalism.

This chapter introduces Mango Mount, a hillside community just outside of Kingston where, as in many rural villages throughout Jamaica, people with considerable material and social differences coexisted relatively peacefully. Villagers in Mango Mount took pride in "living well together," yet underlying this unity in community lay deep fissures along the lines of color, class, and culture. Here, I demonstrate that these fissures were maintained because local institutions—such as the schools and the "square"—reproduced the class, color, and gender hierarchies operating at the national level. Local institutions shaped villagers' choices of friends, the ways they socialized, how they defined who belonged to the community, and the ways they envisioned both individual progress and the development of the community as a whole. Moreover, the differences and distinctions that obtained between community members as a result of their different relationships to these institutions were linked to judgments regarding people's values and progress orientation that also correlated with those circulating at the national level. These judgments were particularly significant in terms of the kinds of relationships poorer villagers have sought to build with middle-class community members. A generational account of some of the poorer families in the district shows that the salience of these relationships has also changed over time. In other words, the socioeconomic mobility many poorer families have enjoyed has diminished the instrumental importance of their ties to particular middle-class community members and, to a degree, their attachment to a vision of progress that articulates with nationalist models of respectability.

Mango Mount: Out of Many, One Village?

From the beginning of the twentieth century, and particularly since the 1950s, the parish of St. Andrew has developed as a sort of suburban satellite community to Kingston (C. Clarke 1975). Upper St. Andrew also includes several rural areas as it stretches northward toward the Blue Mountains. The hillside community of Mango Mount, with a peak elevation of 2,032 feet, is located in Upper St. Andrew about six miles north of Kingston in the foothills of these mountains. The community was, by both popular and archaeological accounts, a Taino Arawak settlement during the period just prior to the British conquest of Jamaica in 1655.[1] During 1996 and 1997, about 5 percent of Mango Mount's approximately 1,400 people were what I designate as "middle class," part of the national stratum of brown, urban professionals and civil servants. The remainder of the community's population was made up of "the poorer class of people," some of whose presence in the village dated to the nineteenth century, and many of whom were either from or had family connections to neighboring rural communities.[2]

With one or two exceptions, the group of professionals and civil servants who moved to Mango Mount from Kingston and other parishes beginning in the 1950s were neither descendants of the planter class nor of the traders from the Middle East who arrived in the mid- to late nineteenth century. Nor were they typically members of the newer generation of business wealth. Rather they formed part of that sector of the national population of (often first generation) urban brown and black Jamaicans, colonially educated and civically oriented, who ostensibly benefited most from independence, in part due to their historical lack of land ownership. These community members shared the apex of the local status or hierarchy pyramid with a handful of North American, Canadian, and British expatriates. Many of the latter were married to Jamaicans who had attended universities in England during the late 1950s and returned with their spouses to live around the time of Jamaica's independence.

Prior to the arrival of these middle-class community members, Mango Mount villagers had been engaged, for the most part, in cash crop farming,[3] with one family manufacturing wet sugar and another running a dry goods shop. Before transportation was mechanized, several villagers also cut guinea grass and sold it to businesses in Kingston that used horse-drawn vehicles, a lucrative endeavor at the time. With the 1936 establishment of the National Water Commission (NWC), much of the district was designated as a watershed area for the Hope River, which, via the Hope Filter Plant and Mona Reservoir, now provides greater Kingston with the majority of its water supply. For this reason, during the 1940s and 1950s private landowners in the area were encouraged to sell their land to the NWC, at which point it was recognized that the majority of those living on the land lacked formal tenure. At the initiative of Norman Manley, who was the Member of Parliament for the rural St. Andrew constituency between 1949 and 1959, NWC properties were made available for leasing. In this way, several village residents obtained 99-year leases for the small plots of land on which they were, in many cases, already living. Other small farmers obtained plots through a land settlement scheme that had been initiated around the same time in another area of the district.

With the drift of middle-class people to the community came various amenities. Prior to the 1950s, only one house at the top of the hill, which had originally been built during the 1880s by the rector of the St. Andrew Parish Church, had a telephone and electricity. Because the Director of Public Works resided in that house during the 1920s, the footpath that had provided access to the hill was made into a driving road. It wasn't until the 1950s, however, that the new middle-class residents established a Citizen's Association, through which they were able to lobby for infrastructural improvements that would benefit the whole community—a paved road, a postal agency, a police post, and a more extensive electricity supply. Land was also donated by one private owner to the NWC for the construction of a water tank, completed in 1967, which thereafter provided the village with a regular water supply. During this period, an Anglican church was also constructed on donated land, the prior church having been destroyed by Hurricane Charlie in 1951. Several of the older men among the "poorer set" attributed the development of Mango Mount to these "outsiders" who "br[ought] the community up to date." The arrival of middle-class people to the hill did provide many with employment opportunities, either in their homes as gardeners or "helpers"—women hired to cook, clean, and take care of children—or in the public and private agencies where they themselves worked or had contacts. Additionally, because the founder of the Citizen's Association coordinated the Farm Work Programme for the Ministry of Labour, she arranged for many of the older men in the village to obtain contracts for seasonal agricultural work in the United States during the 1960s. At a more informal level, middle-class residents often provided the "poorer set" with tips regarding available land and building materials, resources for financing their children's education, or other types of individual assistance.

By the late 1990s, the majority of those among the "poorer class of people" were small landowners or lease holders. These were mostly farmers and tradespeople, some of whose adult children had moved into lower-middle-class and middle-class office occupations. A very small proportion of the "poorer sets" earned their entire income from cash crop farming. Typically, these were older men, many of whom claimed that the younger generation had been seduced by urban jobs and had therefore developed a disdain for farming. The largest local employers during the period of my research were two guesthouses (one upscale and one geared toward campers and other "adventure travelers"), each of which employed about ten to fifteen people from the village. Because there were no major industries in the area, the majority of the "poorer class of people" traveled off the hill to jobs in Kingston. Though a few women worked in administrative positions in business or service offices, most who worked outside the district did so as household helpers or cooks for middle-class residents of other communities. Men, however, were often able to find work in trades or on construction sites. Several community members, and especially those in their sixties, also engaged in the casual farming of fruit and vegetables for their own consumption or to supplement their income. Despite the presence of a couple of dry goods shops that sold fruits, vegetables, and occasionally chicken, most residents also shopped for groceries "on the flat," either in the downtown markets or in the supermarkets in a neighboring community. The community's proximity to Kingston, then, was critical in structuring social relations, occupational opportunities, and evaluations regarding the relative value of goods and services. This point will become more critical in later chapters. For now, I only want to point out that the bright lights of Kingston shaped community members' daily experiences and ambitions to perhaps a larger extent than in other more remotely rural communities throughout Jamaica, particularly with respect to the local development of services, institutions, and industries.

On Belonging

According to the Community Council's archival records, Mango Mount has often been recognized within local and international development circles as a model community in that the relatively rich and poor have been seen as "living well together." Notwithstanding the often significant and affectionate cross-class relationships that existed within the community, however, considerable divisions also existed—and were, indeed, expected. These divisions were usually explained in class terms but were understood to articulate with racial or color terms and were defined through reference to culture. While these separations evoked historically generated color and class hierarchies that also articulated with gender, they were generally experienced as flexible and relational rather than absolute. For example, Matthew—a self-described racially "mongrel" artist in his early thirties who grew up in Mango Mount—parsed villagers' racial and class designations in the following manner:

> I could imagine a situation where people here would see me as a white person. But then I could imagine a situation where I would not be seen this way. If I were with some of the ordinary peasants from the village, black people, and then a Peace Corps worker came by, that person would be white and I would not. Those same people who might call me a white person would now turn around and call that person a white person and call me brown.

Here, Matthew linked color designations not only to phenotype, but also to determinations about belonging. Poorer community members' apprehensions of race, therefore, were also contingent upon their acknowledgment of context. In other words, Matthew's middle-class (and "mongrel") status marked him as "white" in the eyes of the "poorer sets" when compared to other villagers, but his local status marked him as "brown" when juxtaposed with a foreigner.

Furthermore, Matthew argued that it was not only the brown villagers, being on the "border of things," who were contextually colored. He went on to identify specific individuals according to their economic and social behaviors as these have been related to the more general development of Jamaica's population. His comments on this topic were extensive, but I have reproduced them in full here because they flag important issues regarding the persistence of stereotypes related to an historical ethnic division of labor in Jamaica:

> The [white family in the village] is white because they have a long connection with the piece of land they live on and they've always been white. The professionals are mostly brown to white, or brown to black, because they're in some sense detached from the land. They just live here in a house. And the people who farm are black because, again, they're at-

tached to the land. At both ends, there's a meaningful attachment to land, but in the middle, it's not so meaningful. [One of the retired civil servants in the village who is in his late seventies] is black. Except of course he's really brown, but occupationally, he's not brown, he's a farmer. Maybe someone else would think of him as being brown, but I've always known him and his wife as being farmers, very very good farmers, and farmers on a different scale from most of the people here, but to the extent that farming is a black occupation, they are black. [One Lebanese-Jamaican man] is brown, not "Syrian." Here there really aren't the categories "Syrian," "Portuguese," "Indian," "Chinese," those kind of minority categories. In Jamaica generally, yeah, but within this community, in terms of people's relationships with the majority population, there's no real distinction between being "Syrian" or "white" or "Chinese" or whatever because culturally or economically, they don't behave in the way people would expect that group to behave. If you're Chinese in most parts of Jamaica, you have a shop and you live above your shop and you buy bulk and sell small at high margins and make a lot of money. But [the one identifiably Chinese man in the village] doesn't do this, so while people might recognize him as Chinese because of how he looks, since he doesn't run the shop here, he might just be absorbed into "white" or "upper class." The Indian way of life doesn't have any meaning here, there is no Hindu temple or Hosay celebration. So though [an Indian woman in the community] is Indian, because she is not seen as being publicly involved in some of the Indian cultural organizations, and because she's married to a brown man, and because she was born in England, she's seen as "white." [Another woman] is brown, but she's really black. But she's brown because she's married to a brown man and she leads the Anglican church, so her family unit is brown, and therefore middle class, though she didn't grow up that way. It is [her husband's] job that gives the family its status rather than hers. There's this white guy who walks up and down the hill, he doesn't have a car. I don't know what he does, he has land here somewhere, but he is occupationally black, but apparently white, and probably brown, but definitely not middle class.

In this delineation, Matthew has emphasized the fluidity of Jamaica's racial landscape. The crux of his argument revolves around the assertion that individual racial designations could not be defined solely through phenotypic criteria. Rather, racialization was always tied to assessments of social and occupational behaviors, expectations, and practices that were gendered and historically conditioned. Within Matthew's schema, whiteness, brownness, Indianness, Chineseness, and blackness were never givens, but depended upon individuals' relationships to land ownership and cultivation, upon the extent to which individuals associated with their ethnically defined communities, and—for women—upon the status of the men they chose to marry (as well as whether they married at all). That is, although the black woman Matthew mentioned toward the end of his description had working-class roots, because she married a brown middle-class man and because she actively demonstrated her "respectability" through her leadership of the Anglican church, she became socially (and racially) mobile. This, as well as the other aspects of Matthew's demographic analysis, has as much to do with the ways color and class articulate with culture and behavior as it does with the ways social mobility has been correlated with the pursuit of respectability, itself deeply gendered.

Other men and women from the community also tended to describe the village population in these terms, though perhaps not as elaborately. That is, they ascribed some degree of fluidity to Jamaica's tripartite race and class system according to the extent that individuals approximated the behaviors historically associated with class and ethnic groups. More often than not, the "poorer set" in Mango Mount also made individual racial and ethnic designations somewhat fluidly, associating behavior with class and both with race. The flexibility villagers often exhibited when making individual designations based on face-to-face interactions, however, did not necessarily become extended to groups. That is, the significant ties a poorer and black Mango Mount community member might have had to one or another "brown" or white family did not automatically alter their evaluation of "brown" or white people as social and historical groups. In part, this stemmed from their assessments of where individuals were positioned within national color and class hierarchies, but it was also related to expectations among the "poorer set" of how the different groups *were supposed to* behave. For example, if you were a "brown" person but you were not "civic-minded"—in other words, you were not "trying to help the poorer class"—you could become white in the sociohistorical sense of oppressor. In this kind of situation, poorer community members were evoking an ideology, one that had become solidified by the middle of the twentieth century, that placed brown Jamaicans in the role of national and community leaders within both civic and cultural spheres.

Despite this relatively fluid system of racial identification, belonging to the community was generally defined in racially coded class terms. Those in the "poorer class of people" often made distinctions between "Mango Mount people"—those members of the "poorer set"—and "strangers"—those in the middle class who came to live. As one poorer resident put it, "The brown set of people are strangers. Them is really not native Mango Mount, them is 'come here.'" When poorer villagers spoke about the heart of the community, therefore, they typically excluded those in the middle class, regardless of how long their families had lived there. In contrast, the "poorer set of people" figured prominently in middle-class individuals' descriptions of the community. Many said that what prompted them to move to Mango Mount, aside from its cooler climate, "country feel," and their concerns with security, was a desire to live in a community not entirely segregated by class, as many residential districts in Kingston are.

Mr. James, a retired civil servant who was also the president of the Community Council, explained that he saw people's exclusion of the middle-class population when they described Mango Mount as a means of maintaining the identity of what Mango Mount originally was—a group of people originating from one or two families. Despite having significant relationships with several poorer families himself, he noted that no matter how intimate these relationships became, as a "brown" middle-class person he would always be a stranger "because I came here and found them, my father came here and found their fathers, and if it was my grandfather, he would have come and found their grandfathers." He elaborated upon this point by explaining that it was also the case that some of the local residents had sold their land to middle-class people when they felt it was no longer suitable for farming. The new owners, having a different outlook on land use, were then able to build big houses that, in large part, had come to isolate other members of the community through such means as walls, fences, and guard dogs. As a result, individuals among the "poorer set" may have harbored some degree of resentment that these middle-class people were able to live well on "their" land or might have regretted selling it in the first place.

The middle-class residents in Mango Mount, however, were not the only "strangers." Trevor, a black tradesman in his mid-thirties who was born and grew up in the community, remarked that "you have one out of every nation that lives somewhere in a Mango Mount—a white man, a Syrian, an Indian, a Chineyman—and everybody have them own separate culture." Here, Trevor glossed race and ethnicity as nationality, or more accurately, as subnationality since his list was limited to those "nations" that have contributed to the constitution of Jamaica's population. By linking these subnationalities to cultures and by excluding black Jamaicans from his list, he also (perhaps unwittingly) invoked the British colonial ideology that positioned laboring groups arriving in Jamaica after the abolition of slavery as cultureful—that is, as coming from "civilizations" with ancient text-based religions—as compared to transplanted Africans, who were positioned as cultureless and therefore eminently assimilable.[4] Trevor's exclusion of black community members, the most populous within Mango Mount, also situated them as the default against which the separateness of these various groups' "nations" and "cultures" were measured. That is, all the other "nations" were juxtaposed to a norm that was so accepted it went unstated. For Trevor, as for the majority of the "poorer sets" in the community, black people were the "authentic" Mango Mount villagers, the ones who truly belonged.

"Education Gives the Children a Chance in Life"

Other aspects of life that differentiated Mango Mount community members centered around the attainment of formal education and socializing. It has long been noted that education has been seen as the primary route to social mobility in Jamaica, and that in many contexts, it has become the functional alternative to race as the explicit signifier of class position (Kuper 1976; Austin 1984).[5] Parents, on the whole, expressed hope that their children would attain a higher educational level than they themselves were able to because they saw education as providing the children with options and independence. However, it was also true that the likelihood of this happening was, to some extent, predestined among middle-class families and a struggle for those among the "poorer class of people." This is because many among the latter were unable to send their children to primary schools that would adequately prepare them for the Common Entrance Examination (CEE)[6] taken at eleven years of age, an exam that would, in large part, determine the quality of the rest of their education and therefore their future career possibilities.

As anywhere, it was also the case that a family's business and professional contacts went a long way in structuring a child's potential for growth and mobility, a fact that could be particularly stifling in a society where resources are as limited as they are in Jamaica. Indeed, one of the middle-class village residents pointed out that if you came from a "certain background," you would be guaranteed an education, and from there, your opportunities would flow because "you grow with the right people." For the "poorer set," this situation seemed particularly oppressive. They often viewed their potential to "advance in life" as thwarted because they couldn't pay to send their children to "good" schools that would prepare them for the CEE and felt that even if their children passed the exam, they wouldn't be able to afford the fees for high school. Moreover, many argued that "Chiney people" and "Syrians" ran Jamaica's economy. As a result, they felt that even if a "small man" could afford to send his children to good schools, prospective "white" or "Chiney" employers would only employ people they already knew, no matter how qualified their child might have become.

There has been an All Age school (a government-funded school for students aged fifteen and under) in Mango Mount since 1955,[7] and a Basic School (a primary school for younger children), privately owned by the Seventh-Day Adventist Church, was built in 1996.[8] None of the students at these local schools, however, were children of the middle-class residents in the village. Indeed, it was expected that while some middle-class community members would support the All Age school institutionally as board members and, to some degree, financially as benefactors, they would send their own children to private and top-level government schools in Kingston. Because they perceived the quality of education at the All Age school to be poor, many parents among the "poorer set" also attempted to send those children they felt were "brighter" down the hill for both primary and secondary school if they could afford it. This was due, in part, to a lack of faith in the school on the part of the parents, a lack of faith that developed for many when the principal sent his own children away to other schools in the 1980s. Though the principal explained this decision by stating that he had wanted to encourage some distance between himself and his children, many parents decided that if the school wasn't "good enough" for the principal's own children, it wasn't good enough for theirs.

From 1984 to 1985, a study was conducted by two students in the Department of Social Work at the University of the West Indies on the recommendation of the school's board of governors with a view toward identifying problems affecting the school, and, in particular, the high number of children being removed to schools outside the area. These researchers concluded that parents in the village cited poor performance and a lack of interest in children's affairs on the part of the teachers as well as the inability of the school to prepare children for the CEE as reasons for removing their children from the school (Griffiths and Williams 1985).[9] Many of the problems cited in this report were reiterated to me during the period of my fieldwork. Typically, parents found fault with the organization of the school—it was a multigrade school where one teacher attended to children in grades one through three and another to those in grades four through six—arguing that their children did not receive enough attention that was individualized to their specific academic level. One young parent who worked as a household helper had sent her eldest son to live with his father in another parish because his performance had begun to slip at the Mango Mount school. She had also removed her youngest child to the Seventh-Day Adventist Basic School and was determined to remove another because she felt the quality of education the children received did not prepare them for the CEE and therefore wouldn't "give them a chance to move up in life." Several individuals also argued that the quality of education at primary schools in Jamaica generally was better during the colonial period, even though then only "special people" completed secondary school educations. One woman said she felt that "we're almost reaching back to the same situation [as before independence], where only a certain set of people can afford education because it's very hard."

Show Me Your Friends

Since education largely delimited the range of people in children's social worlds, another axis around which villagers' practices diverged was their social behavior, an axis they usually defined as "culture." A few community members suggested that a degree of cultural homogeneity obtained among the different sectors of Mango Mount society because women from the "poorer class of people" cared for middle-class children as well as their own. That is, as household helpers employed by local middle-class residents, lower-class women had a primary role in the domestic social and cultural reproduction of the community as a whole. There is a degree of historical precedent for this practice, but by the late 1990s the local significance of this pivotal relationship had shifted because the bulk of the middle-class children raised in Mango Mount were in their thirties, and those who were still resident in the community had not yet had children of their own. Furthermore, despite this important point of connection, most villagers argued that the "upper set" and the "poorer set" socialized differently. Both middle-class and poorer community members rooted this difference in an understanding of class relations between social groups that was antagonistic and immutable—that is, it was ever thus and will be ever thus. In other words, social contact is not the same as socializing, and the difference has to do with how racial and class distinctions continued to structure social relations of power at the local level. This may seem to contradict my earlier assertion that poorer community members made racial designations somewhat fluidly. However, their apprehension of class relations as fixed and eternal reminds us that while individual evaluations were somewhat flexible, these did not tend to alter understandings and expectations of group relations because the latter were generated within national and global color and class hierarchies of which they were acutely aware.

Moreover, the immutability of class was conceptualized as the result of the (ongoing) actions of people, rather than as a divine predestination. "God never make one man rich and one man poor," Evelyn, a black woman in her early sixties who was born and raised in Mango Mount, maintained. "Is man set it, cause from day one, man fight for power, right? We don't know how it come about but it is all in the heart of man." Evelyn's analysis linked class relations to an ongoing, perhaps eternal, struggle for power within which poor people were always at a disadvantage. Other poorer community members agreed with her assessment. "The rich will always be rich and the poor will always be poor," Trevor stated, "and the rich suck the poor." Mr. James, the Community Council President, also concurred. "There are distinct social classes, and the whole country is built around these classes," he argued. "It's part of how we behave, how we are socialized. That is our Jamaican culture." In linking antagonistic class relations to Jamaica's development and culture, Mr. James issued a subtle reminder that contemporary class relations were rooted in the system of plantation slavery. Their persistence, therefore, was the result of a socialization process that was so totalizing and taken-for-granted it remained implicit. Trevor provided further insight into this process:

> You move around in a certain class, your mother and your father brought you up living a certain kind of way. You would have to be a strong headed girl or boy to break away from the rules and guidelines. Not even your

father or your mother set them, you know, but is a ting which come with the class system. You don't really mix with certain people, socially. Your mother and father might not say, "Don't go next door," but you're born and grow up in the system. You know it. Them don't haffi tell you. Or else you would have to be rebellous and decide seh you're going to mix with whomever you choose, regardless of whatever the other people want to think bout you. A so it go.

Finally, some poorer community members' vision of class—and the social behaviors understood to accompany particular class positions—was also one that, to a degree, transcended race. Anthony, a black man in his early thirties who worked in the music industry and cultivated cash crops, explained that "from you have money, you can do all kind of tings, and that doesn't differentiate from white, from black, from Chiney." Anthony's maneuver here divorced class from culture (in the sense of being "cultured," "civilized," and "respectable"), instead rooting position and potential in the acquisition of wealth. This vision of class relations tended to be more commonly expressed by the younger generation of the "poorer class of people." Theirs was not the contention, as has been commonly asserted within various Latin American contexts, that money whitens, with social mobility demonstrated, at least in part, through the acquisition of culture (again, in the sense of civilization, respectability), and therefore whiteness. Rather, it was an argument that removed culture from the equation altogether, thereby destabilizing the color, class, gender, and culture nexus.[10]

One of the constants within these variations on the theme of class relations was that middle-class people were perceived as potential benefactors and employers of the poorer class. This was a perception middle-class people ordinarily recognized, and so in order to develop better relations with the "poorer set," many attempted to fulfill these expectations to the extent they could. They offered employment if they were able, rides up and down the hill when public transportation wasn't running, building materials or produce if there was surplus, legal advice or primary health care (or referrals) if these were their professional fields, and other forms of individual assistance. However, they did not generally socialize with those in the "poorer class," nor did they encourage their children to do so. Even though children of long-standing middle-class residents in the community would come into contact with the "local youth" on the road or at church, they did not play with them growing up. Take, for example, the case of Virginia and Jonathan, the adult children of a black Jamaican man and an English woman (both retired doctors). Virginia and Jonathan grew up in Mango Mount but completed their university educations in England. They both recalled childhoods that were relatively socially segregated, despite the lack of residential separation. "A certain financial background sends you to a certain set of people because that's what you have in common to do," Jonathan offered. "We didn't hang out with the poorer kids growing up because there was no forum for communication amongst everyone here." Virginia attributed this situation to the community's proximity to Kingston. "Despite having more interaction between the wealthier people and everybody else than in most communities," she said, "there still wasn't a lot of mixing because richer people were in town [Kingston] all the time. [Mango Mount] was a place where middle-class people lived rurally, but didn't necessarily work or go to school rurally."

As a result of these social separations, people in the village had developed theories about "how the other half lived" and why they did so. However, middle-class villagers knew more about how the "poorer class of people" lived and socialized than vice versa because the social lives of the "poorer set" were considerably more public and, among the youth, usually centered around the "square."[11] The square in Mango Mount was actually not a square, in the Latin American usage of the term. Indeed, the community had several "squares" that marked the gathering points of neighborhoods within the community, usually housing a dry goods shop and a rum shop and serving as a stopping point for public transportation. The square at the top of the hill was, during 1996 and 1997, the district's main focal point because the bus route ended there, and because behind the rum shop was a "lawn" used for hosting dancehall sessions on Friday nights. During the day, much of the activity in the square centered around the dry goods shop and the bus stop, but in the evenings, the focus shifted to the bar where, on special occasions like the Jamaica versus United States soccer match, the proprietor also set up a television for public viewing. By nightfall, the majority of those who frequented the square were men, with the exception of Sundays when families often walked together to greet each other there. The middle-class community members, with few and infrequent exceptions, did not socialize at the square. Instead, they traveled off the hill to meet friends in their homes or at nightspots in Kingston.

Socializing, then, was often a question of mobility. As Trevor explained, "when you have money, you socialize in a certain way because you have a car." Two middle-class men made similar assessments. "The lower socio-economic group tends to socialize more in the community because maybe transportation is a problem," said one man in his early thirties, "or because there's a common focal point, which would be the square, where they tend to gravitate because that's the only thing of excitement they can afford to go to." For some in the middle class, socializing was also a question of education, and the "culture" (or lifestyle) that was assumed to accompany this education. Mr. Williams, a sixtyish brown man who had been educated at Cambridge and was retired from his post within the civil service, contended that the people who spent time at the square were probably people of a "lower intellectual class" who needed something to occupy their time. For middle-class people, on the other hand, the square was a "less sophisticated place to go" offering only "trivial activities." Children, Mr. Williams said, would take their cue from their parents, but it wasn't that middle-class people despised the people who frequented the square. Rather, they despised the practices that might "catch on" like drinking or ganja smoking. When I asked him whether people from middle-class families didn't drink or smoke marijuana, he replied that those practices would be "more widespread at the lower income level" and that the kinds of functions middle-class people attended would be "more refined." "There is less cussing and less heavy drinking," he explained. Indeed, "richer" and "poorer" alike asserted that middle-class people wouldn't want to be around cursing, drinking, smoking, and fighting. These are practices they saw as common at the square, and practices they usually associated with the "poorer sets."

It was not only the middle-class villagers who regarded the square as an inappropriate venue for socializing. Generational differences, as well as differences in the extent to which they interacted with other institutions within the community, also shaped the assessments of the square among the "poorer class of people." Older people in the "poorer set," as well as those who were active in any of the three churches, did not generally view the square as the seat of their social lives—due, again, to the "undisciplined" practices associated with the square. One woman in her mid-thirties, a leader in the Seventh-Day Adventist church, said that the type of dance people danced in the square, as well as the type of music being played, was immoral. "It wouldn't be brought into the church," she stated, "because in following Christ, there must be a difference." She also said that many people wouldn't like their children to be exposed to the language, dancing, and drinking that went on in the square because "they don't want to send their kids somewhere with people who they must look down to." Despite one older woman's assertion that the "wealthier people" wouldn't want their children to socialize at the square because they were prejudiced and would fear that their kids would be "caught up in the wrong company," she admitted that this was how she raised her children as well. She didn't want them out at the square every night because, as she declared, "the square is not a place for the children of decent people." Some younger people in the "poorer set" also viewed hanging out at the square as an indication that someone lacked ambition. For instance, an intermittently employed twenty-year-old argued, "Dem people not going forward in life. All them do is smoke spliff and drink all white rum and tun themself wutless."

For their part, the middle-class children who were born and raised in the village often said that they didn't socialize at the square because, as articulated by one man in his early thirties who worked as a salesman, "You might try to go out to the square to be friendly, but are then asked to buy a beer for someone":

> There's no real attraction for me there. I don't know how I learned not to go there, it's nothing consciously taught, and I probably know about 30 percent of the people there, while probably 60 percent know me. And I get along well with them, but they're not my friends. One or two would ask me to buy drinks or give them a money, so it might be a pain in the ass to socialize there.

On the other hand, some of the middle-class children had spent time at the square as they were growing up, but this was an experience largely structured along gender lines. Gerald, a man in his early thirties, remembered that when he was an adolescent, he'd sometimes go to the shop and "hang out and drink some beers, smoke a spliff, and look a woman." He argued that "brown men can do things like that but not brown women, and certainly not white women, at least that's what people expect." His sister confirmed this argument and noted that these gendered expectations surrounding class behavior were held and policed by both the "upper sets" and the "poorer sets" in Jamaica. During a "home leave" from her position as a modern language teacher at a private high school in England, where she had been living for many years, she complained that these were the structural limitations that prevented her from wanting to return to Jamaica to live:

> I would like to be able to not have color class me. It's not that I'm denying my class. I know that I'm a privileged child, but that doesn't mean that I only want to talk to or deal with privileged people. That's what I don't like about it. I would like to be able to meet anybody and just establish a relationship, whatever it's going to be, that doesn't have class in it, or color in it. It's restrictive. I mean, if you take [my family's gardener] for instance. He has a sense of humor, he's an interesting person, he must have had an interesting life, but are we ever going to sit down and talk? No. I would never have that opportunity. It would be rejected. It would be rejected by him. And to some degree by me, were I living here. One, because our paths would just never cross, apart from in my parent's yard or at the square when he's drinking. And even then, I've never hung at the square. That's where I go to get cigarettes, but that's me, I go to get cigarettes. I was not brought up to hang out at a square.

Gerald and his sister have raised an important issue regarding the similarities in the socialization of gender roles across different class backgrounds. While "decent" women, whether "rich" or "poor," were expected to frequent the square only to purchase necessary items, greater social leeway was afforded to men of all classes. Here, I do not mean to indicate that socializing at the square was evaluated in the same way for "upper class" and "poorer class" men. Indeed, Gerald clarified that while it may have been acceptable in his youth to have spent time socializing at the square, and while it may even have been acceptable for him or any other of the young middle-class men to have developed an occasional sexual relationship with one of the "local" women, these social interactions would have been viewed largely within the framework of patron-client relationships as opposed to serious—or even casual—friendships between equals. Further, there was an expectation—held by both the "upper sets" and the "poorer sets"—that at a certain age, middle-class men would stop (or at least privatize) this behavior and develop what were considered to be more acceptable partnerships based on expectations surrounding their class position. These gendered expectations have to do with the ways masculinity and femininity have been structured in Jamaica since the slavery period and the ways both have been linked to color, class, and the pursuit of respectability (Alexander 1977a, 1977b; R. T. Smith 1996). Within the community, then, assessments about how people socialized were linked to ideas about respectability that circulated nationally. Therefore, individuals' evaluations of social behavior were shaped by their own class, gender, and generational positioning in relation to national hierarchies.

Dancehall Rock

The other bone of contention middle-class villagers often had with the square had to do with the dancehall sessions held there on Friday nights and on other special occasions such as Independence Day and the night before Easter. This was, in part, because the majority of middle-class residents of Mango Mount owned property along the ridge at the top of the hill, while the "poorer set's" families were clustered in several different areas of the hill. A typical Friday night session at the square began early in the evening as Michael, the pan chicken man, set up his barbecue drum and began cooking the chicken he had been marinating all day. As the music started pumping through the stacks of speakers set up on the lawn behind the rum shop at the top of the hill, community members would gather. At first, older laborers—men who were rum shop regulars—would congregate in the bar, settling in for an evening of white rum and dominoes. Little by little, other villagers would arrive. A handful of young men would drink rum, play cards, and share stories of the week while watching television in the room adjacent to the bar. A group of boys would begin to practice and show off their dance moves in the yard. And eventually, a few young women would join in the dominoes or card games. On most Fridays, there were never more than twenty or thirty people in the square, and by midnight, the music was usually turned off.

Special occasion sessions, on the other hand, usually were much louder and lasted much longer. Held to commemorate public holidays as well as other private celebrations such as birthdays, they also tended to draw many more people from outside the community. As a result, these sessions also provided greater opportunity for villagers to demonstrate—and view— the latest fashions and dance styles. Though the music typically began in the early evening, most of those coming to the dance would not arrive until midnight. Those from Mango Mount tended to congregate together and watch as the posses of other young men and women rolled up in taxis or on motorcycles. Emerging from their transportation fabulously attired in blond bob wigs, or matching red patent leather lace-up boots and g-string, or tiger-print spandex suits, the women would enter the yard and position themselves in groups throughout the space. Men, following the women, also congregated in groups, but didn't tend to approach the women unless clearly directed to do so. The spotlight from the videoman's camera would move around the yard, prompting the younger virtuosos—male and female—to take the lead in dancing.

Ordinarily, the selector[12] would take the lead from particular songs or particular lyrics to encourage or taunt individual dancers, and occasionally, a man "penetrated" one of the groups of women and danced with someone until she indicated that his time had expired. As rhythm and blues and reggae gave way to hardcore dancehall toward the wee hours of the morning, the crowd responded to the selector's electronic gunshots and his various instructions, such as "all [Mango Mount] badman, gun salute to dis one!" or "all fat pussy gyal skin out cuz unoo know unoo run tings!" or "raise unoo 'an if unoo seh batty man fi get shot!" The session would "hot up" to a climax, then would hit that point of diminishing returns when people would drift back home. Because these sessions created more "noise" and drew more "strangers" than the Friday night sessions, they generated considerably more ire from middle-class community members despite their relatively infrequent occurrence.

In order to just briefly foreshadow something I will discuss more fully in chapter 7, I want to draw attention to the selector's provocations. The last phrase translates loosely to "raise your hand if you think gay men should be shot." "Batty" is a Jamaican term for one's behind, and "batty man" is therefore a derogatory reference to gay men. As I mentioned earlier, these kinds of performances of masculinity in dancehall settings reflect values more generally held throughout the population. While the sort of sentiment expressed here was most often interpreted locally as hyperbole (that is, no one I spoke to was prepared to actually make good on the goading and shoot gay men), there is a serious sanction against homosexuality within the community, a sanction that goes hand in hand with the notion that women exert control over men ("run tings") via their sexuality ("fat pussy"). I call attention to it here in order to demonstrate that popular culture provides a space within which people perform, debate, and, to an extent, contest ideas about gender and sexuality.

Junior, a "local youth,"[13] complained that dancehall sessions in Mango Mount were never as good as in other communities because the "rich people" would always call the police to "lock down the music" because "dem nuh like fi see wi do wha we a do." Indeed, the debate within the community over dancehall had been ongoing, in part because middle-class people tended to see quietness as one of the assets of the village. The proprietor of the upscale guesthouse on the hill explained that while sessions were a popular social form of entertainment, they also caused noise pollution and discomfort in houses nearby where people might have been trying to sleep. For him, dancehall had also become a business nuisance, and he worried that the Friday night sessions would detract upper-class Kingstonians from frequenting his restaurant. The "poorer set," on the other hand, saw the village's quietness as evidence that it was a "boring" place to be. Because Mango Mount was so close to Kingston, there was often less happening, in terms of entertainment, in the village itself.

People in the "poorer set" also generally believed that middle-class people didn't like, or couldn't appreciate, dancehall music, instead preferring "soft" music—calypso, American rhythm and blues, jazz, or "classics." Claude, an upwardly mobile tradesman's son who studied architecture at a local university, explained that during the 1970s "upper-class Jamaicans" didn't recognize reggae music, and that as years have gone by, though reggae had become more accepted, they still didn't think of it as "their style." He also said that since middle-class community members didn't generally speak patois all the time, they might not have been able to understand the new dancehall songs' lyrics because the slang changed week to week. Furthermore, Claude argued that even if middle-class people liked dancehall, they wouldn't "keep sessions like we would." Instead of going to dancehall night at a club in Kingston or to a live stage show or sound system clash, he guessed, the "upper sets" might listen to the "milder reggae" at venues such as the hotels in New Kingston (the capital's business and entertainment district) or even dancehall, but usually only at pay parties. Indeed, I was typically the only local middle-class "browning"[14] at any of the sessions organized by the "poorer sets" in the community during the period of my fieldwork.

Another poorer youth asserted that though a few in the "upper set" loved reggae, they'd rather "bruk out" with calypso and "class reggae music as dirty." "They don't understand the type of dancing the people are doing these days, and that's why they call it slack," he argued. Because dancehall is not "fi dem music, dem woulda call it noise. If it woulda did soca, you wouldn't hear a bell ring." In fact, carnival in Jamaica has received more local corporate sponsorship over the years than Reggae Sumfest and Sunsplash—the two summer reggae music festivals—combined. This has generated considerable resentment not only among people in the reggae music industry, but also among many black Jamaicans who view carnival as an unwelcome import from Trinidad that sanctions middle-class "lewdness" while their own dancehall was considered "slack."[15]

Class position was not the only variable that influenced community members' views on dancehall. Many poorer villagers also cited genera-tional differences as being significant, in that the younger generation of both the "upper sets" and the "poorer class" of people both listened to dancehall, reggae, and hip hop. This has been one of the results of the increased access to U.S. media through cable television in the past decade or so. One woman in her early thirties expressed the opinion that "on the whole everybody is adapting to whatever music is being played now." Terry, a woman in her mid-thirties who was active in the Pentecostal church, agreed. She noted that although the "richer people" of the older generation tended to have a problem with dancehall, "maybe due to the volume at which it is played," the younger people like it, "even the rich." However, she also observed that they didn't dance to it in the same way. "Dem cyaan do dem dance deh, dem cyaan do dem late movements," Terry laughed. "Me never see none a de rich people dance yet." Virginia qualified these assertions regarding dancehall's multiclass appeal among the younger generation. "The majority of people who are poor and unedu-cated, their culture, their music, their dance, are appropriated by the mid-dle classes so the middle classes can feel very Jamaican, or very cool, or very roots," she argued. "Yet at the same time, there's a limit to how much they want to identify with those people socially."

It's a Family Affair

Thus far, I have been highlighting the operative divisions between middle-class residents of Mango Mount and the village's "poorer sets," the ways these divisions have influenced community members' assessments of be-longing, resource allocation, and "socializing," and the links between local and national hierarchies of value along the axes of color, class, gen-der, and culture. Significant distinctions also obtained among those mak-ing up the "poorer class of people," especially with respect to their ability to mobilize social and economic resources. Often, these distinctions were related to the length of time a particular family had lived in Mango Mount.

Indeed, the families that were seen as the nine or ten "original" Mango Mount families were those among the "poorer sets" who had been established in the district—as tradespeople, shopowners, and land holders—prior to the arrival of the middle-class community members. Tracing five of these "original" families over several generations provides a sense of shifts with respect to educational attainment, religious upbringing, land ownership, occupational opportunities, and migration. These families' stories manifest a considerable degree of social mobility and tracking this mobility instantiates the national and global transformations that are negotiated at the community level.

During the 1970s and 1980s, despite significant outmigration, the population of Mango Mount grew as considerable numbers of poorer people moved to the area. This trend was usually attributed to people's desire both to escape the increasing violence and crime of Kingston and to obtain a small piece of land, which at that time was easy to do and relatively inexpensive. Because these villagers arrived in Mango Mount subsequent to the initial development of its population, many derived the impression that the "original" families—who intermarried considerably—"ran Mango Mount." This was, to a large extent, because the established Mango Mount families had had the most involvement over the years with local middle-class residents, were those most often called upon by middle-class community members for their input with respect to community concerns, and who tended to espouse a vision of progress and development that dovetailed with that of the middle classes. While several of the more recently arrived families also exhibited the type of generational socioeconomic mobility as the established families, they were as commonly excluded from it, largely due to their inability to acquire land of their own and to achieve an education past the All Age level. Because mobility, or lack thereof, has been a key factor influencing both poorer villagers' constitution of community and their evaluation of the avenues available to them for their own—and their families'—progress, it was the more recently arrived families who articulated the most profound critiques of the ideologies of respectable progress and multiracialism.

Mobilizing Land, Knowledge, and Migration

Only two of the families who resided in the community could trace ancestry born in Mango Mount to the late nineteenth century. Both families lived on land believed to have been given to them by former estate owners. The other families who were considered to be among the "original" Mango Mount villagers all moved to the community either from nearby villages or neighboring parishes during the early to mid-twentieth century. What is known of the eldest members of this first generation—the grandparents of those villagers who were in their sixties and seventies in the late 1990s— provides a sketchy, but relatively typical, pattern of living among the post-emancipation rural peasantry. Small-scale farming (mostly ground provisions but some sugar), animal husbandry, and higglering predominated as occupations. Family members may have also supplemented their income from peasant production with occasional employment on nearby sugar estates, or within other industries (bananas) that were growing during the late nineteenth century. Members of this generation were, in the main, Anglicans and their literacy was most probably a result of their involvement with the church. At least two of the families lived on family land, and most constituted their family through (legal) marriage.

This last point deserves a caveat, one that may also be relevant for the subsequent generation. It is possible that because older villagers remembered little about their grandparents, they would have been more likely to privilege formal rather than informal unions. That is, the purported absence of children born outside of marriage among this generation may be factual, but it might also reflect hopeful lapses in memory. Moreover, since most interviewees did not know the dates of their grandparents' marriages, it is impossible to assess whether they occurred before or after the birth of children between them.

Within the second generation, we see some educational and occupational diversification. While many in this generation still seemed to receive their basic literacy training within the Anglican church, several also attended (and completed) primary schools. And though small-scale peasant production remained an important source of income, it became supplemented by a wider range of other skilled and unskilled occupations. That people were able to find employment as shoemakers, forklift operators, rock breakers, tailors, and telephone line workers reflects the more general modernization of Jamaica's economy as well as its greater infrastructural development during the early decades of the twentieth century. This development did not come without a cost, however. As I mentioned in chapter 1, during this period many women were pushed out of the lifestyle associated with peasant production and into service-oriented occupations such as domestic work, where they were subjected to more immediate surveillance and a more intense class paternalism (Austin-Broos 1997). A few of the women of this generation within Mango Mount shared these experiences.

In this second generation, we also see a simultaneous movement of people from other parishes to Kingston and St. Andrew and from Mango Mount to areas off the hill in Kingston. The latter trend was especially salient for those living on family land, since the land can only hold so many individuals at one time. This movement was part of the trend toward urbanization during that period. At the same time, we see people moving from downtown Kingston to Mango Mount in search of land, also a reflection of the effects of urbanization since as urban employment markets became saturated, many sought greater security through land ownership and small-scale cultivation. As a result, the more recently arrived families either leased or bought plots of their own where they had no family ties. This was also the first generation in which permanent emigration, in addition to more cyclical and contractual labor migration (to Cuba and the United States), became a feature of life among at least one of the Mango Mount families. Additionally, with the introduction of the Seventh-Day Adventist Church in Jamaica, there was some conversion from the Anglican Church. Finally, again among this generation, family seemed to be constituted primarily through marriage.

In the third generation, we see both a consolidation and a dispersal of Mango Mount community members. Their consolidation was facilitated by the establishment of local (or nearby) institutions, most particularly the elementary school at the bottom of the hill. Everyone in this generation completed their primary education at that school. Their dispersal, on the other hand, reflects a pattern of intensified migration throughout mid-twentieth-century Jamaica more generally, both to Kingston and overseas. Of the twenty-one members of this generation (thirteen men and eight women), eleven left Mango Mount (seven men and four women).[16] Within this generation, women typically migrated as young adults and, more specifically, young wives, reflecting the ideology current among those community members who were in their sixties and seventies in the late 1990s that women should follow their husbands. Incidentally, this ideology was not incompatible with these women's simultaneous assertions that women should pursue their own independent interests and income-generating activities. Nevertheless, this generation of women did tend to see marriage as a contract that placed the burden of relocation upon them rather than their husbands. Men's migration, on the other hand, occurred at diverse stages in the life cycle and was spurred by a wider variety of reasons, ranging from domestic situations to labor opportunities.

Of the six men who remained in Mango Mount, three had apprenticed as either masons or tinsmiths and, as a result, were able to find employment locally as the middle-class population in the village grew. This also held true for another man who worked as a general laborer on various projects within the community (cutting and paving the road, building the school, etc.). All four of these men remained on their families' land (either purchased, leased, or inherited) during their prime working years. One of the remaining two men worked for the telephone company, and the other was the delivery man for a business in Kingston. Both of these men purchased property of their own in the district.

Three of the women who stayed in Mango Mount, two of them shop-keepers and one a "housewife," were married to these men. These women had a consistent residential base either on their family's, their husband's family's, or newly purchased land. The fourth woman, though living on family land in her old age, had "boarded out" during most of her upbringing with various aunts and family friends in Kingston. She had three children with three different men and had entered into a series of short-term residential situations. While the other three women supplemented income from their other endeavors by doing an occasional "days work" for some of the middle-class families in the area when they were younger, they were never fully dependent upon this type of work. The fourth woman, however, had to "work out" consistently in order to survive even though her family owned land. This disparity, while in part related to differences in these women's marital status, was ultimately a result of the relative length of time these various families owned their land. That is, while the immediate predecessors of the three married women had acquired the land upon which their families lived, that of the fourth had, by the time she was born, been in her family for at least two generations. As a result, the land (and the family home) was already saturated, a situation that compromised the fourth woman's potential for relative autonomy.

Within the fourth generation of these five Mango Mount families—those individuals in their twenties and thirties by the late 1990s—the trends noted for the third generation intensified considerably. Of the seventy-five individuals in this generation, twenty-nine were either born or grew up overseas, ten in England and nineteen in the United States. Of the forty-six remaining in Jamaica, thirty-nine grew up "full time" in Mango Mount, five lived back and forth between Mango Mount and nearby villages, and two were raised elsewhere on the island. The construction of the All Age school on the hill in 1955 consolidated an internal village focus, and all of the thirty-nine individuals who grew up in Mango Mount attended this school. Of these thirty-nine, thirty-one continued their education at academic secondary schools and five at technical high schools. Eight went on to achieve a tertiary education: four at the local technical university, two in business colleges, and two in universities in the United States.

Six among those raised in Mango Mount or between Mango Mount and villages nearby did not continue their educations past the All Age level. Of these, two women left school to look after their children, two men apprenticed in trades, one man became a musician and full-time farmer, and one man was traveling back and forth to the United States to work in the hotel and construction industries. Five of these six individuals were outside children of the previous generation, but all had access to family or family owned land and have therefore had relatively stable residential situations.

Of the seventy-five individuals in this generation, only seventeen were still living in Mango Mount in 1997. Thirty-four were either raised in the United States or moved there after finishing school, thirteen were in England, one was in Canada, and all but one of the rest lived in Kingston or urban St. Catherine. Those who migrated overseas as adults were equally divided between the technical and service professions (especially nursing and cosmetology), and several were also students. Those living in Kingston typically either ran small businesses or worked in office jobs. With this generation, women's migration patterns changed to more fully approximate those of the previous generation of men. That is, rather than migrating as a result of their marital or domestic status, women as much as men in this generation also emigrated in order to pursue educational or occupational opportunities. To some extent, this change marks an ideological shift, but there are also practical underpinnings. First, by this generation many families already had contact persons overseas who were able to assist additional family members with the migration and sponsorship process. Second, educational and occupational opportunities expanded for women at the same time as significant shifts were taking place within the gendered international division of labor that facilitated the growth of an internationally mobile female labor force, particularly in the service professions.

Eleven of the seventeen who remained in Mango Mount were men. Of these, five shared a household with their parents on the family's land; three had constructed homes of their own on family land; two bought property of their own in the district; and one boarded with another family. Of the six women, one lived with her own daughter in her mother's household on family land; one lived with her child's father and their children in his family's household; one lived with her husband and their children on land they purchased; and three lived together with their mother on family land. Those who remained worked in a wide range of occupations, with men predominating within trades and women within service occupations, though one man and one woman were trained as professionals. Of the men, two were district constables, one was a laborer, one was a mason, one was an architect, one was a mechanic, two were farmers, one did construction work, and two ran the family dry goods shop and bar. Of the women, one was trained as an accountant, one worked as a secretary, one was a housewife, one worked at her sister's dress shop off the hill, one was the principal of the Seventh-Day Adventist Basic School, and one worked in the local upscale guesthouse. Only two of the women in this generation who lived in Mango Mount and who had children sent them to the Mango Mount All Age School. Three of the others had children in the Seventh-Day Adventist Basic School, and the remainder were sent to primary and secondary schools off the hill.

This fourth generation of the "original" Mango Mount families reflects considerable social mobility and autonomy as a result of two key factors: land ownership and education. Access to family land or family owned land has served as a buffer of sorts for those who were not able to continue their education past the All Age level. The majority of this generation, however, had achieved a secondary and, in some cases, tertiary education. While the third generation was never entirely dependent on the local middle class, their children, by virtue of their education, tended to be even more autonomous. Moreover, because so many in the fourth generation had migrated, the third generation's more instrumentally generated ties to the local middle class had also weakened by the late 1990s since they often received money and other necessary items from their children living either in Kingston or overseas. The fourth generation also had weaker connections to the Anglican church, though many were baptized there. Those who did attend church were, in the main, Seventh-Day Adventists.

As a result of their own experiences, these families typically believed that education was the surest route to progress. That the majority of the fourth generation who had children of their own sent them to schools outside the community was a testament to the persistence of this belief. These families also tended to evaluate the relative success of others through the not unrelated variables of their educational achievements and overseas accomplishments. Despite the generational shifts that made them more independent of the local middle class in practical ways, they still generally adhered to the values of thrift, industry, and community uplift as well as the ideology of progress through education, though not without censure. Members of the fourth generation, for example, having come of age during the 1970s and 1980s, tended to be more analytically cognizant and overtly critical than their parents regarding the ways social inequalities have been reproduced through local institutional structures.

These kinds of critiques were issued most powerfully, however, by those Mango Mount villagers who had moved to the community subsequent to the 1970s. Though the patterns described above with respect to educational attainment, professional training, migration and land ownership, as well as the varieties of residential situations, were not uncommon among village "latecomers," it was equally the case that many of the more recently arrived did not experience this kind of mobility. Those who did not had often come to the community as individuals rather than as families, in many cases in pursuit of the simultaneous goals of finding "days work" among the middle-class households—as domestic helpers or gardeners—and of escaping Kingston's violence. Due to a lack of either available funds or available land, these individuals were often unable to buy a small plot on which to build a house, so some either rented rooms or small parcels of land from other Mango Mount villagers, while others squatted illegally. It was generally their children who populated the All Age school, and because the school produced only a few CEE passes in the past twenty-five years, it was viewed as a critical factor in reproducing their own poverty. This generated some degree of hostility toward those who had been able to advance through education, and several—especially young boys—left school at age eleven or twelve after unsuccessfully sitting the exam. Since this exam structured their prospects for progress through education, they were then forced to seek mobility through other means.

This tendency was not unique to Mango Mount, but reflected national trends. Jamaican sociologist Patricia Anderson has linked the reproduction of poverty with the increased labor market imbalances that developed throughout the 1990s (Anderson 2001). She notes that in 1998, the unemployment rate for young men and women (ages 14 to 24) was double the national average (32.7 percent as compared to 15.6 percent), and further, that young women had nearly twice as high an unemployment rate as young men (42.9 percent as compared to 23.9 percent). Unemployment has typically been expected to decline as individuals achieve higher levels of education, but Anderson's research shows that this has not been the case for young men in Jamaica:

> Whereas there is a demand for unskilled male labor, particularly in agriculture, those young men who achieve some secondary education do not find a commensurate increase in their job opportunities. Young males with no secondary education had an unemployment rate of 12.9 percent in 1998, but the rate was more than double for those with some secondary education. This stood at 26.2 percent for young males with four or more years of secondary schooling. (Anderson 2001:6)

Anderson also found that the opposite trends were true for young women. That is, young women ages fourteen to twenty-four who had no secondary education showed an unemployment rate of 51.9 percent, while for those with four or more years of secondary schooling this rate declined to 40.6 percent (2001:6). Nevertheless, as anthropologist Barry Chevannes has found, while boys either tended to leave school to find work, were siphoned off into vocational schools, or were apprenticed to older tradesmen, they were still able find ways to "earn and control money" (2001:49), thereby fulfilling a gender expectation for boys that positions them early on in the role of provider. The girls' long years of schooling, on the other hand, often did not translate into employment. Therefore, many youth in Jamaica asserted that males would "end up better off in the long run" (Chevannes 2001:52).

Indeed, in the view that it would take too long to apprentice in an "old-fashioned" trade (such as masonry, carpentry, or tinsmithing), many poorer Mango Mount community members—and especially young males—opted for employment in more lucrative industries or sought to migrate to the United States via both legal and illegal means. Among these villagers, an ideology of progress through the acquisition of wealth was paramount. That is, they measured their success—and that of others around them—and evaluated their available options through a monetary lens. Money, here, was not an end in itself but was rather a means toward the acquisition of goods (or entrée) that would reflect both status and style. Here is where this sector of the Mango Mount population diverged from those who adhered, for the most part, to an ideology of progress that positioned education at its core. This is a discussion that I will elaborate more fully in chapter 6. For now, I only want to flag that national trends pertaining to educational and employment opportunities have buttressed a vision of progress often associated with poorer (urban) Jamaicans—the generation of wealth and, with it, the ability to cultivate a particular sense of style. This was the vision more often articulated by the strata of Mango Mount community members, both male and female, who were less able to take advantage of educational and other opportunities locally and who exhibited a more general distrust of formal education as an equalizing institution.

Those villagers who remained in Mango Mount, then, typically fit into three (sometimes overlapping) categories: (1) tradespeople, laborers, small farmers, and their children with primary access to land (either family land or purchased property)—many of whom among the older generation had traveled abroad on labor contracts and returned to Jamaica to live permanently by varying degrees of choice; (2) unmarried women in both residential and nonresidential unions who had primary responsibility for child rearing (including younger women who had moved off the hill, become pregnant, and returned to live in their families' homes); and (3) men and women who, for various reasons, received no education past the primary or All Age level and who were not apprenticed in a trade. Individuals who did continue their education (either academically or through professional skills training) and who were not engaged in farming (either full time or to supplement their income), as well as women who married men who were not from Mango Mount, tended to leave the village, either by moving to "town," or by migrating, in most cases, to the United States. These trends have resulted in a situation whereby the majority of educated and/or skilled individuals among the younger generation were absent from the community—a "brain drain" of sorts. Again, this is not unique to Mango Mount, but has been recognized as a more general problem in Jamaica and, indeed, throughout the Global South.

For those who remained in Mango Mount, land ownership remained a critical factor with respect to social mobility and status, especially given the limited degree of access the majority of people had to an education past the primary or All Age level. Indeed, land ownership appeared to be the most salient variable influencing both relative economic autonomy—since those who owned land were able to cultivate cash crops to supplement household income from other sources—and housing arrangements for Mango Mount villagers. In short, those who owned land always had a fallback position, a sense of both psychological and material security that those who didn't own land (and this often included the children of those who did) lacked. However, land ownership, and especially family land, was something of a double-edged resource. This is because though family land is held by all descendants of the original person who had tenure, only a small number of family members can actually live on it. Ironically, though family land tenure offered security on the one hand, on the other it also contributed to draining the community (and the nation) of a skilled or educated younger generation who ascertained that there was limited space (and place) for them within the local economy.

In terms of housing arrangements, unmarried women, even those from established Mango Mount families, frequently had the most tenuous situations unless they had access to their family's home and land. This was especially the case if they had had several children with different men. Characteristically, they would enter a series of short-term residential unions with each of the fathers, who, in turn, may not have been interested in taking on financial responsibility for those children born previous to their union with the children's mother. As a result, children born outside the most recent union were often sent to live with other relatives or family friends. Even those women who had entered residential unions with Mango Mount men with whom they had borne children tended to have less access to family owned land, especially if their children's father was himself an "outside" child. For example, one woman who had attained a relatively advanced level of education lived with her four children and their father in a small two-room "apartment" attached to her children's father's family house. Her brothers, on the other hand, had been able to build their own concrete houses on their father's land. She herself dreamed of staking out a piece of her father's property and building her own house, since she and her children's father were unable to build on his mother's family land. This was in part because his brother had already begun construction on their mother's property as a result of his earnings from construction work in New York, and also because his uncle's legitimate son had opposed any further construction on the family land, despite the fact that he had long before migrated to Canada. However, when she mentioned her desire to build on her family's land to her father, he shrugged and told her she should "follow" her children's father.

Of course, these are domestic, educational, and economic patterns that have been ethnographically documented since early social scientific scholarship in the West Indies. These early studies, however, did not typically address the ways in which migration has both structured and been structured by these patterns,[17] a critical dimension of Caribbean life explored only within the past three decades.[18] Within Mango Mount, the ability to migrate has not only structured the ways individuals and families have amassed resources but has also shaped the ways community members imagined their futures. However, it is also true that not everyone chose to or was able to migrate, and not all of those who did migrate were able to do so legally. As an economic and educational strategy, then, the ability to migrate legally was a resource, much like education, to which Mango Mount villagers had unequal access.

The above discussion shows how individuals among Mango Mount's "poorer sets" were differentiated through their relative levels of educational attainment, land ownership, and the ability to migrate. These differences have, in turn, structured the resources and opportunities available to them locally within Mango Mount society and have led them to express divergent ideologies with respect to individual progress and achievement. While these patterns generally held true, the generation of poorer community members who were (in the late 1990s) in their early to mid-twenties seemed to offer up more uniform evaluations of how to "move forward in life." By this, I mean that even younger members of the more established Mango Mount families seemed to have rejected elements of the ideology of progress associated with middle-class villagers. I make this point to demonstrate that it was not only the "least fortunate" among the poorer Mango Mount community members who had come to adhere to an ideology of progress through the acquisition of wealth. Rather, I am suggesting that a more universal generational shift has occurred.

For example, the wedding of a young woman from one of the more established poorer families demonstrated and maintained her family's prominent standing among the "poorer sets" through its size, its abundance of food, and its attention to details. It also provided the family with an opportunity to display their considerable property and to mobilize their significant transnational ties in a way that demonstrated that not only had members of her family been able to migrate, but they had also been

successful abroad. Nevertheless, several younger members of the family—
including the bride, who had returned to Jamaica from New York for her
wedding—had not pursued the tertiary educations their parents and grandparents sought to provide for them, instead gaining wealth and status
through other, sometimes illicit means. Additionally, among the approximately 150 guests present at this wedding, none were middle-class community members, a fact that reflects a significant shift between the third
and fourth generations of the "established" Mango Mount families. That
is, while the bride's father had cultivated significant ties to the local middle class, his children, who had by then all left Mango Mount, no longer
did. No longer in need of the contacts, opportunities, or practical assistance middle-class villagers could offer, this generation excluded them
from their constitution of community. Finally, the festivities surrounding
the wedding included a dancehall session, and several among the younger
guests seized the ceremony itself as an opportunity to show off their
fashion sensibilities, sensibilities that diverged from middle-class ideas
about appropriateness, respectability, and modesty in self-presentation.[19]
As has already been noted, many critics have viewed dancehall fashion as a
symbol of "moral incorrectness" and dancehall itself as a glamorization of
capitalism, consumerism, and individualism. For younger villagers in
Mango Mount, though, the culture surrounding dancehall music was
often representative of either their experiences or their aspirations. It also
provided a politics of style within which they creatively expressed themselves in ways that were different from those who maintained an ideology
of progress through education and the acquisition of social respectability.

Conclusion

Throughout this chapter I have highlighted the ways Mango Mount villagers have internalized ideologies that linked belonging and progress to a
color, class, gender, and culture nexus in complex ways. On one hand,
because poorer community members viewed local color and class relations as fixed and immutably antagonistic, they evaluated their position
and their potential based on their ability to access the social and economic
resources usually associated with middle-class mobility. These evaluations
were rooted in their apprehension of Jamaica's historical ethnic division of
labor and the country's position within global hierarchies of power and

prestige, but were also experienced and reinforced at the local level as community members interacted with each other and with local institutional structures. On the other hand, however, poorer villagers also mobilized popular ideologies of belonging that were based on historical connections to the land in the district, were generated within the context of continual back and forth movement between local and global worlds, and were rooted in the social and cultural practices associated with black lower-class Jamaicans. Moreover, as they listed the ways they viewed their lives as different from the wealthier people living among them and the features of middle-class life to which they aspired, they spoke primarily in instrumental, not ideological, terms. That is, those who spent hours on three different forms of public transportation in order to buy vegetables at a market downtown were quick to recognize the value of a privately owned vehicle. However, they expressed little interest, for example, in foregoing socializing in the square or at dancehall sessions in order to attend what they assumed were the "stush" private parties hosted by the "upper sets."

What is key here is that changes in the ways Jamaicans have been positioned in relation to the global political economy since independence have diminished the significance of the local middle-class to poorer villagers' ability to obtain employment, educational opportunities, and other material resources. As a result, personalized cross-class ties have weakened, especially among the generation of poorer community members under thirty-five, and thus the legitimacy of the middle class as political and ideological brokers for poorer community members has been challenged. It should be noted, however, that the two value systems and parameters for progress I have been discussing exist relationally, and the espousal of one or the other was usually contextually based. That is, within the contexts of either greater autonomy or critical disillusionment, villagers might have been more likely to espouse—either explicitly or through their actions—an ideology of progress that differed from the local middle-class professionals.

chapter 4

INSTITUTIONALIZING (RACIALIZED) PROGRESS

Significantly, community members' differential ability to mobilize resources also influenced the degree to which they chose to (or were able to) participate in local voluntary organizations—such as the Mango Mount Community Council, the churches, and political party groups. These were organizations through which Mango Mount residents could address their concerns about what was happening in their village (and their nation), could propose and/or implement solutions, could identify and differentiate themselves, and could hold positions of leadership. Through these venues, therefore, inequalities within the community were both institutionalized and challenged. Additionally, community members' interactions (or lack thereof) with local institutions both shaped and were shaped by their understandings of how a national color, class, gender, and culture nexus articulated with belonging, community development, and leadership. These understandings, in turn, were always generated vis-à-vis their assessments of their potential social mobility within Jamaica's—indeed, a global—political economy. In this chapter, I focus on community members' participation in local institutions in order to demonstrate that because poorer community members felt that their prospects were not considerably better in the late 1990s than they had been in the 1960s, they tended to position the middle class—poorer class divide as the primary community-wide division. In other words, they felt that their common blackness tended to trump the other status distinctions among them that were parsed in the previous chapter. This is significant because it is this nod to a deterritorialized racial community that helps to explain both their investments in and divestments from national and local political landscapes.

The Community Council

The differences in education and lifestyle described in the previous chapter have often provoked antagonisms between the different sectors of Mango Mount society, especially toward the middle- and upper-middle-class community members. Many among the "poorer class of people" felt that middle-class villagers "just drove through" Mango Mount and were all "for themselves." While these complaints were rooted in assessments that "some of the upper set of people dem tink dem better than wi," they also had to do with Mango Mount's proximity to Kingston. In fact, Miss Enith, an older woman from one of the established poorer families, mentioned that though other rural areas counted as many "rich people" among their population as in Mango Mount, she felt that these communities tended to "stick together" more. She suggested that this may have been "because they're all black, and maybe because them all farm, them do the same thing fi dem livelihood." What Miss Enith was proposing here was that middle-class community members remained "strangers" not only because of their "brownness," but also because they "drove through" Mango Mount on their way to work somewhere else.

To some extent, less wealthy villagers also felt that the "poorer set" *weren't supposed to* "associate themselves" with the "upper-class people" because they would feel "out of their league." For example, some were ashamed to have middle-class folk visit their homes because of their "living condition." Winsome, a black woman in her early thirties, once asked me to tell her what middle-class people "really" did at parties in their homes other than eat. When I responded, she guessed that if someone like her went to one of those parties, "probably you might feel left out" because the hosts would only talk to the other middle-class people there because that would be "their set." Similarly, a few middle- and upper-middle-class villagers remarked that they've often been reluctant to attend community-wide events because they felt they'd have no one to talk to.

Others in the "poorer set" however—old and young alike—argued that it wasn't that "rich people" didn't "put out their hands to the poor people," but that the poorer folk, due to a lack of education and awareness, felt that whatever was given them was not enough and therefore wouldn't accept what the "rich people put out to better the community." As a young shopkeeper explained, the middle-class villagers "give nuff help and assistance, but the people keep disrespek them" by breaking into their houses, or stealing from their "yards." Indeed, Matthew's mother, a sixty-year-old doctor who married a brown Jamaican man and had been living in the community for twenty-five years, refused to give rides up and down the hill to people she didn't know after her purse was stolen. Similarly, many of the middle-class Mango Mount community members hadn't built fences and walls around their houses or installed security systems until they were broken into. The differences (both perceived and actual) between residents of Mango Mount and the consequences that had arisen from them (theft and some degree of hostility) provided the original impetus for the formation of the Mango Mount Community Council.

Between 1976 and 1978, the administration of Michael Manley was developing new initiatives toward more effective local government and in 1978 published a policy encouraging the formation of community councils. In response, those already active in the Citizens' Association established the Mango Mount Community Council in August 1978 with the following objectives: (1) to develop self-reliance within the community; (2) to identify problems within the community and to find means of overcoming these problems; (3) to guide and assist the development of the district in the interest of the community; and (4) to liaise with government ministries and public and private agencies. The Council received funding in the early years from the Royal Bank Foundation, the British High Commission and other international agencies, and several local individuals and firms and has received more recent assistance from the U.S.-based Institute of Cultural Affairs, which worked with Council members on leadership development. It has also cultivated a relationship with the University of the West Indies, whose Department of Social Work has occasionally placed students in Mango Mount for their practical training.

Initially, Community Council meetings were held at the All Age school, but a land subdivision and the subsequent purchase of an adjacent property resulted in the building of a community center during late 1979 and early 1980. To avoid the pitfalls of political factionalism that so plagued other communities in Jamaica, the center was built entirely without government funds.[1] Local tradesmen volunteered their labor, and the steel structure was donated by one of the middle-class residents through the Anglican Church.

In the early 1980s, the Mango Mount Community Council was identified as one of the three most effective councils in Jamaica, having built a community center and encouraged recreational activities, obtained bus service, opened a small health clinic, and supported a revolving loan fund for small business development. Many of these activities were initiated with the assistance of outsiders, including several U.S. Peace Corps and Canadian University Services Overseas volunteers, and tended to peter out upon removal of outside support. These "outsiders" were also often credited with having significantly diminished the class rift in the village. For example, the first Peace Corps volunteer from the United States initiated a

Girl Guides chapter which was led by a white Scottish woman who had been living in Jamaica since the late 1940s when she married a white Jamaican man whose family lived in Mango Mount. The Girl Guides group attracted the participation of girls across the class spectrum, and so, for the first time, diverse villagers were involved in a social activity together. The president of the Community Council explained that as a result of this initiative, the white family in the village became seen as "normal people" and not as "white kings on top of the hill." He attributed the volunteer's success to her being American, explaining, "While in the u.s. there is significant prejudice along the lines of color, race, and religion, they don't have the class prejudice that we have."

Of the Council's many committees, the Tourism, Recreation, and Environment Committee (TREC) was the one that most closely articulated with national development concerns beyond those having to do with infrastructural improvement. TREC was formed in 1989 after Hurricane Gilbert destroyed many of the homes in the community in 1988. Through TREC, the Council became a founding member of the National Environment and Societies Trust, a coalition of thirty-nine nongovernmental organizations that implemented various projects geared toward environmental activism. Initially, the Council had received funding for TREC from an international agency in order to develop and open two footpaths leading to the Blue Mountains.[2] Through this project, several youth in Mango Mount were trained to become trail guides, and as a result of this training, some were eventually able to make a living within the burgeoning adventure tourism industry. TREC also developed "Project Plant," a program that was designed to educate farmers as to the virtues of environmentally sustainable development, and a demonstration plot was planted at one of the two guesthouses on the hill. From 1993 to 1996 this project continued in Mango Mount—in conjunction with three surrounding rural districts— as the Hillside Agricultural Project (HAP) and was sustained by u.s. Agency for International Development funds through the u.s. Debt for Nature program. As a part of this project, an American expatriate was able to draw a team of researchers from Columbia University in New York to do a feasibility study of environmentally sound farming practices (Brady et al. 1992). She also facilitated the arrival of a group of u.s. fire marshals who trained a local fire brigade to combat bush fires. A video documentary was made about the community during this period by one of Kingston's local media houses entitled The Little Community That Could.

In the early 1990s, the community center was closed and its programs were inoperative. However, in late 1996 the center reopened, and the Council received substantial funding from a number of government and private organizations for projects such as building repair and renovation, the development of sports and youth recreational activities (the Community Upliftment Program, through which I was recruited to teach dance and drama to the children in the district, both at the local All Age school and at the community center), and Project Plant III, the continuation of both the earlier efforts mentioned above. The Mango Mount Community Council, then, was the local organization that reflected the objectives, the structure, the goals, and the values that were foundational to the early work done by Jamaica Welfare and the People's National Party (PNP) study groups. Because the Council represented a significant attempt by middle-class village residents to bridge the divide between the relatively well-to-do and the "poorer set," and because it provided an organizational focus for implementing local development projects and encouraging community unity, we can position the Council as the local embodiment of the creole multiracial nationalist project—"Out of Many, One Village" so to speak.

Despite its various successes, the Council's archival records suggested that from early on, there were indications that it was failing in its objective to be a dynamic catalyst for the development of the district in both the social and economic spheres. The community center was not often used, and there was increasing difficulty in obtaining voluntary assistance for the work of the Council from "local" residents. Additionally, there had been several break-ins at the center itself as well as instances of vandalism. Meeting notes throughout the years documented feelings, among the "local" population, that the "elites" did things only for their personal image and popularity, and that the Council was built by people who treated them in patronizing ways. Further, many among the "poorer sets" felt that the Council had not provided them with enough evidence that it was committed to furthering their interests. Therefore, while both middle-class and poorer villagers generally agreed that the Council was supposed to work for the "betterment and development of the whole community" and to help people "do things for themselves instead of sitting back and relying on the government," it was also the case that its success in doing so had been limited.

Follow the Leader

Those who were, or who had been, involved with the Council in leadership positions explained this limited success in various ways. Some felt the Council had not succeeded in gaining the confidence of the community, despite various attempts to address the nonparticipation problem. They attributed this to people's misunderstandings about the Council's objectives of self-help and self-reliance. Cathy Ann, for example, argued that the Council was there to prove that if you really strive, you can get somewhere. Cathy Ann was a woman in her mid-thirties who worked as a household helper and cook and who became involved with the Council because her daughter and her friends had been complaining that there was nothing for them to do. She often became frustrated mobilizing in her area of the district, she said, because other community members didn't realize that they had to become involved. "People don't understand that it's all about them," she complained, "and not about the people who run it." Another woman in her mid-thirties, a higgler who had been involved in the HAP project, concurred with Cathy Ann's point. Her feeling was that people in the community erroneously believed that getting buses running, getting the roads fixed, and making sure the center was running had nothing to do with them, but that these projects were someone else's responsibility. One younger middle-class man who had become involved with the Council a short time before the period of my research expressed a similar concern:

> The Council is supposed to work for the benefit of Mango Mount residents and help bring people together, but it's not reaching people, not for lack of effort. Maybe we're not talking the right language, but people don't seem to feel a sense of ownership. They sit down and wait and wonder what the big man is supposed to do. Then he does it and feels like he's done something. Maybe people feel like things are given to them, and if they get destroyed, they'll be able to get another.

Mr. James, the Council's president during the period of my research, argued that there wasn't anybody in the community who didn't support the Council's existence, and that if there were a widespread need in the community, people would focus on the Council to meet it. He also explained that people sometimes didn't participate because they were having personal or family problems with others in the community, and so in order to avoid seeing each other they'd stay away from Council meetings. He added that there was "always, always, always a family quarrel." However, he also stated that a perception existed among the "local" population that the Council was supposed to have been providing an income for them, either through direct employment or through other income-generating projects, and so most youth stayed away because they didn't see the Council as being able to provide them with a living. An impression had also circulated among a number of poorer community members that the Council did, in fact, sponsor income-generating activities, but that only select individuals in the community benefited from these. He explained that though this was not true, convincing people otherwise was extremely difficult because "this is how we were socialized during slavery, to always believe that there's been something hidden from us."

Several poorer community members who *were* active in the Council explained that the lack of participation by many among the "poorer set" was due to a lack of trust in the Council's leadership resulting from ongoing class and color antagonisms that they felt had not changed significantly since independence. The failure of certain projects was also attributed thusly. The Neighborhood Watch program, for example, was seen by many as "people with more to lose coming together against their neighbors." Some Council members felt that these kinds of antagonisms were occasionally perpetuated by members of the leadership themselves. For example, the original president of the Council, a brown man in his seventies who was a self-identified dyed-in-the-wool socialist, remarked derisively that there were "certain individuals" involved in the Council who worked toward maintaining a situation in which people would always have to go to them to get things done, rather than providing an opportunity for people to do things themselves.

There were, indeed, differences of opinion among the Council's leaders regarding methodology. Some felt it was better to listen and facilitate, and to encourage people to define, and then implement, the solutions to their problems. Others preferred to solve the problems themselves, thereby gaining recognition and status. Because the Council's leadership had not changed significantly since its establishment, these divisions among the leadership, and therefore the antagonisms and suspicions directed toward the Council that were related to color and class issues, had persisted. The lack of leadership turnover also affected the participation of younger middle-class community members in Council programming. "A lot of the older people in the Council should have stopped being involved, but they didn't because they had the impression that a lot of the younger people like me would not become involved," Virginia contended. "And often," she continued, "we didn't because there were always these older people to do these things and they were going to get done in the same old way, and then you wouldn't get any community involvement anyway."

Many of the controversies related to a general lack of participation that surrounded one man, a long-standing community member in his seventies who was white, owned a significant parcel of land at the top of the hill, had been president of the Council twice, and whom I will call Mr. Simms. Some Council members argued that the resentment toward this man went as far back as the original construction of the community center. A former president recalled that when they were first building the center, there was a tremendous drive and interest among the wider Mango Mount community. When people were informed that the Council didn't have government funds to help with construction, several tradesmen in the community volunteered their services free of charge. On the first and second days, he remembered, there was quite a turnout. However, by the third day, someone within the Council suggested that the tradespeople should get a token payment to recognize their labor. This made people feel like they weren't giving freely of their time anymore but were being paid, and paid unsatisfactorily. Their attendance subsequently dropped. At the same time, it was said that people got wind that Mr. Simms had proposed to change the concept of the center in order to build a factory so that people from the village would have employment opportunities. The "poorer set" opposed this change because they thought the center was supposed to be for recreation and "now he wanted to work them." As a result, many turned against the Council.

In fact, several individuals attributed their lack of participation in Council activities directly to Mr. Simms. For example, Winsome established a drama club independently of the Council. She recounted the following incident by way of explaining why she stopped going to Council meetings. A representative from the American Women's Club had been interested in the work her drama club was doing and donated US$100 in two installments. Winsome used the first $50 to further what they had been doing, but by the time she received the second check, the club had folded. She remembered that Mr. Simms raised the issue at the next Council meeting she attended, and, in her estimation, behaved as though she were going to steal the money for her own personal use since the drama club was no longer in existence. Winsome was so upset by what she experienced as his lack of faith in her, which she attributed to her being poor and black, that she gave him the check to return himself and has not been involved with the Council since.

Another community member in her early thirties recalled that years before, there had been an active youth group within the Council that had established an exchange program with a youth club in England. Young people from Mango Mount would spend eight weeks in various English cities attending churches and youth club events in order to learn about "black culture" in Britain, and those Jamaicans living in England would spend twelve weeks in Jamaica, some of them placed in homes in the community.[3] The youth group had attempted to garner financial support from the Council for this exchange program, but since some within the Council viewed it as benefiting individuals rather than the community as a whole, they did not contribute. This woman, one of the former leaders of this program, attributed the subsequent decline of the youth group to Mr. Simms, whom she saw as fighting them "left, right, and center." Specific incidents aside, many in the community felt that Mr. Simms thought he was "the boss of Mango Mount," argued that if they participated in projects it would only benefit him, and said that they didn't want to be "under the white man."

For his part, Mr. Simms attributed the limited success of the Council to a lack of trust and understanding between the groups of people in Mango Mount society, which he called the "big house principle":

> My family and I have always been employers of labor. We have a bit of property, we employ people and tell them what to do, where to plant, etc. I suppose this goes back to slavery and the post-slavery time. They don't think that people like me are trying to help the district as a whole. The guys in the square perceive the Council as some sort of "Big Man's Club," and that is why they don't get involved. But what can you do except keep trying?

He also stated that he recognized that people in the "poorer set" would have this kind of response to him, because he was white, but not to some of the other leaders, who were brown. In fact, the assistant secretary of the Council reported that more people had become involved since Mr. James had been elected. These tensions in relation to leadership recall Matthew's demographic delineation of Mango Mount, and the ways it was shaped by assessments and expectations of people's positioning within a national ethnic division of labor. With respect to the Council in particular, community members' understanding of general historical patterns informed their experiences and judgments about the motivations of particular leaders and behind particular projects. In other words, it was clear that a large part of the hostility surrounding Mr. Simms was simply due to the fact that he was a white landowner. Their perceptions of his actions and the motives behind them were therefore shaped by their apprehension of the role of white people in Jamaica's history. That Mr. Simms appeared to reinforce some of the assumptions poorer villagers had about "what white people do" and "how white people think" only solidified their previously noted conviction that Jamaica's color and class antagonisms were immutable.

Given this situation, and given the fact that the Council's leaders were elected by the general population of the village, one might ask why they kept electing the same people. Community members explained that the leaders of the Council had to be the "more wealthier people" because they had more time, resources, and contacts than the "poorer set" and were therefore more effective in conducting the Council's business. This belief was not unrelated to a wider and ongoing debate regarding the qualifications that legitimized certain people as appropriate leaders. The colonial visions of the middle class as competent, responsible, and reasonable still held sway among villagers across differences of age, gender, and class due to their positive assessments of middle-class community members' educational achievement, communication skills, contacts, money, and time. For example, a young middle-class businessman who was active within the Council argued that middle-class leaders' advanced education made them more effective in terms of fund raising. "Obviously, they can better raise funds because they can better put forth an argument," he maintained. "Education has taught them that they have a larger responsibility than self because they have money and a certain level of comfort, so they can spend time and energy working for other people." A sixty-year-old hotel worker agreed, saying that "when it comes to linking with local and international NGOs, you have to be able to communicate articulately and effectively to be able to meet their requirements." To be sure, the "poorer sets" recognized the kinds of skills that were necessary to compete at national and international levels for recognition, funding, and policy change and evaluated their leaders according to the extent to which they possessed them. In this regard, Errol, a tradesman in his mid-sixties, emphasized the importance of some of the local middle-class community members' networks outside of the Mango Mount:

> The middle-class people are leaders because it needed somebody responsible to do it and they are the ones who have the outside contacts and can get donations from various companies. If I were president, nobody knows my name, I wouldn't be able to approach companies successfully. That's why you need the more advanced people in leadership roles, people who are more knowledgeable and have more communication with the outside world.

These requirements also meant that community members who were middle class in terms of the wealth they had been able to amass, but not with respect to educational or professional achievement, weren't assessed as positively in terms of their potential ability to "bring Mango Mount up to date."

There *were* middle-class community members, however, who attempted to encourage leadership development among the "poorer class of people." One woman cited her ongoing struggle to get "Mango Mount people" involved at the leadership level within the Council as evidence that "nobody likes to do the work, but they will knock you for doing it." Her frustration was echoed by Ras Rob, a man in his early forties who worked in the tourism industry and who was an avid reader of black nationalist and Rastafarian literature:

> The Council could be more effective, but it needs input from the small people who are supposed to know what them really want out of the Council. And again, most of the people dem, they are not that bright. Them still suffer from the colonial mentality. Rich folks run the Council, and the small people don't want to go up and talk to these people—because them brown or because them rich—because them have a complex. Them nuh waan get involved because them say, "Bwoy, these people, dem nuh waan deal with this, dem nuh waan deal with that." At the same time, none of them going to really hear, and to tell the people dem what dem woulda like to be done. Dem people try nuff tings, but none a de people dem support it. Dem trust dark. Dem woulda rather just stay in them likkle corner and criticize.

A few middle-class community members in leadership positions within the Council suggested that "Mango Mount people" didn't take the lead because "maybe they feel they wouldn't be able to do it." Other community members, however, felt that someone from the "poorer class of people" might actually be able to accomplish more because "they know exactly what is going on and can mobilize people." Winsome supported this argument based on her perception that the two black professionals who had previously been involved with the Council were effective because they worked "more directly with the people" rather than only in a "middle-class atmosphere." She also added, rhetorically, "I don't know if it was because they were black."

Still others among the "poorer class of people," however, feared that if poorer community members were in charge of the Council, it might become too politically affiliated,[4] or that they would do things only to benefit their own family or friends and not the whole community. Arlene, a woman in her late thirties who worked as a household helper, stated that she preferred middle-class leaders for precisely these reasons. "It is better with the upper class of people in charge because if the poorer class of people were in charge, it wouldn't work out well," she said. "People would criticize too much, and those leading would take too much advantage of things." Arlene's own experience in Mango Mount had been relatively difficult because she wasn't from the district, but had moved there during the 1980s and married and had children with a Mango Mount man who died in the early 1990s. Since then, she has remained in Mango Mount with her children, but without family to support her consistently, she has had to rely upon middle-class community members for assistance. In fact, Arlene's daughter received one of the scholarships offered by the American Women's Club through the Community Council because the secretary brought the opportunity to her attention. "She called me to tell me about it since she knows the children don't have a father," Arlene explained. "If the poorer people were in charge, they might just offer those kind of opportunities to their friends or family." Other community members agreed. Mr. Bailey, a retired mason in his late sixties whose family had lived in Mango Mount "since slavery times," expressed his feeling that the middle-class people involved in the Council were more reliable. "You have to have people who have a free mind and conscience," he argued, "people who can see others' needs, not just a friend-friend business." Trevor, too, shared his view that unless the "lower income people" in charge were well known to the "upper class," they wouldn't accomplish more than middle-class leaders "because people would think they would use the money for personal instead of community purposes."

Several poorer community members, both male and female, explained the issue Trevor raised by asserting that people in the "poorer set" didn't like to see each other progress and therefore wouldn't support those who were doing well. "Dem nuh like small people like themselves who know things," Mr. Bailey grumbled. Instead, they would try to pull them back and only help people who were "directly family." These assessments of the potential for lower class leadership reflected that the "poorer sets" exhibited distrust not only toward those in the middle class, but also toward each other, due, in part, to the extremely limited resources available for distribution throughout the community. As a result of these beliefs—defined elsewhere in the African diaspora as "crab antics" (P. Wilson 1973)—the middle-class community members were viewed as appropriate leaders not merely because they had more resources, but because their resources purportedly allowed them to be fairer.

Several villagers also stated that the lack of participation in Council activities was not only due to their opinions of those in leadership roles, but also a result of their evaluations of the Council's relative success. They argued that if they saw more tangible results from the Council's programs, they would get involved. In this respect, many in the "poorer set" felt that the Council made a lot of promises, but that they didn't see many returns. Some argued that this was because the leaders didn't socialize enough with the "poorer class" because "them think them better than wi," and others because though people were happy to see programs start, they were not willing, or able, to put in the time necessary to sustain them. The latter argument suggests that the continuity problem was often linked to the leadership problem. For example, Mr. Simms's wife, the original head of the local Girl Guides group, said that though she had trained a couple of the girls to take over for her, neither did. She explained that this was because one girl, "being one of the bright ones," migrated, and the other didn't receive as much support from the "local people" as she had.

Finally, a few community members suggested that community center projects were difficult to sustain because of disagreements over the kinds of activities the Council was supposed to support. Joseph, a man in his early thirties who worked in the shop at the top of the hill remarked, "As you start anything at the center it just drops. Maybe what the poorer class of people wants to do the upper class of people don't want them to do it." In fact, most villagers agreed on the basic objectives of the Council. They felt it should work toward fixing the road[5] and getting better public transportation for the village as well as more extensive water and telephone service, should initiate both recreational and educational programs for the area's youth such as skills training and literacy projects, and should help farmers and those interested in small business development in their endeavors. However, there have been several initiatives the Council has not supported financially, such as the community soccer team. The rationale behind this decision was the same as that for the earlier decision not to support the youth exchange program—supporting the team would only benefit a handful of individuals and not the whole community. Since soccer was primarily popular among the young men in the district, and since the young men who played on the team were exclusively comprised of the "poorer set," male youth in the community viewed this decision as a conscious attempt to keep them from enjoying themselves and succeeding against other teams in their rural St. Andrew league.

Additionally, the Council's policy with respect to hosting dancehall sessions at the community center provoked a certain degree of resentment on the part of the poorer youth in the area. Archival notes from 1995 documented complaints from one middle-aged middle-class resident about the volume level of the music played at sessions as well as his suggestion that a "code of conduct" be adopted for such events which would "take into account the wishes of all sectors of the community." In fact, a policy on the use of the community center for dances was ultimately adopted in early 1997 precipitated by damage done to the center's roof when community members attempted to make the additional electrical connections necessary to support the extensive speaker system. This policy stipulated that the center would not be rented for dances, by individuals either inside or outside the community, except where a committee of the Council was involved in the event and would thus be able to influence the volume level of the music "and other behavior expected." Mr. James stated that he didn't agree with this majority decision. Rather, he viewed renting the center for dances as one way the Council could earn money for other community projects. However, many other Council members, including several among the "poorer set" who were over thirty-five years of age, supported the decision, largely because of the other kinds of incidents that often occurred when dances were held in the village (such as theft) given that people knew there was no police post in the community. Still, at one meeting, the director of the Community Upliftment Project reported on a request by a member of the community to hold a party at the center and pointed out that the cessation of permitting dances at the center was one of the reasons the younger villagers were not participating in Council programs.

Consolidating a Common Blackness

The Community Council was not the only venue within which Mango Mount residents could mobilize for individual and community development. Local branches of the Anglican and Seventh-Day Adventist churches, as well as the local political party groups, were also organizations through which community members defined and implemented solutions to the problems they faced. While these venues also tended to institutionalize the kinds of evaluative judgments that reproduced status distinctions among the "poorer class of people" and therefore also the divisions between the "poorer sets" and the "upper sets," they were also forums within which the boundaries between community members were debated, development strategies were negotiated, and internal inequalities were sometimes overridden.

Marching unto God

Because the rector of the Anglican parish church for St. Andrew lived in Mango Mount in the late nineteenth century, there has been a small branch of the Anglican Church in the village as long as the oldest generation of the "established" families remembered. Located at the top of the hill, the church was an unassuming white concrete building with louvers. The wooden pews had wicker inserts in the backrests and a simply paneled stained glass window and cross graced the altar. Regular attendance was generally low—anywhere from ten to twenty people, including children. It was often said among the "poorer class of people" in Mango Mount that the Anglican Church was for "big people" (meaning the "upper sets"), while the "small people" attended the u.s.-based Seventh-Day Adventist and Pentecostal churches. In fact, those middle-class villagers who attended services on the hill were Anglicans, and these were also the people who played leadership roles within the church.

When the Seventh-Day Adventist Church was built lower down the hill in the early 1950s, several individuals from the older Mango Mount families defected, as it were, from the Anglican Church. There was also a

Pentecostal group that met at the community center on Sundays and either Tuesday or Wednesday evenings. This group was affiliated with a branch of the Church of God off the hill and was comprised, in the main, of the poorer villagers (and mostly women) who had more recently moved to the district.[6] One man in his mid-twenties explained the shift away from the Anglican Church as follows:

> When we were growing up, I went to the Anglican Church. In those times, it was really fun because you had a lot of young people coming to church. Each Sunday you'd have a full church. Nowadays it's almost empty. It's like, as we grow up we start to wonder what's the significance of going to church and how that will affect your life. What can the church do for you? And I think the church has been too traditional for young people who are becoming more contemporary, and the church, being that traditional, gets boring. Because ever since I was young I would go there and I'd hear the same hymns. And today I will still hear the same hymns. I wanted to hear something new, and a newer form of church that has more life in it in terms of the gospel. And you'd feel the spirit of the Lord more in an Adventist or Pentecostal church than in an Anglican church.

Despite the trends this young man described, there were still several individuals from the "established" families who continued to attend Anglican services, usually those among the older generation, and of these, predominantly women with their young daughters and granddaughters. The Adventist Church, on the other hand, boasted a regular attendance of about sixty to seventy-five people, fairly equally divided between men and women, and there was significantly more active participation on the part of young adults. Since its membership did not include any of the local middle-class families, the leaders of the Seventh-Day Church were the respected men and women among the "poorer sets," with respectability defined here in terms of education and adherence to the tenets of the church. In the majority, these leaders had also been members of the "established" families in Mango Mount.

While both the Anglican and Adventist churches promoted a politics of respectability, the Adventists were perceived by poorer community members as more up-to-date. Moreover the Adventists' emphasis upon personal responsibility and individual behavior was seen as potentially facilitating the mobility they were not able to access through other more traditional paths. In fact, several villagers had received opportunities through the Adventist church for their own personal development, such as sponsored travel to the United States, either for Adventist conferences or for tertiary education. Moreover, though individuals within the Anglican church were, or had been, involved with other community activities (most often through the Community Council), the Adventist Church was more active in Mango Mount socially, organizing events such as beach trips and cookouts to raise funds for the church and the Basic School. This meant that those who were not affiliated formally with the church often became involved with it through their family and friendship networks.

For example, one evening the church sponsored a fish fry and social to benefit the basic school. When I arrived, Miss Agnes (a long-time devotee of the Adventist church) and her friend Mrs. Williams (a member of the Anglican church) were selling fish, juice, cakes, and other food—much of which had been cooked by Winsome, who attended neither of the churches (despite her children's father's family's active involvement)—near the entrance of the school. Miss Agnes mentioned that another Adventist church group from Kingston was walking up the hill to join them. Winsome's children were all present, and several of the youth who hung out at the square also arrived later in the evening.

The church was open, though most people remained outside, either standing and chatting in groups or playing card games at tables and chairs set up on the hillside. A group of older men was listening to the Tyson versus Holyfield fight, which was being broadcast live on the government radio station, on a transistor radio they held to their ears. From time to time, cassette tapes of U.S. religious rock music were piped through the church speakers. When the group from the other church arrived, one of the Mango Mount church leaders announced that it was "ring game time" and encouraged everyone to gather in a circle nearer the church entrance. Because ring games are generally played by children, I was surprised when the adults congregated to sing U.S. campfire songs together. Many of these American songs were accompanied by clapping in a dancehall rhythm, and a few of the lyrics were transformed (e.g., "Old MacDonald had a farm . . . and on this farm he had some girls . . . gimme gimme here and a gimme gimme there . . ."). The gathering went on until about midnight, at which point the youth from the square continued on to a dancehall session that was being held at a nearby lawn.

What was notable about this event was the way in which it engaged the participation of several people in the community, most particularly the youth from the square, who would not ordinarily attend church events. In part, this was a result of the limited options available for socializing within Mango Mount generally. In other words, many of these youth went to the fish fry and social because it was the only show in town. But it was also the case that even though individuals may have formally belonged to (and regularly attended) the Anglican church, they participated in Adventist events because they were family to, or friends with, members of that church. In its construction of community, therefore, the Seventh-Day church in Mango Mount reinforced status and ideological distinctions among Mango Mount villagers at the same time that it opened these same distinctions to challenge by welcoming the participation of the broadest cross section of the community through its social events. Moreover, since men made up half of its congregation and since it boasted a large active youth membership, the Adventist church more equally divided the burden of pursuing, maintaining, and policing the boundaries of respectability between women and men, young and old, than did the Anglican church, which was attended most consistently by an older generation of women and their grandchildren. Finally, as an American-based denomination, the u.s. influence upon the Seventh-Day church in Mango Mount was profound. This was evident not only with respect to the songs sung, music played, and preaching style, but also in terms of the Adventists' emphasis on the individual, which Mango Mount villagers saw as an American importation.

Not Politics as Usual

It was not only the Adventist church in Mango Mount that garnered the participation of a relatively diverse cross section of the "poorer sets" in its activities. The political party groups also catalyzed broad participation, especially during election years. One of the middle-class women in the community suggested that the "poorer class of people" in Jamaica were often more attracted to politics than to working through organizations like the Community Council because "there's often money made available to do things." Both traditional parties' group leaders in the village had, in fact, always been members of the "established" families among the "poorer set," although each party has also had prominent middle-class supporters within the district.[7]

Due to the degree of violence and fraud that often accompanied both the development of voting lists in Jamaica and the elections themselves, there had been heated public debate—in the newspapers, on the radio call-in shows, and on the television forum shows—over whether international observers should be called in to monitor the elections in 1997. Moreover, a citizen's committee was established to help ensure a "free and fair election," in which at least one community resident participated. Mango Mount, however, was often cited as unusual because People's National Party (PNP) and Jamaica Labour Party (JLP) supporters had always lived side by side without the partisan violence (usually termed "political tribalism") that typically accompanied elections in many other communities in and around Kingston. The JLP group leader attributed this to the fact that in Mango Mount, in comparison with other areas in Kingston where he believed individuals were relatively more anonymous, "We know we are flesh and blood." One resident even mentioned that at one time, there had been a known PNP gunman living in the village, but that he never fired his gun within Mango Mount.

Despite the fact that there had never been significant harassment or intimidation at election time, many villagers still expressed trepidation about voting.[8] One woman mentioned that she had thought about asking her daughter in the United States to send her a ticket so she could leave Jamaica at election time because "me cyaan stand the violence and foolishness wha gwaan." Several others said they had registered but that they wouldn't decide whether they were going to vote or not until election day: "When the day come me will siddung outside the center and see if the moment comes for me to cast my vote." Others cited a general disillusionment with politics as having created a situation in which "black people always warring 'gainst one another," or frustration with the way policies have been radically shifted during transitions from one party to the other. One woman said she hadn't enumerated and didn't plan to vote because she didn't feel any of the political parties had a genuine interest in poor people, a sentiment echoed by many others. She argued that party representatives should spend more time going door to door and speaking to people about their concerns, giving them ways to help "lift up themselves" and less time impressing potential girlfriends with "them new car and them fancy fancy dress."

Despite these and other critiques, many more village residents attended the two local political meetings in 1997 than any Community Council meeting, including the Annual General Meeting. One of the meetings that occurred had been organized by the Community Council as a pre-election "meet the candidates" type of affair. The three candidates for the district's Member of Parliament were each invited to present their party's platform for East Rural St. Andrew,[9] and Mango Mount in particular.

The meeting began late due to the Jamaica versus Costa Rica soccer match, and the only candidate who appeared on time was the representative from the new party, the National Democratic Movement (NDM), a "brown" thirty-something dentist. He had brought along the party's spokesperson on national security and had prepared a very organized and specifically detailed presentation on the NDM's general platform for constitutional reform. He began by arguing that the political system Jamaica adopted after independence had failed to benefit the majority of the population, and that the government and opposition both made promises but didn't have the resources to fulfill them. As a result, the system of political representation was in need of change. He continued by saying that the NDM was proposing that there be greater separation of power between the executive and legislative bodies of government, that Members of Parliament (MPs) not also be appointed as government ministers, and that the prime minister be elected directly by the people. He also stated that there should be term limitations imposed for both the prime minister and MPs, that there be a fixed election date, and that 5 percent of the national budget be allocated directly to constituencies. In short, the NDM representative outlined the party's push toward an approximation of a U.S.-style, rather than parliamentary, democratic system.

One middle-class village resident stated that she felt the candidate's focus on macro issues was generally inaccessible to the Mango Mount audience who, though responding politely, would not necessarily perceive how these changes would be immediately relevant to their lives. People did, however, ask several questions pertaining to his presentation, most commonly having to do with their need for infrastructural development within the community, their concerns about escalating crime and violence, and their desire for skills training programs geared toward the youth—the same concerns usually raised in Community Council meetings.

The JLP candidate,[10] a mid-fortyish Jamaican man of Lebanese descent, arrived three-quarters of the way through the NDM representatives' question-and-answer period. He delivered an impromptu presentation that began by discrediting the NDM's platform for constitutional reform. He argued that parliamentary systems were best because they presided over the most dynamic economies in the world and, shifting into patois, stated that "I born JLP and me nah change nuttin." He then went on to speak in vague terms about economic growth, political stability, and integrity among leadership.

During the question-and-answer period, several young people asked about the JLP's intended programs for youth and women's development, as well as for education, and he responded to all of their questions by saying that though the party did have programs, he was unable to define them specifically because he was not the spokesperson for any of those particular areas. When people asked what he had planned for Mango Mount in particular, he alluded to a manifesto for East Rural St. Andrew which he had "written," but never elaborated on the exact points contained therein. Instead, he spoke generally about skills training and infrastructural improvement. When the president of the Community Council asked whether he planned to work closely with that body, the representative answered that yes, the JLP would support and facilitate local organizations such as community councils. Several younger individuals in attendance took him to task for coming unprepared and not being respectful of the occasion, and just as he seemed to be getting into deep (and dissatisfied) water, the PNP candidate arrived. As such, the JLP representative encouraged the audience to express their concerns to him since he was the incumbent MP.

The PNP candidate, a black man in his late forties, had been delayed due to a murder in another area of the constituency and was able to take advantage of people's dissatisfaction with the JLP candidate's presentation by demonstrating his knowledge of the community and its ongoing problems. He emphasized several times that he was from the constituency and living in it, and he began his presentation by arguing that the community's (and nation's) development should no longer occur along partisan lines. In particular, he noted that MPs should not be community leaders, but rather that local organizations, such as the Community Council, should lead communities in conjunction with the MP because their nonpartisan nature, as well as their emphasis on self-reliance and local mobilization, would be more effective in solving problems.

He addressed, with some specificity, the infrastructural problems in the community (the bad roads, difficulties in obtaining public transportation, increased crime, the dilapidated state of the community center, unscheduled water supply) and highlighted some of his achievements (providing gear to the sports teams, some degree of road relief, facilitating house to house phone service). He also underlined the importance of developing skills training programs "because not all children are born bright to be doctors and lawyers." Finally, he concluded by saying that he would not be involved in political tribalism because "we are all black brothers and black sisters here in Mango Mount." This last comment was met with rousing applause from the audience, but angered at least one of the brown, middle-class women in attendance who said she didn't appreciate him "playing the race card," especially since three of the people who had been murdered within the constituency during the previous three years were white. He responded that he was not trying to be "racial," but was more generally addressing the fact that political gang warfare had affected primarily black people. The meeting ended after this exchange, and the PNP candidate—by constructing his legitimacy to represent the community through a definition of belonging that emphasized a racialized commonality—maintained his seat in parliament.

Individual Distinctions versus Collective Difference

What the above discussions demonstrate is that within the local institutional spheres of religion and politics, Mango Mount villagers held positions of leadership that often reinforced the internal status distinctions among them. As I noted in the previous chapter, these distinctions were related to their varying degrees of control over economic and social resources and the mobility this control could engender. Often, those who had experienced some degree of social or occupational mobility—due to a higher level of educational attainment, to having migrated and returned, or, in some cases, to contacts they had made with other individuals (i.e., local middle-class residents, church leaders, political party leaders)—as well as those who owned land (both family land and otherwise) tended to be those most involved with the local churches and party groups, as well as those most often in leadership positions within these organizations. These also tended to be the individuals who adhered most strongly to the values, usually associated with the middle class, of discipline, hard work, and temperance in behavior (including monogamous mating)—the "respectable poor." Those who did not have access to land, who had either not been educated or who had only completed primary or All Age school, who did not attend any of the three churches, and who were unmarried women with primary child-care responsibilities did not tend to participate in other local institutions and were often viewed (by middle-class residents and the "respectable poor" alike) as lazy, uneducated, undisciplined, and backward. These distinctions highlight the perception that there existed an intersection between people's practices and people's values. As one of the adult children of a local middle-class family explained, "The poor background but established families tend to be positive, forward-looking, progressive. They can interact quite easily with both the richer people and the poorer people. But the majority in Mango Mount still eke out a living laboring or planting, cotched in the hillside somewhere."

Here, those among the poorer population in Mango Mount who most easily interacted with the middle-class residents were identified as sharing their "progressive" and "forward-looking" (read, *respectable*) values, which, in their eyes, has led to their "success" relative to other villagers. Conversely, these other villagers' lack of educational or occupational achievement was often apprehended as a result of their attachment to "backward" values rather than to the ways opportunities and resources continued to be unequally structured through local and national institutions. In other words, "success" and "failure" were understood at the individual level largely as the result of progress-oriented actions, actions seen as emanating from an adherence to progress-oriented (middle-class) values. This was the local understanding through which individuals in the "poorer sets" in Mango Mount came to be assessed as either hard-working and reasonable or "wutless" and lazy.

But while there were many experiences and perceptions that divided the poorer population of Mango Mount, others united them. In the case of participation in church events, family and friendship ties overrode other notable differences, such as adherence or lack thereof to the tenets of the church. And in the case of the political meeting, based on the applause that accompanied the PNP candidate's assertion that "we are all black brothers and black sisters," racial designations overrode other economic and social differences between the "poorer sets." At the same time, then, that the local religious and political institutions continued to structure differences among the "poorer class of people" in Mango Mount, they also provided venues through which these differences could be submerged underneath other more significant commonalities.

What I mean to say here is that despite the significant differentiation that obtained among poorer *individuals* in Mango Mount, the *community-wide* difference that remained the most salient was the one that existed between them, as a group, and the "upper sets." This was, in part, because there was greater fluidity among the "poorer sets" in Mango Mount than between them and the "upper sets." That is, institutions like the Seventh-Day Adventist church brought different groups of poorer Mango Mount community members together in *social* contexts, but there was a lack of comparable institutions that did so for poorer and middle-class villagers, since other institutions (like education) continued to divide them. Additionally, and perhaps more significantly, the "poorer sets" in Mango Mount experienced their difficulties with respect to "getting ahead" as being related first and foremost to their common designation within a wider (national and global) racial hierarchy. This was a hierarchy that perpetuated the relative salience of the middle class–poorer class divide, and one that many villagers rooted in the historical experience of slavery. A sixty-year-old black woman from the community elaborated this point as follows: "How I see it, them abolish slavery and it still in the people mind. Some of their ways don't change. In slavery, you have the upper class people better than the poorer class people and it is going on until today. And I don't think it going to change until God take him world because there is a division. Black people don't have no place in no part of the world, because the hate, the color bar, is so strong." In other words, within the context of community (and national) development, "poorer sets" perceived that their common "blackness" trumped their other status-based differences.

Therefore, local status distinctions among the "poorer set of people," while structured by the larger context of Jamaica's class, color, and gender hierarchies and evaluated by the common criteria generated by these hierarchies, arose as most salient in terms of everyday interactions. Because the larger context institutionalized these distinctions, however, it was this context that became most salient with respect to interactions between the "poorer sets" and the "upper sets." Since the same criteria were used to measure internal status distinctions and cross-class divisions, the "poorer sets" were able to recognize their common oppression within the wider system, irrespective of their own differences.[11] Peter Wade has made a similar point in his examination of the relationship between ideologies of blackness and *mestizaje* in a predominantly black community in Colombia's coastal region. He has written that blacks in Chocó participated in two overlapping processes:

> On the one hand, they have culturally adapted to values and norms the basic orientation and tone of which have been set by a dominant majority, directed essentially by elites, whether colonial or republican. These blacks have in the process begun to participate more fully in national hierarchies of prestige and status. . . . On the other hand, blacks have nucleated and congregated together, partly through choice and partly through the actions of the non-black world, and in these situations they have created and maintained cultural forms that are identified as black culture, whether or not this has some traceable African derivation. . . . This black culture, while not divorced from national scales of prestige and status, tends to emphasize the essential human equality of black people in a community. (1993:6)

Here, Wade has rooted a kind of cultural dualism among coastal black Colombians in both relative geographical segregation and the consolidation of elite hegemony regarding the values that buttressed hierarchies of prestige and status and, therefore, the means to social mobility. In Mango Mount as well, community members' individual successes or failures were explained by others in terms of the extent to which they held values seen as progress oriented. As I argued in part 1, at the level of colonial and national policy formulation, evoking values has often been a coded way for people to evaluate the cultural practices and behaviors that have been associated with poorer Jamaicans in particular. Throughout this chapter, I have sought to show that these kinds of evaluations were also operative at the community level. In their day-to-day lives and through their interactions with local institutions, the "poorer class of people" in Mango Mount assessed the class-based hierarchies between themselves and middle-class community members *and* mobilized status distinctions among themselves according to evaluative frameworks established during the colonial period.

At the same time, the acceptance of these evaluative frameworks did not necessarily correspond to a complete internalization of the ways colonial hierarchies of value became mapped onto class-coded cultural forms and practices. For example, the "poorer class of people's" preference for middle-class leadership within the Community Council was not typically based upon a conviction that the latter were the purveyors of better values (and were therefore inherently more competent to lead), but upon the expectation that the wealthier community members *were supposed to* act as advocates for the poorer villagers because they were in possession of greater resources (specifically time, contacts, and money) which, in turn, allowed them to operate more disinterestedly. Virginia summarized this idea as follows:

> When I was growing up, I wouldn't have said that [those who have been presidents of the Community Council] were community leaders. But after I got involved in the Council, I started to look at it as if they felt they had an obligation. And the poorer people in the community also felt that these people had an obligation to do things in the community. So I started to have an impression that these people were more like facilitators, these are the sort of people who went and talked to the member of Parliament, who found out what the Ministry of Agriculture could do for you. Other people in Mango Mount felt that they're the beneficiaries and that that's the way it's supposed to be. They felt that the middle class people are supposed to organize these projects, but not that Mr. Simms or any of the other people had any more status in the community. It was just that that's what they do. There is no additional status associated with it. People don't feel a sense of obligation to them.

Moreover, increasingly, rather than working through local organizations to "bring development to the community," younger members of the "poorer sets" have gone in search of development elsewhere. This has left a leadership vacuum of sorts within a context where the perception that those with more resources and education could afford to be more disinterested (and therefore better) leaders is so strongly held. The kinds of "crab antics" poorer villagers defined, therefore—antics rooted in the tension between a desire for status mobility and egalitarian unity—pose some of the greatest challenges for leadership development within communities throughout the African diaspora.

Finally, the fairly seamless way church events and political meetings brought together diverse groups among Mango Mount's "poorer sets" and the persistent difficulties faced by the Community Council in its attempts to do the same force us to consider the extent to which poorer community members bought into the Council's overarching goal of unifying the community through a common commitment to a particular kind of development. Indeed, despite the determination of many in the middle class to "live well" with their poorer neighbors, many among the "poorer set" argued that it was not particularly important that the different sectors of Mango Mount society "got along." Instead, what *was* important, as Enroy's comments below indicate, was that they minded their own business and stayed out of each other's way:

> Sure many small people would like to do a lot of things like they probably see the wealthier folk doing, but they can't. Still, the rich man going his way and the poor man going his way. It is very rarely they cross path. Everybody just doing their own thing. It's not a matter of rich and poor don't fight against each other ina Mango Mount. Everybody just live their own life. Simple.

What Enroy was pointing out was that the "poorer sets" did not necessarily aspire to a strict *equality* with middle-class people, but rather to an *independent autonomy*. Though the "poorer class of people" desired a more merit-based structure of opportunity, they did not see their own progress as dependent upon their total acceptance of and adherence to middle-class ideologies regarding respectability and social mobility, nor to their visions of development. This is not to say that poor Jamaicans have rejected these ideologies and visions wholesale. The middle classes have been purveyors of ideas and aspirations that have also, to a degree, represented the genuine interests of poorer Jamaicans because they too have a vital stake in the development and modernization project, especially in relation to infrastructural improvement. While this shared interest hasn't implied the absence of class or racial conflict about the forms, bases, and strategies of development, it does provide some additional explanation as to why the leadership has continued to garner mass support, both nationally and locally.

Instead, Enroy's assertion draws our attention to a broader point, which is twofold. While individuals among the "poorer set" may have accepted middle-class leadership and ideologies regarding progress within specific fora, this acceptance should not be mistaken for ideological consensus (Roseberry 1994). Moreover, it stands to reason that if the institutional structures that have buttressed middle-class community members' roles as political and cultural "brokers" (Austin 1984) were to become less salient in structuring poorer community members' potential for social mobility, then this lack of ideological consensus would become even more stark. Given the kinds of generational shifts delineated in the previous chapter, these points have significant implications for the ways poorer community members, and especially for those among a younger generation, evaluated both the legitimacy of particular institutions and the emancipatory potential of development initiatives implemented at both local and national levels. In other words, poorer Mango Mount villagers believed that their opportunities for individual growth and advancement (and, by extension, those of black Jamaicans generally) had not changed significantly since independence due to the institutional perpetuation of colonial hierarchies of value. This is why their common blackness trumped other status-based differences between them. It is also why they had already begun to pursue alternative paths for their own development. Moreover, it is the reason their responses to state-driven cultural development initiatives tended to be lukewarm at best.

chapter 5

EMANCIPATING THE NATION (AGAIN)

When Mango Mount community members discussed the changes in Jamaica since independence, their answers typically encompassed the following: things used to be cheaper; the money used to "value more"; there used to be less crime and violence; there used to be better government facilities geared toward social welfare; there used to be more "peace and unity among the people"; there never used to be a "gun epidemic"; there never used to be a drug epidemic; the youth didn't used to be so hopeless. These were the aspects of life that both middle class and poorer people cited as evidence for a "general breakdown of values," which they saw as the result of a global economy that, despite being more flexible and dynamic, had nonetheless exacerbated already existing structural inequalities and reduced people's sense of security regarding their livelihood and their community. These complaints were not unique to Mango Mount, but were more pervasive throughout Jamaican society.

Political and cultural leaders at the national level worried that as Jamaicans became more and more incorporated within the U.S. sphere of influence, they would become more familiar with (and potentially more committed to) American figures, goods, and services than with their own motto, heroes,[1] and cultural heritage. They worried that in response to local and international developments since independence, Jamaicans had become increasingly cynical and that the symbols of Jamaica's independence hadn't catalyzed sufficient loyalty and pride among the population. For nationalist mobilizers, this lack of engagement with the cultural dimensions of the national project was clearly a problem requiring a fast solution, especially given that 1997 was an election year. In this chapter, I explore the government's reinstatement of Emancipation Day as a public holiday, one of the more recent initiatives geared toward encouraging pride in Jamaica's history and African cultural heritage in order to foster a sense of national belonging among the mass of (black) Jamaicans. As with other cultural development schemes, the implicit message advanced here was consistent with earlier initiatives: look back, take pride, but move forward. In other words, as noted in chapter 2, because prominent members of the nationalist intelligentsia viewed political and economic cynicism as problems having to do, at least in part, with culture, they attempted to address these problems by strengthening the purported links between people's culture and development, their "self-esteem" and national productivity levels.

A focus on local responses to the restoration of Emancipation Day[2] clarifies how community members have apprehended the disjuncture between cultural and economic development policies pursued by successive Jamaican governments. By counterposing villagers' assessments of "Africanness" to their concerns about "blackness" and the ways these two identity formations inform their understandings of Jamaicanness, it becomes evident that poorer Mango Mount residents—whose lives were increasingly urban and transnational—did not conceptualize their problems in terms of "culture," and therefore did not perceive their inability to progress as related to a negative evaluation of Jamaica's African cultural heritage. That is, while they could appreciate the symbolism associated with state-sponsored cultural development initiatives, they didn't envision these initiatives as capable of catalyzing broader structural change or of creating a wider opportunity structure for themselves or their children. The manner in which the poorer sets engaged with Emancipation Day celebrations locally, therefore, challenged the tenets around which creole nationalist cultural mobilizers have tended to organize their initiatives. Specifically, local participation problematized the ways relationships between the past and the present, and between culture and development, have been framed. Community members' lack of engagement with national cultural development initiatives, therefore, should be seen as something other than a lack of self-esteem.

The (Re)Emancipation Movement

1996 Committee to Review National Symbols and Observances

In February 1996, amid talk of constitutional review, P. J. Patterson appointed a Committee on National Symbols and National Observances.[3] The committee was mandated to (1) review the role, significance, meaning, and suitability of Jamaica's national symbols and observances and recommend changes, if necessary; and (2) examine how national symbols and observances could contribute to sustaining cultural unity and assist in the development of the institutional and operational framework for the fostering of civil society (Report on National Symbols and Observances 1996:3).[4] Patterson intended that this process would serve as a potential antidote to the high rates of poverty and crime as well as what he described as the "cultural chaos, the absence of a national identity, [and] the weakening of our values and attitudes." In his view, these social ills had resulted from a sense of social alienation among (especially) young men and had already led to "the loss from the economy of the creative human abilities of thousands in an entire generation" (Report on National Symbols and Observances 1996:2).

The prime minister was not alone in expressing these opinions. Throughout 1996 and 1997 newspaper editorials, radio call-in shows, and popular opinion addressed the upsurge of crime, unemployment, and violence; the widespread indiscipline and disregard for order among both youth and adults; the increase of "incivility" in day-to-day interactions; the breakdown of family life and weakening of kinship patterns (of whatever type); the decline of voluntarism and civic organizations which once fueled service to community development and nation-building; the drop in educational standards; the decline in economic productivity; the increase in materialism and glorification of all that is foreign (read "American"); and the deepening of cynicism. Despite invocations of the beauty of Jamaica's physical landscape, the general assessment seemed to have been that since independence, "Jamaica mash up completely."

Newspaper columnists also cited people's ambivalence toward, or lack of participation in, the celebration of independence as evidence of this growing society-wide disillusionment with the creole nationalist project. One reporter, writing just after Independence Day 1996, argued that the occasion no longer evoked the sense of history and inspiration she felt should accompany nationhood (Stair 1996). Indeed, public figures commented that independence, as well as all other public holidays—with the possible exception of Christmas—had become nothing more than excuses to travel to the north coast to enjoy the amenities of the all-inclusive beach hotels for those who could afford it, or, for those who couldn't, to visit family throughout the country. To the committee, this reflected a lack of propriety, a robbing of the dignified treatment befitting "the triumph of political self-determination over colonial subjugation and . . . the belief that Jamaicans can be the creators of their own destiny" (Report on National Symbols and Observances 1996:29). Furthermore, newspaper commentators argued that Jamaica's economy had been mismanaged since independence and that in this sense, Jamaica would have been better off had it remained a British colony. Citing the devastation of the economy, the crippling of the health care system, and the exponential rise in crime and murder rates, one letter writer went so far as to propose that Independence Day either be canceled or declared a national day of mourning (Daily Gleaner 1997a), and a fifty-six year-old gentleman interviewed by the Jamaica Herald stated that because of the "invasion of other people's culture," the present generation was unable to identify with independence and emancipation (Jamaica Herald 1997:8).

According to committee Chair Rex Nettleford, the way out of this perceived mess had to be "firmly rooted in the belief in self and the conscious return to the values and attitudes, the ideals and vision that helped to start the Jamaican people on the road to that sense of self which is the basis for real productivity" (Report on National Symbols and Observances 1996:7). For Nettleford and the rest of the committee members, the links between national symbols and observances and national pride and identity on one hand and between this pride and a more productive economy on the other were clear. The theory here was that the development of national pride should lead to greater self-esteem and, therefore, to more positive attitudes toward the work ethic. Thus, the committee undertook the task of reevaluating those entities designated in 1962 to represent the new nation.

While many in the media agreed that the national symbols should represent for people a shared set of aspirations and that they should therefore be reexamined from time to time, others felt that the focus on symbols was a diversionary attempt by the government during a period of deep economic crisis. Nevertheless, the committee held fourteen private meetings, four public hearings throughout Jamaica, and three special colloquia designed to elicit the opinions of youth. They invited written submissions from the public (forty were received), analyzed thirty-nine newspaper columnists' publications, and interviewed five public figures known for their varying perspectives on "cultural issues." Though the committee took on everything from the coat of arms to the national bird, I will confine my discussion here to their efforts to restore the celebration of Emancipation Day.

With independence in 1962, Emancipation Day (the celebration of the final abolition of slavery on August 1, 1838) ceased to be a public holiday.

According to columnist Joan Williams, the theory behind this decision held that celebrating Emancipation Day would have ultimately proven divisive for the new nation, constantly reminding the descendants of slaves and slave owners of their history (Williams 1997). By 1997, however, the dominant sense among nationalist elites was that the removal of Emancipation Day as a public holiday had left Jamaican youth without an awareness of their heritage and of the steps in Jamaica's evolution toward modern statehood. For independence to be meaningful, the Jamaican population would have to understand the various steps and struggles toward nationhood. Emancipation Day, therefore, would have to be restored within the collective memory as the first step toward a modern, civil society—a commemoration of the struggle for and achievement of individual freedom, societal liberation (Report on National Symbols and Observances 1996:32).[5]

Not all Jamaicans had ceased to celebrate Emancipation Day after Independence in 1962. Various Baptist churches maintained commemorative services, and the remaining branches of Marcus Garvey's Universal Negro Improvement Association, which had held annual conferences on August 1, also continued to recognize Emancipation Day. Moreover, several groups of Rastafarians had advocated for years that Emancipation Day be commemorated nationally and, therefore, saw its reinstatement as a public holiday as the fulfillment of their efforts. They also tended to position the celebration of Emancipation Day as a catalyst for other kinds of initiatives. For example, the chairman of the Mystic Revelation of Rastafari suggested that roadside expositions be held across the island, that a national competition be launched for the best development plan for the millennium with a $250,000 prize tag, and that Queen Elizabeth be invited to " 'share the joy and appreciation for the good deed done by Queen Victoria in 1938 [sic] in helping to emancipate the slaves' " (Daily Gleaner 1997g). Other Rastafarians, members of the Ethiopian African Black International Congress, used the restoration of Emancipation Day as an opportunity to relaunch their push for repatriation and reparations, a contentious maneuver given that the president of the Imperial Ethiopian World Federation, believing that the dynasty of H.I.M. Haile Selassie should be restored, had long argued that repatriation should not be a priority while the Marxist government was in power in Ethiopia (Daily Gleaner 1997d).

If Emancipation Day were to be successfully restored, however, the business community, in particular, would have to be convinced that the introduction of another public holiday would not further decimate already low productivity levels, and the general public would have to be reeducated as to the real and contemporary significance of emancipation itself. Thus began the propaganda campaign.

Educating the Public

The government established an Emancipation Secretariat to disseminate information and plan events that would foster a sense of history, inspire a vision for the future, and encourage a Jamaican identity. Available from their offices in downtown Kingston were excerpts of published historical accounts of slavery, abolition, apprenticeship, and "full free" written by various West Indian scholars; an ecumenical litany for Emancipation Day; and reprints of Sir Philip Sherlock's vignettes outlining aspects of the abolition process that had appeared in the Daily Gleaner. Also available were copies of the "Footprints on the Road to Emancipation" series that chronicled the process of abolition from the outlawing of slavery in Britain in 1772, through the pressure exerted upon the government by the nonconformist churches—both in Britain and Jamaica, to the Sam Sharpe rebellion and the subsequent abolition of slavery and development of free villages. This series was published in the newspapers and aired on television daily. Additionally, the Emancipation Secretariat commissioned an emancipation song[6] and two pamphlet workbooks for young adults about Jamaica's history[7] and held two televised panel discussions on emancipation and related themes. Meanwhile, the National Pantomime prepared for its production of the play "Augus' Mawnin,'" which would open on Emancipation Day and continue performances throughout the month of August. Finally, the Institute of Jamaica sponsored a series of Speakers' Corners—events to which scholars and activists were invited to speak on a range of topics having to do with emancipation—in the downtown Kingston park popularized as a cultural and intellectual gathering place by Marcus Garvey.

Emphasis during the Speakers' Corners, as generally within events planned by the Emancipation Secretariat, was placed upon culling events from the past that could shape a new contemporary ideological framework. But opening the debate about the significance of history to identity and culture in the present also created a space for the implementation of policies that would address people's material and social realities. For instance, Prime Minister Patterson announced that in commemoration of the holiday, seventeen academic scholarships would be awarded by the government (Daily Observer 1997b) and a minimum of 100 hectares of land in each parish would be divested to individuals within lower socioeconomic groups for farmsteads, cooperative agriculture, community housing, agroindustrial production, ecotourism, and village expansion (Daily Gleaner 1997d).[8] This latter initiative came right on the heels of Operation PRIDE, one of the Prime Minister's land reform initiatives geared toward overseeing "the greatest distribution of land in Jamaica's history" (Daily Observer 1997a:1).

Debating the Meaning of Freedom

The majority of the public debate surrounding Emancipation Day did not take issue with the government's decision to restore it as a public holiday. Rather, it questioned the degree to which Jamaicans had in fact been emancipated from "mental slavery," and the words of Marcus Garvey and Bob Marley were evoked time and time again.[9] According to most editorialists, many Jamaicans remained in bondage, either directly due to the actions of their fellow countrymen and women or indirectly by the beliefs that anything black is no good and that better is always to be found elsewhere (Mills 1997; Richards 1997). For some, the symbolism was rich, but whether it would change the substance of living in Jamaica in the 1990s remained a question (E. Miller 1997). Others mused cynically on the changing meanings of freedom, asserting that while for slaves, freedom meant "the right to self-determination, self-directedness, self-management," it now meant "freedom from want, freedom to be prosperous, freedom to escape hardship, freedom to be looked after by benign Big government" (Henry 1997b:A4). Still others argued that the commentary on emancipation had "sunken into a fit of romanticism" (Espeut 1997: A4), and that Jamaicans were largely ignorant and indifferent to the significance of emancipation in Jamaica's history. These writers tended to position Emancipation Day as irrelevant to the majority of Jamaicans since their status hadn't significantly improved anyway (Neita 1997b). Those who disagreed with the government's decision stated either that greater focus should have been given to Independence Day instead of wasting money on another holiday, or that there was nothing to celebrate since slavery—masquerading in the contemporary period as white supremacy—still existed (Daily Observer 1997c).

Patterson's invitation of Jerry Rawlings, president of the Republic of Ghana, and his wife, Nana Konady Agyeman-Rawlings, as his honored guests during the emancipation and independence festivities also provoked some degree of public controversy. Among those who welcomed Rawlings were some Rastafarians who took the opportunity of his visit to discuss the possibilities of repatriation to Ghana. One business owner in Mango Mount also took advantage of Rawlings's presence. Through his involvement with the Kingston Chamber of Commerce, he organized a breakfast symposium at which the president spoke about his attempts to rid Ghana's public and private sectors of corruption. Others, however, considered the invitation a slap in the face of democracy. One columnist decried him as a "*coup d'etatist*," a military dictator whose presence was not, in fact, justified on the premise of ancestral links (Henry 1997a:A5).

There were some optimists, however, who saw in the restoration of Emancipation Day an "act of nationhood," an opportunity "to help us reshape the moral, economic, and political imperatives which are implied in the notion of freedom" (Bowen 1997), particularly within a global economic context in which "the forces of history are challenging countries like ours to renew our freedom, and to define our own context and space" (J. Edwards 1997:A5). Moreover, one Rastafarian columnist (who confessed that she hadn't attended any of the scheduled events) wrote that the celebrations successfully "re-Africanize[d] the Jamaican population at an important moment in our history" (Blake-Hannah 1997:7). Reported comments from people on the streets were equally mixed, although there seemed to be a consensus on the meaning of emancipation as "freedom for all black people" (*Sunday Gleaner* 1997:5). Those who felt it was important that the holiday be restored generally stated that it was a good opportunity for the youth to learn about Jamaica's history and that more should be taught about it in the schools.

National Commemorations

The actual events that were planned included a vigil in the National Heroes Park organized by the Rastafarian Centralization Organization to kick off their twelve-hour fast and "day of reflection" with a *nyabinghi*, a drum festival at Jamaica House featuring drummers from Suriname and Trinidad as well as the practitioners of local traditional styles; Mello Go Roun' —the annual showcase of winners of the festival competitions in dance, drama, music, and speech; arts exhibitions; a reggae festival; and an Emancipation Day Grand Market.[10] But, the main event on the official calendar was the Emancipation vigil in Spanish Town Square[11] on July 31 from 6 P.M. until midnight. The vigil was to feature addresses by the prime minister, a representative of the opposition, and the Ghanaian president; performances by the Jamaica military band, a mento band, quadrille and maypole dancers, Ivanay (a then popular female reggae vocalist), the National Dance Theatre Company of Jamaica (NDTC), and various choirs from the Spanish Town area; and the rereading of the Abolition Proclamation at midnight.

The event itself, as well as the more general re-emancipation "movement," was recognized by the government as a grand success. Nonetheless, two relatively negative reports on the event appeared in the *Gleaner*. These stated that it was hard to find parking or see the stage, that the crowd seemed dissatisfied with the long ecumenical service, that the speakers were too verbose and therefore the proclamation was not read at midnight as planned, that as the crowd dwindled a Rasta group had set up a drumming circle near the memorial commemorating British Admiral George Rodney and attracted its own following, and that the only thing that drew the crowd back together after the speechifying was the NDTC's performance of *The Crossing*.[12] Though an abeng[13] was blown by a member of the Accompong Town Maroons, church bells did not ring at midnight as planned. One editorial reported that while the emcee was attempting to get the crowd to chant "Freedom!" a young man behind him shouted, "we nuh free yet!" (Henry 1997b). Another writer quoted a Rastaman explaining to some nearby youth that these were " 'official-type people' who were trying their best but did not fully understand" (*Daily Gleaner* 1997b). The audience, one article concluded, "may not have been convinced that what they were witnessing should leave them thinking or celebrating, or feeling any raised consciousness or having any increase in a feeling of self-worth" (*Daily Gleaner* 1997b; see also *Daily Gleaner* 1997a).

Emancipation Day in Mango Mount

Within the village I had been asking people what, if anything, they usually did as a community to commemorate Independence Day and what they thought of the restoration of Emancipation Day as a national holiday. With respect to the latter, several older villagers remembered commemorating the "First of August" (Emancipation Day) prior to independence with family gatherings and picnics. Many of them recalled it as a day to dance, eat, and have fun and only peripherally associated it with learning from their older relatives what black people had "gone through" in Jamaica. As a result, one older villager thought its meaning might have been lost on a younger generation that he felt was more interested in holidays such as the spontaneous "Reggae Boyz" day off Patterson granted upon the soccer team's qualification for the World Cup tournament in France. Younger adults in the village (those between twenty-five and forty-five), however, generally agreed that the idea to celebrate Emancipation Day was a good one, viewing the final abolition of slavery as the single most important date for people of African descent in the country's history. As such, they saw Emancipation Day as a way to remember Jamaica's African heritage. This opinion was also expressed by the president of the Community Council:

> Emancipation takes us back to realize and understand our African heritage. This is important to all Jamaicans because generally, there's a black world and a white world. And this might sound revolutionary, as my cousin says, but I think there's a great conspiracy in the world generally against black people and Africa and it all has to do with slavery and the fact that white people feel some amount of remorse about black slavery but don't want to express it. Even black people—Africans as well as those in the diaspora—to a large extent don't understand the conspiracy. So I think we need to find some common ground where we can identify the problem and find a solution to this great rift between black and white. As black people we should try to remember our Africanism, and this is where emancipation comes in.

Not everyone in the community, however, felt that focusing on Jamaica's historical development would be either profitable or necessary. One middle-class woman in her mid-fifties, a former teacher and administrator at one of Jamaica's tertiary institutions who also tutored the "local" children, expressed the following opinion:

> What I don't like about Emancipation is that we keep looking back and we're not looking forward. It's nice that we know our history, but I don't know, were you ever ashamed of being descended from slaves? I don't know anybody who is ashamed of being descended from slaves. But they keep saying that people are, so maybe they know more than I do.

Moreover, the restoration of Emancipation Day as a public holiday prompted various cynical responses from both the middle class and the "poorer sets," since villagers understood emancipation, like independence, as an incomplete process. Both middle-class and lower-class men and women tended to attribute this to political maneuvering. Mango Mount community members' distrust of politicians and the political process more generally hung like a cloud over their positive valuation of the recognition accorded to emancipation itself. For example, Elliot, who was the twenty-five year-old son of a tradesman and housewife and the only one of his eight brothers and sisters who received a tertiary education, saw emancipation as the transfer of one system of oppression (plantation slavery) for another (Christianity) and felt its reinstatement was primarily an attempt to broaden the political constituency of the People's National Party:

> Emancipation in Jamaica had a lot to do with religion, Christianity, which also has rules and also changes your life. If you were an American Indian and they introduced Christianity to you, all your culture has to be erased. I think this is a very dangerous thing on a whole because it changes your culture. It changes your lifestyle. Men try to control people with Christianity, and that's one of the things they introduced to the slaves. Letting them know that they were uncivilized, they introduced Christianity to them, and so still they were not free on a whole. So restoring Emancipation Day as a holiday was a political move. They use the emancipation thing just to get votes, votes of the Rastafarians, who've been celebrating it all along.

Carolyn, a thirty-something middle class woman who grew up in Mango Mount and received her university education in England also viewed the reinstatement of Emancipation Day as the result of political maneuvering. She argued that the holiday represented a racialization of politics that was intended to distract Jamaicans from the government's inability to implement successful economic policies:

> To me, there is a race versus nation thing going on and it's kind of ugly. It makes this maneuvering and posturing even more insidious and dangerous in a lot of ways, dangerous in the sense of racializing political concepts instead of just leaving them as political concepts. I see Emancipation Day as part of a piece of posturing within the context of competition for positions of power and an impending election. And it's part of

attributing a race, if emancipation is a kind of race celebration as it's being claimed, by a particular political party. So they are racializing their position in the political competition, rather than dealing with society, economics.

More explicit was the commentary offered by Douglass. With family connections in the district, Douglass had lived in Mango Mount off and on for over twenty years working as the gardener for several of the middle-class families in the district. However, he was considered an outsider by other community members and was often the victim of theft. His perspective on the reinstatement of Emancipation Day called into question the possibility of unity among the majority black population within a virulently competitive political system. As he noted, "The same black man did slave black, so when dem say dem gwine celebrate it, how it go? Political war is slavery too."

Several women among the "poorer sets" expressed similar opinions, but most simply dismissed the government's decision to restore the holiday as meaningless and irrelevant. As one young woman put it, "Emancipation is just words. It nuh mean nuttin.'" On the whole, however, women said less about Emancipation Day and did more. That is, their analyses of the ideological and political motivations behind restoring the holiday were of secondary importance to the practical opportunity presented by Emancipation Day to "plan something so the children can occupy themselves." As a result, when a commemorative community event was eventually suggested, women were more fully involved in its planning and implementation than were male villagers.

When I raised the topic of independence celebrations, a few individuals remembered that perhaps some ten years prior, the community held a parade up the hill to the main square, led by the marching band from a neighboring rural village. They described floats depicting various population groups such as the Arawaks and the Maroons and expressed interest that something like that should happen again, either to celebrate the thirty-fifth anniversary of Jamaica's independence or to commemorate Emancipation Day. I did some investigating and then mentioned the idea to the newly hired part-time Community Upliftment project director for the Community Council, a social-work student at the University of the West Indies completing the practical segment of his master's degree requirements. He, in turn, brought it up at the next Community Council meeting.

Response of the Council's Executive Committee to the proposed Emancipation Day community celebration was varied. One woman immediately pounced on the idea as a good fund-raising opportunity. Another doused her fire by saying no one at the meeting would have the time to plan and organize such an event in less than six weeks. The treasurer argued that since the Council had a grant application pending with the Jamaica Social Investment Fund for reparations and renovations to the community center, it might be a good idea to hold an event that could garner some publicity and would demonstrate that the community was on top of what was going on nationally. The social work student expressed his opinion that the event should be first and foremost a community "fun day," featuring games, activities for children, and performances by community members including the "drama club"—students from the All Age school with whom I had been conducting dance and drama classes. When general opinion seemed to stray away from holding an event, the student mentioned that it had been I who had brought the idea to him in the first place, as I had been asking people about how they thought the holidays should be celebrated. The Council's Executive Committee seemed unresolved on the issue, but the next day, I received a phone call from the Director of Business Projects, an American woman with a doctorate in economics who had been living in the community for the previous six years, asking if I would be willing to organize the event myself.

Saying "no" has never been my strong point. So, with extensive help and guidance from the Business Projects' director and several villagers, I went about organizing an Emancipation Day Road March and Community Fun Day based on what people said they wanted. Not that everybody wanted the same thing—many thought the whole thing was a waste of (my) time and energy. But there was enough consensus on the basic structure of the day to keep things rolling. I was advised as to what committees I should set up, whom I should ask to work on the various committees, where to go off the hill for donations of necessary items as well as prizes, where to buy the chickens, how to get more than you pay for, how to make up the budget for the treasurer, how much white rum to buy for the marching band, how to ask the bartender to donate his sound system (and selector) free of charge, who to call on for help at the last minute, and who not to call on at all. These logistical details taken care of (and some of them weren't, of course, until the very last second), I concentrated on the drama club.

By this time, I had enlisted Winsome's assistance (since two of her own plays had been produced at the community center) in order to create a performance with the youth in the village specifically addressing the themes of emancipation and freedom. Some years previously, Winsome had directed a performance of folk songs and dances with children from the All Age school called "Pickney Sinting" (patois for something by or for children) that was performed in the village itself as well as in the surrounding rural communities. She had also established a drama club at the center that, as noted in chapter 4, had folded some years prior to my fieldwork. Winsome recruited approximately fifteen kids for our first meeting, all of whom were children of the "poorer class of people" in the area. Of these, most had worked with her before. A few, however, were brought in from the street, so to speak, where they had been hanging out talking or playing games. As we started the meeting, I asked the kids what emancipation meant to them. Most said they didn't know, some said nothing, and others mentioned "black people improvement" or "freedom." Then I asked if anyone knew who Sam Sharpe was. One of the children pulled out a bubble gum wrapper with his picture on it and said he was one of the national heroes, but couldn't remember what, exactly, he had done to be honored as a hero. After they explained that they didn't learn about these aspects of Jamaica's history in school, I suggested that they do some of their own research into the abolition of slavery in order to determine what they thought should or should not go into the play.

In the meantime, Winsome's vision was to re-create the important moments of emancipation and to encourage the kids to develop their own words and actions within the parameters of scenes she would outline. As she saw it, the story should begin with a group of young men chatting on the corner. Their conversation would be interrupted by the entrance of a plantation owner and his two slave minions who would capture only one of the men and take him back to the mistress of the plantation for "inspection." In the great house, the mistress would be flanked by several house slaves, and the captured slave would make various attempts to calmly explain that he wouldn't work as a slave, at which point he would be taken for a beating while the master and mistress prepared for a ball they were holding for themselves and their other plantation owner friends. During the ball, the slaves would be asked to provide entertainment in the form of dance and music, and I was asked to teach the kids some traditional Jamaican dance steps for this section. At the same time, some of the other slaves would be holding their own meeting (an *obeah* "session") to discuss the possibility of taking their own freedom. The newly captured slave, who was to spearhead this movement, would tell them that obeah was foolishness and "wickedness," and that this was definitely not the way forward. Instead, he would propose burning down the sugar crops and then fleeing into the mountains. The master and mistress of the plantation would not die in the fire, however, because one of the loyal house slaves would be compassionate and would warn them about what was to take place. At the end of the play, there would be a song or dance about the situation in Jamaica today and how emancipation related to what was going on in the late twentieth century.

The kids did an excellent job of rehearsing this and acting out specific scenes for the first two meetings. Though the master and mistress were never explicitly delineated as white people, the children made a big show of overexaggerated British manners and speaking "proper English," to the extent that they had to be told not to say "please" and "thank you" to the house slaves. They did not pick up the traditional kumina[14] rhythm I was trying to teach them (and didn't seem particularly interested in picking it up), so I settled for a dancehall beat, which everybody could carry. Given their fear of those who were said to practice obeah within the community, they were wary about doing an obeah scene. They also had a hard time coming up with ways to express what meaning emancipation could have in the present.

None of this, however, is what actually ended up happening. After our second meeting, the family of one of the youth who was involved in the play showed up at Winsome's doorstep, cutlasses[15] in hands, and falsely accused her children's father of stealing one of their goats. Winsome's children's father's brother retaliated by running after the family with his own cutlass, the police were called, and that was the end of her involvement with the play. She said she just didn't feel like doing anything to benefit the community when the community wouldn't "live good together." As a result, I was stuck on my own with very little time left and a dwindling participation level among the kids and decided to stick with the official version of the story by having those who remained each read from the "Footprints on the Road to Emancipation" series. That those who remained were all girls reflected both the gender bias in educational achievement and the alienation of (particularly) young men from activities associated with the Community Council discussed earlier.

I asked three of the older girls to write a paragraph about what emancipation meant, how it happened, and its significance for them and for

Jamaica. Two of the girls wrote that emancipation occurred because "black people became tired of being bossed around by the whites" and so they decided to burn down plantations and "fight against the white to be free." One continued that what emancipation meant for Jamaica was that "no one [can] be over our back to work for them without pay . . . [and] we are mostly black and live a happy and free life." Sixteen-year-old Adele, a budding historian herself, wrote:

> Emancipation. Every black person should know the meaning. It means to be free mentally, spiritually, and physically from slavery. Where certain rules are abolished to make everyone be equal amongst each other. Freedom has a similar meaning to emancipation. It means to change your way of life from a certain type of bondage, where you are forced to do things you don't want to do, freedom gives you the right to make a choice and give your own opinion. Emancipation came about in the nineteenth century when the African slaves from the different plantations decided to speak up for their rights no matter what the consequences. They fought for what they believed in no matter how hopeless times got but they stuck to their task to be free and finally in 1838, black people in Jamaica got the emancipation. To Jamaicans our emancipation is very important especially to the elder members of our society. Because our ancestors fought very hard to get our freedom that is why it is important for us as Jamaicans. And so we have yearly events to commemorate this special thing that we all as Jamaicans own. So all to me and my fellow Jamaicans I don't think I can explain because freedom has a meaning that is neverending.

These personal statements were to be interspersed among the other readings, and the girls would start and finish the whole thing by singing "Oh Freedom," an African American traditional song with which they were familiar with because they had heard it when the American television miniseries *Roots* was broadcast in Jamaica. Two days before the holiday, they were as ready as they were going to be, and all the other plans were, for the most part, in place.

August Morning

Emancipation Day started off without a hitch. The van driver for the local upscale guesthouse arrived at my house at the scheduled time and we traveled to the neighboring community to pick up the members of the marching band, a voluntary fife and drum brigade of about twelve laborers and farmers fairly evenly divided with respect to generation. They were, miraculously, already playing in their square and ready to go. We took them to the starting point of the road march, and I notified the woman in charge of the marching groups—and, at the last minute, the cooking—that they were ready before I went back up the hill to the community center to see how far preparations there had progressed. They hadn't, really, due to a transportation glitch with the children's ride, but I was assured that everything was on its way to being worked out. About an hour later, I heard the band coming up the hill, grabbed my video camera, and met them halfway. There were about sixty to seventy-five people following the band, mostly children and a few adults (all from the "poorer sets"), carrying banners they had painted with various slogans about freedom and emancipation. As we rounded the corner near the square, one of the kids asked if he could work my video camera, so I gave it to him for the day to record whatever he wanted. We reached the top of the hill, and as we doubled back down to the community center, it began to pour down rain.

The marchers continued until the center was in sight, at which point they broke into a run. The sound system had just been set up outside and had to be carried in, and the marching band, undaunted, continued playing inside the center. When people asked if the band knew anything other than typical marching songs, they insisted they could play mento, calypso, and even dancehall. However, as the day wore on, their repertoire's scope decreased in inverse proportion to the amount of white rum ingested. The rain soon passed, and the games and rides were set up outside. Everything was running smoothly. Ticket sales were going well, and people seemed pleased with the prizes, which ranged from the donated bottles of rum and other liquors to Burger King paper crowns. The sound system had taken over from the band to the delight of the younger people present, and the "numbers" game sold out both times it was played, much to the chagrin of the Business Projects' director who was convinced that if the villagers spent as much money on their kids' education and activities as they did trying to win a prize in a numbers game, the village would be much better off.

Midway through the afternoon, three of the musicians from the marching band approached me to say that they formed an "acting crew" and that they would perform character sketches if I were willing to drive them back to their village to pick up their costumes. We went, and upon our return, it was almost time for the performances to begin. All but one of the drama club members had gathered, and I went to retrieve the absent girl who had gone home to cook dinner. She had apparently been besieged by a last minute case of stage fright. She ultimately returned, though not without mocking me for insisting that she not let the others down.

The "acting crew" started things off. They were dressed as old women and played out a country scene during which someone was accused of "tiefing" one of the women's roosters. Unfortunately, it was very difficult to hear them, and the audience looked a little confused, though they seemed to recognize and appreciate the concept. The drama club was up next, and after their initial reluctance to take the stage and hold the microphone close enough to their mouths so they could be heard, they went through their routine with conviction. The song was on key, and the most reticent of the girls gave the loudest reading. Those who recited with the most unfaltering and "proper" speech were applauded, while those less fluent readers who stumbled over their words or slipped into patois were heckled. The audience's attention waned and they became restless about halfway through, possibly due, in part, to not being able to hear very well. When the girls were finished, the emcee, a self-identified "baldhead" Rasta,[16] spoke for a moment (to a still restless crowd) about the significance of emancipation for Jamaicans, and he exhorted people to remember that this was what had brought us all together for the day. The selector began playing music over his speech, and the emcee announced that the stage was open for anyone who wanted to spontaneously offer a song or dance.

His daughter and her friend decided to sing a song and asked the selector to play the background music for the then popular version of "Killing Me Softly" covered by the U.S.-based band the Fugees,[17] to which they added the vocals in a style almost identical to the group's lead singer. Finally, the floor was opened up for dancing, and the youth, mostly boys, showed off all the latest dancehall moves, while the little girls—mostly under eight years old—were encouraged to "shek it an wine it." The older girls were more reluctant to dance publicly and were not spurred on by the adults to do so. After a while, several adults began cleaning up, and a group of young men gathered around the music selector's table and took turns on the microphone singing or DJ-ing over the familiar rhythmic variations.[18] Eventually, everyone left the center. Some continued the party at the regular Friday-night dance in the square at the top of the hill, and some went home. At the next Council meeting, those of us who had been involved in organizing the event were congratulated on its success, although none of the Executive Committee members had actually attended since many of them had other obligations, such as the annual national agricultural show that also took place during independence weekend in another parish.

Culture and Development

It would be tempting to interpret the events surrounding the government's reinstatement of Emancipation Day as a public holiday and the variety of responses to these events in simply material (and somewhat cynical) terms. That is, when the economy is stable, the state, being strategically self-interested, is not particularly concerned with the politics of culture. Conversely, when the economy is faltering, state officials become preoccupied with culture while "ordinary folk" remain concerned with (what else?) the economy and their inability to make a decent living. Following this line of interpretation, we could argue that though people generally appreciated and even celebrated the symbolic message attached to the restoration of Emancipation Day, they often perceived the fervor with which this message was advertised as hollow and irrelevant to their immediate economic reality. As a result, we would expect audiences at both the Emancipation Vigil in Spanish Town and the community's performance to be restless since commemorating emancipation would not have been seen as addressing their current material needs. To arrive at a more nuanced understanding of community members' responses to Emancipation Day, however, it becomes necessary to look more closely at the links that have been posited between "culture" and "development." That there are links, and that these links are never disinterested, should by now be clear.

To recapitulate the argument of the book thus far, in chapter 1, I showed that after emancipation, the former slaves were confronted by two competing ideological frameworks guiding the transition from slavery to freedom. One, promoted by colonial officials and supported by the local planter class, was geared toward socializing the former slaves into laboring for wages on the plantation and modifying their cultural practices to support this type of work. This project was institutionally supported through restrictive legislation and policies addressing, for example, the purchase of land and political participation. The second framework, pro-moted by the nonconformist churches, supported the development of an independent small-holding peasantry that, through its association with the churches and their schools, would abandon "slave culture" and adhere to those values considered most progress oriented. Among these values were respectable Christian living, thrift, and individual and community "uplift." Additionally, the former slaves were expected to accept the politi-cal and cultural leadership of the educated middle classes.

As noted in chapter 2, the cultural policy that was developed at the time of independence privileged the lifestyle promoted by this latter vision, and took the further step of valuing those cultural practices of the rural peas-antry that the missionary churches failed to eradicate by establishing and supporting institutions that would remind Jamaicans of their African cul-tural heritage. At the same time, the government pursued economic de-velopment strategies geared toward industrial modernization. Herein lies the disjuncture. The cultural policy, even as it has shifted over the years since independence, has attempted to *change people's minds* about Jamaica's African heritage. However, economic development policies—despite the various shifts within the ethnic division of labor that developed as a result of policies pursued during the 1970s as well as later privatization initiatives—have not been seen to appreciably *change people's positions* within Jamaica's color, class, gender, and culture nexus. That is to say, the lives of the "poorer class of people" in Mango Mount remained institutionally struc-tured in disadvantageous ways that were reminiscent of the colonial period.

The nationalist intelligentsia has more readily diagnosed the effects of this disjuncture—manifested through a lack of participation in events like the National Festival of the Arts, for example—as problems having to do with culture and self-esteem than as the inherent contradictions of capital-ist development,[19] potentially because they did not see themselves as able to effect significant changes in the latter. As such, they advanced the following argument: (1) Jamaica's current social and cultural "chaos" is due, at least in part, to a lack of self-esteem and sense of belonging among the mass of (black) people; (2) this lack of self-esteem is due to the historical and current belittling of "things African," which is related also to the persistence of color and class prejudice; (3) to develop self-esteem and a sense of belonging, it is necessary to engage people with events in their history and their cultural heritage with which they should identify; (4) higher self-esteem will result in greater national pride; and (5) greater national pride will lead to a more productive economy. Hence, the tendency among the nationalist intelligentsia has been to plumb the past for "culture" while forging into the future for "development."

Community members, however, did not diagnose their problems in terms of culture, nor did they typically relate the development of self-esteem to positive valuations of their cultural heritage. For them, structures of inequality that they perceived had not changed in their favor since independence were the most relevant factors constraining their own development. In this respect, valuing the past could only do so much, and a usable past for "culture" was less important because they didn't believe that the answer to their problems lay in looking back to find moral lessons. With this in mind, we can better address the following questions: Did the government's restoration of Emancipation Day catalyze a positive valuation of Jamaica's African heritage locally in Mango Mount? More broadly, what was the contemporary relevance of an African heritage to community members? And what were their assessments of the types of "cultural development" initiatives pursued by state-affiliated organizations such as the Jamaica Cultural Development Commission (JCDC), and national artistic entities like the NDTC?

"What Is Africa to Me?"

To a degree, some of the children's unwillingness to perform an obeah scene with the drama club or their lack of interest in learning the traditional kumina dance and rhythm could be chalked up to a more general youthful wariness of what appeared to them to be unfamiliar aspects of a supernatural worldview. Indeed, during a rehearsal when I asked them what they knew about kumina, they stated that they "heard" that when people went to a kumina ritual, they "got crazy," drank goat's blood and carried on, danced around in circles, and climbed trees upside-down. When I asked them to clarify who these "people" were, they said "old people" and "wrap head people." Following the obvious line of questioning, I then asked that if "old people" and "wrap head people" went to kumina rituals, where did young people go? And everybody answered, in unison, "to a dance." Indeed, aside from the various games offered during the local emancipation "fun day," what garnered the widest popular participation was the dancing and DJ-ing at the end of the afternoon. And significantly, the song chosen by the emcee's daughter, a cover version of a song originally recorded by

Roberta Flack, was recorded by a U.S.-based hip-hop group whose own background was Haitian. Moreover, though the Fugees experimented with musical forms originating elsewhere within the African diaspora, the specific song chosen—"Killing Me Softly"—had nothing immediately to do with emancipation or Jamaica's African heritage.

This focus, especially among young people, on popular culture and through it, an engagement with a transnational "black" culture, was often cause for consternation among nationalist cultural mobilizers who worried that rurally based African-derived Jamaican cultural practices would "die out." This was also a concern among older villagers among the "poorer set" within Mango Mount. For instance, a farmer who also worked at one of the local guesthouses argued for the preservation of a cultural history. "It's important to remember the past and pass our Jamaican culture in terms of music and dance on to the children because it's part of our heritage," he said. "If we start forgetting these things, there will be no history left for them." Here, history (and culture) were offered up as possessions that could be as easily lost as maintained. This view resonated with that asserted by members of the nationalist intelligentsia and was one which, as I suggested in chapter 2, engaged the potential for a separation of cultural practices (and the values these embody) into components designated as positive or negative and productive or unproductive with respect to national development efforts. It was also a view that appeared to be less commonly held among a younger generation, especially those who came of age during or after the 1970s. One younger woman even suggested that the focus on an African cultural heritage was redundant. "It doesn't really mean anything to me to think of it as an African heritage," she said. "You nuh black already, and black dohn mean African?"

Even the middle-class children who grew up in Mango Mount seemed less convinced as to the significance of "cultural development" than their parents and grandparents were. Those who were adults and young adults at the time of independence, many of whom had careers as civil servants, tended to offer the opinion that was current at that time regarding the importance of "modernizing with a difference." For example, one middle-aged civil servant offered the standard nationalist argument regarding the link between the past and the future, arguing that "if you don't know where you are coming from, you can't develop a sense of purpose as to where you are going." He continued to say that cultural development initiatives were important "because during the colonial days, more effort was being made to bring home to the people the dominance of the British empire" and therefore Jamaicans seeking independence needed to counter that worldview by highlighting the country's indigenous cultural heritage. A middle-class woman—a teacher for many years—agreed. "The type of dancing the National Company does wasn't showing anywhere respectable before," she noted. "It was seen as country things for the ordinary uncivilized person. That these have been brought in the focus of part of our heritage, and recognizing that they are valuable, have been the greatest contributions." Another woman took this idea one step further, invoking the nationalist premise that because Jamaicans "are as creative as any other group in the world" the state should promote the kinds of dance and music developed locally "and not just borrow from other people."

The sons and daughters of these men and women, however, appeared less moved. One young man countered the view that understanding the past provides direction for the future. "It's good to remember we are descendants of Africans," he said, "but living in Jamaica now it doesn't really affect us. I don't think it's important in a day to day way, doesn't affect our day to day life." He continued by directly contradicting the nationalist common sense regarding the development of self-esteem, arguing "The actions of our ancestors really don't have a great effect on self-esteem. I believe you decide your own destiny, and no one can have direct effect." Another young man invoked changes associated with intensified global economic integration and the effects these have had on people's ideas about the importance of the past in order to issue a critique of some of the more prominent nationalist cultural mobilizers:

> I think the African heritage is important, but I think that we're living in a world that is changing at such a great pace that although generations need to be made aware of it, it's not something that I think is of such great importance that a lot of time and resources need to be spent on it. Because a lot of it doesn't have any bearing on where you're going as a young person in Jamaica right now, going forward in this society or world that we live in. I think that there's an interest on the part of Rex Nettleford and a lot of the other academics and heavily culturally orientated persons from the university who believe that this is of vital importance. But that's because that's what they're into.

Surely, many would interpret these young people's comments as indications of the resurgence of conservatism (read, American materialism and individualism) and neoliberal capitalist development that had occurred subsequent to the 1980 elections. However, I believe this only accounts for part of their apparent indifference to a particular understanding of Africanness.

To an extent, any group of younger people that has come of age either during or after a period during which attitudes and the structures that support them have been challenged takes for granted the aspects of their lives the previous generation had struggled so diligently to change. Those youth quoted above grew up during the 1970s listening to the politicized and sometimes revolutionary lyrics of reggae music, which galvanized a new consciousness of racial and class identity as well as an awareness of Jamaicans' position within a global political economy. Moreover, Marcus Garvey's influence upon the development of an international (cross-class) black consciousness existed within community members' lifetimes and memories. As a result, as one younger middle-class man argued, "People's consciousness of what was African in them existed before you had the state ideology and state symbols." In other words, the "poorer sets" did not need the state to make links between the past and the present or to validate aspects of their cultural heritage in order to recognize their membership in a racial community. Their cynicism about state-driven cultural initiatives was rooted in their assessment that the state had not done much, in their eyes, to dismantle the institutionalized constraints facing them as they attempted to realize their ambitions within Jamaica. Rather than assuming, therefore, that the reason many among the poorer sets did not participate enthusiastically in the kinds of cultural development initiatives sponsored by the JCDC was that they were insecure as to the validity of their cultural practices, it would be reasonable to argue that they were skeptical about the relevance of holding on to "first time" practices because they questioned the link formulated between the preservation of the past and development in the present and future.

Where the unease with "things African" *has* been evident, I believe, was in the ways both middle- and lower-class community members often located development and civilization outside of Africa. Phillip, a retired middle-class brown man in his early sixties, argued, "Jamaica is more advanced at this particular stage than most of the African countries." He went on to buttress his assertion with examples he felt were important:

Their educational problems are worse than ours, and one of the benefits of the British thing here was that schools were run by churches. We were offered greater opportunity than in African countries. There, there were fewer opportunities and British treated them with less respect. Also, we're smaller so we don't have the hundreds and hundreds of illiterate and diseased persons. We have a smaller area in which to do what we have to do and so do it at a higher level. Culturally, we're more advanced. We have direct contact with the u.s. and u.k. which are supposed to be sources of enlightenment. We got a kick start in the modern era.

Here, this man unwittingly replicated colonial arguments linking imperialism with civilization and positioned colonialists and neocolonialists as the catalysts for a modernity marked by Christianization and education. African countries, in his view, being larger and less creolized—and here I use the term creolization to evoke the processes by which transported labor adapted to each other, to a new environment, and to a plantation socioeconomic system—have been more isolated from the kinds of "cultural advancements" that obtained in the West Indies.

Adele, the sixteen-year-old daughter of a hotel worker and a household helper, offered a somewhat different perspective, one that positioned Africa as a fount of (unchanging) cultural wisdom that might help her come to understand who she was vis-à-vis the rest of the world:

> I want to go to Africa because of what my daddy teach me about Rasta. I want to see it. I think that Africa is one of those countries that don't really give up their culture, even though all the rest of the world is turning to new things, they are still keeping the old things and they don't change. They say Africa is the motherland, and I think if I can go to see it I could see what it was like back then because they don't really change very much I don't think. If I see it, I think I'd have a better understanding of what is expected of me as a black person.

In both these assessments, Africa was portrayed not only as not modern, but as ahistorical. By corollary, civilization and enlightenment were Western—British, and lately, American. These kinds of views were partially shaped by negative media portrayals of the continent. As one man in his early fifties put it, "To tell the truth, when I see some of the atrocities going on in Africa, I'm not sure I want to be associated with that. When I look at the children, the suffering of the people, the backwardness, I think what has gone wrong?" In fact, one area of the village was nicknamed "South Africa." Villagers explained this moniker by referring to the more extreme poverty that characterized that part of the district. They felt that community members in "South Africa" were therefore always "warring" and that the children were neither properly clothed nor sufficiently fed—they had "stick-out bellies like the African pickney on TV." Still, villagers appreciated the historical context surrounding economic (under-) development in Africa. That is, their assessments of Africa's problems were not culturally based. Nevertheless, the difficulty of identifying with an African heritage based on what was known about the African present was noted again and again. Moreover, one man made the observation that this was not necessarily the case for Jamaicans descended from other ethnic groups. "If you call an Indian 'Indian,' or a Chinese man 'Chiney,' they recognize it," he argued, "but if you call a black man 'African,' he will say 'a who yuh a talk to, me nah African.'"

The Power of Blackness

While "Africanness" (understood primarily as a cultural identity) invoked a degree of ambivalence, "blackness" (a racial identity) remained an abiding and immediate concern. If consciousness of an African heritage operated primarily on a symbolic level, even within popular expressive culture, racial consciousness was continually reinforced through day to day experiences of color prejudice and discrimination, both in Jamaica and abroad. It also colored Jamaicans' interpretations of world history and current foreign policy, with Haiti standing as an important regional symbolic referent for the more general disenfranchisement of black people. For example, one poorer man in the village, in describing the tribulations facing black people worldwide, linked Haiti's current position to U.S. interference after the revolution in 1804 by explaining that "dem never get a chance to try dey own ting." This was a situation that, in his view, was institutionalized and therefore persisted via, for example, U.S. immigration policy. He compared the treatment of unskilled Haitian migrants to that of Cubans, pointing out that the United States has welcomed the latter because "Castro educate them" and because "dem brown, not black."

As I pointed out in chapters 3 and 4, racial consciousness among the "poorer sets" in Mango Mount was also reinforced through interactions with other local individuals and institutions. For example, Paulette, a woman in her early thirties from an established poorer family in Mango Mount, reflected on her own process of "coming to consciousness" about her heritage and history. She remembered that her parents did not emphasize a "black history" to her while she was growing up. Nevertheless, as she grew older, she began learning more about Jamaican history by listen-ing to Mutabaruka's radio show on IRIE-FM about African and diasporic history[20] and by reading about African Americans, information that was supplemented by the television programs broadcast during Black History Month. "They'd show certain programs on TV and I'd see how they'd handle black people, and I'd get so emotional that I'd turn off the TV," she recalled. "It's just recently I can really sit down and watch. I don't know if it's embarrassment or anger or what. I'd watch these programs and proba-bly go out on the road and see Mr. Simms and just hate him. I'd think, 'you're one of those.'" Paulette also mentioned that she would teach her daughter, who was three years old at the time, about black history in order that she "know and love herself," especially since she anticipated that her daughter would ultimately attend a university in the United States:

> It's important to let her know that OK, she's of a different color, but she has to love self however people might say that you're black so you're not beautiful. Even here now, people are bleaching out their skins and all of that. I have to make her know that regardless of what people might say [in the States], she will be proud of where she's coming from. Because I'm not going to grow her like how my parents just sort of had me and they never really sat and shared a lot of things with me. You have to make them know, and you do this by telling them about the history.

Paulette's personalization of aspects of the history of race relations in the Americas and her preparations for her daughter's expected migration speak to the more general processes by which the "poorer sets" assessed their positions and evaluated their options.

Indeed, Paulette's comments, and young Adele's earlier reflections about Africa, indicate that even among a younger generation, history matters in the development of personal and community consciousness. However, the aspects of history that mattered were those that were seen to provide insight into the kinds of structural inequalities faced by the "poorer sets" in Jamaica and elsewhere, as well as those moments of struggle that could inspire the pride needed for surviving through contemporary experiences of racial prejudice. While the reinstatement of Emancipation Day would appear to fall into the latter category, it did not catalyze the same degree of interest locally as other representations of African descended peoples throughout the Americas such as, notably, the television miniseries Roots. It is my contention here that this is because the majority of the public discourse surrounding the reestablishment of Emancipation Day framed emancipation not primarily as the liberation of black people in Jamaica, but as the first step on the road to national freedom through political independence. Because many poorer community members viewed the achievement of political independence in 1962 as an unfulfilled promise, they have tended to be cynical of cultural development initiatives that foreground the formation of an independent Jamaican state. As a result, while history mattered, community members' assessments of the presentation of that history often challenged the assertion that in order for the majority of the population to develop self-esteem and a sense of national belonging, it was necessary to engage them with events in their history and their cultural heritage with which they should identify. Framed in national rather than racial terms, villagers in Mango Mount—like the audience member in Spanish Town who shouted "we nuh free yet"—found it difficult to reconcile the institutionalized constraints they faced daily as citizens with the rhetoric of national freedom and progress.

Unlike members of the nationalist intelligentsia, poorer community members did not hesitate to evoke "blackness" within the context of discussing the meaning of emancipation. Indeed, Paulette was not alone in the matter-of-fact way she discussed racial politics and interactions. Where color and race have been touchy subjects in the Jamaican public sphere, as among many of the middle- and upper-middle-class village residents, the "poorer class of people" showed a willingness to discuss "blackness" openly and to equate "blackness" with "Jamaicanness." This is not to say that "blackness" was not often used locally among the "poorer sets" as a signifier either for radical consciousness or for poverty, stupidity, or ugliness in informal, and often joking, contexts, again usually based on a local understanding that worldwide, "black people always at the bottom of the ladder." These were not, however, community members' only referents for blackness, which ultimately also signified community and an idealized egalitarianism, despite the kinds of constraints to this egalitarianism I documented in chapters 3 and 4.

Here, villagers' perceptions of Rastafarians are significant since they were seen locally as embodying both an African and a black consciousness. While several villagers expressed the opinion that the handful of Rastas within Mango Mount were "more loving and cooperative than the average Jamaican," they also differentiated between those they saw as "authentic"—the "real Rastas" who "carry the religion"—and those who had adopted the hairstyle and the posture but who had "dutty, nasty ways" due to their involvement with the international drug trade and tourism industries. Bev, an upwardly mobile woman in her early thirties, remembered that when she was younger she had wanted to attend art school, but that her family didn't support this "because a lot of people felt that if you're in the arts, you're probably a Rastafarian." Here, Bev pointed to the links many poorer Jamaicans had come to make between Rasta, Africa, and culture, with "culture" here used to signify both expressive cultural production and an anti-imperialist way of life removed from the corrupting influences of "Babylon." She continued by evoking the additional link, then current, between the latter lifestyle and illicit drug use: "People thought that once you went to art school, you'd eventually be drawn into culture so much that you'd end up with a dreadlocks. And that was a no-no for my family. Rasta was like the talk of the times. If you say Rasta, you just doomed. As long as you're Rasta them just label you as druggist. It's a little different now."

Despite the fact that Rasta had become more locally acceptable during the previous twenty years, it was also true that negative evaluations of Rastafarians' physical appearance had endured. For example, one day Winsome's five-year-old daughter was playing in my hair and said she thought dreadlocks were ugly. Winsome asked her if she was saying I was ugly, and she answered no, but that other people's locks were. This sentiment was echoed and clarified by a farmer in his sixties who argued that "brown people" with dreadlocks look nice, but that black people who wear dreadlocks don't. Instead, they look "powerful" and scary. I asked if I couldn't look powerful, and he said no, because I'm brown.[21] Other negative references to blackness were most common when villagers were describing other people (e.g., "that person good-looking, she brown"), commenting on class-coded behaviors that seemed out of place (e.g., "you too brown fi go barefoot"), or noting a desire for someone, the latter being related to the extent to which it is believed that people with lighter complexions have money, education, or other assets that could lead to social mobility.

Here, several older women identified a gender bias, pointing out that while black men could express their attraction to lighter-skinned women, if black women pursued lighter-skinned men, black men would argue that they were being racist. This bias is related to the well-documented ways in which beauty as well as notions of femininity and respectability have been associated with (high) color (Barnes 1997; Douglass 1992; Edmondson

1999; Ulysse 1999). However, while colonial associations between color, expectations regarding practice, and ideas about beauty, femininity, and respectability have persisted, there also existed alternative frames of reference by which people evaluated each other. As Gina Ulysse has pointed out, for example, due to the entrance of large numbers of poor women into the often lucrative informal importing sector and to the ways that dancehall culture has provided a space to redefine notions of beauty and sexiness, "Many lower-class females consciously reject the middle and upper-class ideals of beauty . . . and reassert their own notions because the former are not simply unattainable, but also undesirable" (1999:167). The point Ulysse makes here regarding the ways "downtown women" negotiate dual notions of beauty can also help us to understand the divergent attitudes regarding "folk blackness" and "modern blackness" between members of the nationalist intelligentsia and the "poorer class of people" in Mango Mount, and among Mango Mount community members themselves.

I'd like to return, for a moment, to the variety of audience responses to the local performances during the community's Emancipation Day celebration in order to reconsider the premise advanced by nationalist cultural mobilizers that the majority of black Jamaicans lacked self-esteem and a sense of belonging and that this lack was rooted in their insecurity vis-à-vis the validity of their own cultural heritage. I want to suggest that if the focus were shifted slightly toward the ways individuals within the "poorer sets" *actively negotiated* the value of their cultural practices, instead of assuming a *passive* insecurity, then it would be clear that black lower-class Jamaicans continually evaluated their own and others' cultural practices not only in terms of their history, but also in relation to a contemporary global political economy of value. In this way, they recognized—sometimes reproducing and sometimes critiquing—the aesthetic and behavioral value judgments against which their practices were measured. Recognition, here, did not imply resignation, but was the basis for the ways they analyzed the relationships between color, class, gender, behavior, and "culture."

For example, during the girls' readings from the "Footprints on the Road to Emancipation" series, audience members applauded "proper" English and reading prowess while heckling patois and semiliteracy. This suggests that within the genre of public speaking, a standard English form has been adopted and valued.[22] But there, of course, are gendered and class dimensions of this adoption. Though patois is the lingua franca of both men and women in the "poorer class of people," it has only recently become acceptable in some public fora as a hallmark of Jamaican identity. This is, in part, because among middle-class Jamaicans, patois was differentially learned. Boys tended to pick it up more than girls— because, as people argued, "they are in the street more"—and because it was assumed that when they became adults, they would use it to communicate with their employees more effectively. Girls, on the other hand, were still admonished to speak "properly."[23] In this setting, then, a public performance of the standard history of emancipation in Jamaica, Standard Jamaican English was privileged over patois. In contrast, in other arenas such as dance and music, fluency in the "vernacular" form was given higher value than fluency in the standard official form. In other words, among the "poorer set," you were seen as a good dancer if you knew the latest popular dancehall moves and could perform them with agility and personal style. Dance was not defined as a formally choreographed activity, but as individual innovation within the established vernacular framework. Singing was not choral or directed, but was an interpretation, sometimes verbatim, of a popular song everyone knew. Acting was not necessarily a formally written and staged play, but a skit with recognizable local themes and characters.

This does not mean, however, that the "poorer class of people" did not also recognize and acknowledge the officially sanctioned performing arts as legitimate representations of Jamaican culture. That is, they knew that the JCDC and the NDTC were organizations designed to represent Jamaican culture both internally and internationally. Yet the majority of the "poorer sets" in Mango Mount had neither seen the NDTC perform live nor participated in any of the Company's outreach programs and therefore didn't see the Company as having anything to do with their lives. And while the JCDC was more familiar to community members, largely because of the National Festival of the Arts, poorer villagers most often translated the JCDC's vision regarding Jamaican cultural development into more individual and local terms. By this, I mean that even when community members had themselves participated in the JCDC-sponsored National Festival of the Arts or in the Grand Gala at the National Stadium on Independence Day as part of the Rangers, Girl Guides, or Boy Scouts,[24] they didn't tend to tie their participation into a broader discourse regarding the development of their own nationalist consciousness. What is especially significant here is that community members critiqued these kinds of cultural development organizations by arguing that their relevance as institutions depended upon engaging more fully with the popular cultural forms with which they were familiar and in which they participated. This critique complicates Bourdieu's (1984) reading of the relationship between a socially recognized hierarchy of the arts and a socially recognized hierarchy of consumers. In this context, "high art" was represented by the concert dance performed by the NDTC. However, because the NDTC was supposed to reflect a national culture, and because community members saw themselves as those who most legitimately represented the Jamaican nation, their critique of the NDTC contained the kernel of the hierarchy's undoing. In this way, they foregrounded a definition of belonging to the Jamaican community that had, at its foundation, class and cultural practices usually associated with urban (and cosmopolitan) black people, caveats regarding Jamaica as a nation of "mixed multitudes" notwithstanding.

Conclusion: Emancipating Blackness

What I am suggesting here is that many poorer community members' lack of engagement with some of the very practices depicted as central aspects of Jamaica's (African) cultural heritage by the state and by organizations such as the NDTC and JCDC can be read as something other than a lack of self-esteem. As one younger villager put it, "Tradition [is] not an intelligence thing." In other words, the skills involved in performing renditions of cultural practices associated with the past were not seen as particularly useful in the contemporary context. In my codirector's original concept for the play, "tradition" was apparently also not a "progress thing," since she envisioned the newly captured slave *chastising* the other slaves for attempting to secure their freedom by means of an obeah ritual, arguing that "first time" practices like obeah couldn't provide road maps for the future. At the same time, her original script outline recognized these African-derived dance and music practices as having provided entertainment for those in the planter class. Again, good enough to showcase, but not good enough to live by.

Why not? Why is it that many Mango Mount community members viewed rural Afro-Jamaican cultural practices as backward rather than as instruments through which to reclaim a history? Because their social worlds were increasingly urban and transnational and because they had apprehended the fundamental disjuncture between political and economic development strategies and cultural development initiatives (look back, take pride, but move forward). As such, villagers appreciated (and reproduced) middle-class expectations with respect to progress and modernization via education, even where these expectations had not been reinforced by actual experience, and even though they maintained practices and exhibited a creativity that might not have been considered "cultured" by middle-class standards. They acknowledged the value of middle-class values, so to speak, based on their assessment of what would be necessary for them to "move forward in life." This acknowledgment, coupled with the more consumerist ethos associated with community members' own expectations regarding black progress, entailed a rejection of what "first time" people did, at least in part.

This is not to say that on the infrequent occasions when traditional events were held, they were not well attended and heartily enjoyed. For instance, the death of a well-known and well-respected resident of a neighboring community was heralded by a nine-night celebration that was talked about enthusiastically for weeks afterward.[25] This particular celebration had something for everyone—a reggae and dancehall session adjacent to the drumming and singing circle—and stood, therefore, as an example of how "first time" practices are continually adapted and transformed. Nevertheless, as past practices, they were not integral to the day-to-day social fabric of life on the hill. They were also often associated with an agricultural lifestyle and labor relations that younger villagers did not see as modern, desirable, or lucrative, a lifestyle that they did not perceive as germane to success within the contemporary global political economy. Can we therefore assume, as Don Robotham has suggested, that black Jamaicans want blackness as an identity, but a blackness understood as "modern?" Urban, not rural? Educated and professional, not "folk?" In other words, do they want a blackness able to hold its own in the white world of global capitalism? Robotham sees this as exactly what should be expected from a black diasporic population "who owe their very location in Jamaica to the long history of international capitalism; who do not have an autochthonous tradition; and who are deeply embedded in the global system" (1998b:30). Even the Jamaica's Jubilee authors were anxious to demonstrate to a British public how far they had "progressed" in the fifty years between emancipation in 1838 and the book's publication in 1888, how much they had adopted modern ways of life.

Indeed, given the recent changes in Jamaica's political economy, we should *expect* that the "poorer sets" in Mango Mount would not perceive the aspects of Jamaica's cultural heritage promoted by state institutions and other nationalist elites as fully relevant to, or representative of, their current experiences. We should *expect* that the "poorer sets" would not look to the rural models of folk culture that have been presented by the nationalist intelligentsia to represent themselves or to provide them with inspiration or understanding about why things are the way they are now. And we should take seriously the racialized visions of progress and modernity they espouse as alternatives, visions that are preeminently transnational.

PART III

The Local-Global

chapter 6

POLITICAL ECONOMIES OF MODERNITY

I think because Jamaica was settled to make money, to be a factory, people who were brought here were brought here because of their economic utility. They were brought here to work. And in that sense, it was the first experiment in modern industrial relations, and because they were such small islands you could get total societies. Societies that were totally about modern industrial relations, or almost. And then when you consider what happened in the late nineteenth century after emancipation, with the freeing of this labor from the bonds of the plantation, and then this labor just generally going off wherever in the world to labor, some of it, quite a large proportion of it, went elsewhere. Jamaica has always had people going elsewhere and looking for work. What you have there is something very modern. It's people saying OK, this is a good option, this is a reasonable option, I am labor, I am going where I will be paid. To me, that's a very modern concept of who you are and what your meaning is in terms of the social and economic order of things. And these people were prepared to lift up out of Jamaica and go to Panama, where they don't speak the language, and go to the States or to England, where it's cold, just pick up and go. That is an incredibly modern idea. In most countries, people don't make those kinds of international decisions. They make very local decisions. Jamaica was modernized very early as a labor pool. A long time before it was recognized anywhere else.

When I started traveling through Africa and Asia, it changed my interpretation of history from the one I had, which was a very deterministic interpretation, that is, the idea that we are the way we are because of slavery or because of this or because of that. Instead, I started to get this impression that, in fact, these are very new, very modern, very unusual societies in the Caribbean. Not so much because of the racial mix, but because of this thing of everybody coming from somewhere else, being one of the few places in the world where everybody comes from somewhere else. And people have picked and chosen their traditions. I was very surprised to see in various countries in West Africa things that I recognized from here, and then realizing all the stuff we didn't keep or didn't take. On the one hand, I could say that we lost that, that the reason we don't have all these traditions is because they were lost, not permitted in slavery. But then in going to India and Pakistan and other places, you suddenly realize that the Indians, the Chinese, they had a lot more choice. They came in a more semi-free way. They could bring families with them. And yet they didn't bring their culture wholesale. They dropped a whole bunch of stuff as quickly as possible, by choice it seems to me. So my impression started to be that Jamaica and the Caribbean are these terribly free societies, that we have this tremendous freedom because we are without tradition. And that changed my view from the idea that traditions were lost or destroyed, particularly those of African descendants. I felt that, no, actually this is great. Tradition pretty much stinks and this is exactly what you want to be able to do. And that people who actually live in ancient cultures and in their own history have a big problem because it's so hard to modernize, it's so hard to change. And a lot of the things about the modern world, particularly the value on the individual as against the community, is just incredibly hard, particularly for young people, and there's a tremendous stress. This is very different from my experience growing up in Jamaica which was almost that we think flux and change are normal. Our language changes, our music changes, and nobody thinks that's a big deal. And then you realize in other places, when this sort of thing happens, there's a whole body of the community that feels alienated and that this shouldn't be happening and tries to prevent it. This process that we've gone through and the way of our society is something that is happening all over the world now. There's tremendous migration of people, there's tremendous mixing of races. So really, the Caribbean experience is in a way just a distillation of something that is now becoming a terribly common experience whether you're from Bali or South America, you know? This is becoming almost characteristic of our modern societies, people who don't live in their own country. So I stopped thinking that we were more unique, but that maybe we've just gone through this first.

These lengthy interview quotes, musings on modernity offered by two of the middle-class children raised in Mango Mount currently in their thirties, introduce the main preoccupations of part 3: What does it mean to be modern? How should modernity be achieved? How should it be represented? Here, both Matthew and Virginia suggest that Jamaica's modernity is rooted in the dialectical relationship between postemancipation negotiations of capitalist labor relations internationally and the constancy and change of cultural practices. Indeed, community members—and Jamaicans more generally—are intensely aware of their own relationships to a changing global political economy. This last section explores how this awareness influences Jamaicans' evaluations of their political options, their economic opportunities, their social potential, and their cultural choices. It also examines how community members' entanglements with contemporary processes of globalization have influenced their assessments and representations of nation and race—Jamaicanness and blackness, as well as their sense of both social and physical place—locally, nationally, regionally, and globally. Part 3, therefore, explores and explicitly defines the transition I've been flagging throughout the earlier sections of this book as a public shift from the creole multiracial nationalism that was consolidated in the mid-twentieth century to what I call the "modern blackness" of the late 1990s. These two chapters concretize the constituent parts of "modern blackness"; that is, they define both modernity and blackness from the perspectives of Mango Mount community members. Ultimately, part 3 considers some of the implications of the public ascendance of modern blackness for both nationalist institutions and alternative grassroots ideological and material expressions of belonging.

At the end of the previous chapter, I argued that community members' lack of meaningful and consistent attachment to the "folk blackness" promoted by nationalist cultural mobilizers was the result of their own increasingly urban and transnational experiences. These experiences have led them to apprehend a disjuncture between the Jamaican government's increased adherence to policies facilitating intensified global capitalist articulation and the cultural development strategies pursued by the state and other independent institutions. In this chapter, I want to enrich this picture by providing a window into community members' own definitions of political and economic modernity in order to demonstrate that analytically speaking, people's political and economic ambitions on one hand and their sociocultural beliefs and practices on the other cannot be reduced to a one-to-one relationship. For example, despite villagers' disillusionment with the promises of independence, we are confronted with an intense yet taken-for-granted commitment to the idea of political autonomy. And though intensified "Americanization" often topped community members' lists of negative changes since Jamaica's independence in 1962, we nevertheless must come to terms with the increased desire—especially among youth—to consume American products and to enter into a migratory cycle to the United States, whether temporary, seasonal, or permanent. These contradictions, if we choose to label them as such, are not unique to the experiences of Mango Mount community members, but face us all. The challenge here is twofold. First, we need to understand seemingly contradictory responses such as those listed above as part of the two-sidedness of processes of globalization themselves, especially when these processes are experienced from the vantage point of people who have long been marginalized from global centers of power, yet integral to the creation and maintenance of their dominance. Second, we must develop a nuanced analysis that clarifies the ways people manipulate and take advantage of the structures of opportunity surrounding them—sometimes transforming and sometimes reproducing relations of power and inequality—rather than positioning people either as duped or as powerless to resist, reinvent, or renovate.

This chapter begins by outlining the various dimensions of community members' increasing lack of faith in the nationalist project, ultimately teasing out the ways villagers have experienced and assessed the changes in Jamaica's political economy that were outlined in chapter two. By examining community debates and expectations regarding economic development and modernization, we get a sense of the various strategies that were employed by poorer villagers to "move forward in life." These strategies were differently pursued based on individuals' status and gender, but across the board, the most prominent among them was migration. Ultimately this was a strategy that was supported by the intensified privatization and capitalist integration of the 1980s and 1990s. One of the results of community members' migration was that poorer Mango Mount youth depended to a lesser extent upon the contacts and resources of the local middle-class population than did their parents because they were often able to advance their own educational and economic ambitions by leaving the village rather than through improving its infrastructure. As a result, these community members' strategies for advancement were less mediated in the late 1990s than they had been during the 1950s and 1960s. This generational shift is key because it also influences the balance of power between a nationalist ideology of respectable progress through education and a working-class ideology of progress through the generation of wealth.

Dreams Deferred

When asked to define how Jamaica became politically independent in 1962 and what this independence meant for the population, Mango Mount community members offered up a range of arguments that parallel those ordinarily advanced by scholars. For example, several middle-class villagers connected Jamaica's independence to England's declining position in a global economy, arguing that "Britain had made up its mind that it couldn't afford a colonial empire." Andrew, a retired civil servant in his late fifties, argued that "independence wasn't good or bad but was inevitable, long before World War II started:"

> The British decided they were going to dispense with Empire, and there were pressures for independence long before it was ever attained. Behind the scenes, the Americans were prodding the Brits to get rid of empire because Americans regard colonialism as tantamount to original sin.

Not everyone, however, rooted their opinions in economic expediency. Many community members nuanced this kind of reading by highlighting the dialectical nature of the decolonization process. For instance, a mason in his early forties indicated that "*People recognized the need*, and Britain couldn't really bother to have Jamaica pon them plate anymore." And a middle-class secretary in her late forties argued that "Britain was getting rid of her obligations at the same time that *all colonies worldwide were beginning to fight to be rid of outside control*" (emphasis added). The inevitability of independence was also invoked by a woman in her late sixties who had worked her entire life as a domestic helper. "Independence was a good thing," she said. "If it don't even good to wi, we have to take it." Implied within her statement is the acknowledgment that political independence was seen as a necessary strategy for recognition among an international community of nations, an understanding made more explicit by other Mango Mount community members.[1] "To be a part of the world systems, you have to be independent," a mechanic in his mid-thirties noted. "At least we know seh we a Jamaicans." This view was echoed by Matthew, who defined political independence as facilitating Jamaica's entrance within powerful networks, both locally and internationally: "The world expects you to have a nationality, expects you to have a passport and a place where you come from. If you are independent, then you can, within your own environment, form relationships with power. That's what independence is about. Whereas if you are a colony, by definition within your own environment, you can never form relationships with power."

These community members' remarks demonstrate an ideological attachment to nationalism, a taken-for-granted acceptance of the idea that the politically sovereign nation is the most appropriate and inevitable form of social organization within a modern world. Their attachment to this idea was rooted in their convictions that it was better to "manage your own affairs" than to be "governed by remote control," and that it was essential to aspire to determining "your own agenda inasmuch as the rest of the world will allow it:"

> A lot of people saying it better if we were still under England. But then, I have to look pon it from a African standpoint. Because way down ina Jamaica, living under some other people rules, Jamaica don't really belong to us. So it is better for we to rule weself and make mistake than people ruling over you. As a nation, you've got to determine your own way. Because even England want to keep themselves a England, right? American love American first and everybody after. And learning what all went down, every nation should try to control tings for themselves.

These kinds of comments demonstrate the pervasive power of the *idea* of nationalism, a power that is evident in its having become common sense.

Community members located the *real* power of nationalism, however, in both the practical and psychological effects that were expected to accompany independence, effects that many villagers experienced as intertwined. For example, community members argued that independence enabled more Jamaicans to gain access to land that had previously been owned privately, to attain a "certain amount of civil liberties," and to have opportunities—such as government service in positions previously filled by the British—that "removed that feeling of subservience" and "helped develop self-respect," particularly for those among the middle classes. Moreover, they argued compellingly that independence allowed for the more profound self-actualization of individuals. However, community members also argued that independence was to have transformed Jamaica's social and economic hierarchies. Because this expectation has remained largely unmet, villagers expressed a more general disillusionment with the creole multiracial nationalist project. This disillusionment was rooted in community members' belief that their positions within Jamaica's socioeconomic hierarchy had not significantly changed since independence and that therefore political autonomy had not been instrumentally beneficial to the majority of the (black) population.

Disillusionment among the population with the promises of nationalism was not limited to the community of Mango Mount. Since independence, several local and international scholars have noted high levels of cynicism among the population vis-à-vis the nationalist project. In fact, two sociological studies conducted during the early and mid-1960s culled opinions from both "elites" and grassroots leaders, as well as "lower class" respondents, that would also be echoed later by Mango Mount villagers (Bell 1964; Mau 1968). The findings of both these studies suggest that during the years immediately after independence, Jamaicans did not see the political transition as having resulted in any significant change in the economic and social spheres of life.[2] These sentiments did not wane with time, nor was their expression limited to academic work.[3] The main complaints articulated within the scholarship and within newspaper editorials—continued eurocentrism among the Jamaican elite and middle classes; lack of economic growth, autonomy, and compensation; and persistent violence, repression, and brutality—were also advanced by Mango Mount community members. In a somewhat rhetorical give and take, Mr. and Mrs. Williams summed up the opinion of many villagers quite simply:

MR. W: What have we achieved since independence?
MRS. W: Nothing.
MR. W: What we get?
MRS. W: Hardship.

The belief that nothing had changed positively for black Jamaicans since independence persisted despite the assertion of a few that since independence opportunities for educational and economic advancement had, in fact, grown. Even those who emphasized that independence made it possible for many poorer Jamaicans to have unprecedented access to educational and occupational opportunities were quick to point out that these individual gains had not translated into a fundamental shift in power relations on a national level. Nor had they altered Jamaica's disadvantageous position within a global hierarchy of nations. Community members concluded, therefore, black people worldwide were still unable to control substantial resources other than their own labor, despite some changes within Jamaica's political economy since the 1960s and despite the accession of P. J. Patterson to the leadership of the People's National Party (PNP) in 1991.

Indeed, many poorer Mango Mount community members had expected that the achievement of political independence would have been, in some way, a fulfillment of a racial destiny begun with the abolition of slavery. That is, they felt that independence should have bestowed a more total emancipation upon the majority of the population. "Independence was the fulfillment of the wishes of our ancestors for full freedom," Anthony asserted, "freedom to carry on life without having to answer to oppressors, freedom to live life without restrictions." Adele also argued, "Independence was a great thing because without it, black people wouldn't really know where they are coming from or where they are going." She continued by indicating that while independence was important for "the black nation" because it connoted the attainment of equality with "the other nation, the other race, the white man, the Chiney, the Indian," this vision had been thwarted. "It hasn't really turned out that way," Adele lamented. Adele's father Trevor elaborated upon her point. "For our likkle nation, maybe one of the most important thing, speaking from the African standpoint, is having a black prime minister," he said. "I think most African hopes did kind of go up. But I don't see where he being there bring anything good for the people dem because things remain as they were." Here, we are confronted with a sense of political impotence, with a vision of promises unkept. Because poorer community members felt that their expectations of social transformation and racial reparation were frustrated —even with the election of a black prime minister—many like Trevor were cynical regarding the commemoration of independence:

> Me see people a celebrate independence, road march business and street march business. But we look on those ting now with a critical eye. You understand? Because learning what went down, the simplest ting is for them to put on a jump up business to distract you from the real issue. Getting independence from England is one thing, but celebrating it, what we celebrating? Yes, physically them nuh hold us anymore, right? And mentally, we can figure out one and two things weself, but them still hold you. Economically, them hold you same way. Because we still have to work hard for them and them still nuh waan pay we. You still haffi buy them clothes and you still haffi buy them tings because we're not producing for weself as a people. So what are we celebrating?

Middle-class Mango Mount residents typically advanced similar arguments regarding the lack of a fundamental transformation in social relations since independence. Andrew went as far as to say that there had been no significant changes in the relations of power within Jamaica since the slavery period: "In the eighteenth century, people at the top lived in perpetual fear of a slave uprising. Now in 1997, the people at the top live in perpetual fear of a slave uprising. In two hundred years, the social situation hasn't changed a whit. The solution is to emigrate." Here, Andrew portrayed Jamaica's social, economic, and political hierarchies as hopelessly static, with the only hope for transformation being rooted in individuals (who migrate), not in collectivities (who remain). Virginia's sister, an economist in her mid-thirties, also asserted that apart from the replacement of Britain with the United States as the primary external influence, Jamaica hadn't changed that much since its independence. "There are still the same nice things, there are the same tensions," she said. "Jamaica's still very violent, music is still the main cultural expression in people's lives, we still eat the same food, the same institutions are still here, there are still the same schools." Her conclusion, therefore, was that Jamaica was still in the period of change that began when she was a child. As evidence of this assertion, she noted that middle-class Jamaicans still attempted to maintain their positions by emphasizing their "values" and background, and that poorer Jamaicans, to some degree, also accepted these principles as the proper measures of status and potential. Andrew added that despite the revised constitution that was adopted at independence, Jamaica's fundamental "social fabric" remained largely unchanged during the first decade of political sovereignty:

> The only exception was in the civil service, which was known as the avenue for advancement, but even there, the upper ranks were brown rather than black. This sort of thing didn't change a lot during the 1960s. Because the economy was expanding, blacks started businesses, but on the whole, commerce remained in the hands of the people who had always controlled it. In the 1970s, black people sort of finally found their feet in all branches. Still, it was due to the erratic policies of Michael Manley and his so-called government, which led many to leave the island with his esoteric brand of socialism. Now, we have an esoteric brand of capitalism. Since independence, we've had a lot of commercial development, and it's hard to believe that with such enormous growth, we've moved backwards economically per capita. There has been no corresponding development of basic infrastructure. Education hasn't improved and has probably gotten worse, because politicians are frightened by the idea of an educated population, and quite a lot of politicians aren't very educated themselves.

Like most Jamaicans, Andrew evoked the 1970s and Michael Manley's experiment with democratic socialism and renewed popular political education as the main period during which there was an attempt toward significant socioeconomic and political transformation. However, he was also quick to indict Manley's policies as "esoteric," impractical, and therefore unsustainable. Several poorer Mango Mount community members also remembered the 1970s as a "failure," indicating that it was difficult to sustain revolutionary ideologies and practices when "a man haffi go home to him wife who will tell him his pickney hungry." Despite these difficulties, poorer and middle-class community members agreed that the social policies that were initiated during the 1970s (but largely dismantled during the 1980s) had been designed to improve the conditions of poor, black Jamaicans, especially women. Middle-class villagers, in particular, looked with scorn upon those with resources and skills who "abandoned" Jamaica during this period.

Nevertheless, several middle-class community members also perceived that the increased politicization of black and brown Jamaicans during the 1970s, though generally positive, resulted in an increased animosity between black and non-black Jamaicans. For example, Mr. Simms, the white landowner and guesthouse proprietor who had been involved with the Community Council, remembered that "anyone who was brought up to believe in Fabian socialism believed that the world was moving towards a state where there was universal good will, that countries were going to be governed for the good of everybody, that we would be able to look after everybody from the cradle to the grave." Mr. Simms had been in England during World War II and was profoundly influenced by the ideas underpinning the growth of the British welfare state at that time. When he returned to Jamaica, he was an ardent supporter of Norman Manley. "He was just the kind of man who should have been guiding Jamaica," he asserted. "Without question, I voted for the PNP in the first three elections, but when we got independence and we didn't get into PNP hands, it still seemed the JLP had good ideas. So when we changed governments again in the 1970s, I hadn't appreciated that there was going to be all this hatred generated [toward white and other Jamaicans who weren't black]. It came as a surprise to have people shouting at you, treating you as an enemy. I didn't feel I was anybody's enemy."

Virginia framed this increased public hostility and the long-term impact of the significantly different development approach that was attempted during the 1970s as the result of efforts by those who were able to garner a modicum of power after independence to simultaneously maintain and obscure their new public status. She argued that after independence, "brown" Jamaicans were able to snatch some of the positions previously held by white Jamaicans or colonial representatives. "They couldn't own anything," she explained, "but they could be in the civil service and in politics, as long as they recognized the dominance of the white Jamaican." She continued to say that during the 1970s, Manley "threw that whole system up in the air, and that's why people either love him or hate him." What ensued, in her estimation, was a battle to realign Jamaica's ethnic division of labor that was fought in terms of culture and values:

> Manley exposed that there was a struggle going on, that the majority of people didn't like their place. Once middle-class people began to feel threatened, they began to say what they really thought. They tried to define all of the other groups in terms that could never change. Like black people, they're stupid, ignorant, they just think about money, they're violent, they have too many children. That's their box and if we could just keep them in that little box everything would be fine. What happened in the seventies is that a lot of black people "got out of their place" while others were trying to maintain their place in the system. A lot of black people started their own businesses and got good jobs and made a lot of money and so on, totally out of their place. And Chinese people went into banking, which was a white people thing. A lot of what's happening now is people trying to go back to pre-1972, people settling racial scores about all these people who got out of their place, particularly the black businessmen.

Here, Virginia was setting the socioeconomic stage for the ideological battle that she saw as having persisted from the colonial period through to contemporary times. She defined "staying in one's place" as following the rules, rules that had been set by a British colonial system intent on maintaining white superiority and economic dominance. Moreover, she evoked the sort of "ghost hegemony" Williams discusses (1991) by pointing out the difficulty of working outside of these "rules":

> A lot of black Jamaicans also have a very strong sense of the rules as well, and that's where a lot of the envy and distrust of a lot of Jamaicans who have made it comes from because so many people, I think, are brought up with this idea of [staying] in your place. It's like, "I've been good and I've stayed in my place and he's wrong, he shouldn't have what he has, he shouldn't have been successful because that was not what was there for us." And then the people who have made it look around and they see

that that's what people's attitude is to them, that people really think that the person who is lighter skinned than they are really is better, that people feel more attached to his success than to yours. So I think a lot of the insecurity and all that comes out of us not having found our way past this sort of British system, and this thing that was told to us about each of the races and what you can do, what's your place.

Despite the intense—and in many cases, still visceral—responses generated by the mention of Manley's PNP of the 1970s, the initiatives of the decade appeared in both middle-class and poorer community members' more general comments about change since independence as blips, however positive and meaningful, within a longer narrative of economic marginalization and social stagnation. As a result, one factor uniting all Mango Mount community members—men and women, young and old, "upper sets" and "poorer sets"—was a sense that their expectations of political independence had not been met.[4] Their comments suggested a common ideal vision of general social equality, of a nation in which the black majority would have greater access to state power and education, as well as greater control over economic resources. Their common vision, therefore, was one of institutional change, of a dismantled colonial class and race structure and of the attenuation of some of the values that support this structure. However, they felt that despite this vision, Jamaica's colonial color, class, gender, and culture nexus had endured and continued to constrain people's potential for socioeconomic mobility. As a result, community members' ideological attachment to the idea that nations should be independent had not been matched by enough experience that independence was instrumentally beneficial to the majority of the (black) population. For this reason, many believed that Jamaica would have been better off had it remained under British colonial rule.

"Bad to Bad, at Least We Woulda Had Someone fi Look after We"

Though many older villagers remembered that at the time of independence, they felt that being "ruled by Jamaicans" would have been better than retaining British colonial rule "since they born here and know about Jamaica," their experiences since independence have led them to conclude that the country was not "ready" for independence because its leaders were "never mature enough." As a gardener in his mid-forties argued, "From these people run the country things shabby. All they do is twist up the people dem brain, give all the man dem guns to kill off each other. It's not that Jamaicans can't do better," he continued, "They can do it. But some wrong business a gwaan." Another community member, a retired laborer in his early seventies, even argued that British colonial rule was better for black people. "If the white people woulda rule wi, we'd be better off," he insisted. "Them have more sympathy." These kinds of arguments bring us back to the way community members' chose leaders of local institutions such as the Community Council in chapter 4. There, it was noted that in a situation of limited resources, those not enmeshed in a system of exchange guided by kinship ties—and within a national democratic context, party allegiances—were often seen as fairer and more disinterested with respect to distributing what resources existed. Furthermore, the perception that the British colonial office was more "sympathetic" to the concerns of black people living in Jamaica is not unlike the view put forward in chapter 1 whereby the Queen (and, by extension, the British government) was seen as protecting the interests of the slaves and ex-slaves from direct persecution by local elites. In other words, the argument that outsiders' "rule" would be better for poor, black Jamaicans has had a long history.[5]

The vagaries of both local and national political leadership notwithstanding, the most common reason villagers gave to explain their belief that Jamaica should have remained a colony was an economic one. That is, in their assessment, "England money big," and by corollary, Jamaica's money was "small" in the global political economy. In the main, community members felt that since independence, the cost of living had risen to a level at which people were no longer able to meet their basic needs. Many felt that this would not have happened had the pound remained Jamaica's local currency. One younger Mango Mount resident extended this argument to say that "most countries, when they become independent, go bankrupt." Thus, despite an ideological consensus that independence was good and necessary, people's experiences since independence led them to determine that Jamaica "wasn't yet ready" for it.

Readiness, according to community members, was defined through education, economic development, and managerial experience. Several villagers maintained that at the time of independence, the educational system had not yet been sufficiently accessible to the majority of the population—"We were just beginning to get a chance to go to the better off schools"—and that, therefore, it only perpetuated a class-stratified system with respect to social, economic, and political mobility. Additionally, several middle-class and poorer villagers alike expressed the opinion that the majority of the population had not been sufficiently *politically* educated. That is, they felt that the majority of the population did not have a clear picture of their civic responsibilities, as voters and as workers, within an independent nation. Nor did many poorer community members feel that Jamaicans had been adequately informed of their rights, or lack thereof, as delineated within the constitution adopted at independence. Readiness was also often understood locally within an evolutionary framework. That is, one became "ready" for independence through tutelage by those more "civilized" or more experienced. For example, Claude, an upwardly mobile twenty-five-year-old from the "poorer sets" provided some insight into a belief that was also more generally held within Mango Mount:

> If we had developed, if we had remained with the British government, the country as a whole would be better off today socially and economically. Because they have hundreds of years of experience running countries and we had little or none. What we should have done is allowed slavery to totally abolish, and allow black people to climb the economical ladder. From that, we would say, yes, we have an experience. Then we could go out on our own.

What is especially significant about villagers' discourse on Jamaica's state of "unreadiness" or its lack of sufficient "development" or "modernity" prior to the attainment of political independence is that they used it to explain what they described as a more "general breakdown" locally in Mango Mount. That is, in their estimation, it was this lack of readiness that weakened Jamaica, preventing the government from being able to resist intensified global capitalist integration throughout the second half of the twentieth century and thwarting a more substantive transformation of Jamaica's power relations. The result of this, villagers noted, was an increased materialism and individualism that they attributed to the influence of the United States. One poorer Mango Mount resident argued that the pace of life in Jamaica had changed "due to how TV has opened us up so much." "We're Americanized," he said, "so you haffi move fast." Others, and especially older community members, mourned a loss of community spirit. As Evelyn, a black woman in her early sixties, lamented, "Nobody looks out for anybody again. Used to be you had to be responsible to any adult, but now the younger generation gets away with murder." Similarly, Evelyn's sister-in-law expressed the opinion that "Jamaicans were traditionally very caring people, but now that has changed and people mind their own business. Jamaicans have adapted so much American qualities," she continued, "and this is one of them." Men in Mango Mount made comparable remarks. Virginia's brother Raymond noted that "the community used to be much closer, but with the advent of, I guess, progress—in communications, in transportation—the younger people have grown up and don't care much about their neighbors and the area they live in, but are more interested in the fast life and fast cars." Likewise, Trevor argued that contemporary youth were a distinct generation due to their increased materialism and purported lack of "manners":

> Nowadays, the behavior of the people dem is totally different. People don't respect no form of principle. This generation just believe seh that plenty of ting we live by in olden times are not necessarily to them anymore. That is old time tings. A man will tell you seh him cyaan live offa good manners, or him cyaan go a supermarket with good behavior, so it is all going back to the materialistic way of thinking.

These kinds of sentiments—a sort of generational anti-individualist nostalgia—are neither new nor unique to Mango Mount. My sense, however, is that their intensity in the contemporary period is rooted in a feeling of acute powerlessness related to the new global challenges facing Jamaicans at the turn of the twenty-first century. At the same time, what scholars and community members alike refer to alternatively as globalization, neocolonialism, or the new imperialism was not the only cause of their powerlessness. Villagers also attributed the trends toward materialism and individualism to a political system they saw as having divided the country instead of unifying it.

"A Nuh People Mash up Jamaica, You Know. Yes People, but Mainly the Politicians"

As discussed earlier, one of the ideological tenets of the nationalism that developed in Jamaica during the 1940s was the assertion that Jamaicans were competent to run the nation because the leaders held the requisite formal and informal qualifications—education, proper socialization, and an ability in public affairs. Within the colonial context, these qualifications stood for equality in opposition to the prevailing notions of race and color, notions that connoted an essential inferiority or incompetence. However, vitriolic distrust was the most often expressed sentiment regarding politicians and Jamaica's political system at all levels of Mango Mount society in the late 1990s. Villagers argued that politicians kept all the money for themselves and didn't distribute it through their constituencies, bought multiple houses and cars instead of fixing roads, and only accounted for funds when the opposition asked them to. Community members described politicians as corrupt, dishonest, and selfish. Mr. James, the then president of the Community Council, painted a picture of Jamaican political leaders as power hungry and therefore as preventing the majority of the Jamaican population from achieving any sort of real self-determination:

> Thirty-five years ago we thought we were heading in a direction of prosperity, the eradication of poverty. We thought we were heading towards a situation where we would develop and have a particular identity of a Jamaican type development that was different from everywhere else. Today, although we have a stronger Jamaican identity and a greater recognition in the world than thirty-five years ago, as a country we are more impoverished. And at this point, I'm not sure we have a solution or know what directive we should take. We have allowed politicians to lead us how they want to lead and we have left our future to people who are selfish and only a few of whom have had any vision of what Jamaica should be or how to do it. We have allowed these politicians to develop a politics of power for themselves, of leadership and sovereignty over people, and Jamaican people as a whole have never really had political power. It has always been in the hands of a few, and the constitution has promoted this.

Other community members echoed this view, arguing that politicians didn't tend to link their own power to a sense of responsibility.

Moreover, despite the fact that Jamaica was often lauded within international fora for having regular and purportedly democratic transfers of political leadership, villagers indicated that they ultimately experienced these transfers as disruptions, since the ideological battles between the PNP and the Jamaica Labour Party (JLP) tended to mitigate against consistent policy development:

> Our problem with our politics is that after every five years if the party changes, you find that certain things that one party had started don't continue. I think that contributes to a lot of downfall with the Jamaican

economy because the opposition don't really follow up. PNP start this and it's a good program and the other party say "Bwoy, really and truly this was a good thing that the PNP was doing but because my leader say him nuh tink this ting a go work out," then they stop it. Or they don't want the other party to get the praise so they probably change the name of the program, start something new on it and mess up the whole thing.

Finally, on the whole, Mango Mount residents held politicians responsible for the increased crime and violence throughout Jamaican society. "The rise in crime was caused by the political parties dishing out all gun an dem tings dere," Anthony asserted. "We don't see the three of them warring. The people of Jamaica throwing stones at each other and they sit down drinking champagne while we out there killing each other."

Though villagers in Mango Mount linked many of Jamaica's problems to the actions of individual politicians, they nevertheless recognized that these individuals did not act independently of a global political and economic system. Mack, a laborer in his early thirties, issued an almost sympathetic indictment of Jamaica's political leaders. "Our leaders past and present had a responsibility to do the best job," he said. "But sometimes you start out good and end up bad because of bigger forces like America. If Busta [Alexander Bustamante] and [Norman] Manley did set the right trend, maybe it woulda end up all right, but maybe they were controlled by a bigger system." Here, we again see community members connecting Jamaica's lack of political autonomy directly to the influence of the United States, and to a global political and economic system in which Jamaica is positioned disadvantageously.

By now, it should be eminently clear that community members shared an acute awareness that the "local" was always conditioned by the "global" and that their disillusionment with the creole multiracial nationalist project had as much to do with their assessment that Jamaica's position within a global political and economic hierarchy has constrained independent action and economic growth, as it did with their condemnations of political mismanagement and corruption. Their primary frustration, then, was that political autonomy had not been matched by economic self-determination. An independent nation, they complained, was supposed to be self-reliant, supposed to be "more prosperous," but "we cyaan rely pon ourselves even for a second." One poorer villager in his mid-twenties summarized this paradox cogently by arguing "GATT and all those treaties are making you economically dependent while being politically independent." Here again, we are faced with a profoundly lucid and critical understanding of the inherent contradictions of neoliberal capitalist development and the ways this development has unequally structured access to resources and opportunities across the globe. Moreover, it is not unusual that a young Mango Mount community member whose primary socialization and education occurred outside of formal educational environments should have articulated such an analysis. This is because the livelihoods of those who began the twentieth century positioned at the outposts of empire and who have ended it in the margins of globalization depended upon keeping on top of the vicissitudes of the global political economy.[6]

As Mango Mount community members articulated a vision for Jamaica at independence, so too they offered several solutions to Jamaica's contemporary problems. They made appeals for greater unity, better management, good leaders whom they could respect and trust, affordable and accessible education, the initiation of more social programs creating jobs and other opportunities, and the establishment of more factories and increased industrial development. They argued that the government should control the dollar and revalue it, reduce the amount of guns on the street, build confidence among the youth—"make them know that when dem leave school there's a purpose in Jamaica for them," get rid of the "drug business," make people realize they have to work for what they want, focus on the positive instead of the negative, sever their link with the trade unions, and encourage the consumption of locally produced items rather than American imports.

They were also eager to "fix politics" and had several suggestions as to how this might occur. Many recommended that Jamaica should abolish the two-party system and instead have one party with one president, and that the government should develop a constitution that would ensure more democratic participation and the observance of civil rights. In addition, not a few women proposed that Jamaica "try a woman prime minister because a woman know suffering" and would therefore attempt to initiate policies designed to lighten the load upon the shoulders of poor, black Jamaicans. Finally, a solution to Jamaica's enduring class and color hierarchies that was widely envisioned by the "poorer class of people"—both men and women—though seldom articulated publicly within the community was for black people to mobilize nationally along racial lines toward their own social development and economic autonomy. Trevor advanced this argument in the following manner:

Only that can help the African ina Jamaica. We trade with other people yes, and we work with other people, but we got to have our own. We can live ina Jamaica still, we can live mongst every other people. All other set of people organize themselves, African Jamaican must organize themselves. They say the whole a Europe a go use one money now, that is an example. American money spend anywhere in the world, that is an example. And if we as a people should come up, we haffi learn seh that we organize weself. China, Japan, India, all a those country go through similar experiences like even the African in Jamaica or the African people. Them start and them build slowly, and organize themselves until them reach where them reach now. Nobody can oppress them again. Look pon likkle Cuba, them organize themselves and go through still, nuh true? Well the African in Jamaica need to get organized and have a charted course.

Progress Redefined: Bright Lights, Big City

While to this point, I have been addressing community members' views regarding what constitutes political modernity, I now wish to elaborate their definitions of economic modernity and progress. Earlier, I mentioned that within Mango Mount, the very small proportion of the "poorer class of people" who earned their entire income from cash crop farming were typically older men. These men often complained that contemporary youth disdained farming,[7] and argued that since Jamaica was "naturally" an agricultural country, the government and local institutions should develop the opportunities available to small-scale cultivators. Over the years, locally led development organizations such as the Mango Mount Community Council had, in fact, sponsored several agriculturally oriented projects such as the Hillside Agricultural Project, but as noted above, these initiatives had often met with only limited success due to the very low levels of participation among farmers in the community.

As the project's coordinator within the Community Council, Virginia explained the lack of participation by conceding that the project had generated a degree of resentment among community members. She noted that while the original goal of the project was to reforest the area with fruit trees, what actually ended up happening was that people planted coffee, which was ultimately more lucrative for farmers despite the fact that it took three or four years to bear. The project's leadership was disappointed by the fact that people were not interested in planting mango and apple trees. Moreover, since part of their objective was to introduce more environmentally friendly farming habits, the preference among village farmers for coffee, which required the use of various pesticides, was derided. "There was always a bit of tension," Virginia explained, "with people saying that we didn't have to live by this means so we could afford to have all these airy fairy ideas about the environment. So there was this gap between people who had to deal with reality, and their reality was conditioned by what was going to make the most money, which is coffee." Here, the divergence between people's attitudes toward the role of agricultural development is clear. Those who conceptualized the project viewed it as a way to beautify the district in an environmentally sustainable way, while providing long-term benefits to the community through the potential development of cottage industries, such as, for example, a jam factory. Those doing the actual planting viewed the project as a means toward sustaining themselves financially in the short run, based on both their own traditional farming practices and on their knowledge of the global market price for Jamaican coffee. Many in the community viewed this kind of disjuncture as playing a role in younger community members' lack of participation in agriculturally oriented development projects.

Older farmers also accused the youth of being lazy and used this to explain their disinterest in farming. A retired mason who cultivated several acres of land maintained that young people didn't know the meaning of hard work. His assessment was that youth wanted material things—like "big sneakers from America"—but didn't want to put in the work to get them. It was not only Mango Mount's older generation of farmers, however, who argued that community youth didn't try to "better themselves" through hard work. One Pentecostal woman in her mid-thirties who had moved to Mango Mount when a church contact made her aware of available land also remarked that Mango Mount youth were less "progressive" than youth in other closeby rural areas:

> In [a neighboring village], you can see a lot more progression with the poorer class of people who build a little house and uplift themselves. The youth either farm or try to develop a skill. Here it's easier for them to hang out on the corner and know that their parents will put down dinner for them. Most of them still live with their parents and haven't ventured out on their own. In other rural areas, youth achieve things earlier. As a youth leave school, he looks to buy a car and set himself up, maybe throw

a little partner.[8] If you try to tell these youth about partner, they tell you if they can't get the first draw, they won't throw in.

Other community members attributed the youth's lack of interest in farming, as well as their desire for "name brand" goods, to the community's proximity to Kingston. For example, Terry, one of the leaders of the local Pentecostal church group, suggested that within other communities, young people were more oriented toward farming as an occupation because "their foreparents led them into it." In Mango Mount, on the other hand, many of the older generation worked "off the hill" in Kingston and "so the younger ones don't grow up with it." Trevor agreed with this assessment and also made a case for the attractiveness of the symbolic cosmopolitanism associated with Kingston: "Most people believe that ina the city, everything is there, and if we're not a city folk, we are missing a lot of thing. Because the glamour ina the city still. And most people like the excitement so they wouldn't really want to be described as village people. Village people to them is like old people, backward people." Connected to the belief Trevor pinpointed here was people's conviction that what lay outside their community was better than what was there, a conviction that could be inferred by the fact that in the main, people traveled off the hill to get what goods or services they needed, even if these were available in Mango Mount. Sometimes this was because people felt they could get what they needed cheaper off the hill, but this was not the only reason. For example, many explained that they didn't attend church locally because they knew how their neighbors lived day to day. In other words, they didn't want to give others the opportunity to slander them as hypocrites. Additionally, while one of the Mango Mount Community Council's earliest initiatives was the establishment of a local health clinic, it soon closed due to lack of use. For four years a midwife had been stationed in the community and during that time, she delivered only one baby, and that was because the transportation the mother had arranged to take her off the hill had broken down.

In their own defense, many youth agreed that while it was true that Mango Mount's proximity to Kingston played a significant role in their decision against farming as a primary (or even supplementary) occupation, they also complained that the community was stagnant because those youth who did want to buy land couldn't get it since the majority of the land in the community was either family land or was owned by the government. Further, they claimed that the larger landowners wouldn't sell smaller parcels to young people who wanted to farm. In the main, however, these youth didn't want to farm because they no longer saw small-scale farming as a viable means to develop themselves, their community, or the nation, given the effects of 1980s and 1990s privatization drives locally and the move toward a service-oriented economy globally. The interaction that follows between Selwyn (a mechanic in his late thirties), Clyde (a sixty-ish Rasta who delivered the newspaper within the community and often spent time relaxing in Selwyn's garage), and Jason (a youth in his mid-twenties who drove one of the local minivans) illustrates some of these points:

SELWYN: Me remember clearly some a de policies me did see the government really implement ina the seventies. When you look pon it today, look like it really woulda guide wi on the right path. But others try to disencourage people, disencourage the people dem from farming, dem say slavery come right back. That time you couldn't go ina de bank and say you did want a loan for farming.

JASON: But you can't reach nowhere from farming.

SELWYN: But you not fi tell people that.

JASON: Nobody dohn haffi tell me. Me can see it. My parents a farmers and we still live ina one room. Why should I want to farm?

SELWYN: But if it was supported by the government, then you could buy all ten thousand apartments. Dem say dem a try fi give local farmers opportunity to produce more. We shoulda try fi produce more and market the things we have better so we can buy the things we need fi buy.

CLYDE: But American man will say that you not fi produce tomato because you fi buy his.

JASON: Me a driver still, me nuh waan no land. How they put it across to the youth is fling pick, fling pick, but from me born me see my people fling pick and them nuh get nowhere, so let me try something else. If the youth did see success from farming that is how he would go. You never need no big education fi farm. If you come up and see the easier way, siddung in office and pen and paper, you nah go waan go back to the hard way.

CLYDE: But the farmer is the one that feed the nation.

JASON: But the farmer don't get no rating, that's why the youth don't check it.

SELWYN: Me tell my son that nothing dohn come easy. Me assist him fi know that him can drive any of these cars here. Him did used to do a likkle farming too but dem a tief him banana.

JASON: But him wouldn't take farming over a first class trade.

SELWYN: But some people make nuff money. Go a Manchester or St. Elizabeth [other rural parishes in central and western Jamaica] and you cyaan talk to a man if you cyaan talk bout farming.

JASON: But the ones who work for coffee, them nuh get pay nuff. That's why the youth waan get some brain.

SELWYN: Me see people do domestic work have better house than secretary.

JASON: Nah. A domestic helper must get help, from her people a foreign, from her husband. Domestic work cyaan hardly buy her food.

CLYDE: Jamaican woman ingenious you know.

SELWYN: Domestic work my old lady used to do and if she never sick we wouldn't be below anyone now. Me never get no fucking help from my father, not even advice him gi me. A man can do anything him want. The mind is the most powerful thing. Marcus Garvey educated himself so if a man ever tell you him cyaan get education because him parents cyaan send him go a school, it a fuckery. Me a try fi send fi my own a school because the more education, the better you can live, but them must decide how them waan fi live. Me can tell them but it don't necessarily mean them will do it.

JASON: A dat me a say. Education is power. Dat a de way of the world, computers. Education.

SELWYN: But food a more fucking power because whether a man can read or cyaan read, a man haffi eat, and how a man supposed to eat if him dohn produce? Still, you have a whole heap of educated fools.

JASON: But nobody head for the hard work no more.

The conflict here between Selwyn's and Jason's perspectives was largely a generational one. Selwyn, old enough to have been significantly influenced by Manley's policies and outlook during the 1970s, viewed the government as an influential facilitator (or inhibitor) of people's potential progress. Jason, on the other hand, was too young to have personally experienced either the consciousness-raising movements or nationalist outlook of the 1970s. Having come of age during a period when Jamaica's economy was becoming increasingly integrated globally, both through trade arrangements with the United States and through debt arrangements with international funding agencies, his faith in the government to effect change was minimal. Both Selwyn and Jason, however, seemed to agree that currently, poor Jamaicans would have to fend for themselves. That they differed on the means of doing so was reflective of the global transformations in information technology, and of the kinds of knowledge and skills necessary for employment as a result of these transformations, that have occurred since Selwyn became an adult. Incidentally, the emphasis both Selwyn and Jason placed on education is instructive here, and to some extent ironic given the national and local trends that I outlined earlier, trends that directly refute the common-sense idea that a higher degree of education leads to greater employability for males. I flag this here in order to demonstrate the continuing pervasive power of the ideology of progress through education, despite the fact that I am arguing for the ascendance of an alternative ideology of progress through the generation of wealth. The ambivalence implied here is an issue to which I will return in the next chapter.

As suggested from Jason's perspective, when asked about their employment preferences, younger men in the community typically cited either learning a trade (such as masonry, carpentry, or tinsmithing) or developing the skills for an office job. At the same time, however, older tradesmen complained that youth in the village didn't, in fact, approach them to develop master-apprentice relationships and that those who did complained that the process of learning took too long. I mentioned this to a woman in her early thirties, herself the daughter of a mason who was working as an office secretary, and she complained that too many youth wrongly thought that office jobs like hers paid more than trades work. In fact, she insisted, good tradesmen earned twice her weekly salary putting in half the time. However, she felt that this kind of work wasn't attractive to upwardly mobile, status-seeking youth first because tradesmen were seen as manual laborers, and second because she felt youth didn't want to work "under" someone else. The consequence here, as she explained, was that if someone in Mango Mount needed a plumber or a mason, they would often have to employ someone from outside the community because the local tradesmen were consistently overbooked.

In Search of the Mighty (U.S.) Dollar

Due to the lack of available land, the perceived lack of training or employment opportunities locally, and the view that it would take too long to apprentice in an "old-fashioned" trade, many young males opted for employment in more lucrative industries or sought to migrate—either to Kingston or to the United States—via both legal and illegal means. Indeed, everyone in the village with whom I had contact had at least one, and usually several, family members abroad, primarily in the United States, but also, in some cases, in England and Canada.[9] There had also been a transition in migration patterns. While some poorer villagers in their fifties and sixties had brothers and sisters who initially migrated to England during the 1950s and early 1960s, since that time, the majority of poorer community members and their children have increasingly traveled to America instead.[10] Several community members also migrated to the United States "seasonally"—younger men for temporary work on construction sites and older women to work in the home health care industry. Many of those who traveled for this type of seasonal work were not documented employees in the United States but had obtained their positions through their contacts with underground networks of employment agencies, contacts which were usually offered to other friends and family members upon their return. The frequent travel back and forth necessitated by this kind of seasonal labor migration was facilitated by the fact that the national airline, Air Jamaica, offered direct flights to London, Toronto, Los Angeles, Chicago, New York, Newark, Baltimore, Philadelphia, three cities in Florida, and several other U.S. locations as well as deals such as free stopovers in any other U.S. city with a round-trip purchase.

A middle-class community member in his mid-thirties, himself a business owner, explained the trend toward intensified migration by arguing that many Jamaicans knew that while they may not have had "the social or educational skills to advance in Jamaica's relatively small economy," if they were prepared to work hard and hustle in the United States, they would have the opportunity to get ahead and make some money. Though many youth among the "poorer set" commented that in recent years obtaining a visa for travel to the U.S. had become more difficult (in part due to the U.S. government's response to Jamaicans who had been involved in the drug trade), they continued to perceive migration as a way to "move forward in life." This perception was evident in the interaction below, again between Selwyn, Clyde, and Jason:

SELWYN: People migrate for economical reasons and nuff people go up because they see people come back and say it so easy.

JASON: America better financial wise.

CLYDE: A the headquarter of the beast.

SELWYN: You have Jamaicans in the U.S. who live worse than they ever would here, and they can't come back.

JASON: But you have worse than them out here.

SELWYN: I knew a man, taught him my trade. Him make nuff contacts with nuff people. Him was one a de first black man in Jamaica to drive a new VW bug. After him do all this, him gone to America and him nah do well. Him have a gas station there, shack up with some Yankee girl and smoking crack. Him woulda be a multimillionaire in Jamaica right now, but him go America and make himself wutless . . .

JASON: That musi be [must have been] when it was a dollar for a dollar. You cyaan stay ina Jamaica and get rich.

SELWYN: . . . And I can tell you bout a whole heap more. Some people from here hoity toity accountant and go up there and have to be domestic. There you have to pay rent, light bill, everything.

JASON: America more a fast get through thing.

SELWYN: America just fuck up people. Whole heap of people wha did deh yah worse off. You can do anything you want right here ina Jamaica.

JASON: But if you go there, what you gwine do?

SELWYN: Me woulda haffi work in someone else garage, and me nah go do that.

CLYDE: Them tek you fi slave.

JASON: But the man who is street sweeper in Jamaica will always be a street sweeper in Jamaica, but if you is street sweeper in America, you can move forward from that.

SELWYN: Me dohn waan wealth over health. Me see people come back after thirty years and sixty year old look like him ninety.

CLYDE: All the evil wha go on in the world today, America is the cause. A dem bring drugs come a Jamaica. A dem bring guns come a Jamaica. A dem inspire violence ina election time.

JASON: But Americans living condition better than Jamaica.

SELWYN: A nuh so it go. My brethren have six family members living in America for how much years, and him gone up and only one sister could give him $150 . . .

JASON: But when dem come back dem live like king.

SELWYN: . . . Is credit card. America is the cause of everybody debt crisis. America support Jamaica to be wutless.

JASON: But there you have opportunity.

SELWYN: No, there the same as here. Babylon all over. You make yourself what you is.

JASON: But people dead fi hungry here.

SELWYN: But dat happening all over the world.

JASON: But why?

SELWYN AND CLYDE: It a de system.

JASON: What is the system?

CLYDE: Capitalism.

JASON: So it better off in communist countries?

SELWYN: People there poor too.

JASON: So is not capitalism or communism, it's just people wicked.

Here, we see Jason's belief that possibilities exist for advancement in the United States based on his perception that America's occupational class structure is not as rigid as Jamaica's. His buy-in to the "American dream," however, was largely instrumental in that his vision of migration was not one which would lead to building "a better life" in the United States. Rather, it would facilitate a return to Jamaica to "live like king." Another youth who was seeking a job in Kingston's hotel industry elaborated on this point, stating that while "the primary reason for migrating is that 99 percent of the people dem waan come back a Jamaica and set themself up better," many "don't make the money them want so them stay over there." In other words, in order to avoid the embarrassment of exposing the tenuousness of community members' American dreams and their own expectations, they remain in the United States. Nevertheless, he continued, for those who were able to return, "Them build up a nice house, set up a nice business. It always show when them come back." Moreover, these migrated youth were able to send money and other items to their families, though some more regularly than others. In fact, this practice had become so standardized a way to shore up the resources of extended families that those youth who had to be prodded to send remittances were considered unsuccessful, "wutless," and "all for themselves," especially if family members in Mango Mount were fostering their children.[11]

"Woman a Put Dem Foot Forward Now"

To this point, I have been pointing out some of the strategies of young men to "move forward in life." I have focused in this way because when older villagers complained about the younger generation, they typically spoke of "youth," a gendered term most often signifying males between puberty and the age of thirty. Moreover, within Mango Mount, farming was an occupation ordinarily pursued by men. Those women who were engaged in agricultural pursuits tended to be over the age of thirty-five and were primarily involved at the level of selling produce from the land in markets. Women also tended to care for small animals, like chickens, but this was not a pursuit that was exclusive to them. Several men also kept chicken coops, and like women, sold the eggs locally and in markets off the hill. As a result, older men's complaints regarding what they (rightfully) perceived as a declining interest in small-scale farming among youth were directed primarily at young men.

Women in the community confronted different sets of expectations and had different kinds of concerns. First, girls and young women were expected by both their mothers and fathers to stay in school, since without a formal education fewer options existed for them than they did for young males. Again, Barry Chevannes has made this point for poorer communities elsewhere in Jamaica, arguing that education was "the main conduit through which women have been able to acquire and display intellectual and professional leadership . . . [and] the main means whereby [women] rise to community, national, and even international leadership in the arts and sports" (2001:214). In Mango Mount, poorer villagers also anticipated that young women who became pregnant during their secondary school years would complete their diplomas or certificates in one manner or another after they gave birth. In fact, the criticism directed by older community members to young women that was most parallel to that indicting young men's purported disinterest in hard work was that which assailed young women who had borne children and were living in their family's homes but who did not, as far as older family members were concerned, take appropriate measures to care for the child. Most often, this meant that older family members felt that the young woman was neither actively pursuing educational and/or other training opportunities, nor stable employment options, and, in some cases, that she went out dancing too often, leaving her child with family as she enjoyed herself. Sometimes, if these complaints escalated enough, the young woman would be asked to leave the house, but usually family members were able to strike some kind of conciliatory balance, however grudgingly.

Like many male youth, girls who did not continue formal schooling past the All Age level pulled together earnings from a variety of sources, such as small-scale cultivation, higglering, daytime child care, and contributions from family members or baby-fathers. Nevertheless, even those who enjoyed relatively stable living situations had difficulty achieving any degree of economic security. Their educated counterparts, on the other hand, attempted to find consistently paying work in their field, supplementing this with a variety of other income-generating activities based on their own skills and interests. For example, Marvette, who grew up within one of Mango Mount's poorer families and was in her mid-thirties in the late 1990s, passed the Common Entrance Examination and began attending a prestigious high school for girls in Kingston. However, she became pregnant and because the school was religiously affiliated, she was asked to leave. After some time, she finished her secondary education at a well-known technical high school and then became certified as an accountant after completing a two-year course at a local business institute. She was employed steadily as an accountant, but could not make ends meet with this work alone. As a result, she earned additional funds by baking wedding cakes or doing other odd jobs for people. As has already been noted, this kind of occupational diversity often served as a type of insurance for community members, a buffer should there be a downturn in any one of their occupational sectors (see also Bolles 1996a). However, by the mid-1990s, Marvette was finding it increasingly difficult to keep herself, her partner, and her children economically afloat and therefore began evaluating her options for seasonal migration to the United States on labor contracts.

As noted earlier, migration patterns have been somewhat different for men and women. If girls remained in Jamaica past their primary education years—that is, if their parents didn't migrate themselves or send their kids to family abroad to "have a better chance" and a broader range of options—those who passed the Common Entrance Examination tended to finish their secondary education and attempt some advanced training. Like Marvette, as these women entered their thirties toward the end of the twentieth century, they became frustrated when they saw their economic options contracting. As a result, many have attempted to garner labor contracts abroad. While older women, and by this I mean women in their fifties and sixties, typically pursued work within the home health care industry in the United States, younger women had more recently begun to take advantage of new overseas employment programs initiated by the government in order to jump-start their mobility and increase their economic and social resources. For example, the Hotel Workers Programme,[12] implemented through the Ministry of Labour, sponsored the seasonal contract migration of women to work in hotels throughout the United States. As a result of their participation in these programs, these women's economic roles within their families were augmented, and their visions for their own future possibilities were significantly expanded. This future did not necessarily entail permanent migration, however. Rather, they saw their participation as a means to achieve their ends in Jamaica. Like the male youth, these women's view was that the United States was the place to make a living while Jamaica was the place to make life.

Though both men and women from Mango Mount have sought to "better themselves" and their families through migration, they have tended to do so in different ways. First, because women who stayed in Mango Mount through their early thirties were more likely to be primary caretakers of children than their male counterparts, they tended to look for opportunities to migrate for short and structured periods of time rather than indefinitely. In most cases, these women's children were already at least old enough to attend secondary school and so were more enmeshed in local educational and family networks that facilitated short periods of absence. Men, on the other hand, tended to have a more limited educational background, but a greater array of possibilities as migrants due to the kinds of labor-intensive industries in the United States that tend to hire undocumented workers at relatively high wages. These local trends draw attention again to the fact that within the contemporary global economy, achieving an education is not a guarantor of success. That the "poorer sets" within Mango Mount understood that intensified globalization was associated with a decline in local channels for development and social mobility should be clear by their pursuit of more individually oriented, global-looking strategies, rather than locally rooted community-based development.

It is important to point out that despite the lure of easier access to U.S. dollars, migration was seen as a difficult path. For many of the poorer villagers, and particularly those over thirty, the "American Dream" was not without its nightmarish qualities, in part, due to their familiarity with American-style racism. Several men and women alike expressed the opinion that black people "know them is nothing in America" and that "if you don't have a godfather up there, it's better not to go" because "everywhere now, people having things hard." One poorer woman in her mid-thirties clarified this sentiment by explaining that intensified global capitalism has widened the gap between rich and poor, not only between the United States and the rest of the developing world, but also within the United States itself. "Them having problems like the whole of we. And them complain and say people coming in and taking away their little jobs," she said. "The other day I was watching the television and this company that made staples for fifty or sixty odd years, now them haffi move to Mexico.

So a lot of people living worse, it's hard all over. I wish we would all understand that going to America is not easy." If this assessment were pervasive—and it was—why did the idea that things are better elsewhere, and particularly in the United States, persist among so many Mango Mount villagers? Why did they continue to see migration as a positive option for their own development? Why would, as community members argue, Jamaicans who migrate work much harder than they do in Jamaica, perform tasks they wouldn't even consider doing at home (such as cleaning toilets), and put up with things they wouldn't put up with in Jamaica (such as overt racism and "feeling like a second class citizen")? Because they perceived their options in Jamaica as being limited by an occupational and social class structure which they regarded as more rigid than that which prevails in the United States. Because enough Jamaicans have "done well for themselves" abroad to sustain their own rags-to-riches aspirations. And because they saw their migration as temporary, even if it ended up being permanent.

One significant result of the increased migration of the younger generation among poorer Mango Mount community members, both to Kingston and overseas, was that the older generation, once primarily dependent upon the local middle class for the development of their village, both in terms of infrastructural amenities and employment opportunities, now also received assistance (in the form of money, school clothes and books for children, job contacts for seasonal work, etc.) from family members abroad. What this has meant is that while the influence of the local middle class was still often critical with respect to interacting with public agencies locally—and among those very poor who were either unable to migrate or whose families, once migrated, didn't or couldn't help them—it was less generally critical than during the 1950s and 1960s. As I demonstrated in chapter three, the generation that was in their sixties during the late 1990s had relied to a much greater extent upon local middle-class individuals and families for jobs, educational and scholarship opportunities, and contacts (both to national and international agencies) than did the generation in their twenties and thirties.[13]

It is particularly important to point out here that this diminished influence of the local middle class within the lives of the "poorer sets" was also related to an altered assessment of the ability of middle-class individuals to catalyze significant change given the contemporary context. That is, it was not only the case that some poorer families had been able to do fairly well for themselves and therefore no longer needed the practical assistance of middle-class community members, but also that in the late 1990s, the "poorer sets" were less convinced of the ability of the middle-class villagers to substantially alter the scope of their possibilities. In other words, from the perspective of the "poorer class of people" in Mango Mount, the power of the local middle class and the power of the Jamaican state were linked, and therefore their lack of confidence in the state's capacity to create meaningful change in their lives was also mapped onto local middle-class individuals, many of whose contacts and resource bases were generated primarily through their access to state institutions. This material and ideological shift has meant that the role of the local middle-class population as the legitimate leaders of the community—politically, economically, and culturally—was in flux. Even so, it had also become increasingly difficult to facilitate leadership development among the "poorer class of people" in Mango Mount because many of those who might have been targeted for such encouragement were those among whom migration was a real and desired option.

What I mean to draw out from this discussion is a generational shift in the ways community members were evaluating their economic potential in the late 1990s that is related to other generational shifts I've been describing. That is, while "older heads"—from both the "upper sets" and the "poorer class of people"—complained that younger people didn't want to farm and decried the "idle youth who don't want to work," these same youth apprehended the shifts in the global political economy during the past two decades and evaluated the range of opportunities available to them accordingly. By the late twentieth century, then, many male youth and women in their thirties perceived that their opportunities for growth in Jamaica were limited due either to their inability to attain an educational or skill level that would allow them to compete in Jamaica's marketplace, or to the lack of availability of land which was obtained, for the most part, by their parents' generation. As a result, those who were able migrated, either for temporary employment or educational advancement.

Conclusion: Migratory Dreams

Throughout this chapter, I have sought to trace the ways community members discussed their experiences of, and articulations with, the political and economic changes within Jamaica since independence that were outlined for the national level in chapter 2. Villagers' experiences provide the framework for their definitions of what it means to be modern. In the quotes that opened this chapter, a modern nation was defined as one in which "everybody comes from somewhere else," in which "flux and change are normal," and in which there exists "tremendous freedom because we are without tradition." Economically, modern people were said to have made "international decisions" regarding the potential value of their labor and were therefore able to "go off wherever in the world" to work, a "tradition" of sorts that began in the late nineteenth century and that continues to the present. As we have seen, modernity was also defined by community members as political sovereignty, and villagers' vision for an independent Jamaica was one based in a commitment to reforms that would ultimately afford all citizens a bigger stake in Jamaica's future. It was believed that the expected prosperity this project promised would, in turn, diminish the inequalities inherent within the class, color, gender, and culture nexus that developed during the slavery and postemancipation periods.

Because these expectations were largely unmet, there was a general disappointment with the transformations—or lack thereof—since the achievement of political autonomy in 1962. This disillusionment with the promises of independence has been the result of the government's inability to (1) significantly transform the colonial institutional and ideological structures that have constrained the advancement of the majority of the population and (2) to diversify a predominantly agricultural economy in a way that would curtail the increased dependence upon Jamaica's northern neighbor and, therefore, the reproduction of Jamaica's subordinate position within a global economy. On the whole, while community members remained attached to the *idea* that nations should be independent, they had lost faith in the creole multiracial nationalist project as it had developed in Jamaica. It is no wonder, then, that the symbols of Jamaica's independence and heritage offered up within the national public sphere wouldn't consistently catalyze the kind of pride and hope for the future envisioned by nationalist elites at the local level. By this, I mean to say that locally, while people were concerned with cultural politics and representations of national belonging, this was usually less critical than their preoccupations with their potential for survival and growth in the contemporary global political economy. As a result, while I have been framing this discussion in terms of a loss of faith in creole multiracial nationalism, what I'm really talking about here is a disappointment in the declining power of the state in the globalized world of the late twentieth century. Unlike the

1960s and 1970s, when people held high hopes for the power of the government to create significant social change, community members in the late 1990s were convinced that the state could no longer do anything for them. True modernity, therefore, would necessitate the transformation of socioeconomic inequalities globally.

At the same time, or perhaps in the meantime, villagers intensified their engagement with the global economy, endeavoring as individual men and women to reap some rewards for their entrepreneurialism. As they have done so, they have sometimes challenged and sometimes reinforced—at the individual and family as well as broader structural levels—ideologies surrounding class, status, gender, culture, and progress (see also Freeman 2000). What has been particularly striking in the context of Mango Mount is that processes of globalization have tended to erode the traditional patronage relationships between the middle class and the "poorer sets." This erosion has been the result of two divergent, yet successful, paths to progress pursued by the "poorer class of people." The first of these paths, of course, was to pursue a good education, and a few youth from the more established poorer families were able to take advantage of the expansion of local educational opportunities that accompanied independence. The second path, highlighted in the latter part of this chapter, has been the attempt to generate capital through seasonal or "permanent" migration. Both of these strategies have occasioned a decline in the centrality of middle-class villagers to individual and community development within this generation.

However, the diminution of the patron-client relationships between the middle and lower classes has not generated a greater equality between these groups since the local effects of global processes over the past two decades have also reinforced and sharpened both the *class differences* between the "upper sets" and the "poorer sets" and the *status distinctions* among the "poorer class of people." In fact, there has been further division at the community level between those among the "poorer sets" who have been "more established" and those who have become "more marginalized" precisely because the ability to migrate has become such a central resource within the contemporary global economy. The modernity of modern blackness, therefore, is not only decidedly self-conscious and transnational, a modernity both constituted by and constitutive of an acute awareness of local-global relationships—politically, economically, socioculturally, and racially. It also embodies, at one and the same time, both the inequalities that have shaped Caribbean societies over the course of five hundred years and the desire to overcome and transform them.

Finally, because so many community members have focused their eyes toward America—and toward the possibility of entering into a lucrative migratory circuit—it is not surprising that they have also tended to dismiss agricultural paths to progress within the contemporary global order. As a result, cultivating the kind of "respectable" and "vindicationist blackness" outlined by both the late-nineteenth-century *Jamaica's Jubilee* authors and the mid-twentieth-century creole nationalists has not been particularly attractive to them. Neither have they tended to engage with some of the more politicized aspects of the "revolutionary" blackness of reggae and Rasta that have advocated black people's triumph over white oppression. Instead, they have developed a racialized working-class expression of the dominant elite ethos of globalization, even as they have simultaneously exposed, critiqued, and satirized that ethos. In other words, they have identified the acquisition of wealth as an equally valid route to progress as the achievement of formal education or the development of agricultural autonomy, the routes usually advocated by sectors of the nationalist elite. While this ideology is not new among poor black Jamaicans, its ascendance during the 1990s reflects their increased autonomy, itself reproduced by current neoliberal trends.

Simultaneous to these various transformations, another variant of cultural capital has become more publicly acceptable. As I show in the next chapter, this variant does not look toward the models of progress advanced by members of the professional middle classes. The modern blackness of late-twentieth-century youth, then, is urban, migratory, based in youth-oriented popular culture and influenced by African American popular style. It is individualistic, radically consumerist, and "ghetto feminist." Most importantly, as an ethos that has been defined by lower-class black Jamaicans, it is expressed through their cultural idioms and innovations. Modern blackness, therefore, reflects a broader transformation in terms of who (and what) has public power to define and represent Jamaican culture in the contemporary era.

chapter 7

MODERN BLACKNESS; OR, THEORETICAL

"TRIPPING" ON BLACK VERNACULAR

CULTURE

The previous chapters have explored structural and ideological differences among community members in Mango Mount, especially in relation to how they have influenced individuals' experiences and their visions of progress, modernity, and development. In this final chapter, I'd like to return to a discussion of representation—the question of legitimate and current portrayals of Jamaicanness. Here, a local theatrical production serves as a jump-off point for a critical engagement with the ways community members negotiated the publicly powerful ideologies associated with modern blackness locally, as well as how they related them to their own lives and experiences. It also introduces a more general analysis of modern blackness in national and transnational public spheres, addressing a series of questions that have animated this project: Where does modern blackness stand in relation to earlier black nationalisms? In relation to the cultivation of respectability? What are the visions of America and Americanization, cultural imperialism and appropriation, consumerism and individualism that are embedded within formulations of modern blackness? How best might we theoretically unpack the terms I have used to describe modern blackness, such as "radical consumerism" and "ghetto feminism"? Finally, where does modern blackness stand within a continuum of lower-class political visions and action within Jamaica?

Throughout this discussion, the issue of cultural duality and its relationship to the politics of national belonging emerges as key. Using the cultural duality problematic forces us to consider whether, and the extent to which, the contemporary context in Jamaica might alter the way we think about the relationships that scholars have often posited between cultural representation and political progressivism among Afro-Caribbean populations.[1] In other words, because global capitalist expansion has been

uneven, it has generated numerous contradictions that people have attempted to exploit in order to advance their own economic ambitions.
These contradictions have facilitated the elaboration of a complex field of
cultural practice and cultural production that defies neat categorization as
either imitative or oppositional. Aspects of modern blackness such as
radical consumerism and ghetto feminism can both challenge and reproduce timeworn tropes about black vernacular culture—such as hyper-
sexualization and duplicity, for example—constantly sampling from the
past to create something new. As a result, modern blackness does not
present some kind of totalizing and coherent ideological framework for
understanding why things are the way they are among poor, black Jamaicans. Nor does it necessarily provide a blueprint for (revolutionary) action.
Instead, modern blackness emerges as a framework within which present
and future possibilities are evaluated.

Can Blackness Unite?

For many, the transition I've been pointing to throughout these pages—the
public ascendance of visions of community founded upon racialized and
to some extent deterritorialized conceptualizations of citizenship—has
been cause for significant concern, the exposure of a "crisis" in the postcolonial state.[2] This "crisis" has, at its root, the inability of creole multiracialism to catalyze a sense of national unity that would overarch persistent racial, class, and gender inequalities—legacies of the colonial and
slave-holding past that have been reproduced (though in somewhat different ways) by contemporary processes of globalization. These inequalities have shaped a cultural system that maps diverse practices, aesthetics,
and belief systems onto a hierarchy of value, which, though dynamic, has
nevertheless constrained the degree to which Jamaicans have been able to
identify common political interests.

This has long been a concern among scholars within the region, and the
existence of divergent value systems and sets of practices among differently positioned sectors of the populations has had significant implications for both nationalist practice and scholarship in the British West
Indies. During the mid-twentieth century when these societies were undergoing the gradual decolonization process, the dominant view within
the social sciences held that social systems needed to be integrated around

a common value system in order to exist in equilibrium without an over-arching (and often external) system of power and control. As a result, arguments over whether West Indian societies exhibited an incompatible social and cultural plurality or a creolized stratification had to do with assessing the potential success or predicting the foreseeable failure of nationalist projects to unify diverse sectors of postcolonial populations.[3]

While many scholars addressed pluralities within the institutional struc-tures of West Indian societies in terms of their implications for national cohesion, others began attempting instead to define the shared distinc-tiveness of subordinated West Indian populations. Several historians be-gan to reconstruct the social worlds of the black lower classes in an effort to ferret out and highlight examples of practices and values that would vindicate the racial humanity and demonstrate the complex creativity of people of African descent living under the oppressive conditions of slavery and colonialism.[4] Simultaneously, ethnographers began a research focus on cultural duality with the intention of identifying tensions that have been central to Afro-Caribbean societies—those between egalitarianism and hierarchy, respectability and reputation.[5] Here, cultural duality is under-stood as a practice of code switching, maintaining and enacting one or another repertoire of behavior that is considered appropriate for a situa-tion, given a common comprehension of locally specific relations of both material and symbolic power. Yet, because the persistence of cultural du-ality has implied the maintenance of a sociocultural space separate from and alternative to the dominant norm, it has also been seen as embodying a space in which these dominant relations of power could be undermined. In Jamaica, as elsewhere in the West Indies, the dynamic tensions between respectability and reputation, egalitarianism and hierarchy, continue to shape the range of possibilities for action for all members of the society.[6] And attempts to understand the processes by which these tensions are negotiated has been a key aspect of scholars' endeavors to identify the political implications of black lower-class cultural practices and aes-thetics.

This preoccupation has also been a core concern underlying analyses of the creolization process. Much of the early attention to creolization em-phasized the processes of rupture and creativity, and stressed the develop-ment of a shared cultural and social repertoire that could provide the basis for a national identity.[7] In this way, the actual conflicts that occurred and power relations that shaped this development were sometimes obscured

(Bolland 1997; R. Price 1998). In fact, the process of creolization has taken place *within* historical and contemporary relations of domination and subordination at local, regional, national, and global levels (Mintz 1996; Mintz and Price 1992), and these dynamic relations of power have constrained the extent to which the various visions, practices, and aesthetic norms of lower-class black West Indians have been represented within the creole formation at any given moment. As a result, cultural dualism has persisted alongside creolization, now positioned as a "process of *contention* between people who are members of social formations and carriers of cultures, a process in which their own ethnicity is continually reexamined and redefined in terms of the relevant oppositions between different social formations at various historical moments" (Bolland 1997:25).[8]

If we agree that the maintenance of an alternative, potentially oppositional worldview occurs alongside the adoption, adaptation, and modification of previously "foreign" cultural forms and practices, then we should not be surprised that the kinds of political visions generated by lower-class black Jamaicans have been simultaneously radical and pragmatic, utopic and conservative (Burton 1997); nor should we analyze them in terms of an essentialized "being," but instead as always "becoming" (S. Hall 1990, 2001). This is how I would like to approach modern blackness. Though its ascendancy within the public sphere does not exemplify a Wilsonian (1973) triumph of collective egalitarian struggle, it does represent at least a partial eschewal of colonial and nationalist respectability and a public valuation of *fi wi culture*.[9]

"What Is Jamaica to Me?"

When I asked poorer community members in Mango Mount what kinds of cultural representations they felt were typically Jamaican, it was not surprising that reggae and dancehall music topped their lists. Specific songs cited included anything by Bob Marley; Tony Rebel's song released just prior to the elections that advocated an end to political violence and argued that the unity obtained during the soccer team's "Road to France" should prevail;[10] Buju Banton's "Deportee" which chronicles the story of a Jamaican who had "lived large" in the United States, but was deported and returned to Jamaica penniless because he did not "lay a foundation" for the future; "Boops" by Supercat, a song that cautions a man about spending too much money on his various girlfriends since they might also be sleeping with others; and Bounti Killer's "Poor People Fed Up," which is self-explanatory.

They also listed the movies *The Harder They Come* and *Smile Orange* as well as the locally produced television show *Royal Palm Estate* as accurate depictions of Jamaican culture. *Royal Palm* is an hour-long evening (melo)drama about a rural estate community whose characters rang true for Mango Mount community members. For example, the show's household helper was the illegitimate daughter of the original estate owner and one of his workers. She worked on the estate and acted as if she were part of the family, bossing around the other workers. She also bore a son by the man who inherited the estate from his father, but her son was not aware of his father's identity. The son, in turn, impregnated the daughter of another household helper despite the fact that he had a girlfriend. Moreover, the pastor, who typically found it difficult to suppress his sexual attraction to various parishioners, was in constant competition with the local obeah woman for villagers' souls. One of the (black) children who grew up on the estate migrated to the city to pursue his dreams of establishing himself, one way or another, in the music industry. The expatriate woman who was married to the estate owner killed her husband and attempted to outsmart the local detective investigating the case. And finally, several of the policemen were involved in the drug trade. Though villagers felt that *Royal Palm*'s exclusion of portrayals of urban life was unrealistic, when they defended the show's Jamaicanness, they often insisted that "dem ting really happen."

Poorer community members also cited *The Young and the Restless* and other American soap operas as typically representative of Jamaican culture. This may seem surprising given that the lifestyles depicted on these shows appear to have nothing to do with Jamaica. However, their justification for these choices centered around the ways characters on the soap operas treated each other, and particularly the ways they betrayed each other in love relationships. Additionally, because local programming was scarce and expensive to produce in comparison with the relatively low cost of syndicated programming from the United States, community members' favorite shows also included ABC and CNN news broadcasts; *New York Undercover*; *NYPD Blue*; *Walker Texas Ranger*; *Beverly Hills 90210*; *Sunset Beach*; *Hanging with Mr. Cooper*; *In the House*; *The Oprah Winfrey Show* (though they often argued that Oprah was "too boas'y because she only interviews the upper class and superstars"); and *The Montel Williams Show* (whom they generally liked because they felt he interviewed "the more average, from the middle class to the smallest class of people, the ghetto and third class people"). That many of these programs had prominent African American characters or depicted African American lifestyles is not insignificant and is a point to which I will return later in this chapter. In addition to these various media, community members listed "roots plays" as accurate performative representations of "things as they are in Jamaica today."

Roots plays are part of the culture that has developed around dancehall music.[11] This is a culture, as I have already argued, that supplies a public forum through which ideologies alternative to those professed by the creole professional middle classes are articulated. These popular plays, performed in patois, draw from a variety of stock characters to humorously present situations familiar to their largely lower-class audiences. They also tend to intersperse popular dancehall songs throughout in order to push the action along or to underline a particular theme. Middle-class theatregoers often malign these plays as "trashy." That is, they do not consider roots plays to be *real* art and argue that they do not reflect appropriate values or desirable lifestyles. Yet, successful roots plays can be very lucrative for their producers, promoters, and performers. Roots plays are important, then, not only because their narratives offer aesthetic representations that are often typical of the experiences of many lower-class Jamaicans, but also because the social context in which most roots plays are produced and viewed provides a public forum for internal dialogue and dispute. Examining both the text and context of a roots play written and produced by one of the Mango Mount community members will help unpack the term "modern blackness" by grounding creative productions of identity at the most local level.

Winsome, the Mango Mount community member who had established a drama club at the community center, wrote and produced her own roots plays as a means of expressing her vision of Jamaican life and of earning additional money to supplement her income as the accounts keeper for a public institution. Thematically, Winsome's plays explored the intersections of sex, money, and power in human relationships—themes she felt were relevant to the day-to-day experiences of the majority of the population. In 1997, she was working on a play entitled *Ruff Rider* which was ultimately performed in three venues outside of Kingston. *Ruff Rider* is the story of the making and unmaking of a household that includes Monica, her husband Earl, their son Skim Milk—so named for his penchant for ingesting the family's supply of milk powder—and their niece Bella. The story ultimately is a morality tale about the consequences of sexual betrayal and dishonesty.

Ruff Rider

The play begins by establishing the characters of Monica as the hard-working long-suffering wife, Earl as the ever-philandering (and therefore fast-talking) husband, and Skim Milk as the fun-loving and mercenary son. When Skim Milk discovers his father attempting to have sex with Bella, he extorts money from both of them—first from Earl, who insists he keep his mouth shut, and then from Bella, who entreats him to tell his mother the truth. When the moment of reckoning arrives, Skim Milk betrays his promise to Bella, and Monica threatens to throw Bella out of the house for attempting to seduce her husband. Bella pleads with Earl, saying she'll do anything for him if he can convince Monica to let her stay in the household. Earl grabs his crotch and asks "Anything . . . including this?" and Bella agrees.

Later, we are introduced to Sarah Bunjaws, recently arrived from the country to work as the family's new (and not-so-bright) household helper. Sarah, too, becomes the object of Earl's advances, but is ultimately protected by Bella, who reluctantly agrees to let Sarah tag along to her job. Bella works in a club as a go-go dancer alongside Mystic, a dancehall DJ upon whom she has a crush. At the club, much to Bella's chagrin, Sarah and Mystic become smitten with each other. Bella, therefore, resolves to remove her competition, both from the house and from Mystic's life. She discovers a love letter that Sarah had written to Mystic and deviously changes Mystic's name, addressing it instead to Earl and leaving it where Monica will see it. Indeed, Monica finds the letter and throws Sarah out of the house. Bella then goes to visit Mystic who refuses her advances, arguing that he could never forgive Bella for the devious way she got Sarah kicked out of the house.

Meanwhile, Earl returns unexpectedly from a temporary labor gig "in foreign" and wants to sneak "a stab" from Bella before Monica knows he's back in Jamaica. As they moan and groan in the bedroom, Monica arrives home early from work and discovers them. She runs after both of them as Bella pleads, "Auntie, me tell yuh but you never waan believe me and me haffi do this to stay ina the house." The scene ends with Monica pummeling Earl with a piece of board. The last scene takes place in the club where, thanks to Skim Milk's encouragement, Sarah and Mystic have reconciled. Monica enters on the arm of a tall, dark, and handsome stranger. Eventually, Earl also arrives and begs for Monica's forgiveness. Monica, however, tells him that on top of everything else, he can't even satisfy her in bed, and so she has found another man. The play ends with the commotion that ensues when Earl picks up a cutlass to threaten Monica's new man.

There are several thematic threads within Ruff Rider that are key to a more general discussion of modern blackness. Winsome has presented a world where the more lucrative economic opportunities are generated either by migrating or by working within the popular culture industry. She provides insight into the ways in which both of these dimensions are gendered. That is, the young rural woman comes to the city and finds work as a household helper, but the "man of the house" seeks labor contracts abroad; the young urban woman finds a job as a go-go dancer, but the male youth tries his luck DJ-ing. Monica's work, on the other hand, remains unspecified, providing the most consistent income for the household but apparently without any glitz or glamour. Ruff Rider also explores ideologies about appropriate female behavior. For example, Bella's lifestyle is portrayed as exciting, but also unfulfilling. Sarah Bunjaws is depicted as slow and unsophisticated, but the "good country girl" ultimately gets her man. Though Winsome renders an intense distrust between women and men, she also leaves the audience with the idea that "true love" triumphs over adversity and repels pretenders, who are ultimately left to fend for themselves in the sexual marketplace. In this way, Ruff Rider seems to recuperate the respectability narrative. At the same time, it also challenges the unquestioned acceptance of male dominance through Monica's ultimate rejection of Earl at the end of the play. Indeed, her final insult—that Earl couldn't satisfy her sexually—resolves the issue of male infidelity not through an appeal to some abstracted sense of morality but by publicly validating female sexual desire and pleasure. The "happy ending" of Ruff Rider, then, rests on everybody getting what they deserve. Sarah and Mystic find true love with the encouragement of Skim Milk; Bella and her aunt reconcile; Earl is left frustrated; and Monica can finally balance her hard work with some love and pleasure of her own.

Winsome has written other plays—as well as a children's novel—that address similar themes and issues. In all of her work, the sympathetic characters are those she portrays as struggling to balance their own pursuit of individual gain with "living well together" with others. As they negotiate the fine lines between egalitarianism and hierarchy, her characters also contribute to the public debate regarding the gendered dimensions of respectability and reputation. These are themes that I will elaborate more fully below. First, however, I want to identify additional elements of roots plays that are central to a discussion of modern blackness, elements that are embodied through the processes of production and performance.

Rehearsing (and Producing) Roots

The rehearsal and production processes for roots plays are substantially different from those of national, institutionally established performance groups. For the production of *Ruff Rider*, Winsome rehearsed her actors at public parks in Kingston, and during rehearsals, most of the time was focused on making sure people knew the script. There was some attention to directing the manner in which specific lines were delivered or in blocking particular actions, but most of this was left up to the actor. In Winsome's case, rehearsal time was a luxury so a "good actor," in her view, was one who could fend for him or herself, and one who could develop his or her own appropriate "body language" without extensive direction. Consequently, each actor needed to be familiar enough with what they were portraying to be convincingly funny and human. Additionally because there was little time for an extended rehearsal process, and because the group couldn't enter the performance space prior to the day of the show, the actors rarely rehearsed "full out," that is, they seldom practiced the play straight through at performance level. This meant that even Winsome was never quite sure what she would ultimately get from actors with whom she had not previously worked.

To produce her plays, Winsome made all the arrangements with the venues and handled all the publicity herself. Occasionally, but not often, she was able to obtain sponsorship for a portion of her expenses, and one or two of the middle-class Mango Mount community members helped her from time to time. She complained that her children's father didn't really support her involvement in theatre and that he had become jealous of the time it took her away from him, time spent developing close relationships with others. With one or two exceptions, he hadn't attended her productions, and as a result, she felt that he didn't "stand up beside me like a man." She argued that this had also caused her financial problems from time to time. One of Winsome's more successful plays, for example, didn't make as much money as she had expected because at every venue where it was performed, someone stole either the bar or the admission money, which at one location was approximately US$1,700. In her estimation, this wouldn't have happened had her children's father been keeping an eye on the cash box. Still, she maintained that she wouldn't give up her theatre for anyone because it was what she could do to express herself, something just for her.

Winsome found it difficult to produce her plays in Kingston. This was, in part, because the cost of renting theatres in the city was prohibitive and because the theatres, usually booked months in advance, didn't generally rent their space on a per night basis. Additionally, some of the managers of the more popular theatre venues in Kingston were hesitant to produce roots plays because, as they argued, the plays were "too loud" and "too focused on sex." Winsome dismissed this argument, suggesting that roots plays were no louder than u.s. movies and were far less sexually explicit. In her estimation, "uptown" theatres in Kingston discriminated against roots plays because they did not want to portray the lives of the "poorer class of people." As a result, she usually had more luck in rural areas.

To produce *Ruff Rider* in one venue, Winsome contacted the director of a local community center and youth association on a tip from one of her actors. They negotiated a rental fee that included a small charge for the building of "security" thatching around the playing field so that people could not enter without paying to see the show. He also gave her a contact for the owner of a sound system. When these arrangements were settled, the information (date, time, venue, play title, characters' names, and the name of the sound system) was painted on banners (white sheets) and wooden placards brought from Mango Mount, which were then tacked onto light poles along the main road between the village and the main town.

The actors themselves, in conjunction with supportive family members, supplied their own costumes, built the sets, arranged for lighting, and brought props from home. On the night of the performance when the actors were ready, the selector stopped the music that he had been playing and announced that it was "showtime." Throughout the play, there was substantial involvement on the part of the audience who, far from being passive spectators, commented on the action and interacted with the characters. For example, they enthusiastically encouraged Uncle Earl in his sexual advances toward both Bella and Sarah, especially when he returned unexpectedly from "foreign" to "get a stab" from Bella, by shouting "yu cyaan come from foreign and nah get nuh pussy!" However, they objected to Skim Milk's attempts and argued that he should get out of his father's way. They also condemned Bella's efforts to come between Mystic and Sarah, yelling out "lef' it man" when she discovered Sarah's love letter and "you cyaan get him back" when she went to Mystic's house. Audience members also let the cast know when they couldn't hear ("use the microphone!"), and cued the individuals in charge of the lights and music ("play selector!"). The actors also interacted directly with the audience. For example, the character Earl shushed the audience when he was trying to trick Bella into having sex with him while she was asleep, and when the audience said they couldn't hear, the actors on stage moved closer to a microphone and passed it back and forth between them to deliver their lines. Additionally, about two-thirds of the way through the performance when someone backstage received word that several people were still arriving, the actor who was playing Earl asked the audience whether they would mind if they started the play again from the beginning since so many people were just coming. The audience agreed, and so the actors took it from the top.

This kind of dialogic and participatory relationship between the performers and audience members has long been seen as characteristic of black vernacular cultures throughout the Atlantic world. It is a relationship that does not mark the performer off from his or her community and also one that encourages real-time reinterpretation, admiration, and critique. In Winsome's play, by addressing the audience directly and starting the play over, the actors broke the "fourth wall," that symbolic boundary that typically separates performers from spectators. Of course, this "wall" was also broken by audience members who shouted directions and commentary to characters and technical staff. The rural outdoor setting facilitated this kind of interaction, which, though characteristic of roots plays more generally, was more boisterous than is the tendency in indoor venues.

Moreover, the structure of roots plays allows for a degree of improvisation within the script. This improvisation might be spurred by a comment made by a particular audience member or by other concurrent events. For example, during the intermission for a play performed in the rural parish of Manchester, someone from the community was shot in the town square. When the play resumed, the actor who played the character of the strong, tough mother figure chastised the "bad boy" character, asking "was yu kill de man ina de square?!" The "bad boy" character denied the accusation, and after a bit of improvisation about what had just happened outside the theatre, the actors resumed their written lines.

Though many roots plays are performed in theatres in Kingston, low-budget and community-oriented performances like Winsome's neither approximated nor sought to emulate the production standards associated with more established theatrical venues. Instead, cast and audience members worked together with what was common to their community to generate an alternative institutional framework for their own creative expressions.

Winsome's plays, together with the popular music, films, and both locally produced and u.s.-based television shows listed above, provide examples of representations of Jamaican culture that were considered legitimate by the "poorer sets." As a result, the themes raised within the roots play discussed here and the process by which it was performed open a window to engage in a more abstractly analytical discussion about the various dimensions of modern blackness. At the end of the previous chapter, I defined modern blackness as urban, migratory, based in youth-oriented popular culture and influenced by African American popular style, individualistic, radically consumerist, and ghetto feminist. I will now explore these various dimensions in more detail.

Modern Blackness Defined

Reconstituting an Autonomous Aesthetics and Politics

First, the modern blackness of late-twentieth-century Jamaicans diverges from both "folk" and "revolutionary" blacknesses. In order to achieve their political goals, nineteenth-century black nationalists and mid-twentieth-century creole nationalists spoke as "insiders" to "outsiders" in a manner that would be understood by those formulating policy that would affect their futures. However, as Kwame Dawes has pointed out in his recent book on the "reggae aesthetic" in Jamaican literature (1999), the 1970s in Jamaica were a watershed decade in terms of how black Jamaicans articulated and mobilized around their concerns. Dawes argues that reggae music, while garnering significant international appeal, was primarily a musical genre that spoke first to Jamaicans, in Jamaican language, and only secondarily to the rest of the world. Unlike earlier nationalists, these artists' portrayals of working-class lifestyles and philosophies were neither explanatory nor vindicationist. In this way, reggae musicians defined the terms of engagement with both the music and the messages encrypted within it.

Dancehall music, the soundtrack for modern blackness, has taken this trend one step further to reassert, as Louis Chude-Sokei has put it, the "cultural barriers between blacknesses" (1997:222). By this, he means that the identity and political space of dancehall is less easily appropriated by other sectors of the society in the way that some middle-class Jamaicans who were politicized during the 1970s adopted reggae music to embrace their blackness and to champion the cause of Jamaica's "sufferers" (Austin 1983; Stolzoff 2000; Waters 1985). Furthermore, though dancehall culture is a space that is constituted transnationally, its ideology and politics are not available to all African-descended folk throughout the Americas because it has generated a new definition of diaspora. This is a definition, Chude-Sokei continues, that subverts Rasta's emphasis upon an African ethnic and cultural identity, instead championing "a postcolonial underclass navigating a global network of immigrant communities" (1997:218). This kind of nontranslatability is illuminated, for example, in the controversy surrounding the 1993 U.S. release of Buju Banton's "Boom Bye Bye," a song whose violently homophobic lyrics mobilized intense public condemnation and censure within African American and, to a degree, Jamaican American communities. As Patricia Saunders has evocatively argued, Buju Banton's refusal to apologize showed Jamaicans that "despite the power of American markets to make or break imported products and even entire markets, dancehall music and culture would reflect Jamaican sentiments and culture, no matter where it traveled" (2003:96). In other words, his stance mediated the hegemonic force of economic (market) values by refusing to compromise what has been seen as a Jamaican cultural value. The relative autonomy that dancehall music and culture have reestablished for lower-class black Jamaican aficionados has not only been generated within the realm of aesthetics, but also within the realm of politics. As political scientist Brian Meeks has argued, dancehall has provided "an impenetrable retreat in which the poor spoke to the poor without the interpolation of the traditional Left, or any outside source with their preconfigured, structural, and linear view of progress" (2000:12).

Because dancehall is not merely a response to hegemonic power but marks the changing aesthetic and political space that both contests and (re)produces broader relations of power, the space of dancehall—and of modern blackness more broadly—is not monolithic. As with any sociocultural and political trend, there is a great deal of internal ideological debate. Indeed, in recent years there has been a "roots and culture" revival among some dancehall artistes, suggesting that in some circles, sustained public criticism of "slackness" from both within and outside of the music industry has taken its toll (Whyte 1997a). Some observers have met this revival cynically, arguing that it reflects the interests of a new cohort of state and media managers and provides a "purer" antidote to the fusion of reggae and hip-hop that has emerged over the past decade or so as part of a transnational Jamaican American culture (Ross 1998). Others have advanced more optimistic opinions, seeing in the "roots and culture" revival a rejection of neoliberalism and an exposure of the limitations to the economic and social opportunities purportedly offered by globalization (Meeks 2000). What the roots revival reveals most strongly, I believe, is that debates about the ways popular cultural forms represent life in Jamaica are ongoing, both internally among *artistes* and externally throughout the broader society.

If modern blackness is unlike both "folk" and "revolutionary" blacknesses, it is perhaps most similar to the "rude boy" phenomenon of the late 1960s and early 1970s. As indicated earlier, prior to the ascendance of reggae's rejection of Babylon's vision of progress, rudies—influenced by American westerns (and potentially also by the "blaxploitation" film genre)—had captured the imagination of lower-class black Jamaicans, especially those who were recent urban migrants. Emerging within a growing yet increasingly polarized economic climate and a progressively more violent political atmosphere, rudies also challenged the politics of respectability but in a drastically different context and with different results. Because images of rudies and dancehall dons are circulated, canonized, and revised within popular culture, we can also look to popular media to illuminate some of the ways "rude boy" blackness diverges from "modern blackness." By juxtaposing the representations of lower-class black life in The Harder They Come (1973) and Dancehall Queen (1997),[12] the two most popular Jamaican films that bookend the period I'm considering here, it becomes easier to see the continuities and changes in the ways lower-class Jamaicans' conceptualizations of national belonging have (dis-)articulated with the Jamaican state.

The Harder They Come tells the story of a young man named Ivan who travels from the country to Kingston in order to make it big in the music industry. Exploited by his record producer, he eventually becomes involved in the drug trade in order to earn *real* money. Noticing that he and the other members of his crew were also being exploited as petty sellers in an industry that generated vast sums of money both for the local elite and for Americans, he begins to agitate for a bigger share of the profits. His agitation disturbs the equilibrium of the relationships that had been established between local networks of drug vendors, the police, and the music business. As a result, Ivan becomes a police target. To escape their various attempts to catch him, he ends up killing several cops. For these exploits, he emerges as a popular hero as he orchestrates his own rise to the realm of public figures by personally providing editors with news clips and photographs. Meanwhile, the police put the squeeze on the local drug trade with the hope that material deprivation will force Ivan's crew to give up his whereabouts. In the end, Ivan's plan to escape to Cuba is betrayed by his child's mother who rationalizes, "Every game I play, I lose." He dies in true gangster fashion, emerging alone and unafraid from his hiding place only to be gunned down by a police posse.

Produced almost twenty-five years later, *Dancehall Queen* recounts the tale of Marcia, a pushcart vendor in Kingston attempting to support three children on her own. Marcia's problems begin when she and her crew witness a murder. Priest, a street-wise "badman," has killed one of Marcia's friends. Eventually, we find out that Priest has been working for Larry, a male "friend" of Marcia's who provides school fees for her daughter, expecting that she will welcome his sexual advances as she gets older. Indeed, one evening Marcia's daughter returns home from Larry's house livid, shouting at her mother, "You knew this would happen!" and vowing never to take a penny from Larry again. Marcia pleads with her daughter, but soon realizes she will not budge, and so she sets out to find another way to provide for her family. One night, after watching the glamorously dressed women dance in a competition at a local dancehall club, Marcia determines that this might be the way she could make enough money to set her family straight. Meanwhile, Priest has begun threatening Marcia's family in order to ensure that they keep their mouths shut about the murder, and Marcia's brother becomes so traumatized he turns mad. Realizing she has to do something to get Priest off her back, Marcia enlists the help of the woman who sewed her dancehall outfit to devise a plan to both usurp the reigning dancehall queen's title and win the prize money and set Priest and Larry against each other. By this time, she has found out that Larry earns his money through go-go clubs and shady land transactions, and that he is the one behind her friend's murder. She tricks both of the men into thinking she wants to be their girlfriend, approaching Priest as herself and Larry disguised as the "Mystery Lady." She also plants the idea in Priest's mind that Larry is going to betray him. She arranges to meet both of them backstage on the night of the competition in which she will dance. As Marcia is backstage getting ready to perform, Priest and Larry arrive for their respective dates and discover only each other. Priest attacks Larry with a knife, and Larry pulls out his gun and kills him. Meanwhile, the none-too-gracious reigning dancehall queen finds out Marcia's true identity as a "lowly street vendor" and attempts to humiliate her publicly. This plan backfires, however, because the crowd, many of them vendors themselves, had already discovered that the "Mystery Lady" was Marcia. Marcia wins the competition and the audience heartily cheers the victory of the common woman over the uppity former queen. In the end, then, Marcia pulls a fast one on Larry, removes Priest from the streets, and wins money, fame, and respect.

There are several important differences between these two films' portrayals of working-class life in Jamaica, all of which reflect the changes in Jamaica's political economy during the intervening twenty-five years. The first, and most obvious, is that while both lead characters mobilize popular imaginations about "getting over," Ivan dies, leaving his family destitute, and Marcia wins. In The Harder They Come, agents of the state are ultimately able to neutralize Ivan and all he stands for, while in Dancehall Queen the police are portrayed as a bumbling, if menacing, presence unable to effectively do much beyond intimidating community members. Second, there is a notable absence of "brown" middle-class gatekeepers in Dancehall Queen. Where the fate of Ivan and his crew was, in large measure, related to decisions made outside of their purview, Marcia's world is represented as a largely autonomous domain where individuals are left to fend for themselves and take care of each other. Moreover, those who control significant resources in Dancehall Queen are not linked to the institutional structures of either the state or civil society. As noted earlier, this reflects a more general decline in the influence of the middle classes as cultural, political, and economic brokers in the lives of working-class people. Additionally, it is not incidental that with the more general proliferation of the service sector and the feminization of its labor pool throughout the 1980s and 1990s, we should see a woman in the role of the popular hero. However, though Marcia receives fame by the end of the *Dancehall Queen*, unlike Ivan, she was not initially questing it. She, like some of the female characters in Winsome's plays, was seeking to increase her autonomy (from men) in her efforts to raise her family safely. Ivan, on the other hand, is ultimately portrayed as seeking fame for fame's sake, despite his initial attempt to destabilize the hierarchy of networks in the marijuana industry. He is, in the end, unable to provide for himself and his family, despite his ultimate assertion "Star Bwoy cyaan dead."[13]

I do not wish to make this analysis of filmic representations of Jamaican culture too triumphal or conclusive. As noted earlier, many among the "poorer class of people" in Mango Mount still cited *The Harder They Come* as an accurate reflection of life in Jamaica today. Furthermore, with respect to *Dancehall Queen*, they argued that "in real life," Larry would never have let Marcia off the hook after tricking him (instead, he would have killed her too), and that "not everyone can become a dancehall queen." Nevertheless, I believe the two movies do manifest important public shifts in the ideological legitimacy of "modern blackness" as well as in both the composition and the relative power of the state between the 1960s and the late 1990s.

America the Beautiful, or the Belly of the Beast?

In the previous chapter, I noted the pervasiveness of migration and how this has been related to a generational difference with respect to ideas about how to "move forward in life." Here, I want to focus on the ways this intensified migration has shaped local meanings of "America" since this is such an important component of modern blackness. In Mango Mount, community members' view of America as a "land of opportunity" coexisted with the view of the United States as an "evil empire." The latter was, in large measure, due to its position in the global political economy and the impact this has had on economies like Jamaica's. In fact, when villagers identified the "global economy," they typically spoke of "America" (and very occasionally, Japan). Moreover, "Americanization" has often been seen as the latest in a long line of oppressions, and Americans have been viewed as degenerate cultural influences.[14] Indeed, villagers often attributed the perceived increases in consumerism, individualism, materialism, and a desire for instant gratification to American influence.[15]

Nevertheless, many villagers also indicated that in the United States, they experienced an ease of movement they didn't in Jamaica. This ease was both literal—as a result of more extensive infrastructural development—and social—due to what they believed was a greater potential for upward mobility and a less rigid system of social stratification. Whether or not the latter was actually true, the belief that social mobility was possible in "America" was, in itself, significant. Therefore, as I suggested in chapter 6, increased access to the United States has opened an avenue for Jamaicans to evade the colonial race and class structures that were institutionalized by the British.[16] Notably, however, the "America" community members invoked was not the actual New York City neighborhoods where their families and friends lived in cramped apartments alongside African Americans, other West Indians, Puerto Ricans, Dominicans, and West Africans. Nor did it necessarily include Hartford, Miami, New Jersey, or anywhere else they knew Jamaicans lived or worked. Rather, the quotation-marked-off place "America,"[17] the "America" of the "Dream," was upwardly mobile and phenotypically white, if not the green of the almighty dollar itself. Hip-hop and rhythm and blues were not really part of this "America," though they formed a significant part not only of the immigration experience of (especially) younger community members, but also, as I mentioned earlier, of the media experience of Jamaicans of all ages. As a result, the "America" of immigrant dreams was bifurcated—a white America where they might work hard and earn enough money to "move forward in life" and a black America where they might live. Often, the images of these two Americas became more integrated once someone had actually migrated and had to confront America's promises and prejudices for him or herself.[18]

It is also worth pointing out here that while community members' most common invocations of the influence of the United States referenced a global economy of politics and culture, it was also the case that the adoption and modification of American institutions locally within Mango Mount had created additional options for poorer community members to express themselves and their views. This was less explicitly discussed, but as I pointed out in chapter 4, the establishment, for example, of the Seventh-Day Adventist church provided community members with an alternate religious and social forum within which they might hold positions of leadership and influence. Moreover, many villagers saw in the National Democratic Movement (NDM)—the new political party that emerged in late 1995—a chance to alter the course of party politics in Jamaica by changing the parliamentary system of government in a manner that would approach the democratic system as it is practiced in the United States. In this case, moving away from "politics as usual" was not only related to putting an end to the bipartisan violence that has characterized electoral politics in Jamaica, but also as moving toward an American style of government.[19]

Finally, many village youth identified dancehall as a cultural expression that has united youth of different colors and class backgrounds. In part, this was the result of the growing power of dancehall within the public sphere of cultural production in Jamaica. It has also been due to an increasing socialization of American racial ideologies that have inscribed "brown" people into the category "black," a socialization that began with the Black Power movement during the 1960s but that has intensified since the 1980s. This does not mean that Jamaica's tripartite color and class system has been dismantled, nor that color and class prejudice have disappeared among younger people, as these biases are not absent within African American communities. Additionally, though there may be greater cross-class and cross-race interaction among youth in school, by the time they begin looking for employment or spouses, boundaries often become redrawn. Nevertheless, the purportedly greater cross-class appeal of a popular cultural form associated with lower-class black Jamaicans marks a situation in which the colonial color, class, gender, and culture nexus has become increasingly unstable at a time when "America" has become increasingly ascendant within Jamaica's cultural, political, and economic spheres.

Jamaicans' long-standing love-hate relationship with "America," then, is an integral element of modern blackness. On one hand, lower-class black Jamaicans have adopted and adapted some of the trends offered up by the popular African American sitcoms on TV, through the collaborations between dancehall DJs and hip-hop artists or on the streets of New York themselves. On the other hand, the difficulty of extracting personal and national development goals from the shadow of the United States has perpetuated an ongoing resentment. This resentment has occasionally also been extended to black Americans who, despite the stylistic appeal of African American popular culture and despite the political appeal of transnational racial solidarity, nonetheless are sometimes suspected of carrying the banner of the United States.

Radical Consumerism:
"Sim Simma, Who Got the Keys to My Bimma?"[20]

Within this context, it is especially important to note that many younger community members believed that as much as America had influenced Jamaican culture, Jamaicans also influenced culture in the United States. As one younger man put it, "Jamaicans want American style but Americans want to talk Jamaican, to walk Jamaican." He continued to argue for the elaboration of a critical distinction between learning from Americans and thinking like Americans:

> It's not like we're just taking information and they're just fooling us into thinking one way. They're changing because of us. It's a two-way thing. America right now is supreme, but not everybody is thinking like them. But we're learning from them. Everything has its good and bad and it's for us to decide what we want out of it. Some people might say we're picking up their culture, but if you look on some of the Americans, what they're doing is what we've been doing from long time, especially in terms of the music and the dancing. And I'm sure it's Jamaicans going to America that made it a big thing. It's a younger generation of people.

What is notable about this young man's statement is the extent to which he viewed cultural appropriation as a selective two-way process, albeit one that is uneven. This explains why some youth, in contrast to either the older generation of middle-class professionals or the generation of working-class Jamaicans politicized by the various movements during the 1970s, might not have seen America as an evil empire encroaching from the north. Contrary to the dominant image of the culturally bombarded and besieged Jamaican, powerless either to resist or critique that which is imposed from "elsewhere"—the image often proliferated by those who disparaged the growing influence of the United States—youth asserted that David could not only challenge Goliath, but could also influence what Goliath listened to, how he dressed, and what he liked. This has been an important element of how Jamaicans view themselves and their importance on a global scale. The facts that "likkle Jamaica" is known worldwide for its music and its elite athletes (even, perhaps especially, its bobsledders), and that this recognition is completely out of proportion with the island's size, are noted in both public fora and private conversations over and over again. The frequency of these invocations also suggests a need to carve out spaces in which Jamaicans feel, and indeed have, power and recognition within a global public sphere.

Even more importantly, the perspective offered by these youth reinforces the importance of a dialectical reading of the relationship between capitalist globalization and local cultural practices and between consumerism and cultural imperialism. It also nuances the assertions of scholars who argue that global capitalism and its development models are destroying cultural diversity and creating a monoculture (e.g., Escobar 1995) and who identify "Americanization" as solely imperialist and nonnegotiable (e.g., Jameson 1998). What Mango Mount youth argued instead marked an attempt to reinscribe and re-create their own agency through the process of consumption itself. In other words, while coveting American "name brands," they were also quick to point out the extent to which they defined consumer trends (in music selections, linguistic repertoires, clothing styles) within Jamaica and to extend this power to Jamaicans overseas. This is what I am calling "radical consumerism." It is not only an eschewal of middle-class models of progress through moderation and temperance, but also an insistence that consumption is a creative and potentially liberatory process and that the ability to both influence and reflect global style is, in fact, an important public power.

Other scholars have made similar assertions. For example, anthropologist Daniel Miller's analysis of consumption practices within contemporary Trinidad demonstrates that the process of consumption is not everywhere identical but that Trinidadians creolize as they consume, thereby defining modernity for themselves (1994). Film scholar Manthia Diawara has argued that rather than being arcane manifestations of "tradition" to be swept away through the process of modernization, West African markets actually provide a serious challenge to both processes of globalization and the nation-state itself (1998). This is because, within the context of severe structural adjustment, West African markets "give back to people what the state and the multinational corporations take away from them, that is, the right to consume" (1998:120). Historian Robin D. G. Kelley has also emphasized the strategic and creative dimensions of African Americans' "self-commodification of play" (1997:45). Here, he has defined "play" as those aspects of leisure, pleasure, and creative expression that circulate within African American popular culture and provide a few—a very few—with income. For Kelley, "play" is "more than an expression of stylistic innovation, gender identities, and/or racial and class anger. Increasingly it is viewed as a way to survive economic crisis or a means to upward mobility" (1997:45).

What these scholars are pointing to is the need to read capitalist consumption dialectically within the context of specific histories and political economies. This kind of analytic framework engages the possibility for alternative readings of "getting my share now, what's mine,"[21] readings that position what may look like crass (and perhaps imitative) materialism on the part of lower-class black Jamaicans instead as racially vindicating capitalist consumerism. Further, the basis of this consumerism—the ideology that positions progress as the result of amassing wealth—is not now limited to the Jamaican working classes. As David Scott has also pointed out, the new black middle class has been "less concerned with the virtues of taste, or the nationalist ideal of a cultural consensus, and more with markets and money" (2000:295). In other words, this emphasis on capitalism and consumerism has, more recently, been linked to the elevation of a racial identity.

A dim view of these ideological shifts is often promulgated within both academic and popular fora. However, taking "radical consumerism" seriously may reveal that the lower-class black Jamaican man driving a "Bimma" has more on his mind than individualist conspicuous consumption.[22] Instead, he could be refashioning selfhood and reshaping stereotypical assumptions about racial possibilities through—rather than outside—capitalism. That is, black Jamaicans are simultaneously critiquing, selectively appropriating, and creatively redefining those aspects of the dominant capitalist ethos that they believe benefit themselves and their communities, both materially and psychologically. By making this argument, I do not mean to discount the effects of a globally hegemonic Americanism whereby the viability of global markets is secured for U.S. consumers and capitalists by any means necessary (including, or more accurately especially, military intervention) in ways that exploit and reproduce the relative weakness of states constrained by the International Monetary Fund and the World Bank. What I am trying to stress is that within this context, individuals do find ways to resignify dominant ideologies and practices in order to resituate themselves as powerful actors within their own transnational spheres.[23]

Ghetto Feminism: "Yuh Nuh Ready Fi Dis Yet, Bwoy"[24]

Peggy Antrobus has remarked that while she was working as the first director of the Jamaican government's Women's Bureau during the mid-

1970s, she discovered that black lower-class women identified sexuality (as distinct from sex) as one of two primary sources of power in their lives (personal communication 2001).[25] By highlighting the centrality of sexuality to women's power, she has drawn attention to what I am calling "ghetto feminism." The concern with "slackness" in dancehall has not only been related to the glorification of materialism and violence, but also to the public emergence of ghetto feminism, most clearly embodied through the persona of the scantily clad and sexually explicit female DJ. In fact, the term "slack" itself is gendered, as its definition in the *Dictionary of Jamaican English* reads "a woman of loose morals" (C. Cooper 2000).

The public emergence of this persona within popular culture has been critical precisely because her gender politics challenge two primary aspects of the creole nationalist project—the pursuit of respectability and the acceptance of a paternalistic patriarchy.[26] As I outlined in chapter 1, the respectable blackness advocated first by the nonconformist churches and then later by the nationalist elite envisioned a particular ideological and material structure within which men and women would create families and contribute to community and national life. The emphasis on the creation of nuclear family households continued throughout the early twentieth century and was intensified after the 1938 labor rebellions. This emphasis was based upon a view of the family as the determining institution of sociopolitical and economic stability, but this was a family in which males were central as breadwinners and where women were primarily concerned with social reproduction in the private sphere. That this arrangement has never been hegemonic (nor even necessarily desired) within the British West Indies is a commonly stated fact. However, within the context of mid-twentieth-century nationalism, privatizing women and cultivating respectability within the domestic sphere was part of a more general concern with state formation, and, by extension, cultivating respectability within an international public sphere, which, by the end of World War II, extolled the nation as the most sovereign and modern form of social organization.

The changes that have occurred within Jamaica's political economy and occupational structure since independence have opened the door for lower-class women to redefine their public image on their own terms. During the 1970s, significant numbers of women entered the informal economy as international "higglers" (now designated by the government as Informal Commercial Importers), buying commercial goods in Miami and other u.s. (and Caribbean) cities at wholesale prices and reselling them, at considerable markup, in markets throughout Jamaica. Because their overhead expenses are nominal, these vendors have successfully captured clientele from established formal import businesses, in some cases, acquiring enough capital to move their families into more middle- and upper-middle-class residential neighborhoods in uptown Kingston. Further, women service workers swelled the ranks of both national and migrant labor forces throughout the 1980s and 1990s.[27]

In conjunction with the rise of dancehall, these developments have also been harbingers of an important social shift. In her ethnographic research among Informal Commercial Importers in Kingston, Gina Ulysse notes that while in the past, economically successful women might have attempted to cultivate the social standards of femininity associated with upper-class "ladies," the "downtown women" she observed didn't bother. This was because they no longer viewed the consequences of failing to assimilate to middle-class gender ideals as critical to their economic survival, and so eschewed them. Instead, they were actively "recreating different sites of power and redefining the meanings of respect" (Ulysse 1999:168). In other words, black lower-class females were not particularly interested in conforming to middle- and upper-class standards of femininity and respectability. At the same time, middle- and upper-class "ladies" have been forced to acknowledge the power of these women "if for no other reason than because they now also possess and manipulate the hegemonic u.s. dollar" (Ulysse 1999:168).

Ghetto feminism also issues a critique of patriarchy, principally through its public affirmation of female agency, especially as this is related to sexual desire and fulfillment. This critique is most evident in the work of female dancehall DJs such as Tanya Stephens and Lady Saw, and more recently, Ce'Cile. For example, Tanya Stephens encourages women to chastise men for satisfying themselves but leaving them "hot like a ginger"[28] and tells men that the consequences of such behavior are that women will find their satisfaction elsewhere:

> Have yuh ever stop to think wha mek a gal cheat
> Yuh need fi check yuhself before yuh start kiss yuh teeth
> Caw yuh nuh ready fi this yet bwoy
> Have yuh ever wonder what mek a girl cum
> A woman fus fi satisfy before yuh say yuh done

> Yuh cyaan say a thing if yuh end up a get bun
> Caw yuh nuh ready fi this yet bwoy
> —Tanya Stephens, lyrics from "Yuh Nuh Ready"

Similarly, Lady Saw enjoins women to take material advantage of the power embodied within the commodity they control—access to sexual favors:

> Mi have mi light bill fi pay man haffi mind mi
> Man haffi buy mi everyting before dem wine mi
> Mi have rent fi deal with all tomorrow morning'
> So no likkle fool caan strip mi
> Me waan go a Bahamas pon Sunday
> An come back to mi husband Monday
> But 'tis a fool mi a look fi nyam out him bank book
> If dem know what me know dem jus 'low mi"
> —Lady Saw, lyrics from "Man Haffi Mind Wi"

Finally, emerging star Ce'Cile's song "Do It to Me" has recently generated a fair amount of controversy. This is because the lyrics not only encourage her male partner to perform oral sex *with her*—a sexual act widely considered in Jamaica to be both physically unclean and morally reprehensible—but also publicly refutes men's claims that they don't engage in oral sex *at all*:

> Watch dem a talk bout no but a dem a dweet
> Watch dem a talk bout how dem woulda never dweet
> When di fire start bun dem a go feel di heat
> Watch dem a talk bout no, under cover freak eh
> Bwoy stop lie, truth u fi speak
> Bwoy no haffi hide ca mi know u a freak
> Gwaan use u (tongue) caz mi love when u dweet
> Whe mi a lie fah? Love di man dem whe eat
> Some a talk bout oh no
> Nuff a dem a chat but dema go low
> From a gal u love nu fear
> So when selector talk bout who nah dweet hand ina di air
> Bwoy keep u hand dem a u side beca di gyal dem no care
> —Ce'Cile, lyrics from "Do It to Me"

Here, Ce'Cile not only endorses female sexual pleasure. She also exposes male sexual hypocrisy.

What the discourses expressed through the work of these female dance-hall artistes publicly counter is an unchecked male dominance, a dominance that is related to particular ideologies about Jamaican masculinity that emerged within the context of plantation slavery and have been perpetuated without significant modification through the contemporary period.[29] Lisa Douglass has argued that these ideologies are generalized throughout the male population and contrasts this to how ideas about femininity constitute class-specific attitudes and behaviors that are linked to color and are valued differently by the society as a whole:

> Part of what makes a man a man is this prerogative to receive the services and request the attention of a woman. Where a man lacks other types of power, he can gain social or reputational power and control over women simply by virtue of being a man. Men of the lower classes are less likely to achieve this type of power, of course, than their higher-class counterparts. But differences in the assertion of masculinity vary by degree rather than by type. Men measure themselves according to a more uniform scale than do women, that is, there is a single standard of masculinity. Whereas men differ by *degree* of masculinity, then, women differ by *type* of female behavior. (1992:251)

Therefore, when a woman decides to make the level of her attention contingent upon the extent to which a man can provide her with what she needs or wants—or worse, when she publicly insults a man's sexual ability —she destabilizes the ideology of male supremacy. This is because she is asserting a threat not only to that individual man's masculinity, but also to the patriarchal ideological framework that positions this masculinity as transcendently powerful. That this destabilization operates primarily at the ideological, and not the material, level does not diminish its importance because what is key to our purposes here is that the ghetto feminism proclaimed by a Tanya Stephens or a Lady Saw eschews the model of privatized female sexuality associated with the middle-class femininity and respectability that has provided a critical foundation for the creole multiracial nationalist project. Ghetto feminism, then, is a type of what Elizabeth McAlister has called "sexualized popular laughter" (2002:61), a way in which women "read" and critique the social order. I am not suggesting here that Jamaican women have only recently begun to use these tactics to carve out spaces for their own power vis-à-vis the men within their intimate social worlds. What I am noting, however, is that dancehall has created a space for a new *public* advocacy of these tactics by women for women. Further, this is a space that exists beyond the realm of intimate relations, and as such it has the potential to infiltrate a more general political vision.

The obvious contemporary parallel to the ghetto feminism of modern blackness in the United States is hip-hop feminism. As has been the case with dancehall, several scholars have argued that while hip-hop can present images of women that are offensive, it also allows women "a way to defy traditional gender roles, assert independence, and demand respect" and "provides a forum for feminist action" (Grappo 2001:27; see also Rose 1994; J. Morgan 1999).[30] For these scholars, irreverent and sexually explicit rappers like Foxy Brown and L'il Kim are not merely pawns of a sexist recording industry—indeed, a sexist culture—that can't get enough of brown-skinned T&A. Instead, they are independent, they demand respect, and they refuse to discount women's sexual desires and pleasures. That is, they are part of a more general, and ongoing, struggle for control over black female sexuality.[31]

I am aware that locating women's attempts to redefine their own sexual imagery as a feminist practice is controversial, especially if these redefinitions seem to reproduce some dominant tropes about black women even as it challenges others. Indeed, black feminists in the United States have been wary of condoning the use of erotic power as a means of battling sexism expressly because of the historical legacies enfolding black female sexuality. Moreover, as journalist Joan Morgan has pointed out, "Without financial independence, education, ambition, intelligence, spirituality, and love, punanny alone isn't all that powerful. The reality is that it's easily replaceable, inexhaustible in supply, and quite frankly, common" (1999: 224). Similarly, Patricia Saunders has tempered some of the liberatory discourse about women and dancehall by arguing for a reconsideration of the ways "discourses of resistance also work to reinscribe hegemonic practices" (2003:114). This is a reconsideration that would make central the links between gender, sexual politics, and nationalist constructions of sexuality, which, as I have also been arguing, have defined the contours of respectable citizenship.

At the same time, it is true that hip-hop feminists and dancehall divas push the envelope, generate public debate, and broaden what is possible in terms of public behavior for women. The extensive public controversy about the representations of women and female sexuality that surround such *artistes* as Lady Saw, Ce'Cile, and Tanya Stephens, therefore, has to do with the perceived threat they issue to middle-class morality, to lower-class visions of black female integrity and respectability, to many Caribbean feminists' visions of transformation, to male supremacy, and to the project of state formation itself.

The Politics of Modern Blackness
and Hegemonic Reordering in Jamaica

In rethinking the relationships among freedom, subjectivity, and power, Paul Gilroy has argued that black intellectual and expressive cultural production elaborates a "counterculture of modernity" (1993:1). Gilroy considers black music, in particular, to constitute an "alternative public sphere" ([1987]:215). This is because among black Atlantic populations, the production and consumption of music (like that of roots plays) has blurred modern Euro-American boundaries between ethics and aesthetics, life and art, and performer and crowd. For Gilroy, public expressions of blackness are correlated with the values of egalitarianism, community, and reciprocity. Insofar as these values represent challenges to dominant norms associated with the effects of slavery and capitalist development—hierarchy, individualism, and greed—they have been held up as evidence of resistance (with a capital "R"). However, the popular music and plays associated with dancehall culture represent and reproduce aspects of contemporary dominant systems of belief—such as "making it" in the marketplace—and these aspects also embody particular political visions. The questions that remain, then, are as follows: If modern blackness is supposed to be countercultural, where is its counterhegemonic politics? If it marks a new kind of representation holding a new public power, does it embody a new mode of articulating protest? Does it carry a particular vision for the future?

While black expressive cultural forms reflect an alternative historical consciousness and provide the means to articulate and maintain oppositional identities and values, they have also always existed "partly inside and not always against the grand narrative of Enlightenment and its operational principles" (Gilroy 1993:48). Within this context, we are usually quick to recognize that compliance has not always indicated consent. However, it is also true that noncompliance does not always translate into resistance. Inheritors of the contradictory legacies of the Enlightenment and slavery, democracy and imperialism, scientific rationalism and racism, the descendants of Africans throughout the Atlantic world have been forced to develop a worldview that enables them to negotiate Western tenets of civilization while at the same time creatively critiquing them. This inherently double-sided structural formation has meant that for black people, *at least* dual visions, lifestyles, and consciousnesses are not only possible, but also necessary. I emphasize the "at least" in this sentence to suggest that neither the DuBoisian "double consciousness" framework nor the various iterations of cultural duality can fully account for the complexity of the material and ideological cultural formulations I've described in these pages. Like other anthropologists, I am interested here in moving beyond structuralism's legacy, in insisting that we contemplate the relatedness of binary terms "rather than consider them in terms of simple oppositionality" (Murray 2002:19; see also Carnegie 2002; Glick Schiller and Fouron 2001; McAlister 2002; Palmié 2002). From this perspective, modernity and tradition, global and local, secular and sacred, state and nation, and, yes, hegemony and resistance are fluid *relationships*, mutually constituting conceptual tools rather than oppositional categorizational poles.

For anthropologist Stephan Palmié, this is a theoretical move necessitated by the particular historical formation of what he calls "Atlantic Modernity." His use of this term delineates not only the intricate web of political and economic relations that formed the Americas in relation to Europe, Africa, and Asia, but also "the heterogeneous, and historically contingent aggregate of local discourses and practices reflecting on, engaging, and thereby both shaping and transforming this basic structural constellation" (2002:15). The legacy of this formation, Palmié argues, urges an increasingly dialectical conceptualization of the relationship between global processes and human agency. It requires an exploration not only of countermodernities or alternative modernities, but of the "internal fissures, contradictions, and discontinuities" (2002:16) within the terrain of the modern itself, of the ways the "periphery" permeates the "core." In this way, he argues, we move away from a tendency toward categorical separation whose oppositions create their own hybrids and instead "repatriate the seeming chaos, ambivalence, and hybridity of the Caribbean to where it belongs: into the midst of the very forms of knowledge and discourse that produced the distorted image of a foiled African American, and, most specifically, Caribbean modernity in the first place" (2002:52).

Though Palmié is concerned with Afro-Cuban religio-scientific knowledge and practice, his observations hold for the Jamaican context as well. Intellectuals and activists alike have been concerned to assess the transformative potential of popular cultural practices and representations in Jamaica because of their power to reveal the ways nonelites have negotiated the systems and opportunities institutionalized by local leaderships and multilateral financial agencies, while at the same time maintaining their own ways of living and values, even as these are modified with time, technology, and experience. In attempting to pinpoint key aspects of popular political consciousness that have provided a foundation for counterhegemonic material and ideological strategies among Jamaicans over time, several scholars have identified black lower-class politico-religious ideology as embodying transformative spiritual, cultural, and political agendas simultaneously (Bogues 2002; Carnegie 2002).[32] Within other spheres, late-twentieth-century lower-class urban black Jamaican cultural production and sociopolitical practices have been seen as embodying an increased "cultural confidence," a confidence that has occasioned an "expansion of their social autonomy, and a meteoric rise in their social power" (Gray 1994:177).[33] While these formulations help us to discern some of the ways people marginalized from the formal institutions of power create sociocultural, economic, and political openings for themselves, they can only tell us part of the story. This is, in part, because even when considering transterritorial or diasporic formations, they tend to situate counterhegemonic cultural production within narratives of national or racial progress that are ultimately territorially based (Carnegie 2002).

The profound restructuring of the link between territory and nationalism throughout the Caribbean by the end of the twentieth century has had ramifications that could not be mitigated by, say, politicians' attempts to encourage dual citizenship or absentee voting. While migrants have historically forged multiple political, economic, and social ties across territories (Glick Schiller et al. 1992; Basch et al. 1994), because of the intensification of migration, because of P. J. Patterson's attempts to incorporate migrated Jamaicans and African Americans into the national body of Jamaica, and because of the greater penetration by U.S. (and in many cases African American) media, Jamaica is now wherever Jamaicans are. This means that the processes of Jamaican racial, class, and gender formation—both in Jamaica and in diaspora—are always negotiated in relation to those processes occurring elsewhere. The emergent politics of modern blackness is therefore neither univocal nor univalent, but nevertheless has the potential to alter Jamaicans' political and social possibilities in the twenty-first century as significantly as the explicit conceptualization of the African diaspora as a common community did in the late nineteenth century and early twentieth. This is because it is a politics that is rooted in the changing ways people define community, restructure their lives in order to survive, and reorganize racialized, classed, and gendered identities within the public sphere. The narratives of duality and double consciousness can only partially capture the complexity and dynamism of these imaginative and material worlds that are sometimes created through surprising collaborations.

If we approached a more complex understanding of the politics of popular culture, we would, for example, reveal the emphasis on consumerism as something more than false consciousness and a capitulation to Americanized commodifications of desire. Instead, we might apprehend it as a desire for a particular kind of modernity that in specific social realms is "coproduced" with other diasporic communities. Here, I am borrowing the idea of coproduction from Elizabeth McAlister, whose discussion of Haitian Rara in New York City marks a tension between the concepts of diaspora and transationalism. Noting that Rara in New York is in dialogue with the Haitian branches of dancehall and African American hip-hop culture, and explicating the complex and changing relationships forged between Haitian and Jamaican migrants in Florida and Brooklyn (indeed, between newly arrived Haitians and established Haitian Americans), McAlister arrives at the important insight that "the process of identity building is coproduced with other minority communities, and not just against hegemonic groups" (2002:198). In other words, there is a complex historical political economy that surrounds the respatializations and resignifications of Rara, and its meanings are generated not only among Haitians in relation to elites (in Haiti) or whites (in the United States), but also laterally among other diasporic populations. In the case I am examining here, modern blackness becomes coproduced with urban and primarily working-class African Americans who live in Jamaicans' social worlds—both real and imagined—as media producers and neighbors as well as in relation to middle- and upper-class Jamaicans in Jamaica and West Indians and Euro-Americans in the United States and elsewhere.

Within this somewhat broadened context, modern blackness emerges as complex, but not necessarily contradictory. On the one hand, it provides visions for upward mobility within today's globalized economy that are alternative to those professed by professional middle-class Jamaicans. On the other, these visions don't necessarily open the door to long-term transformations in social, political, and economic hierarchies. For example, while the entrepreneurial zeal with which people in Mango Mount seek to take advantage of migratory possibilities has facilitated their relative success within a global labor market, it has also drained the community of young people with skills, has presented serious challenges to the development of leadership locally, has further disadvantaged those community members who are not able to migrate, and has perpetuated an outward outlook whereby local ambitions require foreign realization. At the same time, migration is a critical opportunity within a context where, in spite of increased access to education, Jamaicans cannot find remunerative work locally that is related to their specific skills.

The complexity of modern blackness is also expressed within its popular representations, such as dancehall culture. Winsome's play, for example, both celebrated the culture of dancehall and recuperated aspects of the culture of respectability. Among female DJs themselves, we hear lyrics that destabilize the normalcy of male infidelity while others support it. Similarly, while many women appreciate aspects of these DJs' politics, very few emulate their self-presentation in a daily fashion. Instead, their attraction to Tanya Stephens, Ce'Cile, or Lady Saw is more akin to living vicariously through the images they present. As Carolyn Cooper has suggested, dancehall is perhaps best understood as an "erogenous zone," a "liberatory space in which working-class women and their more timid middle-class sisters play out eroticized roles that may not ordinarily be available to them in the rigid social conventions of the everyday" (2000).

Because modern blackness is a part of and itself embodies the cultural plurality that frames the range of ideological and political possibilities for contemporary Jamaicans, it is less a stable and coherent ideological framework for action than a way of seeing, organizing, and imagining that can negotiate and incorporate other ways of seeing, organizing, and imagining. Modern blackness, then, embodies not a crisis, but a public power previously unattained, one that encompasses a framework for facing a global political economy in which Jamaica is never as powerful as it exists in the imaginations of Jamaicans. Indeed, because the conditions of neoliberal capitalist globalization have intensified older hierarchies of class, color, gender, and culture and have created new tensions and conflicts between ethnic and national groups, and because subordinated people have little control over how the broader parameters of their lives are being determined by today's economic and political structures of power, the public ascendance of modern blackness signals a significant change. This is true whether aspects of cultural production associated with modern blackness are evaluated as challenges or capitulations to dominant ideologies and practices. Popular cultural production in contemporary Jamaica, then, must be positioned neither as a kind of contradictory false consciousness, nor as inherently or hopefully resistant or revolutionary. Instead, we must take note of its complexity and particularly of its reflection of the changing balance of power between the respectable state and popular culture. In this way, we can more easily see how a decline in the public power of middle-class respectability might constitute something other than a crisis.

conclusion

THE REMIX

In November 1997, Jamaica's soccer team qualified for the 1998 World Cup finals in France. This marked the first time ever that a team from the British West Indies reached the finals and only the second instance that the Caribbean region would be represented.[1] During the Jamaican team's "Road to France," many newspaper commentators saw the fervor of national spirit that was generated as an example that Jamaicans could be unified across the bitter divides of color, class, and culture that ordinarily structured relationships between them. Moreover, this "one glorious moment of 'Out of Many, One People'" (G. Brown 1997) was viewed as transferable to other arenas of life such as politics and economic development. Several commentators suggested that the team's success could be an antidote to the "rampant individualism" seen as characterizing Jamaican society since it highlighted the importance of working together, discipline, striving for excellence, and patriotism (Stair 1997a). Others portrayed it as hopeful evidence that "we are capable of going up against anything the rest of the world has to throw at us and to succeed in the face of it . . . an essential trait required for surviving in a global economy" (Semaj 1997). The match against the United States team in Washington D.C., in particular, was popularly and publicly understood as a contest between "David and Goliath" in which the Jamaican team stood in for the regional interests of all West Indians in America.

However, a few were more skeptical about the long-term possibilities of the upsurge in national pride. One columnist predicted that the burst of "flag nationalism" accompanying the team's success would be tenuous, individualistic, and short-lived:

> The sense of success will not translate into everyday behaviour because the emotions associated with the sporting success are the very antithesis of the experiences of day-to-day existence. Consequently, when the celebrating is over, people return to everyday survival as if nothing had happened. . . . Sports may be used as a temporary distraction and offer hope for progress, but true national unity will only come about when people see real changes in the quality of their lives at all levels. (Boxill 1997)

These "moments" of apparent national unity are few and far between in Jamaica and their consolidation, as in most societies, often requires the appearance of an external threat. In this case, that threat was represented by the United States's soccer team, with the team itself standing in for America's current dominance on global political, economic, and cultural playing fields. The tied match was celebrated as a victory in Jamaica, evidence of David successfully confronting Goliath on Goliath's turf. This was not, as has been the case with cricket, seen as an example of the colonies beating the empire at their own game.[2] On the contrary, it was an indication that Jamaicans could keep the (new) empire at bay in a game associated with Third World excellence. That the Jamaican team itself was largely culled from the black working-class population is not incidental in this respect. As I have been arguing, while the cultural practices associated with poor black Jamaicans were often those popularly considered to represent Jamaica within the international arena, rarely had they catalyzed solidarities among the entire population locally. Here, then, was a moment in which blackness stood in for Jamaicanness, available to all Jamaicans as a symbol of temporary triumph over foreign domination. Throughout these pages, I have been examining the ways these fleeting moments might, when amalgamated and contextualized within broader processes of change, point us toward deeper understandings of social transformation at various levels.

For the past twenty years or so, anthropologists have been attuned to the efforts of those engaged in defining public concepts of national cultural identity worldwide (Mahon 2000). We have asked questions regarding the larger economic and sociopolitical conditions, both locally and globally, surrounding shifting attention to people's history and their self-consciousness of that history. We have sought to account for the agency of social actors by identifying the people or groups who have made decisions to elevate certain practices at certain times to the status of representing a national or community ethos. We have also analyzed the ways in which these decisions have been institutionalized, both at the national level and through everyday practices. And we have, for the most part, celebrated these contradictory processes as social movements that have ultimately benefited the "folk" by giving official legitimacy to some aspects of their lifestyles, even as we have identified the ways global social hierarchies have remained stubbornly persistent and economic inequalities have increased. We have only recently turned our attention to the uneasy relationships between state-driven "identity politics" and "development politics," and the ways both may contradict the actual lifestyles, experiences, and desires of a populace. We are also now more clearly elaborating the specific institutional and temporal contexts in which these relationships develop and change.

Throughout this book, I have taken a long view of institutional change and its potential for social transformation at various levels. The questions that have concerned me have had to do with the implications of democratizing institutions, and by this I mean not only broadening the cultural content upon which nationalist institutions bestow legitimacy, but also increasing their access to people previously excluded. More specifically, I have asked whether increased access to institutions has necessarily entailed a fundamental shift not only in the content and values they promote, but also in the viability of the institutions themselves. I have sought to identify the contexts in which, and the processes by which, institutions gain and lose relevance. And I have attempted to clarify the fate of nationalist institutions within the current context of intensified globalization as the power of individual states to socialize and provide for their citizenries has changed. What I have presented here is merely one case at one particular historical moment that marks a partial hegemonic reordering in postcolonial Jamaica by grounding individuals' choices, beliefs, and experiences within both a changing local, national, and global political economy and a shifting geography of race, class, gender, sexuality, and generation. To do so, I have attempted to portray a situation where everything is "slightly—but not completely—tilted toward incompleteness, instability, and change" (Ortner 1996:18), in this way trying to emphasize moments of creativity and transformation.

I have argued that there has been an important transformation in post-independence Jamaica, a generational change whereby lower-class black Jamaican expressive popular culture has emerged as paramount in the public sphere and has thereby surmounted the Creole nationalist emphasis on "folk" cultural forms. As lower-class black Jamaicans have adapted and subverted the new reconfigurations of power emergent as a result of contemporary forms of a globalized capitalism, lower-class blackness has become the most common signifier of what it means to be Jamaican today. This means neither that Africa—as a symbolic trope—holds no meaning for working-class Jamaicans nor that Jamaicans don't affirm a diasporic consciousness by celebrating their Africanness. Throughout the Americas, "Africa" has been wielded as a political and cultural weapon to resist white oppression both in the past and currently. But this has less to do with the contemporary realities facing African peoples and more to do with the challenges confronting black people in the modern West. Efforts to elevate Jamaica's African cultural heritage, then, have simultaneously engaged and rejected Western visions of progress and development. Over time, they have also simultaneously modified and solidified Jamaica's colonial hierarchies. Because these are hierarchies that have been reinforced by contemporary global processes, history lives on in the present, and Africa remains a salient symbolic referent for diverse sectors of Jamaican society, though in different ways. For the majority of Jamaicans, however, everyday experiences of racial discrimination—both locally and globally—reinforce a more immediate sense of identity that is rooted in the modern transnational familial, educational, occupational, and media circuits that encompass their lives.

Within the current context of a more general disillusionment with the promises of anticolonial nationalism around the globe and a growing frustration with the constraints to structural change presented by the contemporary neoliberal global economy, it has been useful here to emphasize transformations in specific institutions. Such a focus has helped to specify the processes by which, and contexts within which, power relations are both produced and transformed since, as we know, power is not possessed; it is exercised.[3] Additionally, by historically grounding the changing political economy of institutions, it has been easier to see institutional transformations as signs of broader hegemonic shifts, shifts that constitute (and that are reproduced through) the relationships between nationalism and popular cultural production.

In the case I have outlined here, we are seeing two moments of important social and institutional transformation in Jamaica, the first from the period of Crown Colony rule to independence and the second from independence to the late twentieth century. The former placed emphasis on the "folk," on defining what was indigenous, understanding that these "folk" forms also manifested Jamaica's African heritage. Mid-twentieth-century nationalist cultural mobilizers hoped that this reconstituted past, in publicly recognizing the contributions of Africans and their descendants to the historical and cultural development of the Jamaican nation, would provide moral codes for its future. As a result, their efforts were also, at least in part, geared toward changing working-class culture to be more "respectable"—that is, more in line with the logics of gender roles and family structures promoted by American (and British, during the late colonial period) models of development. Indeed, creole nationalists distanced themselves both from the perceived "backwardness" of Africa and from the rural and urban proletariat whose practices—and values—were seen as disruptive to a modern social order over which middle-class professionals would preside. Within the context of anticolonial struggle, the assertion of an equal and legitimate cultural heritage was designed to prove Jamaica's political and cultural maturity. By developing institutions that would increase Jamaicans' potential for upward social and economic mobility, creole nationalists were also attempting to socialize the population simultaneously into a particular vision of their own cultural distinctiveness and into the values of service and voluntarism they considered crucial for the building of the new nation.

The second moment of transformation, that from independence to the present, reflects a vastly different political, economic, and ideological context and emphasizes the role of popular urban lower-class cultural productions. Despite the enduring influence Rastafari has had upon Jamaicans' sense of themselves and their influence globally, by the end of the twentieth century, Africa was almost absent from popular cultural projections. Instead, blackness was the most common signifier of Jamaicanness. These postindependence transitions represent a more general generational shift whereby popular urban cultural forms have emerged as paramount within the public sphere of national representations. At the same time, the political and economic strategies of lower-class black Jamaicans have also gained new legitimacy and proliferated publicly. The combined effect of these changes has been that the hegemonic values and institutional arrangements of the creole period have been challenged.

As I have indicated, these shifts have occasioned intense and sometimes moralistic debate, both popularly and within academic arenas, regarding *values*. This is, in part, due to the ways newly ascendant gender, racial, and consumerist ideologies and practices have destabilized two primary aspects of the creole nationalist project—the pursuit of respectability and the acceptance of a paternalistic patriarchy. What is really at stake in these debates is the integrity of the postcolonial nation during a period of intense disillusionment with the nationalist state. Indeed, the new context of late twentieth and early twenty-first century globalization has diminished the power of individual states—and some states more than others—to socialize and provide for their citizens. In many postcolonial countries, recent privatization drives have come on the heels of constraints encouraged through the development agendas of international agencies such as the World Bank and the International Monetary Fund.[4] The "crisis," then, really has to do with the viability not only of the nationalist ideologies established during the anticolonial period, but also of the state itself.

Is there a way, however, to interpret these transformations as constituting something other than a crisis? While it is true that current processes of globalization have widened income gaps, intensified racialized and spatialized hierarchies internationally, and increased the insecurity and marginalization of the most disadvantaged groups in the labor market, it is also the case that the new global political economy has opened other opportunities. The current context of global capitalism, while it leaves little room for collective "counter"-anything, has also generated new avenues through which many individual lower-class Jamaicans are advancing their economic ambitions and elaborating alternative cultural frameworks. Within the context of intensified transnational migration, they are increasingly able to circumvent the local middle- and upper-class Jamaicans upon whom they were previously more dependent politically and economically. Moreover, an amplified racialized diasporic consciousness has enabled lower-class Jamaicans to publicly challenge the creole nationalist view of "folk" blackness and therefore subvert the ideologies of those who in the past few decades have had immediate power over their lives. In other words, the current context has opened a space in which aspects of colonial color, class, gender, and cultural hierarchies that had been reproduced by the nationalist elite are being challenged and sometimes eschewed. The key to pulling the analysis of postcolonial hegemonic shifts in Jamaica out of a crisis-oriented discourse that foregrounds values, therefore, is paying greater attention to the ways people manipulate the broader political, economic, and ideological contexts in which these shifts have occurred. This helps us to see new possibilities.

What the Jamaican case illustrates is that the context of anticolonial struggle facilitated a hegemonic reorientation toward the nationalist state as the guarantor of increased democratic participation in all aspects of society and as the symbol around which pride could be mobilized, intense debates regarding policy agenda notwithstanding. This trend is rooted in the late-nineteenth-century ideology that sovereign nations should have not only territorial but also cultural borders, that states are the most modern form of social organization, and that progress is marked by the extent to which an engaged citizenry voluntarily participates in the state's institutional structures. The context of globalization, on the other hand, has oriented citizens away from the nationalist state and toward other avenues for individual, family and household, and community development. Modernity is marked through urban cosmopolitanism, citizenship has come to be experienced transnationally, and progress is defined through the power to consume. Concurrently, publicly hegemonic ideologies regarding national cultural belonging have also shifted. In Jamaica, the multiracial harmony envisioned by mid-twentieth-century creole nationalists was upstaged, during the 1990s, by an unapologetic blackness. Urban sound system dances have stolen the limelight from rural Jamaicans' "folk" forms as Jamaican bodies—still racialized, still classed, still gendered—keep step with global time.

These processes should make it clear that to continue to hang national development upon the hook of a creolized unity is to chase a phantom, to reproduce the racial distinctions that the rhetoric of cultural amalgamation obscures. If the transcendent unity envisioned at independence has not, some forty years later, fundamentally transformed colonial color, class, cultural, and gender hierarchies, can we not give up the ghost and reinterpret racially based claims to national belonging as something other than inherently dystopic? David Scott has also argued that the contemporary context in Jamaica forces us to let go of the Parsonian integrationist model once and for all, to eschew the idea that a community requires a single unifying structure of values and an underlying social contract to secure and guarantee order (2000:286). He suggests that instead, we adopt a concept of community "that hangs more on provisional decisions, contingent reasons, practical knowledges" (2000:298) and, therefore, a concept of politics as strategic practice, negotiation, and compromise. This is a concept of community that has, in fact, already been realized by many poorer Jamaicans struggling to sustain themselves within a global political-economic context that itself tends to reproduce the very inequalities creole multiracial nationalism sought to combat.

What I am insisting here is that modern blackness is neither intrinsically divisive nor exclusionary. What modern blackness chiefly challenges is the subordination of black people—politically, socially, economically, culturally—that was established during slavery, *persisted throughout* the creole nationalist era, and has been *reestablished*, though in somewhat different ways, by globalization, privatization, and structural adjustment policies. In this sense, modern blackness is not so much a threat to national unity, but an indictment of the effects of global capitalist integration, an exposure of the ways institutional structures established during the colonial period have continued to reproduce racial and class inequalities *despite* efforts on the part of state leaderships to change them. Modern blackness, then, is a call for the fulfillment of a promise that has remained unrealized. It is neither a manifesto for the dismantling of the nation nor a resignation to the attenuated power of the Jamaican state and its institutions. Instead, the modern blackness of transnational, diasporic, and cosmopolitan Jamaicans simultaneously reflects the failure of creole nationalism to turn all subjects into true citizens in postindependence Jamaica, late-twentieth-century transformations in global capitalist development, and the creative "anancyism"[5] of Jamaicans worldwide. By tracing the emergence of new popular subjectivities like modern blackness, while still grounding them in a history of changing social relations over time, we are able to see more clearly how relationships among networks of individuals, the state, civil society, transnational organizations, and global capitalism are configured in the contemporary period.

epilogue

The shifts I have noted throughout this book are by no means unique to Jamaica, though the specific forms some of these generational transformations have taken require contextually based readings of the relationships between local political economies and social and cultural ideologies. They should also be regarded as shifts that are still shifting, transformations still in motion, for the endpoint of the research for this book does not mark the end of these discussions. Many changes have already occurred since the end of 1997, both locally and nationally.

For example, by the summer of 2003, there had been two significant leadership transitions within the Community Council in Mango Mount. The first occurred in 2001 with the election of a new Executive Council. The new president was a forty-year-old middle-class community member who grew up in the village. He was neither a civil servant, nor a professional, but rather owned his own security company. At times, his business responsibilities prevented him from being able to attend all Council meetings, and when he was not present, the new senior vice president, a woman from one of Mango Mount's established poorer families who had been active in the Council for years, presided. She was also the Council's Community Development Officer—a newly created, salaried half-time position—responsible for developing and implementing programming for all age groups at the center. It was perhaps due to her more institutionalized involvement, and to the efforts of a remarkably energetic and thoughtful U.S. Peace Corps volunteer to organize by subcommunity, that there had been a slight increase in participation in Council meetings and a more significant increase in community residents' use of the center facilities. More of the district's young children seemed to spend afternoons at the center, and a few of the male youth in the community had become more active. Overall, however, there still seemed to be a relatively low level of participation in Council programs, and the same generational conflicts tended to arise regarding the kinds of programming that were suggested and the ways these programs were implemented.

Though the center itself was refurbished in 1999 to serve as a location for computer literacy and income-generating projects, these projects had not yet gotten off the ground by the summer of 2001. Additionally, the revolving loan program was terminated as interest seemed to wane and participants defaulted on their payments. Nevertheless, fund raising for new programming was an ongoing endeavor. There had also been an attempt to build an endowment in order to become less dependent on outside grants, especially since these rarely covered general operating expenses. Toward this end, during the summer of 2001 the Council hosted a special benefit performance of one of the theatrical productions running at a nearby venue at which they raised close to one-fifth of their target. Unfortunately, for various reasons, this funding—and therefore the projects it was meant to support—did not materialize, a fact that ultimately led to the second leadership transition within the Council. Currently, the president and the secretary treasurer are both black professional women in their late forties/early fifties. With the exception of one or two community-wide events (such as the twenty-fifth anniversary of the Mango Mount Community Council that occurred early in the summer of 2003, and an ongoing karate class), the Council seems to be in a lull phase. The center is no longer open every afternoon, Council meetings are poorly attended, and fund-raising activities have stagnated. The community development officer, though no longer salaried, opens the center when she can on a voluntary basis in an attempt to keep a degree of momentum going among the children.

Beyond the community center, additional significant changes have transpired in the village. With the closure of both guesthouses in 1998 (the only local businesses), community members were left without local sources of employment apart from working, as individual laborers, for other community members. The Basic School attached to the Seventh-Day Adventist Church had also closed because the school director's husband was relocated to another parish. While the migration flow out of Mango Mount had remained steady, there were also many new faces within the district. For the most part, these were people without significant ties to the village, and many community members believed that they were criminals who were being sheltered from law enforcement authorities by friends. This resulted in the intensification of a local discourse that blamed "outsiders" for an increased atmosphere of fear—as community members said, "You don't know who is who anymore." At the same time, a murder within the community in 2001 was followed by silence rather than the usual community gossip and speculation, a fact that suggests that villagers knew who was responsible and that that person was local. A spate of thefts—some accompanied by violent attacks—occurred in the area until the perpetrators were caught and arrested in late 2002, after which point things returned to a relative calm.

There had also been an increase in the number of dancehall sessions in the district. However, because the bar next to the dry goods shop in the square at the top of the hill had closed, sessions were no longer held on the ridge of Mango Mount—the area closest to the majority of middle-class community members. Instead, they took place in either of two lawns, both of which were relatively remotely located. Consequently, fewer sessions were locked down as a result of middle-class residents' complaints to police about noise.

Community members had also continued their commemorations of Emancipation Day and Independence, which, organized mainly by the community development officer and her daughter, had increasingly come to reflect the social and aesthetic preferences of the "poorer class of people." For example, though Emancipation Day in 2001 was marked only by the showing of a movie at the community center (*Charlie's Angels*, by popular demand), Independence Day was a full-blown community fun day that culminated in a talent show organized by the youth. The community development officer enlisted the help of several young men to cook the fish tea and fried chicken that were to be sold, to organize the games and athletic competitions that took place throughout the day, and to emcee a talent show. The show began at nightfall before an audience of between two and three hundred community members, and featured several singing, dancing, and DJ-ing acts. The dance pieces choreographed by the girls were mainly routines they performed to then-popular U.S. rhythm and blues songs like Destiny's Child's "Independent Woman" and "Bootylicious" that were nonetheless dominated by dancehall moves. The boys, on the other hand, chose dancehall songs (the most popular of which in 2001 was the remix of U.S. rhythm and blues artist R. Kelly's "Fiesta"), and their routines were noticeably less choreographed and rehearsed than those of the girls. Several community members who were known to be singers also performed. The young women tended to perform the slower U.S. rhythm and blues songs, while the young men either sang their own reggae compositions or DJ-ed. This gendered distinction was complemented by a generational one, as the more "conscious" reggae offerings were made by older community members and were respected, though not cheered as vigorously as the younger DJs.[1] After the show, prizes were distributed to the winning athletic teams. The whole event, which didn't end until about 11 P.M., was considered a success—both financially and socially.

These changes at the local level not only draw our attention to the continued urgency of strengthening local infrastructure, Jamaicans' persistent pleasure in resignifying African American popular culture, the complex negotiation of the ways gender ideologies are inscribed through popular cultural production and participation, and the ongoing (and ever more difficult) search for local avenues through which economic advancement is possible. Local changes also reflect the relatively greater degree of institutional autonomy and influence enjoyed by lower-class community members as well as the significant transformations that have also occurred at the national level as the state has endeavored to catch up with its population.

Of central importance here is an apparent shift in emphasis on the part of the Jamaica Cultural Development Commission, the Jamaica Tourist Board, and other organizations from promoting festivals highlighting "folk" traditions or "heritage" events, to those based on the food specialties of particular locations throughout Jamaica. This shift has also been spurred by community-based efforts to find innovative ways to raise funds for local initiatives or to increase awareness for community projects. For example, the first Busso² Festival in Portland in 2000 originated out of the community's efforts to promote local development and began as a yearly homecoming celebration for people who had been raised in, but who had since migrated from, the Swift River area. Similarly, the Citizen's Association and Youth Club of a small town in the parish of Trelawny hosted a Corn Festival in 2001 in order to promote corn as an alternate crop for the region. Westmoreland's Curry Festival in 2001 was planned to raise funds in order to upgrade the local high school sewer system, and the benefits from the Manchester Potato Festival in July 2001 went toward the construction of a new post office and health center to serve the needs of area residents. Community volunteers handled much of the work leading up to and during these festivals, and local businesses and restaurants also pitched in their support.

Many other yearly food festivals have been inaugurated since 2000, including the seafood festival in Alligator Pond, Manchester; the Crabfest in Westmoreland; the Shrimp and Yam festivals of St. Elizabeth; the Old Harbour and Port Royal Fish and Bammy festivals; the Breadfruit Festival of Westmoreland; and the Kumento Festival of St. Thomas (Wray 2001). Perhaps the most popular—and most well attended—festival of the summer has been the Jerk Festival in Portland. When it was initiated in 2000, the festival attracted three times the projected attendance of 5,000. By 2001, event planners moved the festival to an alternate location in anticipation that they would have even more traffic than the year before, which they did. The 2001 festival boasted countless food and beverage vendors, with chefs improvising on the usual themes of chicken and pork to also prepare all manner of nontraditional meats, and even some vegetables and tubers, in the jerk style. There was also a stage where groups performed throughout the day, beginning with local school children's renditions of ring games and ending with the calypso band, Byron Lee and the Dragonaires.

Most of these kinds of festivals are sponsored by community organizations in collaboration with both public and private institutions such as the Social Development Commission, the Jamaica Cultural Development Commission, the Jamaica Information Service, the Jamaica Tourist Board, Alumina Partners of Jamaica, Air Jamaica, and other local corporations. Moreover, as events, they are primarily targeted toward augmenting domestic tourism and also toward luring migrated Jamaicans back home to assist in the local development process.[3] In these festivals, "folk" traditions are a part, but not the centerpiece, of the day's activities.

The year 2000 also saw the return of the Independence Day street dance. Prior to the intensification of political violence in Jamaica and the advent of indoor clubs and private fetes, these public dances were the most popular way to celebrate Jamaica's independence. In 2000, the main street in Kingston's commercial district was blocked to traffic, and some 35,000 people gathered to bring back this tradition. The next year, the event was planned by the Ministry of Local Government and Community Development and sponsored by local radio stations, newspapers, hoteliers, and businesses as well as local franchises of international businesses like Kentucky Fried Chicken, Wendy's, and Burger King. The 2001 Independence street dance provided something for everyone. Veteran singers performed alongside gospel stars, dancehall DJs, and "old-fashioned" entertainment like the Rod Dennis Mento Band, the Tivoli Gardens Marching Band, the Humming Bird Steel Band, and the Jamaica Military Band.

Despite the popularity of the 2001 Independence celebrations, there was also much talk of a "muted sense of national confidence about the future"

(Daily Gleaner 2001b). This was due, in part, to the intensification of political violence that began in April 2001 after the murder of a well-known political gang leader from one of the downtown garrison communities. It was also, however, the result of an increased sense of frustration regarding the lack of opportunities for advancement locally and the consequent reliance on migration as both an individual and national development strategy. That both of these factors were understood as indicative of the relative weakness of the Jamaican state—in both local and international arenas—was evident in the titles of several newspaper editorials and letters to the editor during that summer, such as "The State Is Collapsing" (Vascianne 2001b) and "Jamaica: A Dying State" (Hewitt 2001). Arguments from these and other commentators examined the deleterious effects of rural underdevelopment and extensive out-migration, with the latter focused especially on teachers, nurses, business professionals, university graduates, and hotel workers (Davidson 2001; Espeut 2001; Vascianne 2001a). With the departure of approximately 85,000 Jamaican nationals between 1997 and 2000—75,000 of whom were destined for the United States (Vascianne 2001a)—there had developed an intensified concern not only regarding the loss of skills to Jamaica, but also with respect to the effects of migration upon families and households. Government ministers and newspaper columnists alike spoke emphatically about the need to ensure that Jamaica's own development was not sacrificed to the gods of free trade and capital mobility. Within this climate, it was not surprising that English Prime Minister Tony Blair's visit to Jamaica at the end of July 2001 was followed by the Caribbean Community Secretariat's proposal that the "special relationship" between the United Kingdom and the Caribbean be rebuilt in order that England "make its voice count" on behalf of the region during meetings of international trade blocs (Daily Observer 2001).

While this increased sense of hopelessness in the face of the U.S.-dominated global economy was palpable, some commentators also noted that "many more ordinary citizens are demanding change" (Daily Gleaner 2001b). Indeed, several new civil society organizations had emerged since 1997, especially after the gas riots in April 1999.[4] Perhaps the most prominent among these organizations at the national level has been Jamaicans for Justice, a cross section of Jamaicans who work from a human rights perspective in order to bring national and international attention to abuses of power on the part of the government and the security forces. Jamaicans for Justice, however, was only one among many other national and community-based organizations working toward both structural and ideological change.

It remains to be seen what kind of effects these sorts of organizations might have at the national level. To be sure, within Mango Mount, by late summer 2003 there was a greater sense among the poorer community members who had not become upwardly (or outwardly) mobile that fewer middle-class residents were willing or able to help them. This was, in part, because many of those among the "upper sets" who had previously been involved in the Community Council had either left the district or become too elderly to maintain their involvement, and because those among the "poorer sets" who had achieved some degree of mobility had not necessarily become interested in spreading their resources (time, money, skills) laterally throughout the community. As a result, the institutional mechanisms that had existed locally to keep people from completely having to fend for themselves have largely disappeared, and the poorest of community members must once again seek assistance from sympathetic and well-placed individuals who have time and energy to give. The next five to ten years will be critical, therefore, with respect to the cultivation of new leadership and new networks, the elaboration of new models for community development, and the generation of new parameters for what it means to belong—to the community, to the nation, to the world.

notes

introduction "Out of Many, One (Black) People"

1 See Cohn and Dirks 1988; Mitchell 1991; B. Williams 1991, 1996b.

2 An extensive literature has developed addressing the messy relationships between culture and nationalism and how these relationships have shifted over time. National citizenries, it has been shown, have been created and consolidated through such means as the codification of language, the standardization of culture, the establishment of civil society, the writing of official histories, and the "invention" of rules and traditions (see, for example, Anderson 1991; Corrigan and Sayer 1985; Hobsbawm 1983; Hobsbawm and Ranger 1983; and Nagengast 1994). Many have demonstrated that in the processes of codifying national symbols and writing national histories, racial, gender, and class inequalities are often subordinated to national concerns, and cultural change is often conceptualized as loss (see, for example, Alonso 1988, 1994; Babadzan 1988; Chatterjee 1993; Foster 1991; Fox 1990a; Handler 1988; Keesing 1989; R. Price 1998; Quintero-Rivera 1987; Swedenburg 1990; Verdery 1991). Nationalist cultural production, then, is both a material and ideological process that reflects the changing interests of the state and its citizens. The processes of imagination, invention, and memory represent attempts at the "naturalization of the arbitrary" (Brow 1990:4), and the ongoing conflicts involved in creating and disseminating representations of the nation are practices by which time and space become bounded to serve particular political goals.

3 Jamaica (1962), Trinidad and Tobago (1962), Barbados (1966), and Guyana (1966) gained their independence before many of the smaller Caribbean nations like Antigua (1981), the Bahamas (1973), Belize (1981), Dominica (1978), Grenada (1974), St. Kitts and Nevis (1983), St. Lucia (1979), and St. Vincent (1979). Several Anglophone Caribbean territories still maintain colonial status with Britain (Anguilla, the British Virgin Islands, the Cayman Islands, Montserrat, and the Turks and Caicos Islands), and the diversity of political arrangements with former imperial nations throughout the Caribbean is staggering.

4 The 1991 census indicates that of the 2.3 million people that comprised Jamaica's population, 90.5% identified themselves as black; 7.3% identified themselves as of mixed racial descent; 0.2% as white; 1.3% as East Indian; 0.3% as Chinese; and 0.5% as members of other ethnic groups, including Syrians, Lebanese, and Jews (Statistical Institute of Jamaica 1991).

5   The "African cultural heritage in Jamaica" or "Jamaica's African cultural heritage" refers to that set of cultural and social practices evolved by black Jamaicans during the period of slavery. This set includes, but is not limited to: kumina, a Congolese-derived ritual involving ancestral communication through dance and music that is practiced predominantly in the eastern parishes of Portland and St. Thomas; nine-nights, the set of rituals attending death; dinki mini, a celebration similar to kumina that acknowledges deaths, births, and other significant events within the community; gerreh, another community-wide ritual practiced primarily in the Western parishes; jonkonnu, originally a religious practice connected with West African secret societies that evolved into a secular masquerade normally occurring during the Christmas season; burru, a secular celebration about whose origins little is known, but whose drumming was the only music officially tolerated on the plantations as it was used to set the work pace of the slaves; ettu, another community gathering related to death; bruckins, a "party" that imitates (and satirizes) the British royalty and plantation life; revival, a Jamaican interpretation of Baptist practices; and, later, nyabinghi, a Rastafarian style of drumming and chanting, so named after a secret anticolonial society originating in the Congo and Uganda and later led by H.I.M. Haile Selassie, the Messiah of Rastafari (the term nyabinghi is itself interpreted in Jamaica to mean "death to black and white oppressors"). For lengthier discussions of the origins, development, and social role of these (and other) practices, see Beckwith 1929 [1969]; Bilby 1985; Brathwaite 1971b; Carty 1988; Chevannes 1998; and Murrell, Spencer, and McFarlane 1998.

6   Benedict Anderson's definition of the nation as "an imagined political community" (1991:6) realigned the ways in which anthropologists approached the subject of the nation-state. But if the nation is an imagined community, then what is imagined? By whom? And to what end? These are critical questions because, as Arjun Appadurai has so aptly put it, "one man's imagined community is another man's political prison" (1990:6). Scholars concerned with state formation have drawn heavily from Antonio Gramsci's (1971) and Nicos Poulantzas's (1978) reformulation of the relationship between the state and civil society, Gramsci's concept of hegemony as further elaborated by Raymond Williams (1977), Phillip Abrams's deconstruction of the unitary image of the state (1988), and William Roseberry's attention to both material and symbolic processes and practices (1991). For these scholars, the process of state formation is always anchored in relations of inequality that are institutionalized through everyday state routines, rituals, activities, and policies that constitute and regulate the social formation of citizens through technologies of power (Corrigan and Sayer 1985; J. Scott 1998). As a result, state formation is a process that is always in tension with emergent popular cultures, a continued struggle for hegemony (Joseph and Nugent 1994).

7 Also salient here are the ways nationalist elites have sometimes generated new dimensions of inequality through their ambivalence toward Western modernity. For example, in *The Nation and Its Fragments*, Partha Chatterjee outlines what he sees as an essential difference between Eastern and Western nationalisms in order to establish a trajectory of anticolonial nationalist struggle that diverges from the models delineated in Anderson's book. He argues that "anticolonial nationalism creates its own domain of sovereignty within colonial society well before it begins its political battle with the imperial power" (1993:6) and demonstrates that in India, this was done by dividing the universe of social institutions and practices into two domains, the material and the spiritual. In the material domain—that of economics, politics, and science and technology—the superiority of the West was conceded and its example followed. In the spiritual domain, however, the distinctiveness of an autonomous and essential cultural identity was cultivated to serve as the foundation for a "modern," yet non-Western, national culture. Chatterjee contends that the creativity of anticolonial nationalist projects lies within the elaboration of this spiritual realm where "the nation is already sovereign, even when the state is in the hands of the colonial power" (1993:6). Elsewhere, he demonstrates that this division is established and reproduced in gendered terms, as men become the movers and shakers within the material arena, while women are relegated to and regulated as guardians of the spiritual sphere (1986, 1989). It is interesting to note that Audrey Wippers made similar points some twenty years earlier. In exploring the constraints upon the ideological resistance of nationalist elites in East and West Africa during the early 1970s, she investigated their concomitant assertions of competence (within the realms of political and economic leadership) and superiority (within the sphere of culture). Wippers shows that in attempting to reevaluate and revitalize precolonial practices, however, these nationalists also encouraged women to return to the home, lower their hemlines, stop using cosmetics, and stop straightening their hair. "Although highly critical of Western countries," Wippers writes, "African governments are also highly sensitive to their judgments. Knowing the negative image many Westerners hold of their countries—the equating of nakedness with primitiveness, for instance—and determined to change this image, they feel that they must suppress aspects of traditional life that reinforce this image. On the one hand, they wish to preserve traditional culture, while on the other, they wish to become a modern nation. In one breath, they castigate women for changing too much and in the next, they castigate tribesmen for not changing enough" (1972:35–36). The difference between Chatterjee's and Wippers's accounts, it would seem, lies in the divergent ways African and Indian populations have been positioned within global imperialist discourses regarding civilizational hierarchies. That this difference is of critical relevance to the Caribbean con-

text becomes evident when one examines the cases of Trinidad and Guyana (see, for example, Munasinghe 1997).

8 Within the Spanish-speaking Caribbean colonies, this has not been the case. There, the metropolitan government exerted stronger controls over local policy, and the irregular establishment of the plantation system was reflected in the development of the population. Because large European settler populations had stabilized before the expansion of the plantation in the late eighteenth century, nowhere and at no time did African slaves ever outnumber freemen of European origin. Several scholars have argued that this, in combination with the paternalistic social integration of the hacienda system, weakened the development of class and race solidarity and led to greater local institutional uniformity between different sectors of the population, especially in the areas of law, language, and social customs (Knight 1990; Mintz 1971; Safa 1987). This creolized institutional integration, in turn, has also served as the foundation for the ideology of *mestizaje*, an ideology of mixed-raceness that inscribes the Hispanophone Caribbean into the rest of Latin America. Here, the image of the peasant, the symbol of *indigenismo* self-sufficiency, has been elaborated as the most salient referent of a national heritage. For comprehensive discussions of ideologies of race and nation in Latin America, see de la Cadena 2000; Graham 1990; Skidmore 1993; Stutzman 1981; and Wade 1993:3–47. See also Garcia (2000) for an insightful analysis of how indigenous rights activists in highland Peru have mobilized racial and ethnic designations in order to define themselves as both "modern" and "traditional."

9 While the focus in Gilroy's work is the "Black Atlantic," similar processes have also been outlined for indigenous populations. In the Australian context, for example, several scholars have analyzed the ways people use both old and new technologies to construct and distribute ideologies about community, difference, and social meaning through artistic practice. In the contemporary period, therefore, Aboriginal artists are simultaneously engaged in the process of rewriting dominant images locally and circulating them transnationally in art galleries and on movie screens (Ginsburg 1991, 1993; Myers 1991, 1998).

10 A growing body of literature addresses these concerns. Analyses that have shaped my own thinking on these issues include Averill 1997; C. Cohen 1998; Daniel 1995; Davila 1997; Glick Schiller and Fouron 2001; Maurer 1991; McAlister 2002; D. Miller 1994; Munasinghe 2001; Murray 2002; Olwig 1993a–c, 1999; Pacini 1995; R. Price 1998; Reddock 1998, 1999, 2001; Segal 1994; Stolzoff 2000; Stuempfle 1995; Trouillot 1990; B. Williams 1990, 1991; Yelvington 1993a; and Young 1993 (see also Aparicio 1998; Guss 1993, 2000; Savigliano 1994; Wade 1993; Wilk 1996).

11 Though many scholars have provided insights into the various transformations in the global political economy since the 1970s, my own understand-

ing is based primarily on the work of the following scholars: Appadurai 1990, 1996; Comaroff and Comaroff 2001; Friedman 1993, 1994; Ferguson 1999; Gupta and Ferguson 1992; S. Hall 1997; Harvey 1989; J. Petras 1990; Sassen 1994, 1998; and Trouillot 2001. While it is not my intention here to enter current debates regarding the "newness" of globalization, see Bill Maurer's (2000) cogent rethinking for a refutation of the argument that late-twentieth-century capitalist globalization is no different from the late-nineteenth-century move toward free trade imperialism (see also Hardt and Negri 2000).

12 The gendered dimensions of these processes have been illuminated by several scholars. See, for example, Bolles 1983, 1996a; Deere et al. 1990; Fernandez-Kelly 1983; Harrison 1988b; Kempadoo 1999; McAfee 1991; Mies 1982, 1986; Nash and Fernandez-Kelly 1983; Ong 1987; Safa 1981, 1995; Sen and Grown 1987; Ward 1990. These scholars have shed light on the processes by which the exploitation of young Third World women workers within off-shore multinational capitalist production has both articulated with local gender ideologies (but see Freeman 1998 for a different context), and generated the opportunities for women to organize as women and as workers (see Enloe 1990 and Mohanty 1997 for analyses of women's activist strategies). A literature has also developed on women's migrant labor as domestics (see especially Aymer 1997; Colen 1989; Colen and Sanjek 1990; Gill 1994; Parreñas 2001), often focusing on the ways ethnicized, racialized, and nationalized labor has enabled the upward career mobility of white American (and European) women, thereby solidifying hierarchies between women. Scholars have also demonstrated the ways in which migration, especially to the United States, has reproduced, transformed, and generated new gender ideologies and practices among immigrant women (see, for example, García Castro 1985; Georges 1992; Glick Schiller and Fouron 2001; Lamphere 1987; Pessar 1996; Soto [1987]; Wiltshire 1992).

13 Arjun Appadurai (1990, 1996) has been the main proponent of this position within anthropology. His analysis of contemporary global processes emphasizes the role of "disjunctive flows" (1990) and "objects in motion" (2001) in what he understands to be a new deterritorialized condition of imaginative resources and practices. Several scholars have taken Appadurai to task for what appears to be an elision of the context in which these flows occur, an unbounded discussion of imaginative and practical possibilities that ignores the political economy of time-space compression in specific locations, his implication that everyone can equally avail themselves of the opportunities of and for mobility, and the mistaken assertion that transnationality has been liberating for all. Aihwa Ong has argued particularly vehemently that his account of cultural flows doesn't identify the processes that increasingly differentiate the power of mobile and nonmobile people

and that his formulation "begs the question of whether imagination as social practice can be so independent of national, transnational, and political-economic structures that enable, channel, and control the flows of people, things and ideas" (1999:11; see also Rofel 1999:12). Appadurai's more recent version of his argument pays somewhat more attention to the ways various flows are situated in what he calls "relations of disjuncture" (2001:5), yet he does not provide any specifics about these relations and continues to celebrate imaginative deterritorialization as part of a newly emancipatory politics of globalization (2001:6–7).

14   This is, in part, the point of scholars who have examined emergent transnational forms of family formation, economic advancement, political organization, mobilization, and practice. This is a growing body of literature that encompasses work on transnational migration (for example, Basch et. al. 1994; Chamberlain 1997; Glick Schiller et al. 1992; Glick Schiller and Fouron 2001; Kasinitz 1992; Kearney 1991; Nagengast and Kearney 1990; Rouse 1991, 1995; Savishinsky 1994; Sutton 1987, 1992; Sutton and Makiesky Barrow 1987; James 1993; Mohanty 1991; M. P. Smith 1995; M. P. Smith and Guarnizo 1998), as well as that addressing diaspora (Beriss 1993; Clifford 1994; S. Hall 1990; Wiltshire 1992).

15   Lila Abu-Lughod has argued that the search for everyday struggles among subordinated populations has led many scholars to romanticize resistance rather than examine the specific strategies of power implemented locally (1990). Tim Mitchell, too, has critiqued the tendency toward a scholarly romanticization of popular struggle, arguing that this perspective—itself grounded in the dualisms of persuasion:coercion; ideological:material; mind:body—fails to show how modern mechanisms of control "create the apparently two-dimensional world that our everyday metaphors of power take for granted" (1990:548). Mitchell maintains that by attempting to show that marginalized groups do, in fact, possess historical consciousness, many scholars have relied on these oppositions in order to argue that power is an external process that can constrain behavior without necessarily controlling the mind. To get beyond these conventionally employed dualisms, he argues that it is necessary to demonstrate how power *creates* these dualisms in order to appear external to practice.

16   I began research for this project during the summer of 1993, made brief visits in the spring of 1996, then returned for the period between October 1996 and December 1997. The bulk of the data presented in this book was collected during this period. I have since returned several times for short periods and took students with me for two months during the summer of 2001.

17   Mango Mount is a pseudonym.

18   I should note here that in my interviews, both with members of the artistic community and in the village, I gave my word that I would shield individ-

uals' identities. This is something often more easily promised than done, particularly when those being interviewed are nationally recognized public figures. In chapters 1 and 2, where these individuals are explicitly representing themselves or the institutions they direct, I have identified them. Otherwise, I have made attempts to preserve their anonymity. In the community ethnography, names (where they are used) have been changed. Comments offered by one individual have sometimes been attributed to another of a similar social standing or have been divided among several. Conversely, statements articulated by several individuals have occasionally been amalgamated into one voice.

19 Most of the information on the early history of Mango Mount that appears here and in chapter 3 is derived from oral histories conducted with community members. However, I also found a variety of archival sources helpful for contextual data (see especially Higman [1976]; Maryland Plantation Estate Book; Jamaica List of Properties 1921; and Return of Properties 1882).

20 Trouillot uses a Nation-World-Village structure to frame his overarching argument that worldwide industrialization has not converted peasantries into proletariats and that therefore peasantries cannot be analytically severed from the wider world of capitalist production because they always constitute part-economies, a point first made by Sidney Mintz (1989).

chapter 1   The "Problem" of Nationalism in the British West Indies

1 The creole multiracial nationalist perspective on Jamaica's independent development was also significantly challenged during the 1940s by a more explicitly Marxist (and communist) vision, but as I discuss later in this chapter, those advocates of this position were marginalized within mainstream political institutions after their expulsion from the People's National Party in 1952.

2 Historian Nigel Bolland has critiqued Brathwaite's formulation on the grounds that because it presents a dualistic vision of Jamaican society, it fails to appreciate the broader relations of power structuring interactions between Afro- and Euro-Jamaicans during the period under review. He argues that a more dialectical reading of the relationship would allow for an analysis of power and inequality, while still foregrounding the creativity of Jamaicans in forging their own cultural complex (1997).

3 Britain abolished the slave trade in 1807, but slavery itself was not ended until 1838. In 1834, colonial officials agreed to a modified abolition of slavery, inaugurating a period of "apprenticeship"—during which time the attempt was made to socialize slaves into a free labor force—that was to last six years, but ended after four.

4 Gordon had become an advocate of black peasants in St. Thomas, imple-

menting his own land reform schemes by buying and leasing land, which he then subdivided and sold or sublet.

5   I have relied primarily on the perspectives of Heuman 1994, Holt 1992, and Robotham 1982 to relate the story of the Morant Bay rebellion.

6   Various strains of Social Darwinism emerged between the mid- and late nineteenth century, the nuances of which I don't address here. See Baker 1998 for a more extensive exploration of Social Darwinism and its relationship to anthropology.

7   Mia Bay, in her book *The White Image in the Black Mind: African-American Ideas About White People, 1830–1925*, makes a similar point in her discussion of the racial vindicationist discourse African Americans employed to refute both scientific racism and Jeffersonian theories of polygenesis in the mid-nineteenth-century United States. She argues that these black intellectuals' attempt to argue for both cultural and environmental difference within the context of the unity of mankind placed them perilously close to the ideological underpinnings of "Jim Crow" (Bay 2000, especially 36).

8   A version of my analysis of the *Jamaica's Jubilee* text previously appeared as "Modern Blackness: 'What We Are and What We Hope to Be,' " *Small Axe* 6 (2): 25–48, 2002. "Colored" people—meaning mixed "brown" folk—were not invited to contribute to this volume in the view that black Jamaicans would more forcefully reflect the impact of emancipation and missionary activity on the population of ex-slaves. In the preface, the authors insisted that they should not be seen as exceptions within the race. Rather, they wanted the British public to know that there were many others like them who also would have been able to write the book. *Jamaica's Jubilee* is hereinafter referred to as JJ after quoted material.

9   Specific biographical information on the contributors can be found in C. Wilson 1929.

10 That expectations of the progress of the ex-slaves might have been too high among visitors and commentators since at the time of emancipation they were only a few generations removed from "savagery" is a recurrent theme (Vernill 1931:135). Bigelow was the only contemporary writer to offer an alternative development strategy that would have potentially improved conditions on the island, allowing former slaves the opportunity to demonstrate their "capabilities" through industrial employment (1970 [1851]: 156).

11 A Scottish-born historian and essayist and a leading figure during the Victorian era, Thomas Carlyle is perhaps best known for his antidemocratic stance and racism during the later years of his life.

12 John Jacob Thomas, a schoolmaster in colonial Trinidad, and T. E. S. Scholes, a black Jamaican writer, both critiqued Froude's assertion that Negroes were intellectually inferior by delineating the achievements of the former slaves since emancipation (Scholes 1899; J. J. Thomas [1889]). Eliz-

abeth Pullen-Berry, an Englishwoman who published two books about her travels throughout Jamaica and the United States South (1903, 1971), also rejected many of Froude's interpretations. Nevertheless, she too concluded that "the black is at his best under British rule" and that if left to themselves black people would "revert" to a state of savagery (1903:26).

13 Of course, these were not the only intellectuals to find themselves and their arguments limited by the context in which they worked. Lee Baker makes the point that Booker T. Washington also couched his own thesis regarding the separateness but interdependence of the races within Social Darwinist terms (Baker 1998:62; cf. Bay 2000).

14 Holt's argument here is that the abolitionists and policy makers were prepared only to accept a definition of freedom that was determined by a liberal democratic ideology in which humans' behavior was believed to reflect primarily their acquisitive, materialist appetites. This liberal democratic thought was part and parcel of the rise of industrial capitalism and helped to justify the emerging bourgeois social relations of the seventeenth and eighteenth centuries that had produced the English working class (1992).

15 See, for example, Thome and Kimball (1838), Phillippo (1969), Bigelow (1851 [1970]), and Gardner ([1873]). For the most part, these writers were anxious to demonstrate that, contrary to prevalent fears, the transition to apprenticeship in 1834 and to "full free" in 1838 occurred peacefully, unaccompanied by either mass rioting or a complete abandonment of the estates.

16 See Douglass Hall (1959) and Swithin Wilmot (1992) for an elaboration of these arguments.

17 We should also remember that the Baptist communities did not exist outside of the estate system. In fact, there was a degree of interdependence between the plantations and free villages because the villages were purposely established close to plantations to provide employment buffers for former slaves (Phillippo 1969:430).

18 By the mid-1890s, 81 individuals had become owners of 97% of the area of rural land offered by the government for sale (Satchell 1990:21). Moreover, between the 1860s and 1880s, women played a significant role in the growth of the peasantry, with the majority of the land they conveyed constituting transfers to peasants (Satchell 1995:224). However, during this period women acquired much less land than they transferred, with 70,872 acres gained as compared to 225,699 acres transferred (1995:227). This means that while women played a significant role in the growth of the peasantry during the late nineteenth century, they themselves were forced to seek avenues other than land ownership for their own survival.

19 Bryan Edwards notes the existence of this belief among the slaves as early as 1792, a belief that is rooted in the fact that the local white oligarchy was

relatively autonomous vis-à-vis the Crown: "I have not the smallest doubt that the negroes on every plantation in the West Indies were taught to believe that their masters were generally considered in the mother country as a set of odious and abominable miscreants, whom it was laudable to massacre" (1818:553).

20 Michael Craton (1982) has also made this point with respect to the ideological foundations of revolts during slavery.

21 Some diasporic blacks even discussed potential black colonization of Africa. The first attempt to resettle Africa from the Americas in 1899 combined a desire to provide land for entrepreneurial West Indians and other blacks with educational and missionary functions for Africans themselves. These early pan-Africanists, not surprisingly, used much of the language of the British imperialists (Bryan 1991:258).

22 This is an argument that Gilroy also makes in his discussion of Martin Delany's ideas about pan-Africanism and black nationalism during the same time period in the United States (1993).

23 Born in the Bahamas, Dr. Love worked as an Anglican priest and medical doctor in the United States and Haiti before arriving in Jamaica in 1890, five years after the implementation of constitutional changes allowing for limited local representation in the Legislative Council. Dr. Love believed that "the best hope for black people lay within the British legal and political system and that his job was to encourage them to strive to take their rightful place within that system" (Lumsden 1987:136). Toward that end, Love began publishing the Jamaica Advocate in December 1894, a newspaper that ran weekly for almost eleven years. Love promoted the ideas of fair taxation, popular education, constitutional rights, and access to unused government lands for peasants. He also encouraged the backing of black political candidates as well as the more general liberal-unionist platform. Most significantly, he advocated self-government within the context of empire, founding the National Club—Jamaica's first nationalist organization —in 1906. In addition to developing his own political career, Love was also involved in activities that opened opportunities for black participation in an alternative politics. He established the Jamaica Advocate Co-Operative Association, played a significant role in the relatively brief existence of the Pan-African Association in Jamaica, and was involved from its inception with the Jamaica Union of Teachers. Love also founded the People's Convention, an organization that was originally established to celebrate the sixtieth anniversary of emancipation but grew between 1898 and 1903 to mobilize black Jamaicans to express views on current sociopolitical and economic issues. Despite Love's highly developed racial and national consciousness, he accepted the superiority of European civilization and therefore asserted blacks' equality with whites by insisting that blacks were capable of reaching the standards of European civilization. He was there-

fore interested neither in the surviving aspects of African religion, nor in a return of black people to Africa. Instead, he urged black Jamaicans to equip themselves with the tools of European education in order to advance their progress toward self-government.

24   The founders of Rastafari—generally identified as Leonard Howell, Joseph Hibbert, and H. Archibald Dunkley—like Bedward before them, had all been influenced both by Garvey's organization and by their own migratory experiences. Howell had spent time working in the United States; Hibbert had resided in Costa Rica, and in 1924, joined the Ancient Mystic order of Ethiopia, a U.S.-originated Masonic group; and Dunkley had served as a seaman on Atlantic Fruit Company liners.

25   Garvey's participation in nationalist political struggle perhaps began within the National Club, Jamaica's first nationalist organization founded in 1906 by Robert Love and Sandy Cox, for which he served as an assistant secretary. The National Club movement died when Cox migrated to the United States in 1912.

26   For more on the legacy of Garvey's work, see Lewis and Bryan 1991.

27   Sam Sharpe, a slave who had been involved with a local Baptist group, led the 1831 rebellion that marked the beginning of the end of slavery in the British West Indies. Originally planned as a sit-down strike over the Christmas holidays, the revolt took on a life of its own as slaves burned plantations throughout western Jamaica.

28   These funds would increase again with the 1945 revisions to this act.

29   Interestingly, one of the first activities of the Colonial Development and Welfare office staff in 1941 was to visit the mini–New Deal programs of the Roosevelt administration in Puerto Rico and the U.S. Virgin Islands, visits that were organized by the Rockefeller Foundation. This is significant because it reflects a consideration of the Puerto Rican model of development not only with respect to industrialization but also in terms of social development. The United States, however, did not adopt a welfare approach. Instead, they took a scientific approach, establishing population control policies and institutionalizing home economics education. By the mid-1950s, based on research conducted in Puerto Rico and Jamaica funded by the U.S. Conservation Foundation (Blake 1961; Stycos and Back 1964), the general agreement was that overpopulation was the main reason for the region's economic problems, and the Puerto Rican model (sterilization among lower-class women) was put forward as a viable alternative (Reddock 1994:213,224).

30   See also Blake 1961; E. Clarke 1966 ; and Henriques [1953]. I will not go into a detailed delineation here, but the West Indian literature was also influenced by psychologically oriented studies of family life in the United States (Dollard [1937]; Powdermaker [1939]), as well as the "culture of poverty" literature (Cox 1948; Davis et al. [1941]; Liebow 1967; Warner et al. 1941).

31 M. G. Smith, of course, did not agree with the stratification model, instead arguing that differences in cultural practice reflected incompatible differences in social institutions and that therefore West Indian polities were held together not by a common value system, but only through the political and economic domination of the white minority (1962, 1965).

32 Later studies modified the early Eurocentric stress on male dominance and the nuclear family by suggesting that lower-class family forms were creative adaptations and solutions to problems faced in other spheres of their lives (Dirks and Kerns 1976; Gonzalez 1970; Greenfield 1966; Rodman 1959, 1971; Rubenstein 1980, 1983). More recently, scholars have returned to Herskovits' (1990) proposition that West Indian family forms are modifications of West African forms (Kerns 1989; Sudarkasa 1988; Sutton 1984; Sutton and Makiesky-Barrow 1977). For a cogent review of the literature on the theoretical shifts within studies of West Indian family and kinship practices, see Christine Barrow's work (1996, 1998a).

33 There has been significant debate regarding these points. Mavis Campbell has seen the free colored population as having developed strong "caste" solidarity during the period of slavery, but also as always willing to unite with slave masters against blacks during slave rebellions, maroon wars, and peasant uprisings. She has argued that since they accepted colonial ideas regarding natural racial superiority, "They failed totally to make what could have been a great contribution to the transformation of the society from a state of slavery to freedom and stability" (1976:367). Her position has since been tempered by Gad Heuman, who has countered that despite their bias toward gradual political change, the colored class—both before and after emancipation—formed a significant opposition to the white planter class and that their ideas did not demonstrate an unreflective adoption of European attitudes (1981).

34 It bears noting here that not all Jamaicans were equally able to find a voice within the principal form of popular collective mobilization (trade unionism) and leadership structure that had emerged by the late 1930s. Women, for example, were largely excluded from trade unionism because they were leaving the rural agricultural workforce at precisely the time a limited degree of representation became available for those who stayed on the land, and because there were no unions yet organized for those women who became domestic servants or vendors. Indeed, the welfarist approach institutionalized through colonial policy stressed women's service while obscuring demands for women's rights (Austin-Broos 1997; Ford-Smith 1997; Reddock 1994; Vassell 1995).

35 When the JPL was launched in December 1937 in Jamaica, the Colonial Office opened a file labeled "Anti-British Propaganda." The organization, however, was dismissed as a potential threat after an investigation of their activities.

36 For additional archival materials on the history of Jamaica Welfare, see *Daily Gleaner* 1938; *Daily Gleaner Supplement* 1987; Girvan 1962.

37 In fall 1943, Barbados Welfare was founded, and in 1944, experienced staff members of Jamaica Welfare were requested to visit Trinidad, Barbados, and Guyana. Additionally, archival records show numerous visits to the Jamaica Welfare offices and project sites by representatives from Pakistan, Uganda, and Ghana.

38 Though the PNP did not advocate immediately for self-government, it eventually committed itself toward that ultimate goal. In 1941, the party declared itself socialist, viewing national liberation as the first step toward the development of a socialist state, a position from which it backed away toward the late 1940s. Beyond the pamphlets I have listed in the bibliography, for more on the early PNP, see Nettleford 1971.

39 These included standard wages for relief work; wage increases to meet increases in the cost of living; the establishment of industrial courts; improved workmen's compensation; the formation of a government bank; less taxation on food and clothing; higher income tax and death duties; abolition of property tax, instead taxing land on unimproved value; the implementation of land reform schemes by which more land would be made available for peasant settlement; the fostering of collective and cooperative systems of settlements; the creation of more technical and advisory services; more agricultural credit; more and better marketing facilities; state aid for local small industries and trades; state industrial development; island slum clearance and re-housing; the development of water resources for power, irrigation, and home use; swamp reclamation; reforestation; state ownership of public utilities and sugar factories; the establishment of an institute for agricultural and industrial research; the initiation of old age pensions, more free medical, health, and nursing services for the poor; unemployment assistance; rent restriction and tenancy reform; the creation of a statistical department; an immediate census; the rapid development of junior vocation and agricultural schools as well as the development of more opportunities for higher education; universal suffrage and self-government by dominion status (PNP 1940).

40 It has been argued that Bustamante was encouraged by the British to form another political party in order to split the nationalist movement. By the 1960s, the constituency of West Kingston was becoming a volatile social and political flashpoint, and by mid-June 1966 the JLP versus PNP street war had been consolidated, leading ultimately to the October 1966 declaration of a state of emergency (Lacey 1977). Several additional neighborhoods in downtown Kingston have since become known as political garrisons, areas in which the leadership of opposing political parties developed constituencies through promises of patronage. It has generally been argued that these areas were subsequently militarized and that this process had

engendered the considerable electoral violence that has occurred in Jamaica's recent political history, as well as the increase in the drug trade. For
a fuller discussion of the more general impact of political garrisons in
Jamaica see Figueroa 1996, and for a scholar-journalist's account see Gunst
1995.

41 I thank Don Robotham for helping me to clarify these points.

chapter 2   Political Economies of Culture

1 See, for example, M. Lewis 1969; Wright 1966.

2 See, for example, Beckwith 1929 [1969]; Brathwaite 1971b; Craton 1978;
Jekyll 1907 (cf. Genovese 1972; Levine 1977).

3 Unless otherwise noted, much of this brief outline of cultural development
initiatives prior to the mid-twentieth century was culled from Ivy Baxter's
account (1970), though consultation with other archival sources and individuals who were involved in some of the cultural initiatives she describes
has led me to modify some of her dates.

4 For example, Herbert De Lisser, a writer and then director of the Institute of
Jamaica, founded *Planter's Punch* during this period; Edna Manley initiated
the publication of *Focus*; and Una Marson began editing *The Cosmopolitan*.

5 Held in 1952, this festival was funded by the u.s. government, the Puerto
Rican Tourist Board, and the Alcoa Steamship Company.

6 This competition, sponsored by the Gleaner Company's afternoon daily
newspaper, the *Star*, listed these ten types as follows: "Miss Ebony, a Jamaican girl of black complexion; Miss Mahogany, a Jamaican girl of cocoa
brown complexion; Miss Satinwood, a Jamaican girl of coffee-and-milk
complexion; Miss Apple Blossom, a Jamaican girl of white European parentage; Miss Pomegranate, a Jamaican girl of white-Mediterranean parentage; Miss Sandalwood, a Jamaican girl of pure Indian parentage; Miss
Lotus, a Jamaican girl of pure Chinese parentage; Miss Jasmine, a Jamaican
girl of part-Chinese parentage; and, Miss Allspice, a Jamaican girl of part
Indian parentage" (*Star*, July 26, 1955, p. 3). The contest was open to
anyone born in Jamaica ages eighteen to twenty-five, and was to bestow
1,300 pounds of prize money. In 1960, an advertisement for the Miss Mahogany contest also offered the winner a free trip to Trinidad's carnival. For
an extensive discussion of the "Ten Types, One People" contest as well as
the issues raised by Jamaican beauty pageants more generally, see Barnes
1997.

7 The Ministry of Education wrote the syllabi for music, art, and craftwork;
and Rex Nettleford (who would later found the National Dance Theatre
Company of Jamaica) and Joyce Campbell, then the assistant community
development programmer for the Jamaica Social Welfare Commission,
developed the syllabus for Dance.

8   Since 1963, the National Festival of the Arts has broadened to include a festival song competition, popular and mento music, costume queens, drum corps, and steel band contests as well as roadside concerts and street dances. In 1968, the Jamaica Festival Commission was established as a policy-making body, replacing the old Festival Office; and in 1980, responsibility for the National Festival of the Arts was given to the newly formed Jamaica Cultural Development Commission (JCDC).

9   In 1962 Rex Nettleford and Eddy Thomas established the NDTC, a company that did not seek government sponsorship but whose work fell within the parameters of Seaga's vision. Both Nettleford and Thomas had participated in the various artistic efforts prior to independence geared toward defining and promoting an indigenous cultural aesthetic through research and performance. Viewing dance as a catalyst for social change, they sought stylistically to evoke Jamaica's multicultural history. Further, in establishing the Company, their goal was to provide an institutional model for Third World performing arts organizations that would be "community-oriented in objective, national in scope, international in recognition, professional in standards, and amateur in status" (Nettleford 1985:272; see also Nettleford 1969). Over the years, the NDTC has worked to change the Eurocentric orientation of cultural institutions in Jamaica toward one that would more accurately reflect the cultural history of the Caribbean by using the rurally based dance and music forms associated with various sacred and secular ritual practices as the basis for creative or modern dance choreography. Members of the NDTC have also created impressive institutional linkages with the festival movement sponsored by the JCDC, with the educational system, and with various local media houses. Elsewhere I discuss the NDTC and its institutional web in much greater detail (Thomas 2002a).

10 There have been two major periods of increased U.S. capital investment in Jamaica. The first, discussed in chapter 1, occurred during the mid- to late nineteenth century and was directed toward the development of the banana industry (as well as a concomitant early foray into tourism). The second began after World War II and was geared toward the expansion of bauxite mining (the demand for aluminum had been stimulated by the Korean War and the space exploration program) and tourism. While Canadian companies also held significant interests in bauxite mining (Alcan), by independence Jamaica's economic relations had been substantially reoriented toward the United States. In 1962, 39% of Jamaica's total foreign trade was with the United States (Beckford and Witter 1982:72).

11 The initial suggestion that the British West Indies follow Puerto Rico's "Operation Bootstrap" model was issued by Nobel Prize winning economist W. Arthur Lewis. When the PNP lost the elections leading into independence, the Jamaica Labour Party (JLP) also followed these policies. From 1944 to 1949, the JLP argued against state intervention in private

enterprise along the lines proposed by the PNP, and Bustamante cited the 1944 report from the Colonial Office as having already established the unfeasibility of a Jamaican manufacturing sector. However, by the time of independence, the JLP reversed its position.

12   In the 1930s, black Jamaicans constituted only 1% of the middle class, but by the 1960s this number had expanded to 10% (Stone 1991:251).

13   I thank Don Robotham for pointing out that this view has not been unique to the JLP. There was also, during this period, a conservative group within the upper middle class, usually associated with the PNP, that had embraced the preservation of "folk" culture as a way to inoculate the peasantry and the urban poor against Marxism. The promotion of "folk" culture, for them, became a reliable bulwark against any radical modernizing ideology emanating from their political enemies in the middle or working class.

14   The PNP nationalist middle class and the left have traditionally been strong in Kingston.

15   Since then, the party has comprised several distinct social groups: those among the rural working class and peasantry who derive from the trade union wing; those among the urban poor; and those who derive from the ruling commercial and landed group. Again, I thank Don Robotham for clarifying the intracacies of some of these political and economic shifts and their relationships to cultural development initiatives during this period (Robotham 1998 and personal communication).

16   The first Jamaican branch of the Ethiopian World Federation was established in Kingston in 1938. After 1949, Jamaicans were among those who became interested in repatriating to Africa as a result of Selassie's donation of a land grant in Shashamane for all Africans throughout the diaspora. The Rastafarian community in Jamaica petitioned the government to explore the possibility of repatriation, and finally in 1961, a delegation was sent to meet with Selassie and other Ethiopian government officials. More extensive discussions of these events can be found in Nettleford 1970 and C. Price 2003. In 1983, the Ethiopian World Federation's Jamaica chapters modified their charter to become the Imperial Ethiopian World Federation, which is now a political party that mobilizes to have representation for the Rastafarian community in Jamaica's parliament.

17   Here, I am referring to U.S. Black Power and cultural nationalist movements, as well as the Négritude advocated by Leopold Senghor and Aimé Cesaire. As far as I know, Seaga's efforts to establish exchanges with cultural institutions in West African countries were never realized.

18   Both Barry Chevannes and Brian Meeks have suggested that Henry's goal of repatriation was strategic and primarily symbolic, but that the ultimate aim of the Henry Rebellion was to build Africa in Jamaica. Chevannes argues that this aim became clearest upon Henry's release from prison, after which point he dropped the back-to-Africa position and began working on com-

munity development schemes. Additionally, in 1969, Henry released a pamphlet recognizing Michael Manley as the man chosen to free Jamaica from racial hatred. Chevannes views Henry's entrance into the political mainstream as confirming his commitment to Jamaica (1976). Chevannes's and Meeks's excellent discussions of the Henry Rebellion also highlight the New York City connection among movement participants and illustrate some of the tensions between Jamaicans and African Americans within this transnational—perhaps pan-African—coalition (Chevannes 1976; Meeks 2000). Terry Lacey also devotes a chapter to the Henry Rebellion in his discussion of violence and politics in Jamaica during the 1960s (1977), as does Obika Gray (1991).

19 The backlash against Rastafarians after the Henry Rebellion led not only to their request that the university undertake a systematic study of their lifeways and worldviews in order to provide legitimacy for their beliefs, but also to their distancing from the violence of Henry's group. The resultant study was carried out by M. G. Smith, Rex Nettleford, and Sir Roy Augier, and was published in 1961 as the *Report on the Rastafari Movement in Kingston, Jamaica.*

20 See Lacey for a fuller discussion of this (and other) incidents during the 1960s and of the Jamaican state's response to them.

21 These disturbances brought commercial life in Kingston to a standstill for a day, paralyzed the bus services, necessitated the mobilization of the Police Riot Squad, and occupied both the police and the Fire Brigade in the Kingston and St. Andrew corporate area for days (Lacey 1977).

22 Gray argues that the torrent of "Westerns" was a negative influence upon Kingston's poor youth as they "stimulated the formation of gangs among working-class youths and marked them with a fateful recklessness" (1991: 75). His claim here is part of a long-standing discourse blaming American cultural influences for antisocial behavior in Jamaica.

23 Mento was the popular musical form associated with rural Jamaicans during the 1940s and 1950s. For more on the development of Jamaican music, see Bilby 1995; Chang and Chen 1998; S. Davis 1992; Lewin 2000; Neely forthcoming; Stolzoff 2000; White 1984; Witmer 1989.

24 Here, Obika Gray celebrates Rudies' "resistance" to Jamaica's social status quo, but Garth White has gone one step further. His seminal article on ska and rude boys places rudies in the role of Fanonian revolutionary (1967).

25 Jamaican political scientist and celebrated pollster Carl Stone has offered much more scathing evaluations of Seaga's policy (Stone 1973, especially 98, 100).

26 Socialist activism reemerged in Jamaica after independence in 1962. It is not my intention here to delineate the various strands of socialist and communist mobilization throughout the 1960s and 1970s, but see Gray 1991 for a more comprehensive discussion of organizations established, constituencies mobilized, and goals pursued.

27 See Stephens and Stephens for a more detailed description of Manley's policies (1986).

28 There is extensive debate as to whether the CIA was indeed involved in destabilizing Manley's PNP government. Stephens and Stephens (1986) suggest that evidence supporting this claim is inconclusive. Bolles, however, reports former CIA operative Phillip Agee as having confirmed that the United States made deliberate attempts to undermine democratic socialism (1996a). What is important here is that locally, Jamaicans *believe* that the CIA did, in fact, play a role in ousting Manley. This is a belief that is commonly held across class, race, and gender divides and has contributed to anti-American sentiment among the population.

29 George Beckford and Michael Witter argue that the evangelical sects were the most hostile to the government during this period. They also allude to reports that "agents of destabilization" were using the evangelical movement as a cover for their activities (1982).

30 Of course, black businesses were not the only interests that were adversely affected by Seaga's policies, but as Carl Stone points out, "Because many had recently come into business, had borrowed heavily to make this move, and were operating in very vulnerable sectors, the effect was greater on black businessmen as a whole than on the other ethnic groups owning enterprises" (Stone 1991:257).

31 For more extensive discussions regarding the impact of structural adjustment policies on women in Jamaica, see Bolles (1996a), Harrison (1988a, 1988b, 1997), and Mullings 1999. See also Narcisse et al. (1995) on the ways women's organizations in Jamaica have attempted to alleviate the effects of structural adjustment.

32 For example, Women's Media Watch and J-FLAG, an advocacy organization for gay and lesbian Jamaicans, have publicly denounced certain songs and lyrical phrases.

33 UNESCO sponsored the 1996 Consultations on Cultural Policy in Jamaica. Significantly, it was also UNESCO that organized and financed two worldwide conferences on cultural policy during the 1970s and 1980s that resulted in the publication of dozens of monographs identifying the cultural distinctiveness and development policies of the countries involved (see N. Dawes 1977).

34 In response to the "crisis of underdevelopment" occasioned by universally applied policies intended to support economic growth, there has been a more recent emphasis among multilateral organizations that development should be culturally contextualized and locally rooted. "Culture," thus, began to be seen as the foundation of this process, and, as such, could be either a positive or negative force.

35 This is not a suggestion given to either studio or community groups performing Jamaican creative folk dances, a fact not lost on spectators at

JCDC events. One of the camera operators filming Mello Go Roun,' the annual showcase of selected winners from the Festival of the Performing Arts, responded to one of the Jamaican folk dances in which dancers sometimes face each other, touching at the hips while "wining" up and down, by arguing that it was hypocritical to celebrate that kind of movement within the folk pieces while decrying it in the dancehall. Indeed, no JCDC representative suggested that the kumina dancers "tone down" or "find ways to creatively apply" what could be perceived as sexually suggestive movements.

36 Aisha Khan also makes this point in her discussion of the creolization concept as it has been related to the Caribbean (2001:279). Of course, not all change implies loss, just particular kinds of change. As I hope has been evident throughout this discussion, certain histories are always engineered out of the nationalist public sphere.

37 For a full outline of the concerns and recommendations in each area of focus, see the 1997 report published by the Ministry of Education, Youth, and Culture, 4–15.

chapter 3   Strangers and Friends

1 Arawak middens have been identified at two locations in Mango Mount, and the community was listed as the highest known Arawak site in Jamaica by Dr. James Lee at the Jamaican Archaeological Society. Artifacts recovered included scraps of pottery, seashells, and bones of a small animal (Aitken n.d.). The ethnohistorical description of Mango Mount that I present here draws from community members' oral accounts as well as archival sources available at the Kingston and Spanish Town branches of the National Library.

2 Indeed, census figures indicate a relatively broad class spread within the village. Of 228 households, the majority of which were detached private houses, about half had public water piped into the house; the remainder either had water piped into the yard or used public standpipes (Statistical Institute of Jamaica 1991: 472). One hundred seventy households were wired for electricity, and while 120 used gas fuel, 55 used wood or charcoal and 36 used kerosene (ibid. 559, 588). In terms of educational attainment, 13 males and 25 females had received only a nursery or infant school education; 225 males and 183 females had attained a primary education; 140 males and 149 females had gone to secondary school; 30 males and 36 females received a university education; and 45 males and 31 females had no formal education at all (ibid. 233, 263). Despite the numerical preponderance of males, then, females in the village tended to attain a higher level of formal education. This is part of a national trend I will explain more fully in the next chapter. Of the working age population (14 and over), 312 were

men and 298 were women. One hundred eighty-one men and 131 women reported having worked during the week prior to the census, and 39 men and 11 women were seeking work (ibid. 310, 340).

3 "Cash crops" are typically vegetables and fruits that can be grown small-scale, but sometimes people also use the term to refer to marijuana cultivation.

4 For analyses of this point within the Trinidadian context, see Munasinghe 1997; Wells 2000; Yelvington 1993a.

5 Austin's seminal study of two communities in Kingston argues that "Educational values have become incorporated in an ideology of class . . . the notion of the 'uneducated' in Jamaican society has come to carry the ideological burden once associated with color discrimination. The uneducated it is often suggested deserve their position at the bottom of society, and thus does a laudable aspiration come to serve the cause of class subordination" (Austin 1984:xiv).

6 The Common Entrance Examination (CEE), originally established to expand higher educational opportunities to a broader base of Jamaica's population, determines scholarship placements in government secondary and high schools throughout Kingston. Children no longer sit for this exam, as the system was modified in 2000.

7 Available records from the Mango Mount All Age School show that it opened in 1955 with 34 students in its first term. Before its establishment, most of the villagers were educated at a primary school off the hill, to which they traveled by the bridle path. As a government school, Mango Mount All Age was provided with a curriculum guide for each grade. The government also owned the building and paid utilities and teacher's salaries, staffing the school based on enrollment levels. The government's continued support of the school was contingent upon the continued need for a school in the district and on its assessment of the ability of the school to meet students' needs. A panel of the Ministry of Education's team of Education Officers arrived once every three years to check the performance of the students, evaluate the principal's record keeping, and make sure the curriculum was being followed.

8 The Seventh-Day Adventist Church was built during the 1960s and was affiliated with a branch off the hill.

9 When this study was conducted in 1984/5, it was noted that the school had failed to produce a CEE pass since 1972. Moreover, though ten students sat for the CEE in 1997, only one passed.

10 The implications of this maneuver are various and will be discussed more extensively in subsequent chapters.

11 This situation contrasts with that which is often evoked within the American context. That is, it has been argued extensively that in the United States, poorer people tend to know more about the lives of wealthier people be-

cause they work in their homes. What is different in the context I am describing here is the comparative lack of residential segregation.

12 The term "selector" refers to that person choosing and mixing the records at a dance. Selectors usually also offer running commentary upon what is happening at the dance, what people are wearing, how people are moving, and current events.

13 The term "youth" in Jamaica is generally used to refer to anyone under thirty, though it is often more associated with young men than young women.

14 "Browning" is a Jamaican racial designation that references a light-skinned female and usually connotes at least a middle-class background.

15 Begun in 1991 by Byron Lee, carnival in Jamaica has been seen largely as an "uptown event"—that is, an event for the "upper sets"—and not, as in Trinidad, as a party for "the masses." In recent years, however, carnival seems to have become slightly more integrated, and several younger villagers among the "poorer set" admitted that they liked soca, but only "seasonally." Two even paid the J$600 (US$17) each to attend one of the Sunday night J'Ouvert parties during the 1997 carnival season. See Edmondson (1999) for a discussion of the ways Jamaicans have appropriated carnival and how this appropriation has transformed the racial and class foundations that prevail in Trinidad's carnival.

16 Of these eleven, only one (a woman) has remained in Jamaica, while the others have gone to live abroad—seven in the United States (five men and two women) and three in England (two men and one woman). Of the men who migrated, two did so as children when the unions that produced them dissolved. Both of these boys were sent to live with family already living in England. Another man was sponsored, after his retirement, by one of his children already living in the United States. The remainder traveled to the United States based either on potential employment contacts made through peers or those developed as a result of previous farmwork contracts. Three of the four women left Mango Mount as a result of marriages to men from other communities, and one seems to have migrated in order to leave her husband and join her family in the United States.

17 Edith Clarke's ethnography of three communities in Jamaica provides a partial exception to this point (1966). See also P. Wilson 1973.

18 See, for example, Sutton and Chaney 1987; Glick Schiller et al. 1992; and Basch et al. 1994.

19 There is an extensive literature on dress and the politics of self-presentation among working-class communities throughout the African diaspora. For analyses pertaining to the Caribbean context, see, for example, Austin 1984; Cooper 1993; Douglass 1992; D. Miller 1994; Neptune 2001; and Ulysse 1999.

chapter 4   Institutionalizing (Racialized) Progress

1   In 1996, however, the Council decided to begin taking advantage of government funding through the newly formed Jamaica Social Investment Fund, a World Bank funded program developed as part of the government's efforts to alleviate poverty. As a World Bank program, the Executive Committee determined that sponsorship of projects through the fund would not hinder their efforts to remain nonpartisan.

2   This program has subsequently received substantial funding from the Environmental Foundation of Jamaica and the Canadian Green Fund.

3   This program ended because several Jamaicans ended up staying in England illegally after the exchange was over.

4   Though Mango Mount has not been a politically volatile community, because of the more general climate surrounding elections and party politics, many people are still hesitant to affiliate themselves with politicians, and most associate political violence with poorer folk rather than with middle-class people.

5   On the other hand, a few of the middle-class landowners in the community suggested that the bad roads—the most often remarked upon community hazard—were, in a way, a mixed blessing because they prevented outsiders from wanting to come and settle.

6   Unfortunately, due to time constraints, I was unable to give equal time to all three church organizations, in part because I attended church services with those villagers with whom I had the most sustained contact. As a result, I have extremely limited data on the Pentecostal group beyond that which is anecdotal.

7   The 1997 elections marked the emergence of a new political party—the National Democratic Movement (NDM)—whose major supporter and mobilizer in the village was a member of the middle class.

8   I want to note here the extreme difficulty of talking to people in Jamaica about their political preferences—even in the village—due to the history of election violence. Even community members with whom I had developed close relationships were hesitant to speak about who they might or might not support when the election date was announced and would laugh and tell me, "I hope you're not going around asking everybody this." It was possible, in a limited way, to track political persuasions by knowing the group leaders and by going through voting lists with residents who were familiar with families' involvements with one or another of the parties. However, much of this information was provided with the caveat that it remain completely confidential.

9   Politically, Mango Mount is part of the East Rural St. Andrew constituency created in 1959 from the old East St. Andrew seat that was established in 1944 and which had occupied about 55% of the entire parish. With an

average voter turnout of 72% since 1944, East Rural St. Andrew is the largest constituency in the corporate area, and is historically a PNP area, but generally a PNP swing seat. (In fact, Norman Manley was the MP for the area between December 1949 and July 1959.) The PNP is generally strong in Harbour View, Bull Bay, Constitution Hill, Kintyre, Mt. Charles, and Content Gap; and the JLP used to be strong in Gordon Town, Mavis Bank, and Irish Town and currently has heaviest support at Hall's Delight, Bloxburgh, Seven Miles areas, Woodford, and Maryland, the last two being neighboring communities of Mango Mount. The constituency has had only two female candidates in over 52 years, but has a reasonable history of third-party and independent participation, including the Jamaica Democratic Party (JDP), People's Political Party (PPP), and the Jamaica United Party (JUP). During my fieldwork, the area was represented by a PNP Member of Parliament (Caine 1997).

10 After this meeting, the JLP candidate for the district was changed.

11 Nancy Foner's early ethnography examining status and power in a rural Jamaican community came to similar conclusions regarding the ways villagers evaluated status at the local level and the articulation between village-based systems of status distinction and the color, class, gender, and culture stratification system operating at the national level (1973). What appears to have changed by the late 1990s is the extent to which community members were willing to challenge the values of national society and the legitimacy of institutional structures.

chapter 5   Emancipating the Nation (Again)

1 The pantheon of national heroes was delineated at independence in 1962 (though some were added later) as the group of leaders who were important to Jamaica's development as a modern nation. They include Nanny (a celebrated Maroon leader and the only woman hero), Sam Sharpe, George William Gordon and Paul Bogle (leaders of the Morant Bay Rebellion), Marcus Garvey (leader of the Universal Negro Improvement Association), Norman Manley ("father" of the nation and leader of the first political party), and Alexander Bustamante (Manley's cousin and first prime minister of independent Jamaica). Over the years, there has been much debate about whether to instate Bob Marley as a national hero, and with Michael Manley's death in March 1997, some speculation as to whether he would be added to the list.

2 Emancipation Day has also been adopted as a public holiday in several other Caribbean nations. See, for example, Bogues 1995; Bryan 1995; and C. Cohen 1998.

3 A version of my analysis of the Emancipation Day celebrations was published in *Identities: Global Studies in Culture and Power* 5 (4):501–42.

4 Committee members included Rex Nettleford, O.M., chair; Joyce L. Robin-

son, O.J., vice chair; Danny Roberts (Joint Confederation of Trade Unions); Minna McLeod (Association of Women's Organizations of Jamaica); Horace Summers (Jamaica National Youth Council); Sherlock Allen (Jamaica Teachers Association); Sonia Jones (Institute of Jamaica representative); Rev. Ernle Gordon (Jamaica Council of Churches); and Gregory Roberts (Guild of Undergraduates, University of the West Indies).

5   The 1997 reevaluation of the commemoration of Emancipation Day was not without historical precedent. For the sixtieth anniversary of "full free" in 1898, Dr. Robert Love founded the People's Convention in order to introduce solemnity and reflection into Emancipation Day celebrations that those involved felt had become increasingly secular and disjointed since 1838 (Lumsden 1987; R. Lewis 1987). The convention itself was conceived largely as an association of black middle-class Jamaicans advocating on behalf of the black majority. Many of Love's written statements that inaugurated the convention at the beginning of the twentieth century were echoed almost word for word, though usually unacknowledged during the summer of 1997.

6   "Our Freedom Song" was written by Noel Dexter and was available on tape from the Jamaica Information Service, the official information agency of the government.

7   These two workbooks were *Freedom Story 1494–1962: Activity Book for Children Ages 6–12* and *Freedom Road: Emancipation to Independence, 1494–1962* and were published and produced by the Jamaica Information Service for the Emancipation Secretariat. The starting date for both these books was the date of Columbus's landing in 1494, I believe, in order to be able to include the original inhabitants of Jamaica, the Taino Arawaks, in its history.

8   This announcement prompted one columnist to point out that while the poor in each parish receive 100 hectares of land, the wealthy get a bailout of J$30 billion, likening the then current bailout of the financial sector by the government to the British compensation of the planters at emancipation (Stair 1997b).

9   "Redemption Song," written by Bob Marley, is the song of freedom that contains the oft-cited lyrics inspired by one of Marcus Garvey's speeches: "Emancipate yourselves from mental slavery, none but ourselves can free our minds."

10 The events listed were some of those planned at the national level. Many parish and village events were also planned through local and already existing civic committees of the Jamaica Cultural Development Commission (JCDC) and Social Development Commission.

11 Spanish Town was the capital city of Jamaica at the time when the Abolition Proclamation was read publicly on the steps of the old courthouse.

12 *The Crossing* is a dance choreographed by Rex Nettleford and was performed by the NCTC for the 150th anniversary of the abolition of slavery in Jamaica. It attempts to chronicle, in dance, the history of Jamaica's development as a plantation colony.

13 The abeng was the conch horn blown by Maroon communities in order to alert each other. This practice is still current.

14 Kumina is one of the religious practices that developed on the plantations during slavery and is said to be of predominantly Congolese origin.

15 A cutlass is a machete, the ubiquitous all-purpose chopping tool shaped like a scythe.

16 As is well known, one of the visible trademarks of the Rastafarian faith is the wearing of dreadlocks (see Chevannes 1998 for a historical account). However, many poorer men who sympathize with the ideology of Rasta but do not dread their hair call themselves baldhead Rastas.

17 "Killing Me Softly" was originally recorded by Roberta Flack.

18 When a Jamaican speaks into the microphone over a beat, it is called DJ-ing rather than rapping (or MC-ing), as it is within African American hip-hop.

19 The latter argument is, of course, the one that has been advanced by the (marginalized) left in Jamaica.

20 Mutabaruka is a Rastafarian dub poet known for his afrocentric (and revolutionary) lyrics.

21 Here, this farmer was also perhaps unwittingly invoking the view current during the slavery period that mixed-race (or "brown") offspring were weak and therefore useless for field labor. Of course, others—especially male youth more drawn to the kind of "rude boy" culture described in chapter 2—elaborated more positive interpretations of looking "powerful and scary."

22 See Roger Abrahams (1983) for a detailed and comparative discussion of the importance of public talk and performance throughout the West Indies.

23 This gendered differentiation among the middle classes was changing among those under the age of twenty. This was partly due to the prevalence of dancehall culture. It was also true that often, when middle- and upper-class Jamaicans migrated to the United States or United Kingdom, they tended to speak patois more often in order to assert a Jamaican identity.

24 These were all groups that were no longer active in Mango Mount in 1997, and the Grand Gala has not occurred for several years. Additionally, while the All Age school had formerly received announcements regarding the National Festival of the Arts competition, in recent years they had not.

25 Traditionally, nine-night ceremonies are held on the ninth night after a death and are community gatherings including drumming and singing designed to send the person's spirit on to the next life.

chapter 6   Political Economies of Modernity

1 For a similar argument, see Olwig 1993c.

2 See also Foner 1973 for an excellent treatment of the ways an expanded educational and political system after independence opened greater opportunities for grassroots participation in national institutional frameworks

and social and economic mobility, while at the same time generating new dimensions through which status disputes and frustrations—and therefore disillusionment with political independence—were expressed at the local level within a rural community.

3   See, for example, *Abeng* 1969, *Sunday Gleaner* 1972:8, and Buckley 1987.

4   Here, it is important to point out, especially with respect to the "poorer class of people," that this is what they said in the late 1990s, but not necessarily what they thought at the time that Jamaica was undergoing the transition to self-government. That is, while several may have had faith in the possibilities of political independence, there is also evidence from anthropologists working in other areas of the region during the period just before independence of a substantial degree of concern that the nationalist leadership would not do well by them (Sutton 1970).

5   I never heard this argument articulated by poorer community members under the age of thirty.

6   A number of formal and informal institutions exist to facilitate this kind of knowledge sharing, primary among them in the contemporary period being the morning and afternoon radio call-in shows.

7   There were a few younger people in the village who farmed at least part time, some of whom cultivated marijuana in addition to other cash crops, which made it more lucrative for them. However, one youth explained that one of the reasons "money is tighter now" was because whereas ten years prior, "most people hustled some ganja," more recently the government had been cracking down on this. He saw this as related to U.S. influence and events in Colombia and argued that those who previously hustled don't necessarily have the education to do anything else.

8   Partner is the rotating lending and savings circle whereby a group comes together and contributes a certain amount of money in each specified amount of time and then, at designated intervals, each individual receives the whole pot.

9   The pattern of migration for the children of the middle-class professionals living in the village differed from these patterns. If they had migrated to England or the United States, they tended to stay in order to further either their educational or professional goals and to raise their families, while their parents remained in Jamaica. Moreover, whereas the generation of middle-class villagers now in their fifties and sixties might have gone to England to further their education or their careers, several of their children have instead traveled to the United States.

10   This destination switch has been due, in part, to changes in immigration legislation in the United States and the United Kingdom during the mid-1960s and is also related to the changing position of the United States within the global economy.

11   For more on child fostering practices, see Soto [1987].

12 These types of programs, and in particular the Hotel Workers Programme, form the basis of my next research project. I am particularly interested in what impact these women's participation in the Programme will have on their families and on the community as a whole in the long run; whether their intensified mobility ultimately increases their autonomy and power in relation to men; and the effects of women's increased migration upon community and leadership development locally (Thomas 2001).

13 It is also true, however, that the personalized ties between the "poorer class of people" and the local middle class in Mango Mount were only one or two generations deep. As a result, it is possible that the "poorer set's" autonomy was more profoundly rooted—both materially and ideologically—to begin with.

chapter 7   Modern Blackness; or, Theoretical "Tripping" on Black Vernacular Culture

1 By Afro-Caribbean, I mean to include the formerly British, French, and Dutch West Indies and to some extent, the u.s. Virgin Islands, but not the Spanish-speaking Caribbean. This distinction is important because cultural duality is one theoretical and social dimension that distinguishes the Hispanic Caribbean from the West Indies. This is not to say that Spanish-speaking Caribbean people do not engage in such practices as code-switching. However, outside the Spanish-speaking Caribbean, the differences between the cultural and social institutions of different sectors of the society are more marked due to the different experience of colonization, especially the much earlier implementation of monocrop export-oriented plantation agricultural development under conditions of slave labor.

2 This view is put forth (with varying degrees of alarm) by several scholars, including Charles Carnegie (1996), Brian Meeks (1994, 2000), Don Robotham (1998a), and David Scott (1999, 2000). It is also a view that is propagated within the public sphere—and discussed at the local level—since newspaper and radio commentators often remark upon the "crisis" confronting Jamaica.

3 What I am referring to here is M. G. Smith's plural society theory (1955, 1962, 1965), the various kinds of critiques it engendered (Austin 1983; Cross 1971; S. Hall 1977; Robotham 1980), and the stratification model that was subsequently developed to explain the persistence of inequalities within a context of national integration (R. T. Smith 1967, 1996).

4 See, for example, Brathwaite 1971b; Craton 1978; Genovese 1972; and Levine 1977.

5 I am using Peter Wilson's terms here because his ethnographic account of respectability and reputation was the most seminal early exploration of

West Indian cultural duality, and the most contested (1973). For important critiques of Wilson's formulation, see Barrow 1998a; Besson 1993; Douglass 1992; D. Miller 1994; Sutton 1974; B. Williams 1996b; and Yelvington 1995. I also thank Kevin Yelvington for reminding me that Melville Herskovits's formulation of "socialized ambivalence" predates Wilson's cultural duality framework and for suggesting that I think through the political economy surrounding this kind of knowledge production. His own work on Herskovits's Haitian field research in 1934 locates the conceptualization of socialized ambivalence both in relation to the development of historical explanations for black cultural difference and behavioral and political shifts (seen as "instability" at that time) and with respect to the close associations Herskovits had with local black (as opposed to "brown") intellectuals like Jean Price Mars (Yelvington 2002). For Yelvington, then, socialized ambivalence and cultural duality emerge primarily as intellectual tropes designed to make sense of (and shape) particular political struggles.

6   By separating the structural and cultural dimensions of Afro-Caribbean dualities, I do not mean to suggest that they are not related. My intention is to reflect the differences between work like that of Chandra Jayawardena (1963)—who emphasized the structural foundations underlying the simultaneous desire among subordinated populations to achieve both status and collective solidarity (egalitarianism versus hierarchy)—and that of Peter Wilson (1973)—whose analysis attempted to position a code-switching cultural duality at the core of individuals' worldviews.

7   This was in contradistinction to scholarship that was designed to identify and trace the African roots of West Indian societies (e.g., Alleyne 1988).

8   I thank Connie Sutton, Sue Makiesky-Barrow, and Diana Wells for helping me to clarify my understanding of cultural duality, creolization, and double consciousness.

9   This is a patois phrase that is used by black lower-class Jamaicans to refer to their own cultural practices.

10 In November 1997, Jamaica's soccer team qualified for the World Cup tournament to be held in France in 1998. I discuss some of the ways this event was analyzed within Jamaica in the conclusion.

11 Roots plays are the closest Jamaican equivalent of the African American theatre genre known as the Chitlin' Circuit. For a description of this type of cultural production in the United States, see Gates 1997.

12 Both of these films were released by Island Jamaica Films, a subsidiary of Island Records. In 1960, white Jamaican Chris Blackwell established Island Records to record and distribute Jamaican music worldwide. The company's headquarters moved to London in 1962, and throughout the 1970s, Island Records brought popularity to reggae music, in part by marketing LPs in the same manner as were American record producers. Island's first film project was The Harder They Come. In 1989, Island was bought by the

Netherlands-based conglomerate Polygram, but Blackwell remained the head of the Island companies until November 1997 (after the release of *Dancehall Queen*), when he left Polygram.

13 For a somewhat different reading of these two films against each other, see Scott 1999: 212, n52.

14 There is a long history to this perception of Americans as uncivilized. When the tourism industry began in Jamaica during the late nineteenth century, while Americans were heralded as positively infusing Jamaicans with a "go-getter" spirit, they were also viewed as culturally coarse (Taylor 1993). This view has persisted. Harley Neita's "Interesting Historical Highlights" published in the *Daily Gleaner* cited a 1958 tourism-related incident in the north coast: "The Montego Bay Chamber of commerce calls on Government to help rid the town of 'the nuisance of scantily dressed tourists roaming the streets in bathing suits and shorts.' Members are concerned because the example is being followed by Jamaicans, and the secretary is instructed to write the Ministry of Home Affairs asking that a notice be placed at the Airport asking visitors to wear swim suits only at the beaches and short shorts on the hotel premises, for as one member said, 'it is not everything foreign that is good to follow' " (Neita 1997a).

15 Mary Waters makes similar arguments for West Indian migrants in the United States (1999).

16 Historian Harvey Neptune makes a similar argument in his analysis of the role of the United States within Trinidadian nationalist struggles during the colonial period (2001).

17 John L. Jackson uses this term—a "quotation-marked-off place"—to describe the ways Harlem residents and media moguls evoke the mythical Harlemworld of second Renaissances and souped-up Range Rovers as against their own Harlem realities (2001).

18 Many scholars have addressed the ways West Indians have both assimilated with and distanced themselves from, in particular, African Americans. For excellent recent treatments, see LaBennett 2002 and M. Waters 1999.

19 I do not mean to suggest that the NDM was unequivocally viewed in a positive light since many villagers, and Jamaicans more generally, were wary of the NDM's leaders, who had allegedly been intimately involved with the promulgation of political violence during their tenure with the two traditional political parties.

20 The subsection's subtitle is from lyrics to a song entitled "Who Am I" by dancehall DJ Beenie Man.

21 These are lyrics to Jimmy Cliff's "The Harder They Come." My thanks are due here to an anonymous reader for Duke University Press who pointed out that the "now" in this line of the song draws our attention to the continuities between rude boy (1960s) and dancehall (1990s) ideologies in relation to consumerism and immediate gratification.

22   Explicit racialized critiques of white capitalist exploitation of black culture are also common within U.S.-based hip-hop. For example, in the second verse of "Izzo (H.O.V.A.)," Jay-Z raps: "I do this for my culture [meaning, other black people], to let 'em know what a nigga look like . . . when a nigga in a roaster [meaning, a Lamborghini Testarosa]; Show 'em how to move in a room full 'o vultures, Industry shady it need to be taken over; Label owners hate me I'm raisin' the status quo up, I'm overchargin' niggaz for what they did to the Cold Crush; Pay us like you owe us for all the years that you hold us, We can talk, but money talks so talk mo' bucks."

23   I am using the concept of resignification here in the way Kamari Clarke does in her examination of the processes by which U.S.-born Yoruba revivalists in Oyotunji Village re-envisioned the rituals and social organization of Cuban Santeria to institutionalize instead a "purer," more "authentically" Nigerian Yoruba practice (Clarke 2004).

24   These are lyrics to a song entitled "Yuh Nuh Ready" by female dancehall DJ Tanya Stephens.

25   The other source of power she identified was spirituality (as distinct from formal religion). In this discussion, I focus on sexuality.

26   Brian Meeks has also suggested that we can view the collapse of the creole multiracial nationalist project as the collapse of a male project (1994).

27   The success of these women, as well as the more recent success of women within educational and economic spheres, has been part of the impetus behind the recently articulated discourse surrounding the "marginalized" lower-class black man (see de Albuquerque and Ruark 1998 and Barriteau 2001 for rebuttals to the marginalized male thesis). However, Faye Harrison has tempered what has emerged within popular and academic spheres as a kind of celebration of the power and autonomy of lower-class women involved in the informal sector, arguing that it masks the structural realities of poverty faced by most poor women (1988b).

28   These are lyrics to the song "Draw Fi Mi Finger."

29   What I am invoking here is the "dual marriage system" as conceptualized by R. T. Smith (see R. T. Smith 1996, chapter 6; and Douglass 1992, especially 238–242).

30   In the years since the publication of her book (1999), cultural critic Joan Morgan has tempered her position somewhat. Where less than five years ago, Morgan notes, sexism in hip-hop would have been part of a broader conversation that would have also included debates about freedom of speech, the multiplicity of female images available within hip-hop (e.g., Queen Latifah and L'il Kim), and the pursuit of pleasure, the current moment in mainstream hip-hop—marked by increasingly narrow portrayals of skinny, scantily clad white, Latina, Asian, and light-skinned African American women bumping and grinding in videos—has generated frustration among black women (2002).

31 This kind of discourse is not without precedent. Several scholars have demonstrated that a consideration of women's blues during the 1920s and 1930s provides insights into the ideological debates both within and outside of the African American community during that time and illuminates the ways working-class women contested patriarchal assumptions about "a woman's place." See especially Carby 1999 a, b; A. Davis 1998; Higginbotham 1997.

32 For instance, Barry Chevannes has identified the ideological continuities within a number of socioreligious movements in the nineteenth and twentieth centuries, and particularly Revivalism and Rastafarianism, in order to understand both individualism and community egalitarianism as socially transformative (1998). And as mentioned earlier, Abigail Bakan (1990) has highlighted the role of religious idioms, as well as the expectation of and appeal to the British Crown as a fair and benevolent ruler, as thematic continuities within popular protest until the acquisition of formal independence. See also Bogues 2003.

33 Obika Gray argues that methodologically, the politics of the poor is generated through informality, improvisation, attrition, and survivalism, and that it is largely a politics of identity designed to "recover, defend, and preserve their sense of cultural respect and authority" within the broader context of competition for wealth, power, and influence (1994:182). Gray further identifies several channels through which poorer Jamaicans have defined and defended their politics. Among these are evasion and disengagement; "social outlawry" and the rejection of dominant class morality; and the "trespassing" and "colonizing of social spaces," including those spaces associated with party politics, the informal economy, and the domain of "culture"—as he defines it, sports, musical entertainment, dance forms, language, and religious expression (1994:187; see also Gray 1991). "Social outlawry" was the term anthropologist Faye Harrison used to describe the alternative political tactics used by those unable to benefit from the more usual vehicles of empowerment in Jamaica, such as clientelism. Harrison argues that outlawry, unlike patron-clientelism, "represents a more principled form of resistance against established authorities and the oppressive social order they represent and defend; and contrary to many forms of criminality, it opposed the victimization of the innocent and the oppressed" (1988a:259).

conclusion The Remix

1 Haiti's soccer team qualified for the World Cup finals once in the 1970s.
2 There is an extensive literature that approaches West Indians' appropriation of cricket from this perspective (see, for example, Beckles and Stoddart 1995; James 1963; Manley 1988; Manning 1981).

3   See Bourdieu 1984; Foucault 1983; Roseberry 1994.

4   Stephanie Black's recent documentary, *Life and Debt*, is a particularly tren-
chant chronicle of the effects of globalization on Jamaica's major industries
(2001).

5   Stories about Anancy the spider are tales whereby the figure of the trickster
is able to outwit his more powerful opponents through his cunning and
cleverness.

epilogue

1   That these gendered and generational practices reflected expected norms
was evident in the enthusiastic audience response to the various singers.
These kinds of performances remind us that the masculinities and femi-
ninities associated with modern blackness are constantly negotiated with
other expectations surrounding appropriate gender behavior (and particularly feminine behavior), and that these gendered performances are
embedded within global political economies of cultural production. Here,
different genres of African American popular music (rhythm and blues,
hip-hop) became the stage upon which Jamaican gender ideologies were
rehearsed.

2   Busso is a mollusk unique to the area around the Rio Grande in Portland. It
looks like a small snail and is traditionally used in soups.

3   These festivals have not yet begun to attract tourists from overseas, though
there are plans to market them in that way in the future. Additionally, the
Busso Festival has established an internet Web site through which most of
its overseas business is also generated.

4   Spurred by a complex series of gas tax raises in April 1999, Jamaican
citizens protested by creating roadblocks all over Kingston and throughout
the countryside. They succeeded in shutting down commerce for several
days.

bibliography

Abeng. 1969. "Festival and Independence." August 9, vol. 1, no. 28.

Abrahams, Roger. 1983. *The Man of Words in the West Indies: Performance and the Emergence of Creole Culture*. Baltimore: Johns Hopkins University Press.

Abrams, Philip. 1988. "Notes on the Difficulty of Studying the State." *Journal of Historical Sociology* 1 (1): 58–89.

Abu-Lughod, Lila. 1998a. "Introduction: Feminist Longings and Postcolonial Conditions." In *Remaking Women: Feminism and Modernity in the Middle East*, ed. by Lila Abu-Lughod, 3–31. Princeton: Princeton University Press.

———. 1998b. "The Marriage of Feminism and Islamism in Egypt: Selective Repudiation as a Dynamic of Postcolonial Cultural Politics." In *Remaking Women: Feminism and Modernity in the Middle East*, ed. by Lila Abu-Lughod, 243–69. Princeton: Princeton University Press.

———. 1990. "The Romance of Resistance: Tracing Transformations of Power through Bedouin Women." *American Ethnologist* 17 (1): 41–55.

Aitken, Hellen. n.d. *History of Ivor*. Pamphlet.

Alexander, Jack. 1984. "Love, Race, Slavery, and Sexuality in Jamaican Images of the Family." In *Kinship Ideology and Practice in Latin America*, ed. by R. T. Smith, 147–80. Chapel Hill: University of North Carolina Press.

———. 1977a. "The Culture of Race in Middle-Class Kingston, Jamaica." *American Ethnologist* 4 (3): 413–25.

———. 1977b. "The Role of the Male in the Middle-Class Jamaican Family: A Comparative Perspective." *Journal of Comparative Family Studies* 8 (3): 369–89.

Alexander, M. Jacqui. 1997. "Erotic Autonomy as a Politics of Decolonization: An Anatomy of Feminist and State Practice in the Bahamas Tourist Economy." In *Feminist Genealogies, Colonial Legacies, Democratic Futures*, ed. by Chandra T. Mohanty and M. Jacqui Alexander, 63–100. New York: Routledge.

———. 1991. "Redefining Morality: The Postcolonial State and the Sexual Offences Bill of Trinidad and Tobago." In *Third World Women and the Politics of Feminism*, ed. by Chandra T. Mohanty, Ann Russo, and Lourdes Torres, 133–52. Indianapolis: Indiana University Press.

Alleyne, Mervyn. 1988. *The Roots of Jamaican Culture*. London: Pluto.

Alonso, Ana Maria. 1994. "The Politics of Space, Time, and Substance: State Formation, Nationalism, and Ethnicity." *Annual Review of Anthropology* 23:379–405.

———. 1988. "The Effects of Truth: Re-Presentations of the Past and the Imagining of Community." *Journal of Historical Sociology* 1 (1): 33–57.

Anderson, Benedict. 1991. *Imagined Communities: Reflections on the Origin and Spread of Nationalism*. Rev. and extend. ed. New York: Verso.

Anderson, Patricia. 2001. "Poverty in Jamaica: Social Target or Social Crisis?" Paper presented at the Caribbean Studies Association Conference, St. Martin, May 27–June 2, 2001.

Anthias, Flora, and Nira Yuval-Davis (eds.). 1989. Woman-Nation-State. New York: Macmillan.

Aparicio, Frances R. 1998. Listening to Salsa: Gender, Latin Popular Music, and Puerto Rican Cultures. Hanover, N.H: University Press of New England, Wesleyan University Press.

Appadurai, Arjun. 2001. "Grassroots Globalization and the Research Imagination." In Globalization, ed. by Arjun Appadurai, 1–21. Durham: Duke University Press.

——. 1996. Modernity at Large: Cultural Dimensions of Globalization. Minneapolis: University of Minnesota Press.

——. 1990. "Disjuncture and Difference in the Global Cultural Economy." Public Culture 2 (2): 1–24.

Austin, Diane. 1984. Urban Life in Kingston, Jamaica: The Culture and Class Ideology of Two Neighborhoods. New York: Gordon and Breach.

——. 1983. "Culture and Ideology in the English-Speaking Caribbean: A View from Jamaica." American Ethnologist 10 (2): 223–40.

Austin-Broos, Diane. 1997. Jamaica Genesis: Religion and the Politics of Moral Orders. Chicago: University of Chicago Press.

——. 1994. "Race/Class: Jamaica's Discourse of Heritable Identity." New West Indian Guide 68 (3–4): 213–33.

——. 1992. "Redefining the Moral Order: Interpretations of Christianity in Post-Emancipation Jamaica." In The Meaning of Freedom: Economics, Politics, and Culture after Slavery, ed. by Frank McGlynn and Seymour Drescher, 221–44. Pittsburgh: University of Pittsburgh Press.

Averill, Gage. 1997. A Day for the Hunter, A Day for the Prey: Popular Music and Power in Haiti. Chicago: University of Chicago Press.

Aymer, Paula. 1997. Uprooted Women: Migrant Domestics in the Caribbean. Westport, Conn.: Praeger.

Babadzan, Alain. 1988. "Kastom and Nation Building in the South Pacific." In Ethnicities and Nations: Processes of Interethnic Relations in Latin America, Southeast Asia, and the Pacific, ed. by Remo Guidieri, Grancesco Pellizzi, and Stanley Tambiah, 199–228. Austin: University of Texas Press.

Bakan, Abigail. 1990. Ideology and Class Conflict in Jamaica: The Politics of Rebellion. Montreal: McGill-Queens University Press.

Baker, Lee. 1998. From Savage to Negro: Anthropology and the Construction of Race, 1896–1954. Berkeley: University of California Press.

Balibar, Etienne. 1991. "Racism and Nationalism." In Race, Nation, Class: Ambiguous Identities, ed. by Etienne Balibar and Immanuel Wallerstein, 37–67. New York: Verso.

Barriteau, Eudine. 2001. "Requiem for the Male Marginalization Thesis in the

Caribbean." Paper presented at the Caribbean Studies Association Meetings, St. Maarten, May 28.

Barnes, Natasha. 1997. "Face of the Nation: Race, Nationalisms, and Identities in Jamaican Beauty Pageants." In *Daughters of Caliban: Caribbean Women in the Twentieth Century*, ed. by Consuelo Lopez Springfield, 285–306. Bloomington: Indiana University Press.

Barrow, Christine. 1998a. "Caribbean Masculinity and Family: Revisiting 'Marginality' and 'Reputation.' " In *Caribbean Portraits: Essays on Gender Ideologies and Identities*, ed. by Christine Barrow, 339–58. Kingston: Ian Randle.

——. 1998b. "Introduction and Overview: Caribbean Gender Ideologies." In *Caribbean Portraits: Essays on Gender Ideologies and Identities*, ed. by Christine Barrow, xi–xxxviii. Kingston: Ian Randle.

——. 1996. *Family in the Caribbean: Themes and Perspectives.* Kingston: Ian Randle.

Basch, Linda, Nina Glick Schiller, and Cristina Szanton Blanc. 1994. *Nations Unbound: Transnational Projects, Postcolonial Predicaments, and Deterritorialized Nation-States.* Langhorne, PA: Gordon and Breach.

Baxter, Ivy. 1970. *The Arts of an Island: The Development of the Culture and of the Folk and Creative Arts in Jamaica, 1494–1962.* Metuchen, N.J.: The Scarecrow Press.

Bay, Mia. 2000. *The White Image in the Black Mind: African-American Ideas about White People, 1830–1925.* New York: Oxford University Press.

Beckford, George, and Michael Witter. 1982. *Small Garden, Bitter Weed: The Political Economy of Struggle and Change in Jamaica*, rev. ed. London: Zed Books.

Beckles, Hilary. 1989. *Natural Rebels: A Social History of Enslaved Black Women in Barbados.* New Brunswick, N.J.: Rutgers University Press.

Beckles, Hilary, and Brian Stoddart (eds.). 1995. *Liberation Cricket: West Indies Cricket Culture.* New York: St. Martin's Press.

Beckwith, Martha. 1929 [1969]. *Black Roadways: A Study of Jamaican Folk Life.* New York: Negro Universities Press.

Bell, Wendell. 1964. *Jamaican Leaders: Political Attitudes in a New Nation.* Berkeley: University of California Press.

Beriss, David. 1993. "High Folklore: Challenges to the French Cultural World Order." *Social Analysis* 33 (2): 105–29.

Besson, Jean. 2002. *Martha Brae's Two Histories: European Expansion and Caribbean Culture-Building in Jamaica.* Chapel Hill: University of North Carolina Press.

——. 1998. "Religion as Resistance in Jamaican Peasant Life: The Baptist Church, Revival Worldview and the Rastafari Movement." In *Rastafari and Other Afro-Caribbean Worldviews*, ed. by Barry Chevannes, 43–76. New Brunswick, N.J: Rutgers University Press.

——. 1993. "Reputation and Respectability Reconsidered: A New Perspective on Afro-Caribbean Peasant Women." In *Women and Change in the Caribbean*, ed. by J. Momsen, 15–37. London: James Currey.

——. 1992. "Freedom and Community: The British West Indies." In *The Meaning of Freedom: Economics, Politics, and Culture after Slavery*, ed. by Frank McGlynn and Seymour Drescher, 183–219. Pittsburgh: University of Pittsburgh Press.

Bigelow, John. 1851 [1970]. *Jamaica in 1850, or the Effects of Sixteen Years of Freedom on a Slave Colony*. Westport, Conn.: Negro Universities Press.

Bilby, Kenneth. 1995. "Jamaica." In *Caribbean Currents: Caribbean Music from Rumba to Reggae*, ed. by Peter Manuel et al. Philadelphia: Temple University Press.

——. 1985. "The Caribbean as a Musical Region." In *Caribbean Contours*, ed. by Sidney Mintz and Sally Price, 181–218. Baltimore: Johns Hopkins University Press.

Black, Stephanie, dir. 2001. *Life and Debt*. New York: New Yorker Films. [Available on VHS and DVD (2003)].

Blake, Judith. 1961. *Family Structure in Jamaica: The Social Context of Reproduction*. Glencoe, IL: The Free Press.

Blake-Hannah, Barbara Makeda. 1997. "Well Done Jamaican Government." *Daily Observer*, September 8, 7.

Bogues, Anthony. 2003. *Black Heretics, Black Prophets: Radical Political Intellectuals*. New York: Routledge.

——. 2002. "Politics, Nation, and PostColony: Caribbean Inflections." *Small Axe* 6 (1): 1–30.

——. 1995. "The Logic of Freedom and the Jamaican Political Process, An Overview." In *August First: A Celebration of Emancipation*, ed. by Patrick Bryan, 11–22. Kingston: Department of History and Friedrich Ebert Siftung.

Bolland, O. Nigel. 1997. *Struggles for Freedom: Essays on Slavery, Colonialism and Culture in the Caribbean and Central America*. Kingston: Ian Randle.

——. 1992. "The Politics of Freedom in the British Caribbean." In *The Meaning of Freedom: Economics, Politics, and Culture after Slavery*, ed. by Frank McGlynn and Seymour Drescher, 113–46. Pittsburgh: University of Pittsburgh Press.

Bolles, A. Lynn. 1996a. *Sister Jamaica: A Study of Women, Work, and Households in Kingston*. New York: University Press of America.

——. 1996b. *We Paid Our Dues: Women Trade Union Leaders of the Caribbean*. Washington: Howard University Press.

——. 1983. "Kitchens Hit by Priorities: Employed Working-class Jamaican Women Confront the IMF." In *Women, Men, and the International Division of Labor*, eds. June Nash and Maria Patricia Fernández Kelly, 138–60. Albany: State University of New York Press.

Bourdieu, Pierre. 1984. *Distinction: A Social Critique of the Judgement of Taste*, trans. Richard Nice. Cambridge, Mass.: Harvard University Press.

Bowen, Calvin. 1997. "Of Freedom and Nationhood." *Daily Gleaner*, August 6, A4.

Boxill, Ian. 1997. "Beyond Flag Nationalism." *Daily Gleaner*, November 11, A4.

Brady, Neal, Diana Gavina, Michael Kaplan, JoAnn Schop, and Dan Viederman. 1992. "Report of Findings of the Columbia University EPD Environment Team: Mango Mount and the Mammee River Gorge." Unpublished report.

an Alternative Modernity." In *Ungrounded Empires: The Cultural Politics of Modern Chinese Nationalism*, ed. by Ong and Nonini, 3–33. New York: Routledge.

Ortner, Sherry. 1996. *Making Gender: The Politics and Erotics of Culture*. Boston: Beacon.

Pacini, Deborah. 1995. *Bachata: A Social History of a Dominican Popular Music*. Philadelphia: Temple University Press.

Paley, Julia. 2001. *Marketing Democracy: Power and Social Movements in Post-Dictatorship Chile*. Berkeley: University of California Press.

Palmié, Stephan. 2002. *Wizards and Scientists: Explorations in Afro-Cuban Modernity and Tradition*. Durham: Duke University Press.

Parreñas, Rhacel Salazar. 2001. *Servants of Globalization: Women, Migration, and Domestic Work*. Stanford, Calif.: Stanford University Press.

Patterson, Orlando. 1967. *The Sociology of Slavery: An Analysis of the Origins, Development and Structure of Negro Slave Society in Jamaica*. London: MacGibbon and Kee.

People's National Party (PNP). 1938. Inaugural Speeches by Norman Manley and Stafford Cripps. Pamphlet.

——. 1939. Educational Programme. Pamphlet.

——. 1940. Plan for Today, and Money for the Plan. Pamphlet.

——. 1941. Report of Third Annual Conference. Pamphlet.

——. 1942a. Call to the Workers. Pamphlet.

——. 1942b. Danger to the Worker, a Plot: Bustamante and the PNP. Pamphlet.

——. 1942c. Report of Fourth Annual Conference. Pamphlet.

——. 1944. How Can I Help the PNP? Pamphlet.

——. 1945. Programme for Action Now. Pamphlet.

——. n.d. Notes on Socialism. Pamphlet.

——. n.d. What Is Civics? A Guide to True Citizenship and Good Government. Pamphlet.

Pérez, Louis Jr. 1999. *On Becoming Cuban: Identity, Nationality, and Culture*. Chapel Hill: University of North Carolina Press.

Pessar, Patricia. 1996. *A Visa for a Dream: Dominicans in the United States*. Boston: Allyn and Bacon.

Petras, Elizabeth. 1988. *Jamaican Labor Migration: White Capital and Black Labor, 1850–1930*. Boulder, Colo.: Westview Press.

Petras, James. 1990. "The World Market: Battleground for the 1990s." *Journal of Contemporary Asia* 20 (2): 145–76.

Phillippo, James. 1969. *Jamaica: Its Past and Present State*. Reprint of 1st ed., 1843, London: Davisons of Pall Mall.

Piot, Charles. 1999. *Remotely Global: Village Modernity in West Africa*. Chicago: University of Chicago Press.

Pitman, Frank. 1967. *The Development of the British West Indies, 1700–1763*. Hamden, Conn.: Archon Books.

Post, Ken. 1978. *Arise Ye Starvelings: The Jamaican Labour Rebellion of 1938 and Its Aftermath*. The Hague: Martinus Nijhoff.

Poulantzas, Nicos. 1978. *State, Power, Socialism*. London: New Left Books.

Powdermaker, Hortense. 1939. *After Freedom: A Cultural Study in the Deep South*. New York: Viking Press.

Pred, Allan, and Michael J. Watts. 1993. *Reworking Modernity: Capitalisms and Symbolic Discontent*. New Brunswick: Rutgers University Press.

Price, Charles Reavis. 2003. " 'Cleave to the Black': Expressions of Ethiopianism in Jamaica." *New West Indian Guide* 77 (1–2): 31–64.

Price, Richard. 1998. *The Convict and the Colonel: A Story of Colonialism and Resistance in the Caribbean*. Boston: Beacon.

Pulis, John W. 1999. "Bridging Troubled Waters: Moses Baker, George Liele, and the African American Diaspora to Jamaica." In *Moving On: Black Loyalists in the Afro-Atlantic World*, ed. by John Pulis, 183–221. New York: Garland.

Pullen-Berry, Elizabeth. 1903. *Jamaica as It Is, 1903*. London: T. Fisher Unwin.

———. 1971. *Ethiopia in Exile: Jamaica Revisited*. Reprint of the 1905 ed., New York: Books for the Libraries Press.

Quintero-Rivera, Angel. 1987. "The Rural-Urban Dichotomy in the Formation of Puerto Rico's Cultural Identity." *New West Indian Guide* 61 (3–4): 127–44.

Ragatz, Lowell J. 1928. *The Fall of the Planter Class in the British Caribbean, 1763–1833: A Study in Social and Economic History*. New York: Century Company.

Reddock, Rhoda. 2001. " 'Man Gone, Man Stay': Masculinity, Ethnicity and Identity in the Contemporary Socio-Political Context of Trinidad and Tobago." Invited lecture at the Center for the Americas, Wesleyan University, November 1. Series title: "Ethnic Politics and the State."

———. 1999. "Jahaji Bhai: The Emergence of a Dougla Poetics in Trinidad and Tobago." *Identities* 5 (4): 569–601.

———. 1998. "Contestations over National Culture in Trinidad and Tobago: Considerations of Ethnicity, Class, and Gender." In *Caribbean Portraits: Essays on Gender Ideologies and Identities*, ed. by Christine Barrow, 414–35. Kingston: Ian Randle.

———. 1994. *Women, Labour and Politics in Trinidad and Tobago: A History*. London: Zed Books.

Report on National Symbols and Observances. 1996. Kingston: Jamaica Information Service.

Return of Properties: 1882; Parish of St. Andrew. Kingston: Government Printing Office.

Richards, Courtney. 1997. "A New Kind of Slavery." *Daily Gleaner*, August 9, A5.

Roberts, George. 1957. *The Population of Jamaica*. Cambridge: Cambridge University Press.

Robinson, Cedric. 2000. *Black Marxism: The Making of the Black Radical Tradition*. Chapel Hill: University of North Carolina Press. 1st ed., London: Zed Press, 1983.

Robotham, Don. 2000. "Blackening the Jamaican Nation: The Travails of a Black Bourgeoisie in a Globalized World." *Identities* 7 (1): 1–37.

——. 1998a. "Transnationalism in the Caribbean: Formal and Informal." *American Ethnologist* 25 (2): 307–21.

——. 1998b. "Politics, Hegemony, and Color in Jamaica." Unpublished manuscript.

——. 1997. "Postcolonialities: The Challenge of New Modernities." *International Social Science Journal* 153:357–71.

——. 1993. "The Dislocation of Values in the English-Speaking Caribbean: The Jamaica Case." Paper presented at the University of Chicago Alumnae Conference, Department of Anthropology.

——. 1982. " 'The Notorious Riot': The Socio-Economic and Political Bases of Paul Bogle's Revolt." Working paper no. 28. Mona: Institute for Social and Economic Research, University of the West Indies Press.

——. 1980. "Pluralism as an Ideology." *Social and Economic Studies* 29:69–89.

Rodman, Hyman. 1971. *Lower Class Families: The Culture of Poverty in Negro Trinidad.* New York: Oxford University Press.

——. 1959. "On Understanding Lower-Class Behavior." *Social and Economic Studies* 8 (4): 441–50.

Rofel, Lisa. 1999. *Other Modernities: Gendered Yearnings in China after Socialism.* Berkeley: University of California Press.

Rose, Tricia. 1994. *Black Noise: Rap Music and Black Culture in Contemporary America.* Hanover, N.H.: University Press of New England.

Roseberry, William. 1994. "Hegemony and the Language of Contention." In *Everyday Forms of State Formation: Revolution and the Negotiation of Rule in Modern Mexico,* ed. by Gilbert Joseph and Daniel Nugent, 355–66. Durham: Duke University Press.

——. 1991. "Marxism and Culture." In *Anthropologies and Histories: Essays in Culture, History, and Political Economy,* 30–54. New Brunswick, N.J.: Rutgers University Press.

Ross, Andrew. 1998. "Mr. Reggae DJ, Meet the International Monetary Fund." *Black Renaissance* 1 (3): 207–32.

Rouse, Roger. 1995. "Questions of Identity: Personhood and Collectivity in Transnational Migration to the United States." *Critique of Anthropology* 15 (4): 351–80.

——. 1991. "Mexican Migration and the Social Space of Postmodernism." *Diaspora* 1 (1).

Rowe, Maureen. 1998. "Rastawoman as Rebel: Case Studies in Jamaica." In *Chanting Down Babylon: The Rastafarian Reader,* ed. by Nathanial Samuel Murrell and William D. Spencer. Philadelphia: Temple University Press.

Rubenstein, Hymie. 1983. "Caribbean Family and Household Organization: Some Conceptual Clarifications." *Journal of Comparative Family Studies* 14 (3): 283–98.

——. 1980. "Conjugal Behavior and Parental Role Flexibility in an Afro-Caribbean Village." *Canadian Review of Sociology and Anthropology* 17 (4): 331–37.

Ryan, Selwyn. 1972. *Race and Nationalism in Trinidad and Tobago: A Study of Democracy in a Multi-Racial Society.* Toronto: University of Toronto Press.

Safa, Helen. 1995. *The Myth of the Male Breadwinner: Women and Industrialization in the Caribbean.* Boulder, Colo.: Westview Press.

——. 1987. "Popular Culture, National Identity and Race in the Caribbean." *New West Indian Guide* 61 (3–4): 115–26.

——. 1981. "Runaway Shops and Female Employment: The Search for Cheap Labour." *Signs* 7, 418–34.

Sassen, Saskia. 1998. *Globalization and Its Discontents: Essays on the New Mobility of People and Money.* New York: New Press.

——. 1994. *Cities in a World Economy.* Thousand Oaks, Calif.: Pine Forge Press.

Satchell, Veront. 1995. "Women, Land Transactions, and Peasant Development in Jamaica, 1866–1900." In *Engendering History: Caribbean Women in Historical Perspective,* ed. by Verene Shepherd, Bridget Brereton, and Barbara Bailey, 213–32. Kingston: Ian Randle.

——. 1990. *From Plots to Plantations: Land Transactions in Jamaica, 1866–1900.* Mona: Institute of Social and Economic Research, University of the West Indies.

Saunders, Patricia. 2003. "Is Not Everything Good to Eat, Good to Talk: Sexual Economy and Dancehall Music in the Global Marketplace." *Small Axe* 7 (1): 95–115.

Savigliano, Marta. 1994. *Tango and the Political Economy of Passion.* Berkeley: University of California Press.

Savishinsky, Neil. 1994. "Rastafari in the Promised Land: The Spread of a Jamaican Socioreligious Movement among the Youth of Africa." *African Studies Review* 37 (3): 19–50.

Scholes, T. E. S. 1899. *The British Empire and Alliances, or Britain's Duty to her Colonies and Subject Races.* London: Elliot Stock.

Scott, David. 2000. "The Permanence of Pluralism." In *Without Guarantees: In Honour of Stuart Hall,* ed. by Paul Gilroy, Lawrence Grossberg, and Angela McRobbie, 282–301. New York: Verso.

——. 1999. *Refashioning Futures: Criticism after Postcoloniality.* Princeton: Princeton University Press.

Scott, James. 1998. *Seeing Like a State: How Certain Schemes to Improve the Human Condition Have Failed.* New Haven: Yale University Press.

Seaga, Edward. 1963. *Five Year Independence Plan, 1963–1968: A Long Term Development Programme for Jamaica.* Kingston: Ministry of Development and Welfare.

Segal, Daniel. 1994. "Living Ancestors: Nationalism and the Past in Post-Colonial Trinidad and Tobago." In *Remapping Memory: The Politics of Time Space,* ed. by Jonathan Boyarin. Minneapolis: University of Minnesota Press.

Segal, Daniel, and Richard Handler. 1992. "How European Is Nationalism?" *Social Analysis* 32 (1): 1–15.

Semaj, Leachim. 1997. "The Reggae Boyz and the National Psyche." *Daily Observer,* November 14, 6.

Sen, Gita, and Caren Grown. 1987. *Development, Crisis and Alternative Visions: Third World Women's Perspectives.* New York: Monthly Review Press.

Senior, Olive. 1991. *Working Miracles: Women's Lives in the English-Speaking Caribbean.* London: James Currey.

Shepherd, Verene. 1994. *Transients to Settlers: The Experience of Indians in Jamaica, 1845–1950.* Leeds: Peepal Tree Books.

Shepherd, Verene, Bridget Brereton, and Barbara Bailey, eds. 1995. *Engendering History: Caribbean Women in Historical Perspective.* New York: St. Martin's Press.

Simey, Thomas S. 1946. *Welfare and Planning in the West Indies.* Oxford: Clarendon Press.

Skidmore, Thomas. 1993. *Black into White: Race and Nationality in Brazilian Thought.* Durham: Duke University Press. 1st ed., New York: Oxford University Press, 1974.

Smith, Michael Garfield. 1966. Introduction to *My Mother Who Fathered Me: A Study of the Family in Three Selected Communities in Jamaica,* by Edith Clarke, i–xliv. London: George Allen and Unwin.

———. 1965. *The Plural Society in the British West Indies.* Berkeley: University of California Press.

———. 1962. *West Indian Family Structure.* Seattle: University of Washington Press.

———. 1955. *"Framework for Caribbean Studies.* Mona: University College of the West Indies, Extra-Mural Department.

Smith, M. G., Rex Nettleford, and Roy Augier. 1961. *Report on the Rastafari Movement in Kingston, Jamaica.* Mona: Institute for Social and Economic Research, University of the West Indies.

Smith, Michael Peter. 1995. "Transnational Migration and the Globalization of Grassroots Politics." *Social Text* 39:15–33.

Smith, Michael Peter, and Luis Guarnizo, eds. 1998. *Transnationalism from Below.* New Brunswick, N.J.: Transaction Books.

Smith, R. T. 1996. *The Matrifocal Family: Power, Pluralism, and Politics.* New York: Routledge.

———. 1967. "Social Stratification, Cultural Pluralism, and Integration in West Indian Societies." In *Caribbean Integration: Papers on Social, Political, and Economic Integration,* 226–58. Rio Pedras: Institute of Caribbean Studies.

———. 1956. *The Negro Family in British Guiana.* London: Routledge and Kegan Paul.

Soto, Isa Maria. 1987. "West Indian Child Fostering: Its Role in Migrant Exchanges." In *Caribbean Life in New York City: Sociocultural Dimensions,* ed. by Constance Sutton and Elsa Chaney, 121–37. Staten Island: Center for Migration Studies.

Stair, Marjorie. 1997a. "The Road to France—Lessons of Vision, Faith." *Daily Gleaner,* November 22, A4.

———. 1997b. "What Change Since 1838?" *Daily Gleaner,* August 10, A4.

———. 1996. "True Independence." *Daily Gleaner,* August 10, A4.

Star. 1955. "Ten Types, One People." July 26, 3.

Statistical Bulletin. 1999. Ministry of Labour and Social Security. Kingston, Jamaica.

Statistical Institute of Jamaica. Population Census 1991. Parish of St. Andrew. Kingston: Statistical Institute of Jamaica.

Stephens, Evelyne, and John Stephens. 1986. *Democratic Socialism in Jamaica: The Political Movement and Social Transformation in Dependent Capitalism*. Princeton: Princeton University Press.

Steward, Julian, et al. 1956. *The People of Puerto Rico: A Study in Social Anthropology*. Urbana: University of Illinois Press.

Stolberg, Claus. 1992. "Plantation Economy, Peasantry, and the Land Settlement Schemes of the 1930s and 1940s in Jamaica." In *Plantation Economy, Land Reform, and the Peasantry in a Historical Perspective: Jamaica 1838–1890*, ed. by Claus Stolbert and Swithin Wilmot, 39–68. Kingston: Friedrich Ebert Siftung.

Stolberg, Claus, and Swithin Wilmot, eds. 1992. *Plantation Economy, Land Reform, and the Peasantry in a Historical Perspective: Jamaica 1838–1890*. Kingston: Friedrich Ebert Siftung.

Stoler, Ann. 1989. "Making Empire Respectable: The Politics of Race and Sexuality in Twentieth Century Colonial Cultures." *American Ethnologist* 16 (4): 634–60.

Stolzoff, Norman. 2000. *Wake the Town and Tell the People: Dancehall Culture in Jamaica*. Durham: Duke University Press.

Stone, Carl. 1991. "Race and Economic Power in Jamaica." In *Garvey: His Work and Impact*, ed. by Rupert Lewis and Patrick Bryan, 243–64. Trenton, N.J.: Africa World Press.

———. 1973. *Class, Race, and Political Behavior in Urban Jamaica*. Mona: Institute of Social and Economic Research, University of the West Indies Press.

Stuempfle, Stephen. 1995. *The Steelband Movement: The Forging of a National Art in Trinidad and Tobago*. Philadelphia: University of Pennsylvania Press.

Stutzman, R. 1981. "El Mestisaje: An All-Inclusive Ideology of Exclusion." In *Cultural Transformations and Ethnicity in Modern Ecuador*, ed. by Whitten. New York: Harper and Row.

Stycos, J. Mayone, and Kurt Back. 1964. *The Control of Human Fertility in Jamaica*. Ithaca, N.Y.: Cornell University Press.

Sudarkasa, Niara. 1988. "African and Afro-American Family Structure." In *Anthropology for the Nineties*, ed. by Johnnetta Cole, 182–210. New York: Free Press.

Sunday Gleaner. 1972. "Ten Years of Independence," August 6, 8.

———. 1997. "People's Voices: What Does Emancipation Mean?" Portmore Journal, July 19, 5.

Sutton, Constance, ed. 1995. *Feminism, Nationalism, and Militarism*. Washington: American Anthropological Association, International Women's Anthropology Conference.

———. 1992. "Some Thoughts on Gendering and Internationalizing Our Think-ing about Transnational Migrations." In *Towards a Transnational Perspective on Migration: Race, Class, Ethnicity and Nationalism Reconsidered*, ed. by Nina Glick Schiller et al., 241–49. New York: NYAS.

———. 1987. "The Caribbeanization of New York City and the Emergence of a Transnational Socio-Cultural System." In *Caribbean Life in New York City: So-ciocultural Dimensions*, ed. by Constance Sutton and Elsa Chaney, 15–30. New York: CMS.

———. 1984. "Africans in the Diaspora: Changing Continuities in West Indian and West African Sex/Gender Systems." Paper presented at a Conference entitled "New Perspectives on Caribbean Studies: Toward the 21st Century," August 29.

———. 1974. "Cultural Duality in the Caribbean." *Caribbean Studies* 14 (2): 96–101.

———. 1970. *The Scene of the Action: A Wildcat Strike in Barbados*. PhD diss., Depart-ment of Anthropology, Columbia University.

Sutton, Constance, and Elsa Chaney, eds. 1987. *Caribbean Life in New York City: Sociocultural Dimensions*. New York: CMS.

Sutton, Constance, and Susan Makiesky-Barrow. 1987. "Migration and West Indian Racial and Ethnic Consciousness." In *Caribbean Life in New York City: Sociocultural Dimensions*, ed. by Constance Sutton and Elsa Chaney, 86–107. New York: CMS.

———. 1977. "Social Inequality and Sexual Status in Barbados." In *Sexual Stratifica-tion: A Cross-Cultural View*, ed. by Alice Schlegel. New York: Columbia Univer-sity Press. Reprinted in 1981 in *The Black Woman Cross Culturally*, ed. by Fil-omena Steady, Cambridge: Schenkman.

Swedenburg, Ted. 1990. "The Palestinian Peasant as National Signifier." *Anthro-pological Quarterly* 63 (1): 18–30.

Taylor, Frank. 1993. *To Hell with Paradise: A History of the Jamaican Tourism Industry*. Pittsburgh: University of Pittsburgh Press.

Thomas, Deborah. 2002a. "Democratizing Dance: Institutional Transformation and Hegemonic Re-Ordering in Jamaica." *Cultural Anthropology* 17 (4): 512–50.

———. 2002b. "Modern Blackness: 'What We Are and What We Hope to Be,'" *Small Axe* 6 (2): 25–48.

———. 2001. "Seasonal Labor, Seasonal Leisure: The Gruntwork, Goals, and Gains of Jamaican Hotel Workers in the United States." Paper presented at the Caribbean Studies Association meetings in St. Maarten, May 2001.

———. 1999. "Emancipating the Nation (Again): Notes on Nationalism, Modern-ization, and Other Dilemmas in Post-Colonial Jamaica." *Identities* 5 (4): 501–42.

———. 1993. *Defining National Identity through Performance: The Example of Jamaica*. Master's thesis, Center for Latin American and Caribbean Studies, New York University.

Thomas, J. J. 1889. *Froudacity*. London: T. F. Unwin.

Thome, Jas, and J. Horace Kimball. 1838. *Emancipation in the West Indies: A Six Month's Tour in Antigua, Barbadoes, and Jamaica.* New York: American Anti-Slavery Society.

Trouillot, Michel Rolph. 2002. "The Otherwise Modern: Caribbean Lessons from the Savage Slot." In *Critically Modern: Alternatives, Alterities, Anthropologies,* ed. by Bruce Knauft, 220–37. Indianapolis: Indiana University Press.

———. 2001. "The Anthropology of the State in the Age of Globalization." *Current Anthropology* 42 (1): 125–38.

———. 1995. "An Unthinkable History: The Haitian Revolution as a Non-Event." In *Silencing the Past: Power and the Production of History,* 70–107. Boston: Beacon.

———. 1990. *Haiti, State Against Nation: The Origins and Legacy of Duvalierism.* New York: Monthly Review Press.

———. 1988. *Peasants and Capital: Dominica in the World Economy.* Baltimore: Johns Hopkins University Press.

———. 1985. "Nation, State, and Society in Haiti, 1804–1984." *Focus: Caribbean,* ed. by Sidney Mintz and Sally Price. Pamphlet series. Washington: Woodrow Wilson International Center for Scholars, Latin American Program.

Tsing, Anna Lowenhaupt. 1993. *In the Realm of the Diamond Queen: Marginality in an Out-of-the-Way Place.* Princeton: Princeton University Press.

Turner, Mary. 1982. *Slaves and Missionaries: The Disintegration of Jamaican Slave Society, 1987–1834.* Urbana: University of Illinois Press.

Ulysse, Gina. 1999. "Uptown Ladies and Downtown Women: Female Representations of Class and Color in Jamaica." In *Representations of Blackness and the Performance of Identities,* ed. by Jean Rahier, 147–72. Westport, Conn.: Greenwood Press.

United Nations. 2002. *International Migration Report 2002.* New York: United Nations.

Vascianne, Stephen. 2001a. "Aspects of Migration." *Daily Gleaner,* June 25, A4.

———. 2001b. "The State Is Collapsing." *Daily Gleaner,* editorial, July 16, A4.

Vassell, Linnette. 1995. "Women of the Masses: Daphne Campbell and 'Left' Politics in Jamaica in the 1950s." In *Engendering History: Caribbean Women in Historical Perspective,* ed. by Verene Shepherd, Bridget Brereton, and Barbara Bailey, 318–33. Kingston: Ian Randle.

———. 1993. *Voluntary Women's Organizations in Jamaica: The Jamaica Women's Federation 1944–1962.* M. Phil. thesis, Department of History, University of the West Indies.

Verdery, Katherine. 1991. *National Ideology Under Socialism: Identity and Cultural Politics in Ceausescu's Romania.* Berkeley: University of California Press.

Vernill, A. Hyatt. 1931. *Jamaica of Today.* New York: Dodd, Mead, and Company.

Wade, Peter. 1993. *Blackness and Race Mixture: The Dynamics of Racial Identity in Columbia.* Baltimore: Johns Hopkins University Press.

Ward, Kathryn, ed. 1990. *Women Workers and Global Restructuring.* Ithaca, N.Y.: School of Industrial and Labor Relations, Cornell University Press.

Warner, Lloyd, Buford Junker, and Walter Adams. 1941. *Color and Human Nature: Negro Personality Development in a Northern City*. Washington: American Council on Education.

Warner-Lewis, Maureen. 1991. *Guinea's Other Suns: The African Dynamic in Trinidad Culture*. Dover, Mass.: Majority Press.

Waterman, Christopher. 1990. *Juju: A Social History and Ethnography of an African Popular Music*. Chicago: University of Chicago Press.

Waters, Anita. 1985. *Race, Class, and Political Symbols: Rastafari and Reggae in Jamaican Politics*. New Brunswick, N.J.: Transaction Books.

Waters, Mary. 1999. *Black Identities: West Indian Immigrant Dreams and American Realities*. Cambridge, Mass.: Harvard University Press.

Wells, Diana. 2000. *"Between the Difference"*: Trinidadian Women's Collective Action. PhD diss., Department of Anthropology, New York University.

White, Garth. 1967. "Rudie, Oh Rudie!" *Caribbean Quarterly* 13 (September): 39–44.

———. 1984. "The Development of Jamaican Popular Music, Pt. 2: The Urbanization of the Folk." *ACIJ Research Review* 1 (1): 47–80.

Whylie, Dwight. 1997. "The Angry Beat." *Daily Gleaner*, April 14.

Whyte, Justin. 1997a. "Movement of Jah Music, Romance, Religion Replace Lewd Lyrics." *Sunday Gleaner*, November 12, 1C.

———. 1997b. *Sunday Gleaner*, January 26, 1E.

Wilk, Richard. 1996. "Connections and Contradictions: From the Crooked Tree Cashew Tree to Miss World Belize." In *Beauty Queens on the Global Stage: Gender, Contests, and Power*, ed. by Colleen Ballerino Cohen, Richard Wilk, and Beverly Stoeltje, 217–32. New York: Routledge.

———. 1995. "Learning to be Local in Belize: Global Systems of Common Difference." In *Worlds Apart: Modernity through the Prism of the Local*, ed. by Dan Miller, 110–33. New York: Routledge.

Williams, Brackette. 1996a. "A Race of Men, A Class of Women: Nation, Ethnicity, Gender and Domesticity among Afro-Guyanese." In *Women Out of Place: The Gender of Agency and the Race of Nationality*, ed. by Brackette Williams, 129–58. New York: Routledge.

———. 1996b. "Mannish Women and Gender after the Act." In *Women Out of Place: The Gender of Agency and the Race of Nationality*, ed. by Brackette Williams, 1–33. New York: Routledge.

———. 1993. "The Impact of the Precepts of Nationalism on the Concept of Culture: Making Grasshoppers of Naked Apes." *Cultural Critique* 24 (1): 143–91.

———. 1991. *Stains on My Name, War in My Veins: Guyana and the Politics of Cultural Struggle*. Durham: Duke University Press.

———. 1990. "Nationalism, Traditionalism, and the Problem of Cultural Authenticity." In *Nationalist Ideologies and the Production of National Cultures*, ed. by Richard Fox, 112–29. Washington: American Anthropological Association.

——. 1989. "A Class Act: Anthropology and the Race to Nation Across Ethnic Terrain." *Annual Review of Anthropology* 18:401–44.

Williams, Joan. 1997. "A Squandered Legacy." *Daily Observer*, August 4, 6.

Williams, Raymond. 1977. *Marxism and Literature*. Oxford: Oxford University Press.

Wilmot, Swithin. 1995. "Females of Abandoned Character'? Women and Protest in Jamaica, 1838–65." In *Engendering History: Caribbean Women in Historical Perspective*, ed. by Verene Shepherd, Bridget Brereton, and Barbara Bailey, 279–95. Kingston: Ian Randle.

——. 1992. "Black Space/Room to Manoeuvre; Land and Politics in Trelawny in the Immediate Post-Emancipation Period." In *Plantation Economy, Land Reform, and the Peasantry in a Historical Perspective: Jamaica 1838–1890*, ed. by Claus Stolbert and Swithin Wilmot, 15–24. Kingston: Friedrich Ebert Siftung.

Wilson, C. A. 1929. *Men of Vision: A Series of Biographical Sketches of Men Who Have Made Their Mark upon Our Time*. Kingston: Gleaner Company.

Wilson, Peter. 1973. *Crab Antics: The Social Anthropology of English-Speaking Negro Societies of the Caribbean*. New Haven: Yale University Press.

Wiltshire, Rosina. 1992. "Implications of Transnational Migration for Nationalism: The Caribbean Example." In *Towards a Transnational Perspective on Migration: Race, Class, Ethnicity, and Nationalism Reconsidered*, ed. by Nina Glick Schiller, Linda Basch, and Cristina Szanton Blanc 175–87. New York: NYAS.

Wippers, Audrey. 1972. "African Women, Fashion, and Scapegoating." *Canadian Journal of African Studies* 6 (2): 329–49.

Witmer, Robert. 1989. "Kingston's Popular Music Culture: Neo-Colonialism to Nationalism." *Jamaica Journal* 22 (1): 11–19.

Wray, Milton. 2001. "An Array of Tastes, Colours . . . Food Festivals Celebrate Jamaica's Heritage." *Daily Observer*, June 30, 20.

Wright, Philip. 1966. *Lady Nugent's Journal of her Residence in Jamaica from 1801 to 1805*, rev. ed. Kingston: Institute of Jamaica.

Wright, Richardson. 1937. *Revels in Jamaica, 1682–1838*. New York: Dodd, Mead.

Yelvington, Kevin. 2002. "Melville J. Herskovits and 'Socialized Ambivalence:' The History of an Idea in Caribbean Anthropology." Unpublished paper.

——. 1999. "The War in Ethiopia and Trinidad, 1935–1936." In *The Colonial Caribbean in Transition: Essays on Postemancipation Social and Cultural History*, ed. by Bridget Brereton and Kevin Yelvington, 189–225. Gainesville: University of Florida Press.

——. 1995. *Producing Power: Ethnicity, Gender, and Class in a Caribbean Workplace*. Philadelphia: Temple University Press.

——. 1993a. "Trinidad Ethnicity." In *Trinidad Ethnicity*, ed. by Kevin Yelvington, 1–32. Knoxville: University of Tennessee Press.

Yelvington, Kevin, ed. 1993b. *Trinidad Ethnicity*. Knoxville: University of Tennessee Press.

Young, Virginia. 1993. *Becoming West Indian: Culture, Self, and Nation in St. Vincent*. Washington: Smithsonian Institute Press.

Index

Abeng, 76, 166, 303 n. 13

Abrams, Phillip, 280 n. 6

Abu-Lughod, Lila, 284 n. 15

African Americans: hip-hop and, 175, 179, 247, 256, 260, 303 n. 18, 308 n. 22, 308 n. 30; investment in Jamaica by, 84; modern blackness and, 229, 260–61; popular culture of, 23, 73, 260; on scientific racism, 286 n. 7; self-commodification of play and, 251; Universal Negro Improvement Association and, 45

African cultural heritage: Americanization of, 180–81; Crown Colony rule and, 266; Emancipation Day observances and, 165, 167; generations on, 179–80; in government policy, 65–67, 69, 177; Henry Rebellion and, 71–72, 294 n. 18, 295 nn. 19, 20; nine-nights celebration and, 190, 280 n. 5, 303 n. 25; reggae music and, 2, 74, 77–78, 115–16, 181, 242, 273; Rudies, 72–74, 75, 77, 243, 303 n. 21; self-determination of, 73–74; self-esteem of, 177–78, 187–89; state recognition of, 4–5, 22, 280 n. 5. *See also* Black nationalism; Blackness; Rastafarian movement

Afro-Caribbean societies, 230, 232, 258, 305 n. 1, 305 n. 5, 306 n. 6

Agriculture, 215–16, 221, 222; acquisition of wealth and, 229; bananas, 41, 43; capital investment and, 68; cash crops, 97, 99, 213, 304 n. 7; coffee, 213, 217; environmentalism and, 133, 213, 214, 300

n. 2; Hillside Agricultural Project, 133, 135, 213–14; migration and, 43, 46; seasonality of, 98; urban industrial service workers and, 67

All Age School, 105, 121, 122, 171, 223, 298 n. 7

Americanization: of African cultural heritage, 180–81; consumerism, 260; globalization and, 85–86, 250; materialism and, 208–9, 214; modern blackness, 23; radical consumerism and, 231, 250, 251; television programs and, 234–35

American Women's Club, 137–38, 141

Anderson, Benedict, 279 n. 2, 280 n. 6, 281 n. 7

Anderson, Patricia, 123–24

Anglican Church, 102, 118–19, 122, 132, 144, 145

Antrobus, Peggy, 252, 283 n. 12

Appadurai, Arjun, 280 n. 6, 282 n. 11, 283 n. 13

Austin-Broos, Diane, 40, 44, 49, 119, 156, 230 n. 33, 242, 298 n. 5, 305 n. 3

Bakan, Abigail, 42, 46, 48

Baker, Lee, 286 n. 6, 287 n. 13

Banton, Buju, 233, 242

Baptist Church, 6, 32, 39–41, 46, 47, 162, 280 n. 5

Barrow, Christine, 10, 290 n. 32, 305 n. 5

Basch, Linda, 259–60, 284 n. 14

Bay, Mia, 286 n. 7

Beauty, 63, 186–87, 292 n. 6

DEBORAH A. THOMAS

is assistant professor of cultural anthropology

at Duke University.